THE 1000 BHP GRAND PRIX CARS

ACKNOWLEDGEMENTS

This investigation of the Grand Prix cars of 1984 - 1987 would not have been possible without the enthusiastic co-operation of many of those responsible for their design and development.
RACECAR ENGINEERING is particularly indebted to:
John BARNARD, Helmut BARTH, Steve BRYAN, Rory BYRNE, Giacomo CALIRI, Tommaso CARLETTI, Carlo CHITI, Gordon COPPUCK, Ron DENNIS, Gerard DUCAROUGE, Bernard DUDOT, Bill GIBSON, Geoff GODDARD, Steve HALLAM, Brian HART, Nobuhiko KAWAMOTO, Norbert KREYER, Ignazio LUNETTA, John MacDONALD, Brian MASON, Gordon MURRAY, David NORTH, Neil OATLEY, Guiseppe PETROTTA, Maurice PHILLIPPE, Christian van der PLEYN, Mick RALPH, Paul ROSCHE, McLane "Mac" TILTON, Mario TOLENTINO.

The black and white photographs are the work of John Overton, Alan Lis, LAT, IPA and Ian Bamsey. The dust jacket photographs are by LAT and Zooom.

The colour photograph selection is from the John Overton collection.

THE 1000 BHP
GRAND PRIX
CARS

IAN BAMSEY

WITH CONTRIBUTIONS BY
ENRICO BENZING • ALLAN STANIFORTH • MIKE LAWRENCE

Foulis

Haynes

A **FOULIS** Motoring Book

First published 1988

© RACECAR ENGINEERING (Specialist Publications)

Published by
Haynes Publishing Group, Sparkford, Near Yeovil,
Somerset BA22 7JJ, England.

Haynes Publications Inc.
861 Lawrence Drive, Newbury Park, California, 91320,
USA.

Produced for G.T. Foulis & Co. Ltd. by
RACECAR ENGINEERING (Specialist Publications)
6, Foundry House, Stars Lane, Yeovil, Somerset BA20
1N L, England.

Editorial Director: Ian Bamsey
Research Assistant: Alan Lis
Chief Photographer: John Overton

British Library Cataloguing in Publication Data

Bamsey, Ian
The 1000 BHP Grand Prix cars.
1. Formula 1 racing cars. Racing, 1984 - 1987
I. Title
796.7'2

ISBN 0-85429-617-4

Library of Congress Catalog Card number 88-80238

Printed in England by:
Wincanton Litho, Wincanton, Somerset
Origination by:
Graphic Examples, Sherborne, Dorset

CONTENTS ▶

AGE OF TITANS

'Rocket fuel' made it possible. The ball started rolling in mid '83 when BMW countered Renault's use of water injection by fuel technology. Injecting water into a turbocharged engine's 'charge air' did more than merely assist cooling: for reasons that had no formal, text book explanation the water acted as a combustion stimulant, increasing power. Pre war, turbocharged aircraft engines had used water injection to extend payload. Having picked up on the idea, Renault and Ferrari denied that water constituted a power boosting additive: there was no technical explanation to prove otherwise. BMW, on the other hand saw more could be gained through manipulation of the composition of the fuel itself.

BMW drew on the depth of experience of chemicals expert BASF's Winterschall subsidiary. Winterschall produced fuel which, while within FISA's long worded definition of 'petrol', unleashed a significant power increase. It caught Renault out, Piquet's BMW-Brabham surging ahead of Prost's water injected Renault following the introduction of Winterschall fuel at Zandvoort, 1983, to snatch a World Championship crown that had seemingly been destined for France.

Prost won the most races in 1984, and teammate Lauda stole the World Championship driving Porsche/TAG-McLarens running a blend of pump petrol and Avgas. Doctored Avgas was one thing; 'rocket fuel' was another. The difference was toluene. By '85, what was 'petrol' to FISA, to all front runners was a blend of 80% toluene with 20% chemicals to make it 'legal'. Toluene based fuel was not dubbed 'rocket fuel' without good reason - it allowed four figure outputs to be achieved with relative ease. Back in 1983 the maximum power, 750b.h.p. became the minimum figure at the bottom of a straightline power curve.

By late '85 race power had increased from the 650b.h.p. seen early in '83 on unlimited fuel to almost 900b.h.p., in spite of a 220 litre ration, while qualifying power was soaring above 1000b.h.p. BMW had reached the magic 1000b.h.p. first, towards the end of 1984, pouring Winterschall fuel through a rugged in line four boosted to 4.5 bar - four and a half times atmospheric pressure at sea level. Intense turbocharger development was proving necessary and engine builders had to work in close co-operation with turbocharger manufacturers. BMW switched from KKK to Garrett to seek special development work. Through '85 BMW's boost kept on climbing, to exceed 5.0 bar: power went to 1100b.h.p. - and beyond. It had become impossible to measure: the BMW dyno went no higher.

At Monza in 1986 Berger saw a 5.5 bar flash reading from his BMW/Mader-Benetton: Heini Mader estimated over 1300b.h.p. The '85 BMW and '86 BMW/Mader engines regularly qualified at 5.3 bar, and at such extreme levels cooling is everything. For that reason, fuel was gushed through the engine and water was flung at the charge air cooler - three litres a lap - turning to steam and mingling behind the car with a cloud of unburned hydrocarbons from the exhaust pipe: visible horsepower.

It was brutal horsepower, the single turbo equipped four cylinder engine tripling its output from 6000 to 9000r.p.m. Twin turbo equipped V6 rivals enjoyed higher revs and a wider power band. But power was still harsh when Renault, Ferrari and Honda likewise sought four figure qualifying outputs. Renault threw away its turbocharger wastegates for maximum effect and saw 5.2 bar at Adelaide, while screaming to 13,000r.p.m. - well in excess of 1100b.h.p., and again impossible to measure.

All that power went through tyres that were patently inadequate: regulation wheel sizes had been fixed when 500b.h.p. was the norm. Wrestling the beast left the driver pretty shattered. These days, Saturday night on the town was right out of the question! And race day was no less taxing, in spite of the sobering effect of the 220 litre fuel ration, tightened to 195 litres for '86/'87. Toluene fuel was denser than pump petrol, packing more energy in the tank, and its high detonation threshold allowed higher compression ratios, helping to compensate for lower boost.

Having won the '83 World Championship using a maximum of 3.3 bar, BMW had planned to race at that level in '84 in spite of the fuel ration, exploiting comput-

> "with rocket fuel, 750b.h.p. was the minimum rather than the maximum power"

Geoff Goddard
Chief Racing Engine Designer
Cosworth Engineering

erised control to keep it free from a melted piston crown or turbine wheel as the mixture was leaned off. But 750b.h.p. wasn't enough: Porsche/TAG had other ideas. By the end of '84 BMW was exploiting 3.8/3.9 bar, Porsche/TAG 3.6/3.7 bar, both on a 7.5:1 compression ratio. Power was already in excess of 850b.h.p.

As compression ratios increased with toluene fuel and computer control became ever more sophisticated race boost went over 4.0 bar, Honda setting the standard in '86 with something in the region of 950b.h.p. The 4.0 bar restriction for '87 didn't check the rise: compression ratios went even higher and race power crept close to 1000b.h.p. It would never have been possible on pump petrol...

The keys, then, were fuel and computer control. To race competitively it was necessary to run as close as possible to the verge of detonation: that called for a tolerant fuel and sophisticated manipulation of injection and ignition. The lean-running '84 - '87 Formula One race engine lived on the verge of destruction: if the fuelling went wrong it would rapidly melt down. Its micro-processor based control box took readings from a host of sensors monitoring engine operation and regulated the injection and ignition systems according to a sophisticated pre-set programme, which accounted for most operational conditions.

It was very subtle. Ask Renault why Honda had the edge in '86 and the answer is that Honda appeared to have superior control, to be able to run that fraction closer to the thin line between winning power and a detonated engine. Of course, the entire package had to be right: engine (including turbocharger system), electronics, fuel, tyres and chassis, not to mention the driver.

The chassis was heavily restricted in terms of the aerodynamic devices it could employ, yet its aerodynamic form was as important as ever. Top teams were reckoned to spend over 200 days in the wind tunnel each year. Research was carried out using scale models on rolling roads: in effect, the actual cars had become scaled up replicas of wind tunnel models. The 'flat bottom' restriction of '83 might have cut downforce by 60% at a stroke, but come '87 and lateral forces were beginning to approach those of the high-'g' ground effect era, though drag was much higher.

A lot of turbo horsepower was spent dragging big wings through the air. Drag co-efficients appear to have been in the region of 1.0 - 1.5, compared to less than 0.5 for a good road car. On the other hand, a Grand Prix car had at least 50 times the downforce. Downforce was far more important than drag, in spite of the fuel restriction. At Le Mans a 'slippery' car could comfortably exceed 200m.p.h. given 600b.h.p.: from over 1200b.h.p. Berger's record Formula One speed at Monza was 'only' 218m.p.h. Grip was sought at the expense of top speed; was won prodigiously through the ever evolving black art of aerodynamics.

Grand Prix engineers had come to rub shoulders with aerospace technicians in the spheres of aerodynamics and materials technology. Thanks to the involvement of major motor manufacturers there was more money than ever for research, in all areas: engine, turbocharger, electronics, fuel and chassis technology. Grand Prix cars had moved closer than ever before to the sharp edge of technological development.

By the mid Eighties the Grand Prix team had become

an advanced engineering facility working in close co-operation with a major automotive corporation and its hi tech race engine division - BMW Motorsport, Cosworth, Honda R&D and Renault Sport, to name a few - which in turn had turbocharger, electronics and fuel companies as development partners. The 1986 and '87 Constructors Championships were won through the co-operation of Williams and Honda R&D, with help from IHI turbochargers, Mobil and Honda's own Electronics Division. The days of a team building a 'kit car' chassis, buying an engine off the shelf and running it on pump petrol were long gone. Indeed, now the engine manufacturer shopped for the team. Honda had 'bought' Williams in return for an estimated £16 million worth of engines, technical support and financial assistance per annum (and, having won those two championships then went shopping elsewhere).

Thankfully, there was still room for the enthusiastic sportsman in this playground of automotive Goliaths. By and large, the constructors adopted by the likes of BMW, Ford, Honda and Renault were the same as had once bolted a straightforward Cosworth DFV into the back of a relatively unsophisticated chassis (working to a fraction of the budget). And the spirit of going racing for the sake of it, rather than as the representative of an industrial giant, lived on through the efforts of the likes of John MacDonald, Giancarlo Minardi and Enzo Osella. Moreover, the rise of the turbocharged engine had made room for small engine builders, keen to play the role of David: Brian Hart, Carlo Chiti and Erich Zakowski. They didn't have the resources, but they had sheer enthusiasm that helped keep grids full.

Alas, by the mid Eighties it had become clear that tur-bocharged Formula One was steadily pricing itself out of existence: the number of 'haves' was dwindling, and the gap to the 'have nots' was growing. And the sheer performance of the cars was uncomfortably high for safety's sake. It had to end, and did so in 1987. This, then, is a record of an extraordinary era. An era during which brute power went hand in hand with a new level of engineering sophistication. The Age of advanced technology, 1000b.h.p. Grand Prix Titans.

> # "Berger saw a 5.5 bar flash reading... Heini Mader estimated over 1300b.h.p."
>
> Rory Byrne
> Technical Director
> Benetton Formula Ltd

MENU

This book provides an account of all 55 turbocharged cars which contested the era of high boost and fuel restriction and also looks at the principles underlying engine and chassis design in the mid Eighties. The 'Background' section looks at the state of Grand Prix car design immediately prior to our period, while 'Trends '84 - '87' looks at the major features of development through the 1000b.h.p. era. The remainder of the book is divided into 10 sections, one for each participating engine marque.

Each engine marque section discusses the background to the marque's involvement and includes an entry for each engine fielded, with specification and details of design and development. The specification sheets have been standardised for ease of comparison and indicate the specification at the start of the 1984 season (or original specification in the case of later models). The notes on development include a consideration of each team employing the given engine model, charting the team's fortunes, and the section is concluded by a directory of all the chassis in which the engine was employed.

The chassis details include a standard specification sheet. This includes the manufacturer's claimed dry weight which might not be realistic, as the text will indicate. The specification given is that at the time of the first run of the car, and any alterations to it are identified by the text, which looks at key chassis design features and design modifications.

The colour photograph selection features the following:

Page 2 -
Alboreto in the cockpit of the Ferrari F187 at Silverstone, 1987.

Page 3 -
Tambay, Renault RE50 at Brands Hatch, 1984.

Page 6 -
BMW/Megatron cars at Francorchamps, 1987, led by Cheever's Arrows A10.

Pages 10 and 11 (clockwise from top left) -
Study of BMW engine, 1985; portrait of Gordon Murray; Senna, Renault- Lotus 98T; Alboreto, Ferrari F187; portrait of Ayrton Senna; Brabham BT53 racing Renault RE50; the cockpit of Prost's McLaren MP4/2B.

Overleaf -
Honda engine, 1987.

BRUTE FORCE

Background:
Development of
the turbocharged
Grand Prix car pre-1984

In the Sixties Coventry Climax developed two 1.5 litre engines, one having 16 cylinders, the other only eight, each having 32 valves. The lower revving four-valve-per-cylinder engine produced more power thanks primarily to better breathing. Engine power is limited by breathing - more fuel can be introduced almost at will but there must be a corresponding increase of air to burn with it. The four valve option provides a larger valve area within a given bore while small valves flow better than large ones. Further, the mingling of two air streams is thought to be beneficial, as is scavenging on a broad front. Importantly, the four valve layout leaves an ideal central position for the plug. Consequently flame travel is short and equal in all directions, discouraging the formation of end gas - pockets of unburned mixture in remote corners of the chamber which increase the risk of detonation.

Detonation, or uncontrolled burning has to be avoided at all cost. It occurs when a portion of the mixture, usually near the exhaust valves, reaches a critical temperature and burns spontaneously, interfering with the progressive spread of the flame front. In the case of pre- ignition, a portion of the mixture ignites prior to ignition from the plug, due to hot spots in the chamber. Not only is uncontrolled burning inefficient, it causes a rapid rise in cylinder temperature and, sustained for more than a few seconds, is the easiest way to melt a piston crown.

Additional bonuses of the four valve layout are improved valve seat cooling thanks to dual exits and the fact that two small valves together offer less mass than one larger equivalent, so valve train inertia is reduced, reducing strain on the springs - the Achilles heel of any engine. Further, the four valve layout offers scope for better breathing and improved combustion through careful attention to port and combustion chamber design.

The typically over-square Climax four valve engine had a traditional 60 degree included valve angle and a domed piston crown to achieve the desired 12.0:1 compression ratio. The resultant combustion chamber had a less than satisfactory 'orange peel' shape with a high surface to volume ratio. In contrast, a contemporary pioneering Shell sponsored Weslake research engine (built only in two cylinder form) had a narrow valve angle - half that of the Climax - and flat topped piston with shallow valve clearance notches. Deep cutouts can interrupt flame spread and can form stagnant pockets which adversely affect breathing. The combination of a flat piston crown with only small, shallow cutouts and a shallow pent roof provided a compact chamber with low surface to volume ratio minimising heat losses and offering good combustion characteristics.

BMW tried to go further with an 'Apfelbeck' head that had the four valves radially disposed around an ideal hemispherical roof but floundered in the face of a less than ideal piston crown shape, less efficient scavenging and problems stemming from the complexity of the necessary double rocker valve operation. Reverting to valves operated directly by twin overhead camshafts, BMW also tried diametrically opposed inlet and exhaust valves; again, better for top end power, but poorer for torque due to more air friction in the inlet passages, and still needing complex charge and exhaust plumbing which contributed to the system's downfall.

The uncomplicated four valve crossflow head with inlet ports one side, exhausts the other combined with flat topped piston and pent roof combustion chamber was championed by Keith Duckworth through the classic FVA and DFV engines. Adequately fired by its single central plug it offered excellent breathing and combustion characteristics and was the heart of most subsequent Seventies and

Eighties race engines.

The state-of-the-art normally aspirated over square four valve race engine which emerged from the Seventies had a water cooled aluminium alloy block, generally carrying wet liners which were secured at the top by a flange but were free to expand (thanks to flexible O-ring seals) at their lower end. While cast iron offers better rigidity than aluminium alloy, the cast alloy block offered adequate rigidity with superior thermal conductivity: aluminium boasts three times the conductivity of iron. In practical terms, that means it rejects heat to water faster and consequently runs cooler. Most importantly, it offers a valuable weight saving. However, while the normal light alloy piston could run a tight clearance in an alloy bore due to the absence of differential expansion, poor wearing properties mitigated against alloy bores.

The DFV utilised steel, later iron liners while Ferrari chrome plated the bores of its alloy cylinders, a technique once favoured by Porsche. In 1971 Porsche had introduced a nickel-silicon carbide coating developed by piston supplier Mahle primarily for the NSU Wankel engine. This so-called Nikasil coating, unlike chrome plating was not in any danger of lifting, and worked well with aluminium offering excellent friction characteristics. It was employed for an all-aluminium derivative of the DFV, the DFY, reducing oil consumption and the incidence of ring trouble. Mahle's lightweight Nikasil coated aluminium liners were similarly adopted by many other race engine manufacturers.

Typically, in the Nikasil engine a Mahle forged light alloy piston drove a steel crankshaft through a steel or lightweight titanium H-section con rod with a free-floating steel gudgeon pin located via circlips. Above the gudgeon pin were three conventional rings, two compression, one oil scraper, also from a German supplier; Goetze. In the usual vee engine one bank would be slightly ahead of the other to allow conventional rods to be paired on each crankshaft big end journal, each rod secured by two rather than four-bolt caps.

Generous big end and main bearing overlap helped crankshaft rigidity. The crankshaft was forged or machined from a solid billet of steel and was invariably surface treated to provide a hard case while maintaining strength in the core. The slow 'nitriding' process was employed, this taking a number of days to alter the chemical composition of the surface layer through the production of very hard nitrates of iron and certain alloying metals. The nitriding agent was ammonia gas which decomposes into hydrogen and nitrogen at the furnace temperature of about 500 degrees centigrade, below the change point of the parent steel.

Crankshafts incorporated extended balancing webs and ran plain shell- type bearings with a main bearing between each dual big end journal, though Ferrari had toyed with roller mains and ran four rather than seven bearings for less frictional loss in its 180 degree

('flat') V12 engine. The Ferrari engine was also unusual in that, while its heads were water cooled, much of its block (below the hottest upper portion of the liners) was oil (and to a lesser extent air) cooled. Efficient dry sump oil systems, with at least one pressure and one scavenge pump and a chassis mounted oil cooler were, of course, universal.

Hart's unique in-line four

Whether the cylinder configuration was in line or vee, a combined cylinder block and crankcase (strictly speaking a 'monobloc') was employed, with the head (or heads) being detachable. However, in the early Eighties Hart produced a unique in line four with integral head which he dubbed a monobloc and the term went into general usage to describe the fixed head design. The regular detachable head, sealed by a Cooper ring gasket, was cast in aluminium alloy, occasionally magnesium and was fitted with bronze-based valve seats and guides. Separate cam-cum-tappet block carriers were often employed.

Invariably the common vee configuration unit was designed to be run fully stressed, with chassis loads fed into heads and lower crankcase. Consequently, the tappet block had to be very rigid to avoid tappet seizure and the bottom end had to be equally stiff. A flywheel combined with a 7 1/4 inch plate diameter clutch allowed the crankshaft to be set low to keep the centre of gravity as close to the ground as possible and often main bearing caps were formed integrally with a rigid sump. Matra's V12 did not, however, set a fashion with main bearing caps located by interference fit, and by both side and conventional bolting.

Camshaft drive, usually at the front end, was by gears or toothed belts, gears arguably more precise but belts lighter and easier to replace. Gear trains are subject to very severe instantaneous loadings and are heavy and complex arrangements on the engine front and all gears need running clearance on teeth, however small affecting precision. Belts have effectively zero stretch, but operate in torsion which must affect accuracy.

The steel camshafts operated the valves through inverted steel bucket tappets with hardened shims fitted inside the buckets to provide clearance adjustment. The valves were also steel - often Nimonic when facing exhaust heat - and were closed by twin coil springs, located by the conventional split collar. Often the inner coil was a slight interference fit within the outer to damp out surge

- the phenomenon of the coils accelerating on their own account. This shortcoming and the physical limits of the steel employed kept the race engine, regardless of number of cylinders, to less than 13,000 r.p.m. Attempts at higher revs were met by uncontrollable surge - the valve was unable to follow the cam.

R.p.m. was once limited by ignition, traditional contact breaker systems hard pressed to cope with speed in excess of 6,500 r.p.m., let alone 13,000. Early transistor assisted systems retained the points simply as a trigger carrying low current, with the switching of coil current taken care of by a power transistor. In view of the low current needed to trigger the transistor it became possible to exchange the mechanical contact breaker - which has a tendency to bounce at high r.p.m. - for an electro-magnetic pick up on the crank. Often located at the flywheel, this produces a small induced current pulse the appropriate number of times for each revolution. This small pulse is fed to an electronic pulse shaper and amplifier which in turn renders the main transistor conductive at the appropriate time. Such contactless transistorised systems provide more accurate triggering allowing a more powerful coil to be used and cater for higher speeds producing up to 1000 sparks per second - sufficient for an eight cylinder engine to run to 15,000 r.p.m.

The mid Seventies saw the development of the so called 'capacitor discharge' systems, using a condenser, or 'capacitor' in which to store electrical energy as it builds up. Such systems have similar transistorised triggering to the contactless coil system but activating a thyristor condenser which is another form of transistor capable of handling extremely high voltage and currents up to 100 amps. The system incorporates capacitor charging and voltage amplifying circuits, the latter to increase spark voltage to the distributor and offers a higher energy, shorter duration spark. Capacitor discharge systems were developed by Marelli - the Raceplex system, superseding the Dinoplex system - Bosch, Lucas and Honda.

The four valve race engine was traditionally fuel injected via a mechanical system such as that provided by Lucas for the Cosworth DFV. That featured a shuttle-type metering unit which was supplied with fuel at a constant pressure. The throttle slides were linked by a finely adjustable rod to a carefully contoured cam which in turn controlled exactly how far the shuttle - a free floating piston - could move.

As we have noted, more fuel can be injected at will into a cylinder (either directly or, as in the case of the engines under discussion, indirectly via the air intake) but to produce more power, more air must be introduced to allow full combustion. Taking advantage of the good breathing of the four valve race engine, considerably more air was introduced via turbocharging, as pioneered by Renault in the late Seventies. The turbocharger pressurised the charge air prior to intake so as to increase its density and

thus the quantity that could be crammed into the cylinder per cycle.

A turbocharger is an exhaust driven device which employs a centrifugal compressor to provide the air pressurisation. The compressor is directly connected to a gas turbine which is driven by the waste energy passing through the exhaust system. The turbine creates a flow restriction in the exhaust system so exhaust manifold back pressure will be higher in the turbocharged engine. However, provided sufficient exhaust gas energy is converted into compressor work for the charge air delivery pressure to equal or exceed atmospheric pressure at the turbine inlet, the engine's breathing will not be adversely affected. Running with such a positive pressure relationship - 'in crossover' - the turbocharged engine is able to exploit the potential of very dense charge air, assuming, of course, this density is matched by a correspondingly greater quantity of fuel.

The density increase will not necessarily match the pressurisation imparted by the compressor. This is because raising the pressure of any gas increases heat as well as density, any temperature rise being at the expense of density. Nevertheless, feeding the pressurised charge air through an aftercooler (colloquially referred to as an 'intercooler' in the motor racing world and simply a radiator for charge air rather than engine coolant or engine oil) en route to the intake can reduce its temperature sufficiently to win back the majority of the potential density increase.

If there was no density (or any other) loss, a 1.5 litre engine pressurised to 2.0 bar intake pressure would produce equivalent power to a similar 3.0 litre atmospheric engine at sea level, given the same quantity of fuel. The atmospheric engine's intake pressure will, of course, drop with altitude - for example at Kyalami it will be around 0.85 bar, such is the air density loss 1500 metres above sea level. But while the atmospheric engine will lose power, the turbocharged engine can be given a little more boost - adding 1.2 rather than 1.0 bar - to maintain its regular power output on its usual allocation of fuel. Note that subsequent figures for bar boost refer to absolute pressure - that is, the pressure seen in the intake manifold, rather than to the amount added to atmospheric pressure through the process of turbocharging.

Turbocharging was pioneered in the aviation world as a means of maintaining intake manifold pressure at high altitude. Subsequently, in the late Fifties and Sixties it was widely employed as a means of extracting additional power from diesel engines for road haulage work. The turbocharged road car was a rare beast when the Indy Car world took to the technology in the late Sixties and was still an exception to the rule when Renault started the Formula One turbo trend in the late Seventies. Consequently, Renault started with adapted diesel engine turbochargers, as used in USAC, and by itself and Porsche at Le Mans.

The type of turbocharger developed for commercial vehicles clearly had to be relatively cheap to manufacture and reliable. Consequently the standard configuration was that of single stage radial flow gas turbine linked by a short rotor shaft (running in an inboard bearing system) to a single stage radial flow compressor. The typical turbine impeller was of high temperature steel welded to a shaft to form the rotor assembly. The turbine had to withstand exhaust temperatures of up to 900 degrees centigrade and ran within a cast iron housing. Spinning at up to 90,000r.p.m., the shaft revolved in plain bearings fed with engine lubrication oil. The compressor impeller was of aluminium alloy clamped to the shaft by an end nut. It spun in an aluminium housing which incorporated the volute (a carefully shaped outer housing). The impeller blades accelerated the incoming air so as to impart a high velocity to it by centrifugal force, then the air was diffused into the volute, reducing its velocity and thus building up pressure.

It should be noted that compressor action is essentially aerodynamic: it is not a positive displacement device trapping air in sealed chambers before it is compressed. Consequently, as engine speed and load increase its aerodynamic qualities are severely tested. In a Formula One engine a compressor was asked to provide an immense range of airflow from idle to 11,500r.p.m. on full throttle. Critically important is the relationship between airflow and pressure.

If flow is too low for the pressure build up in a system the air can stall and change direction - the phenomenon of 'surge' which can occur violently, causing serious damage. At the other end of the spectrum is flow that is disproportionately high for the pressure build up. Air flow can go supersonic at the inlet, which is inefficient and causes dangerous charge heating. If flow is too high there will be excessive impeller speed for a given pressure delivery, and it is possible to overspeed the impeller, causing it to burst.

Clearly it is desirable to run a compressor as closely as possible to its peak efficiency at all times. Low efficiency causes a disproportionate temperature rise. A compressor's efficiency - its adiabatic (or 'pumping') efficiency - is reflected in the temperature rise it creates. 100% efficiency would see no temperature rise but in practice around 75% efficiency is the best that can be achieved. Running a compressor below its peak efficiency implies a greater power requirement for a given pressure rise. Different turbochargers have different characteristics (usually illustrated by plotting the relationship between pressure and flow on a compressor 'map') but it is difficult to produce a turbocharger which combines high efficiency with the map width needed to accommodate an engine with a wide r.p.m. and throttle range.

Essential is careful matching of compressor to engine, of engine to turbine and of turbine to compressor. Whereas gas flow through the compressor diffuses, flow through

the turbine does the accelerating, and turbine speed is a function of exhaust gas temperature and speed, and of pressure in the exhaust manifold. A turbine can use all the heat it can get - provided it can withstand the temperature. Turbines capable of withstanding 1100 degrees centigrade were the best that had been developed to the end of '83. Exhaust gas speed as felt by the compressor is influenced by the turbine entry nozzle: reducing the size of a nozzle will accelerate the gas at low throttle levels. However, as engine speed increases the gas chokes at the turbine entry, increasing back pressure in the manifold. That pressure rise could eventually overtake the pressure in the inlet manifold.

In practice, a pressure relief valve is usually fitted to bleed excess pressure from the exhaust manifold once inlet pressure reaches a given level. The common diaphragm operated exhaust wastegate is thus a pressure differential sensing device, with a spring loaded poppet valve to bye pass gas from the turbine entry once boost pressure reaches a required level.

Clearly, the speed of the turbine is the compressor speed. Centrifugal forces increase as the square of rotational speed but air is light stuff and in practice the compressor has to run at high speed before anything much happens in the way of significant boost. At low to medium engine speed boost will be modest, particularly as the inlet pressure build up has to be insufficient to cause surge. However, as revs rise pressure will start to rise disproportionately and power will climb quickly and steeply. In the worst case there will be a sudden inrush of power that the driver will find very hard to cope with. Hence the importance of the wastegate if a more civilised engine is desired.

Power is a function of work done on the power stroke (brake mean effective pressure (b.m.e.p.) which, in effect, is an engine's torque) and engine speed. Clearly, the turbocharger increases b.m.e.p. and for greatest benefit it will be matched to an engine's torque curve, with revs used to extract maximum power. As far as possible the turbo will be matched with the wastegate to maintain the desired boost level constantly on a given circuit. However, on almost any road racing circuit there will be corners for which the throttle has to be backed off to the extent that there is insufficient exhaust gas energy to keep the turbine spinning fast enough to keep the compressor within its useful working range.

Opening the throttle again will not instantly speed up the turbine again due to the inertia of the rotor assembly. This delay in reaching useful compressor speed is throttle lag - an inevitable delay between pressing the throttle pedal and power arriving at the rear wheels.

Harsh power delivery and throttle lag are inherent problems of exhaust gas turbo-supercharging. Formula One regulations demanded that the turbo engine produce its performance from half the 3000cc capacity of the regular Seventies atmospheric engine. The smaller mass of the 1500cc block

was offset by the additional mass of the turbocharger system while the drag of aftercooler surface area had to be overcome. In practice the Formula One turbo engine had to produce not twice but at least two and a half times the 175/180b.h.p. per litre of the 3.0 litre four valve race engine to be able to stamp its authority the way it did in 1981/83. And a portion of that extra power was spent overcoming the heavier fuel load needed, though mid race pit stops for fuel and tyres helped on that score.

Aftercooling was effective in gaining density, to the extent that two and a half times the power per litre took little more than 2.5 bar. For example, two and a half times 175b.h.p. per litre is 438b.h.p. per litre, or a total output of 646b.h.p.: BMW actually claimed 640b.h.p. for its 1983 World Championship winning turbo engine on 2.5 bar.

During 1983, with the pit stop strategy, boost was often turned high for at least a short portion of the race, exceeding 3.0 bar and in qualifying went to 3.5 bar, taking power outputs over 700b.h.p. (actually to 769b.h.p. on a hypothetical, idealised linear scale). BMW admits that at late season races it exploited as much as 740b.h.p. on race day, aided by improved fuel. Let's call the 1983 turbo machines 'the 750b.h.p. Grand Prix cars'.

Power through cold air

The race engine turbo system was well developed by 1983, as indicated by the effectiveness of the air:air aftercoolers employed. It has been calculated that a mere 10 degree rise in charge temperature robs 25b.h.p. and aftercoolers were required to reduce charge temperature from 240 degrees to 40 degree while minimising any pressure loss through the matrix. It was also, for example, important to keep charge plumbing and exhaust primaries short to minimise turbo lag. The entire engine and turbo system package had to be designed as an integral component, a key element of which was the plenum chamber above the inlet tracts which balanced charge air prior to induction. It was very difficult to get equal flow to each port. BMW positioned its injectors in the plenum chamber rather than the inlet tract and also ran a throttle butterfly ahead of the compressor intake. Butterflies rather than throttle slides were necessary in the face of highly pressurised air which poses serious friction problems in the movement of the slide plates.

The adapted diesel turbochargers employed in '83 were asked to rev as high as 180,000 r.p.m. and did so still on plain bearings fed engine oil,

although engine builders had come to provide a separate scavenge pump to attend to the turbocharger. The effective aftercooling reduced the thermal loading on the engine, but this was still extreme and effective compression ratios were high.

The geometric compression ratio was 6.5/7.0:1 rather than 12:1 in a typical contemporary atmospheric engine, requiring a gap between the piston at t.d.c and the top of the liner to retain the preferred flat top piston and narrow angle pent roof chamber. Nevertheless on 2.5 bar boost or more the effective compression ratio could be well in excess of 12.0:1. Higher compression on an atmospheric engine running on pump petrol was both dangerous in terms of increased suspectibility to detonation, and in any case led to a falling off of the performance curve. The turbo engine had, in effect, its compression ratio varying with boost but with careful ignition control and running on carefully selected petrol, avoided detonation as the effective compression ratio rose to 16.0:1 and beyond. Nevertheless, the piston had a very hard time.

The maximum thermal loading that an engine can endure is set by the resistance of its pistons, rings, valves and valve seats to thermodynamic stress. To exceed a given level of resistance is to invite a burned valve or melted piston. While the basic four valve race engine stood up remarkably well to vastly increased mechanical loadings on both top and bottom ends, Renault had to do a significant amount of pioneering work with piston manufacturer Mahle, ring manufacturer Goetze and valve spring producer Schmitthelm. Naturally, as those companies supplied the majority of rival engine builders, others benefited as they jumped on the turbo bandwaggon.

Alloy pistons running in Nikasil liners were appropriate for the turbo engine, tight clearance avoiding intense combustion 'torching down' the gap between piston and bore, while good conductivity helped get heat to the water. The majority of heat had to escape through the water cooling system the thermal flow route being from the piston crown out to the ring belt whence the heat is transferred to the cylinder wall and thence to the coolant. In addition, from early on Renault had found it necessary to oil cool the piston crown. It was important to avoid heat build up in the combustion chamber, not only to avoid excessive thermodynamic stress, but also due to the heat intolerance of petrol. Controlled burning is only possible within certain limits defined by combustion chamber temperature, charge temperature and mean effective compression ratio.

At first piston cooling was achieved via a simple spray to the underside of the crown. With higher boost Mahle introduced an oil gallery cooled piston. This set a circular oil channel under the crown a little way in from the ring belt. Oil was sprayed into it through an access hole and circulated as the piston reciprocated in the bore through the so called 'cocktail shaker effect', escaping again through a second hole. Certain diesel engines had a constant supply of oil to the crown fed up the con rod but the oil gallery piston was deemed effective enough, becoming standard Formula One equipment.

Good water circulation around the head and upper portion of the liners was, of course, important, and sodium filled Nimonic steel valves were generally employed on the exhaust side. Renault and others experienced the burning away of valve seats: a phenomenon that could be evident as a car approached the end of a race! More damaging was valve spring failure and Renault had to do a lot of work with Schmitthelm in the face of the savage cams that were necessary to get the required valve opening for its V6.

Interestingly, Renault's arch rival of '83, the four cylinder BMW was an engine which, while it had the guts and head of a contemporary four valve race engine, employed a stock iron block without Nikasil cylinders. Renault had also started out with an iron block but figured that it could get sufficient rigidity with alloy while saving weight and switched during the '83 season, moving into line with the Ferrari and new Porsche-TAG V6 turbos, the Alfa Romeo V8 turbo and the four cylinder Hart turbo. Apart from the 'production based' BMW, only the similarly Formula Two based Honda V6 turbo retained an iron block.

In the face of the forthcoming 220 litre fuel ratio the thirsty Alfa Romeo V8 clearly had little future and in any case it had been overshadowed by the better of its four and six cylinder rivals. The V6 configuration provided a shorter, stiffer crank and an inherently more rigid structure - both the iron BMW and the alloy Hart in line engines were run only semi-stressed, whereas all the V6 engines ran fully stressed. The larger piston crown of the four cylinder engine clearly presented a greater cooling problem, and while it ran a single 110,000r.p.m. turbocharger, the V6 engines ran two smaller 180,000r.p.m. turbos, one per bank, these units offering less inertia and thus providing boost at lower revs and offering a wider spread of power. Additionally, the V6 configuration promised higher revs.

On the other hand, a big single turbo offered superior torque and with four cylinders supplying it a twin entry turbine was employed to harness exhaust pulses so as to increase turbine speed at low engine r.p.m. And if the four cylinder engine had to be boosted to a higher level to provide an equivalent power output, given its lower revs, that was only by a marginal amount. In theory the four cylinder BMW and Hart engines could have run twin turbos for less lag, one fed from each of the two exhaust ports, but early attempts by Hart had floundered in the face of installation problems.

Development of the turbochargers themselves lay in the hands of the turbo manufacturers, due to the difficulties and vast expense of producing bespoke units. Renault's pioneering engine had at first been equipped with the products of

Garrett AiResearch, a Californian company reckoned to be the world's largest manufacturer of turbochargers. Meanwhile, in the sportscar arena, Porsche was working with the German KKK - Kuhnle Kopp & Kausch - firm. KKK went Formula One with Renault following the introduction of twin turbos in 1979, as it could supply suitable smaller units more promptly than Garrett. By 1982 KKK was also supplying Ferrari, BMW, Alfa Romeo and Honda, while Alfa Romeo had started trying units from its sister company 'Avio' and Honda had turned to fellow Japanese concern IHI - Ishikawajima Harima Heavy Industries - reckoning that was the way to get special development work done.

KKK twin turbo regulars Renault and Ferrari were somewhat taken aback when the Porsche-TAG engine arrived in 1983 with what appeared to be bespoke units. Having found KKK's '83 turbos less suited to its own engine than to the Ferrari, Renault turned to Garrett, signing a three year deal for '84 - '86 under which Garrett agreed to carry out special development work. Hart had used Garrett until mid '83 but, frustrated with the off-the-shelf units it had been getting, had switched instead to the British Holset company.

By 1983 throttle lag had dropped dramatically from Renault's frustrating early level thanks to turbocharger development and to more sophisticated injection and ignition control. In addition, various turbo tricks had been employed, such as injecting an extra spurt of fuel as the throttle was opened to create a surge of exhaust gas that would get the turbine spinning. Ferrari had even bye passed compressor air over the turbine while the throttle was shut, injecting extra fuel to burn with it (ignited by the red hot turbine blades). Such ploys were illsuited to the upcoming fuel ration era. Another idea was to fit variable incidence vanes ahead of the compressor to give air a pre-swirl at low compressor revolutions.

The very act of injecting fuel into the air flow offered a cooling effect thanks to its latent heat of evaporation and running rich consequently had a beneficial cooling effect. More so as it speeded up the combustion process: the effect was to help drop both charge and exhaust temperatures. In addition, a large amount of valve overlap could be employed causing a blow through of unburned or partially burnt fuel, which similarly was kind on the turbine as well as helping to keep combustion temperature under control.

A further factor was the composition of the fuel itself. In theory, a fuel's octane rating indicates its resistance to detonation: the higher the rating the higher the resistance and the higher the mean compression ratio that can safely be run. Formula One regulations restricted fuel to: "petrol having the following characteristics - maximum 102 octane; maximum 2% oxygen and 1% hydrogen by weight, the remaining 97% consisting exclusively of hydrocarbons and not containing any alcohols, nitrocompounds or other

power boosting additives". Yet despite the apparent exactness, that definition of 102 octane petrol opened the door to the fuel chemist.

Strictly speaking, "petrol" is but the European name given to refined petroleum (or a synthetic substitute produced by chemical process) as used in motor cars. The act of refining petroleum produces many different liquid hydrocarbons and there are over 200 chemicals present in pump petrol, which varies from manufacturer to manufacturer and from country to country. The Formula One fuel chemist was able to ensure the presence of the precise hydrocarbons which, while not recognised "power boosting additives", work particularly well in the turbo engine.

Examples of hydrocarbons derived from petroleum are octane, toluene and aniline. Octane is commonly found in pump petrol, unlike the other two which are more useful to the turbo engine. High boost slows flame spread. The chemist was able to brew a legal fuel that burned more rapidly, generated more heat energy and had a higher resistance to detonation - in effect, a higher octane fuel. BMW introduced such wizardry during the '83 campaign, working with German chemical giant BASF's Winterschall subsidiary, much to Renault's chagrin. Renault had regularly run a high grade of fuel but explains that this was "very close to pump fuel - not completely chemical like BMW's fuel".

Rich
to
avoid
disasters

However, exploitation of fuel chemistry was still in its infancy, as was control of fuel injection and ignition. Renault had set out on its pioneering route employing Kugelfischer mechanical injection with a "3D cam" to allow response to both throttle position and boost pressure. Boost pressure was sensed by a pneumatic device which rotated the cylindrical cam, while a linkage to the throttle mechanism moved it along its main axis. Nevertheless, the unit was still only responsive to engine load, not speed. The same fuel quantity was injected for a given load at 12,000r.p.m. as at 6,000r.p.m. The fuelling had to be a compromise and as it always had to be sufficiently rich to avoid overheating disasters, it was often too rich causing relatively high consumption for a given power output. Improved control would make an engine more responsive - a crucial consideration given a turbo engine's throttle lag - and more economical. Turbo engine development and the fuel restrictions introduced in the early Eighties, first in the endur-

ance racing arena, helped spur the development of electro-mechanical and fully electronic injection systems.

In an electro-mechanical system an electronic control unit (ECU) takes readings from a variety of engine sensors and controls a servo motor which operates the cam on the metering unit while in a fully electronic system a similar ECU activates triggers controlling solenoid-operated injectors, determining the timing and duration of each injection pulse. An important difference between the two systems is delivery pressure. The computer-timed electronic system works at a far lower pressure than the mechanical metering unit: around 5 bar.

Higher pressure offers superior atomisation: better burning, and better fuel consumption. That was particularly important with pump fuel, for at high boost flame spread was slow and uneven. The combination of the superior fuel preparation of the high pressure electro-mechanical system with the superior control of the low pressure electronic system had proved to be impossible ideal.

Early electronic injection systems were developed by Bosch for road cars - a well known example its low pressure, analogue-based L- Jetronic system, introduced in 1973. The Eighties brought more sophisticated systems in which information from the sensors was converted from analogue to digital values by a digital converter to allow the ECU to incorporate a micro processor. Micro processor control of electro-mechanical or electronic injection could be integrated with ignition control in a full engine management system such as the low pressure Motronic MS3 system developed by Bosch for Porsche, initially for endurance racing application.

A micro processor can cope with information from a great variety of sensors monitoring the engine's operating conditions - fuel pressure and temperature, air temperature, water temperature and battery voltage are read, in addition to load (throttle and boost) and speed. Two half speed sensors are employed, one with a blip for each cylinder, the other with just one blip: the former tells the processor the engine is, say, a four cylinder, while the latter tells it which cylinder is which. Each cylinder is treated individually and the speed sensors tell the processor to keep on running the programme in firing order. Crank angle is established by the sensors and injection and ignition timing can thus be set to relate to it. A low voltage pulse from the ECU triggers the servo motor/ injector drive and ignition amplifier to provide the optimum fuelling and ignition advance/retard for the conditions identified by the various sensors.

The micro-processor, in essence, consists of two chips: a RAM (Random Access Memory) chip to do the calculations and a plug-in EPROM (Erasable, Programmable, Read Only Memory) chip to dictate the ignition and injection settings appropriate for given sensor readings. These various dictates form what is known as a map and are compiled as a result of extensive dynomometer testing. For example, a reading will be taken every 250r.p.m. and every 0.25 bar boost for a given throttle opening to determine optimum ignition and injection settings for given conditions of load and speed. Control of the settings will then be fine tuned by the ECU according to the other sensor readings and the basic laws of physics - for example, low water temperature indicates warm up and the fuelling will be richened accordingly.

Crucial to the whole system is the basic software - and patient dyno testing. However, the plug-in EPROM facility allows fine tuning of the map at the trackside. Originally the map will have been transferred from the main dyno computer and at the track the EPROM can be removed again from the ECU and plugged into a portable EPROM programmer for alteration. For example, major overrun cannot be simulated on the dyno but can be accommodated in the light of track experience.

Clearly the process of mapping on the dyno was exhaustive and ongoing as engine specifications evolved. As maximum performance implied running at the limit, mapping could 'use up' a number of engines! On the track, digital control, while not increasing top end power, offered better response, better low down torque and overall a more drivable turbo engine with improved fuel efficiency. The challenge was to write software capable of doing the job without any 'bugs', to get the mapping right and, perhaps most important of all, to protect the micro processor's sophisticated circuits from interference. These circuits were highly sensitive to 'spikes' - interference in the form of electro-magnetic pulses generated mainly by the ignition system - calling for very careful location and insulation of the ECU and its wiring.

Digital based engine control was still in its infancy in '83 and, for example, the sophisticated Motronic MS3 system was causing Bosch all sorts of headaches, largely due to spikes, following its late season adaptation to the new Porsche/TAG engine. The '83 pacesetters, Renault and BMW, both employed electro-mechanical injection using the Kugelfischer pump, BMW working with Bosch to develop microprocessor control (having run an analogue system in 1982) while Renault did its own electronics. BMW went further than Renault, incorporating a separate circuit board with its own RAM within the ECU for on-board recording of the digitized signals, which could then be downloaded in the pits for subsequent analysis. In its simplist form, this 'logging' process recorded minimum and maximum values for a given parameter. A more complex form was to log how long was spent at a given value, while the ultimate was to log the entire circuit on a continuous time basis, allowing a read out to be available for each parameter at any given point on the track, on any given lap. BMW also experimented with telemetry links - transmitting the ECU signals directly to a receiver in the paddock area while the

car was on the move.

While digital based control was an important factor in turbo engine development, and fuel technology was starting to creep in, during '83 running rich was still the main, and somewhat crude way of pushing up the detonation threshold. Fuel tankage was restricted to 250 litres but mid-race fuel stops were possible and were common in '83 as fuel was used liberally to cool the engine. It was reckoned that running rich could be worth a 100 degrees centigrade drop - around 10% - in exhaust gas temperature. Consequently the mid-race stop allowed a turbo to run higher boost safely while also reducing its starting weight disadvantage compared to a 3.0 litre atmospheric runner. The traditional Ford Cosworth cars' advantages of running lighter and so exploiting softer tyres were reduced and by '83 turbo lag had been significantly cut making turbocars competitive even on slow circuits.

Worst of all for the 3.0 litre runners was the '83 restriction on ground effect technology: no longer could clever chassis engineering overcome a significant power disadvantage. Underbodies had to be flat within the wheelbase so the possibility for achieving downforce from the under car airflow was severely curtailed. The overnight downforce cut was in the region of 60%. Front and rear wings subsequently generated the majority of downforce, as in the days before the ground effect revolution. Wings generate downforce at a higher drag penalty. For a given speed, soaring turbo power could drag bigger, more effective wings through the air and in '83 the Cosworth engine, after years of astute rearguard action, finally met its match.

In spite of the ground effect restriction, the typical '83 chassis outwardly resembled its so called 'wing car' forerunners. Its familiar layout set the fuel tank behind the driver cell in a narrow monocoque tub which was flanked by pods housing the coolers. Sidepods were the logical location for the massive cooler area required by the turbo engine and a narrow nose and inboard front suspension promoted good airflow to them.

Beneath the old wing car carefully shaped tunnels ran back from just behind the front wheels the entire car length either side of the central chassis structure. Each tunnel was shaped to act as a venturi, accelerating air and thus, according to Bernoulli's Law, lowering its pressure, just as air is accelerated to obtain a pressure drop in a carburettor venturi. The air was accelerated into a shallow venturi throat that extended under the respective sidepod, was held at high speed through the throat and was then decelerated in a steeply rising diffuser positioned alongside the drivetrain. The diffuser section was designed to provide controlled deceleration, maintaining airspeed through the throat. It ran as far as the rear wing, the local effect of which helped the extraction process. The front and rear wings were asked to produce very little downforce in their own right, act-

ing virtually as trim tabs, since underbody downforce was won at a lower drag penalty. Indeed, as tunnel performance improved front wings started to fade away altogether.

Although the '83 regulations called for the entire width of the underbody between the front and rear wheels to be a uniformly flat surface, it was possible, in effect, to treat this as a throat through which air could be gainfully accelerated. To do so entailed putting a diffuser behind the mandatory flat area. In its simplest form, the 'diffuser' was merely a short upsweep at the end of the flat bottom area. The upsweep had to be split either side of the gearbox but if so desired could be extended as far as the maximum permissible 600mm. rear overhang (measured from the rear wheel axis).

Kicks for the air

Each of the flat bottom car's twin diffuser upsweeps provided a focus for the general influx of air characteristic of an unsealed underbody region. Air accelerated as it squeezed under the pod floor; got another 'kick' as it squeezed between the rear wheels; yet another as it funnelled into a diffuser entrance. Acceleration of air into the upsweeps caused the biggest pressure drop, and there was the important choice of short 'flip up' or long diffuser ramp. In the case of the former, the area under the rear deck created a vacuum, helping draw air from the underbody. In the case of the latter, the extended ramps drew in air, generally assisted by the action of the exhaust, a principle introduced by Renault during the '83 season.

With exhaust blown diffuser ramps, a pipe was led into the base of each ramp so that the gas flow would help 'activate' the airflow on the underside. It should be noted that a full length diffuser ramp was active on both sides for airflow through the engine bay would create useful pressure on its pronounced upswept upper surface. However, the overall package was very subtle: in each case there was a complex interaction between the 'underwing', the tail shrouding and the rear wing. An extended, exhaust blown diffuser worked well with a pronounced 'bottleneck' plan rear end, as in the case of McLaren MP4, while a 'flip up' worked well with a relatively high and wide tail shroud, as in the case of the title winning Brabham BT52. Brabham could not get an extended diffuser to work without exhaust activation, and had only one exhaust pipe to play with.

While it was possible to decrease

the inherently low pressure under a flat bottom car, the front and rear wings now had to supply getting on for 90% of total downforce (with a front - rear split in the region 30 - 70 to 50 - 50). A return to large front wings was indicative of the renewed importance of wings. It was consequently necessary to ensure the cleanest possible air flow to the rear wing, as well as to provide sufficient cooling to meet the prodigious needs of the turbocharged engine.

Aerodynamic and cooling considerations and ever more restrictive regulations dictated the layout of the new breed of flat bottom car. It was confined to four wheels, only two driven (and all properly sprung): six wheel and four wheel drive experiments were a thing of the past. However, a minimum weight cut for '83 from 580kg. to 540kg. represented a huge challenge in terms of materials technology thanks to the weight of the turbo system - even the old figure had been a struggle with a turbo engine on board.

No limit was put on wheelbase and wheelbase dimensions were tending to increase in the face of turbo power and (given the rear overhang ruling) in the interest of keeping the wing as far back from the engine cowl as possible and, perhaps, of lengthening and thus lowering the fuel tank. In theory, a long wheelbase car enjoys lower slip angles at which a given cornering force is generated and, all other things being equal, will be easier and more forgiving to drive. When Gordon Murray had added a 75mm. spacer to the Brabham BT49 it had gone 1.5 seconds a lap faster, and had been perfectly balanced everywhere. A long wheelbase tends to improve the lift:drag ratio, and Brabham found any awkwardness on tight circuits overcome by a weight distribution which provided better traction. Possible drawbacks of a long wheelbase include loss of rigidity and extra weight.

In the interests of weight distribution and rear wing location a spacer was invariably set between clutch and differential and this extended bellhousing had become a logical location for the oil tank. Weight distribution was a major consideration. The classic front:rear distribution was 40:60 but with increasing turbo power and loss of downforce, as much as 65% was put on the rear in the interest of traction. However, the location of the centre of pressure was as important, as well as that of the centre of gravity, the front:rear aerodynamic split affecting both traction and handling.

Understeer is an inherent danger of a rearward weight bias combined with high power, but traction should be improved. Traction can also be improved, in theory, through lowering the centre of gravity. Running low reduces drag-inducing turbulence and a lower centre of gravity improves cornering power. Further, to create worthwhile downforce, a flat bottom has to be run close to the ground and at a consistant ride height and attitude.

Another consideration is the distribution of masses relative to the location of the centre of gravity - concentrating mass towards it reduces the moment of polar inertia (the so called "dumb bell effect"). In theory, lowering the moment of polar inertia allows faster directional change and reduces the force trying to make the tyres break away under cornering. In that respect a central fuel tank was ideal - a full 250 litre load weighed around 200kg. Further, located near the centre of gravity, it would not upset handling as it diminished. While rival cars clung to the traditional Hewland pattern of longitudinal gearbox set behind the differential, with the passing of the 'wing car' Ferrari set a transverse box ahead of its c.w.p. for a lower moment of polar inertia.

Naturally, under flat bottom regulations any form of skirt was outlawed and wings and other aerodynamic appendages had to remain immobile and were restricted by both front and rear overhang limits and by maximum width dimensions. The rear overhang figure of 600mm represented a cut of 200mm. from the '82 regulations while width was down from 1100mm. to 1000mm. However, maximum height increased to 1000mm. excluding roll bars, a higher set wing considered to be in the interest of rear visibility. The maximum width ahead of the rear wheel axis was 1400mm. this limit extending over the flat bottom area and as far as the front wheels. Front wings could be up to 1500mm. in overall width below rim height, but width ahead of the front wheel axis above that was restricted to 1100mm. Overall width was confined to 2150mm. Use of the maximum available front track was expedient to ensure an adequate airflow to the sidepod mounted coolers.

According to the '83 regulations, monocoque design had to recognise minimum cockpit dimensions and requirements for two roll bars (the second incorporated in the dash bulkhead) and a 'crushable structure' around the fuel cell. In addition, the monocoque had to form part of a so called "survival cell". In essence, the survival cell legislation insisted upon an integral box member running either side of the driver compartment and extending 500mm. ahead of the driver's feet and upon protective panels either attached to the tub or, where pods were carried, forming the pod side panel. The foremost 400mm. of each box member was not necessarily to be part of the monocoque but was to be solidly fixed to it. The box members had to conform to materials and dimensional criteria, as did the side panels which were required to be at least 200mm. high and cover at least 60% of the wheelbase, effectively determining the minimum length of a sidepod.

Access to the cockpit was to be unhindered and in theory the driver had to be able to vacate it in five seconds. Safety belt, life support system, extinguishers for driver compartment and engine, two circuit breakers and dual brake circuits were mandatory and were covered by detailed requirements. Additional safety minded regulations laid down requirements for fuel and oil systems and specified acceptable fluid and electrical lines. The fuel container had to be an FIA approved Kevlar reinforced supple rubber bag located within 400mm. of the longitudinal axis of the car.

Clearly, given the tight dictates of the regulations and the extensive ancillaries of the turbo engine, the mid Eighties chassis designer started with a far from clean sheet of paper. Even the wheel rim size was standardised by the need to slot into the development programme of one of the few tyre suppliers. In view of the practicalities imposed by anything other than an unlimited budget, the overriding considerations were those of wheelbase and plan area, the minimisation and distribution of weight, engine system packaging and aerodynamic form.

Scaled-up replicas of models

Packaging, particularly of engine ancillaries was a nightmare and restricted aerodynamic options. Aerodynamic form was all important and design had to be concerned with every detail, and was a source of constant development. In effect cars had become scaled up replicas of the models exhaustively tested in rolling road wind tunnels such as that at Imperial College London originally used by John Barnard to develop the shape of the McLaren MP4.

The '83 McLaren with large underbody area - sidepods extending forwards alongside the cockpit; the underbody plate carried as close as possible to the rear wheels with wheel 'sealing plates', and prominent, full length, diffusers - was typical of '83 thinking. However, as we have noted, even with an effective underbody the rear wing contributed far more downforce and commonly with turbo cars it featured two or three flaps mounted to the rear of the main element, those rising up very steeply but generating more downforce only at a significant drag penalty. Air leaking through the slot between them helped keep the flow attached to the low pressure underside. The wing was fully adjustable and the number of elements and their sectional shape and relationship could be varied according to circuit requirements.

Unlike the rear wing, the equally important low mounted front wings worked in 'ground effect' and their endplates ran very close to the ground. A single flap was often added to a front wing but it was important not to spoil airflow to the sidepods. The turbo car's fully adjustable rear wing generally carried deep endplates and during the '83 season Ferrari introduced the concept of positioning winglets on it ahead of the rear wheel axis to take advantage of the more generous 1400mm. within-wheelbase width restriction. The rear wing was supported either by a single central post attached to the gearbox or by a horizontal beam running between endplates similarly attached to the gearbox. Front wings were either mounted on a transverse pole running through the nosebox or were part of the nose moulding, with consequently only flaps adjustable.

Drag was created not only by wings and diffuser, but by coolers, and of course the overall fuselage shape, and it was important to shape the latter so as to put the rear wing in clean air, to ensure adequate cooling, and to minimise drag for maximum speed. With the coolers mounted in sidepods the internal flow was crucial and was influenced by the design of inlet and outlet ducting. Smooth air flow maximises cooling efficiency while minimising the inevitable drag penalty. Size of radiator alone is not everything: air has to be persuaded through it and the wake behind a car helps the extraction process. The hot air could be vented upwards into the flow over the rear wing or rearwards, often passing through a shrouded engine bay.

Whereas a four cylinder car requires only one water radiator and one aftercooler, a six cylinder needs one of each per bank. The common four cylinder layout was to position the aftercooler on the left, the usual side for the turbo, with the water and oil radiators on the right, while the logical six cylinder approach was to serve each bank by its respective pod, placing the radiator ahead of the aftercooler. The aftercooler was kept as close to the engine as possible to minimise charge plumbing to the benefit of throttle response. Generally the aftercooler was engine bay vented while radiators were top vented and coolers were invariably of the lightweight aluminium type.

The chassis had to accommodate a number of cooling air flows in addition to those for the engine which, in some cases, was kept unshrouded in deference to an engine designer's wishes. Generally a gearbox oil cooler was carried atop the transaxle while shocks, brakes, not to mention the driver, required cooling flows. Additionally a compressor intake was required, and if the engine bay was shrouded the turbo often required hot air extraction through body vents.

In 1983 Gustav Brunner introduced the concept of shaping the monocoque so as to act as an integral fuselage shroud, such chassis sculpturing being made possible through the introduction of advanced composite materials. Those materials were introduced to save weight and add rigidity to the chassis structure, which in its entieity consisted of the monocoque tub (housing driver, fuel tank and supporting the front suspension), the engine (plus attendant frame in the case of a semi-stressed four cylinder engine) and the transaxle (supporting the rear suspension). It is important that this structure is as rigid as possible, given high power and considerable downforce to cope with. Indeed, even with a low power car only fractional movement of one set of suspension pick up points relative to another will make a mockery of theoretical suspension performance. Lack of torsional rigidity will be perceived by the driver as unpredictable handling and will probably spoil a car's responsiveness to alterations intended to adjust its handling.

The need for a stiff yet slim monocoque saw wing car designers turn from sheet aluminium tubs to aluminium honeycomb - a sandwich of thin inner and outer aluminium skins bonded to a core of paper thin honeycomb-form aluminium foil which acted as a continuous shear web. However, while wing car designers were starting to exploit the inherent stiffness of the aluminium honeycomb composite, moves were afoot that would lead to a switch to resin/fibre skins based on carbon fibre or Kevlar sandwiching an aluminium foil or Nomex honeycomb core, again the core saving weight. Advance composite skins were more tear resistant than aluminium, the product could be moulded to shape and the finished article had less weight and far greater torsional rigidity. In view of the sandwich construction of the outer panels it was no longer necessary to form longitudinal box members to provide the rigidity lost to the monocoque's basic 'shell' through the cockpit opening. However, the regulations continued to insist upon such construction, as we have noted. And the depth of the cockpit was still a significant consideration, low cut sides costing rigidity.

The strength of a resin/fibre composite is in the fibre. These advanced materials have fibres perhaps only 0.005" thick spun from carbon or the DuPont Corporation's Kevlar aramid. While they offer truly exceptional tensile strength and stiffness, they do so in only one direction: axially. Loads have to be fed along the axes of the fibres. Epoxy resin is used to envelope the fibres, after they have been woven into a cloth. The resin forms a plastic matrix which secures the fibres in the proper relationship to one another and bonds several layers together to a required thickness.

Weaves can be anything from a right angle lattice (50/50) to unidirectional, where 95% of the fibres run in one direction with the others merely tying them together until the resin is applied. Broadly speaking, monocoque skins were a laminate of a number of unidirectional layers sandwiched by an inner and outer layer of 50/50 weave. A resin matrix offers no significant strength in its own right yet accounts for a high proportion of the total weight of a composite material. But it plays an indispensable role as, while it transmits loads to the fibres it will not transmit cracks, and individual fibres can fracture without causing significant reduction in component strength as neighbouring fibres will consequently not be affected and will bridge the gap.

Generally a resin/fibre composite is supplied as 'pre-preg' sheets which means that it is already impregnated with heat curing resin and only needs baking in an autoclave (a high pressure, high temperature oven) once it has been worked into the shape of the component. Clearly there is an almost infinite choice of combinations in the fibre (carbon or Kevlar), the weave and the resin in a pre-preg material and thus it is produced to order. The main differences between carbon fibre and Kevlar are stiffness, impact resistance and cost. Carbon fibre is stiffer while Kevlar is less expensive and absorbs kinetic energy better. The combination of carbon fibre and Kevlar offers a good compromise between stiffness and impact resistance.

When in 1981 McLaren unveiled the first carbon fibre car, one week later Lotus unveiled the first carbon fibre/Kevlar car, and it was the latter combination that became the most widely employed in the early Eighties. However, McLaren bonded together five sections (including bulkheads) moulded to shape by American rocket maker Hercules, while Lotus formed its composite tub by folding up two panels to form a shell into which aluminium bulkheads were inserted. Moulding to shape then bonding became the norm, the tub usually split into two main shell halves - either upper and lower or two sides - with bulkheads added, often of aluminium. Where the monocoque was exposed to the airstream, access through the shell structure to dampers and so forth was allowed through removable plates.

With composite material structural options being almost infinitely variable, it is possible to optimise the strength:weight ratio, but to do so is an analytical nightmare without a computer programme to assist. Finite Element Modelling was regularly used in aerospace applications - this breaks down the structure into hundreds or thousands of elements for computer analysis to find the optimum structural solution. The first racing application of F.E.M. was undertaken by Hercules on behalf of McLaren in the development of Barnard's original tub design. That tub was reckoned to be 70% stiffer in bending and torsion and almost 25% lighter than the metal item it replaced.

The crash resistance of composite tubs worried a number of designers while the technology was young. The traditional aluminium sheet monocoque deformed progressively and if properly designed would absorb a great deal of energy while so doing. Advanced composites were acknowledged as stiff but it was feared that they would prove dangerously fragile upon secondary impact. A number of early Eighties tubs were designed with all or some of the outer skin aluminium though in some cases this was due to lack of in-house composite facilities. As we have noted, aluminium bulkheads were common.

A typical arrangement of tub crossmembers saw the front bulkhead carry the forward arm of a wide based lower wishbone and form the front of the pedal box while a double scuttle bulkhead assembly at the rear of the pedal box sandwiched the inboard, upright dampers and carried upper suspension mounts, steering and anti-roll bar while a dash bulkhead carried the rearward arm of the lower wishbone plus the mandatory roll hoop. In some cases the upper wishbone was supported by scuttle and dash bulkheads. Invariably the tub was completed by firewall and rear bulkheads sandwiching the fuel tank, atop which was the main roll hoop. The regulations dictated that the two roll hoops were to be no more than 500mm. apart and that a straight line linking the top of each was to pass over the driver's helmet. The dash roll hoop had to be as high as the steering wheel. The roll hoops could be formed of composite material and a roll pyramid atop the tank was consequently an alternative to the traditional rear braced metal hoop.

McLaren's trend setting MP4 design started the fashion not only for an advanced composite tub but also the use of such composites for body panels, undertray, wings, brake ducts and so forth. For example the radiators were carried in carbon fibre boxes, strong enough to act both as mounts and ducting, replacing conventional metal subframes and g.r.p. ducts. Ahead of the engine was less metal, less weight.

Excess weight is a serious handicap adversely affecting acceleration, braking, cornering performance, tyre wear and overall reliability. Informed opinion suggests every 10kg. excess weight adds 0.2 - 0.3 seconds to a typical lap time. Less well financed cars could be up to 80kg. over the 540kg. dry minimum weight. One important saving was made through the adoption of carbon fibre reinforced carbon (carbon- carbon) discs, originally developed for Concorde and introduced to racing by Brabham. The overall weight saving could be over 20kg., and was unsprung as well, for inboard brakes were generally a thing of the past, primarily due to airflow considerations, though inboard front brakes also represented additional weight and complication with the need for a shaft from the front hub. Carbon-carbon brakes not only saved unsprung weight but also reduced the rotating mass and lower mass means lower inertia: it is easier to accelerate and brake and follows a road surface more closely. However, in practice lessening unsprung, rotating mass was a somewhat marginal gain but the overall weight saving was significant, as was the higher co-efficient of friction of carbon-carbon pads and discs. This combination promised lower pedal effort yet greater deceleration.

Development of carbon-carbon brakes suitable for racing was a laborious process. The brakes introduced by Brabham were produced by Dunlop and featured steel centre discs: later Brabham discs were produced in the USA by Hitco, a division of Armco Steel that had started manufacturing for military aircraft in the late Seventies. Carbon-carbon is difficult and expensive to produce. Essentially it consists of a matrix of carbon/graphite material reinforced with carbon/graphite structural fibres. Production entailed putting a woven web of carbonised rayon or similar fibre in a methane gas filled furnace where, red hot, carbon atoms formed on it in a top-secret process known as carbon vapour deposition. Densification is accomplished by impregnating fibres with carbon during repeated steps at high temperature and the entire process takes many weeks: hence the material's expense. The product has to be machine finished using diamond tooling.

In 1980 Brabham used 0.7 inch thick solid carbon-carbon discs supplied direct by Hitco through an exclusive agreement for development, with Hitco engineers attending Brabham test sessions. The discs operated at a significantly higher temperature than conventional cast iron discs - up to 600 degrees centigrade, not far off the temperature at which carbon-carbon starts to oxidise. It was found almost impossible to dissipate sufficient heat to maintain an acceptable wear rate on slow circuits so Brabham's discs - ten times as expensive as conventional discs but longer lasting - were at first restricted in use.

McLaren was also interested in the development of carbon-carbon discs and in '83 started working with French aerospace company SEP which had a suitable ventilated disc. By the end of '83 both Brabham and McLaren were ready to race carbon-carbon everywhere, using their own calipers. AP Racing shared the rest of the caliper and 'conventional' disc market with the Italian Brembo concern. Cast iron discs were either 1" or 1.1" thick and ventilated by internal radial slots, the thicker discs heavier but longer lasting.

Growing stalagmites and stalactites

The disc was bolted to an alloy bell driven by wheel pegs and was designed to function as an air pump, drawing the air ducted from the brake scoops through the upright and flinging it out around its periphery. Curved internal vanes were standard on cast iron discs by the Eighties and AP had a more advanced 'sphericone' disc which was run by many of its teams in '83. The sphericone essentially consisted of alternate stalagmites and stalactites growing inward from the opposing disc friction plates and was a lighter, cleverly produced design. At one stroke, it both reduced the weight of the disc and increased the heat dissipation area.

Brembo led AP in caliper development. The magnitude of mechanical force exerted by the caliper in response to the hydraulic system relates to piston area. The turbocharged Grand Prix car required four pistons per disc which pre-'83 implied two calipers, one either side of the disc. In '83 Brembo introduced a Formula One 'four pot' caliper, AP following suit later in the season. The main advantage was lightness: each AP two pot caliper weighed 1.5kg., whereas the four pot alternative weighed 2.7kg., and the saving was greater with pads installed. Brembo and AP four pot calipers were cast in aluminium as two halves which were bolted together with steel bolts. They carried aluminium pistons and, for cast iron discs Ferodo copper/asbestos pads. The caliper was bolted to the upright and to avoid interfering with the airflow the brake was buried inside the wheelrim. The standard 11" disc size left little caliper clearance in a standard 13" rim.

A wheel has to allow a free passage of cooling air, be as light as possible, yet must withstand massive loadings (in particular it must be rigid in the plane of rotation to ensure positive handling). Two basic types of wheel were in use in the early Eighties, the cast magnesium alloy wheel offered by UK company Dymag Engineering and the modular cast magnesium/spun aluminium alloy wheel produced by Speedline in Italy. The modular wheel has a sand cast magnesium centre to which inner and outer aluminium alloy rim halves are bolted, these rims absorbing energy well in the event of impact, and distorting rather than shattering or cracking should a driver hit a kerb on a street circuit but has the drawback of a slight weight penalty. A set of Dymags saved around 2/2.5kg. overall. Brabham didn't like Dymag wheels and produced its own one piece magnesium wheel which it reckoned was stronger, and perhaps lighter.

Typically rim widths were 11 - 12" at the front and 16 - 17" at the rear. Overall wheel size was set by the regulations at 18" wide and 26" diameter and rear tyres had been made to those maximum dimensions since the Seventies. The standard 13" rim diameter gave the tyre engineer a preferred aspect ratio while allowing room for adequate sized brakes. A tyre's aspect ratio represents a compromise between controlabillity and outright grip as a higher ratio will have a detrimental effect on the ultimate level of grip attainable but will offer the driver more feel, leaving him more satisfied with handling and braking.

A car can only be as good as its tyres allow, and tyre performance is therefore crucial. Tyre performance relates to shape and size, construction, compound and running temperature and pressure. Maximum grip is obtained at an optimum temperature and pressure but there is evidence to suggest that tyre temperature and in turn, pressure varies considerably as the car negotiates a course. Running a tyre too hot causes blistering while running too cold causes the rubber to roll off. A fall below optimum pressure can lead to overdeflection resulting in excessive heat buildup, which is one cause of premature tyre failure.

It is clear that an underpowered car can be at a significant disadvantage if its tyres have been developed to suit a more powerful rival - it might not be able to get the tyres up to working temperature at all. At the other end of the scale, where more than one highly competitive team runs with a given tyre manufacturer there will always be suspicions that the tyres are better suited to one chassis than another. It is practically impossible to judge if a more successful car has benefited from better chassis development or advantageous tyre development - neither stands still.

Clearly, where a selection of tyre compounds is available it is important that a chassis is able to exploit the fastest available race tyre. A tyre goes through a heat cycle and well before it wears out it will 'go off', significantly lengthening lap times - perhaps to the extent that a pit stop becomes expedient. The ability to make a softer, stickier compound last can be equivalent to running a significant amount of extra horsepower. Generally a well balanced car is easy on its tyres. However, a driver can easily ruin potential tyre performance by driving too hard too soon , particularly on full tanks.

If compound is important, so too is construction and when significant progress is made by a tyre manufacturer it is often a modified construction that is the reason. Clearly, the biggest constructional factor is the choice of crossply or radial. Radials have a more flexible sidewall which can increase "carcase lag" - the time it takes for a movement of the wheel to be transmitted through the carcass to the tread. On the other hand, radials run at a lower slip angle at the limit - less time is required to develop the slip angle which means steering is quicker, more responsive. And the radial sidewall offers a useful damping effect. However, the lower slip angle means that the driver has less warning of imminent loss of adhesion!

Running softer without squirm

Significantly, while the radial sidewall is subject to more distortion under load, the radial's tread area is subject to less. Unlike crossplies, radials do not suffer significant 'tread squirm' which can cause overheating. They offer reduced rolling resistance and enjoy reduced operating temperature and they can more safely run softer compounds. Radials offer more grip under cornering and braking, more traction, more straightline stability and more consistency. In theory at least.

In practice Formula One radial pioneer Michelin had decades of

crossply tyre development to overcome when it set out in 1977. In the early Eighties it showed it had a competitive tyre and was joined by Pirelli. Goodyear would admit a radial's more stable tread area allowed it to run softer compound treads - it had an advantage in the wet. It was also clear that the fact that the radial, unlike the crossply, did not grow at speed was an advantage, particularly on high speed tracks, ride height remaining more consistent.

Radial tyres require more camber change in the suspension, the design of which is closely related to tyre characteristics and took on new importance in 1983. With wing cars there had been little suspension movement - most flex was in the tyre sidewall! With less downforce and more power there were more attitude changes, more suspension movement calling for more precise geometry.

The basic linkage was fairly standard in the mid Eighties with wishbones and some form of inboard damper actuation at each corner. The positioning of suspension pick ups was primarily influenced by tyre architecture. The front suspension invariably featured an unequal length wide based lower wishbone and narrow based upper wishbone. At the rear the usual practice was to utilise a pair of unequal length wide based wishbones plus a toe in control link.

Ground effect considerations had led to the widespread adoption of inboard suspension in the late Seventies. Initially necessarily beefy rocker arms replaced conventional upper wishbones: a better solution was to fit either a tension link to pull on a short pivoted arm at the base of the damper or a compression link to push a compact bell crank atop the damper. Being loaded in either purely tension or compression, such links could save weight and were not subject to flex, the unavoidable handicap of a conventional rocker. The rocking pieces were compact so bending loads were not a problem. By changing the rocker the ratio of wheel movement to spring/damper movement could be readily altered.

Although a tension link could be thinner than a compression link, with the former clearance is required below the damper for the rocking arm. In both cases the system can offer rising rate geometry which helps minimise pitch change under acceleration and braking.

Koni oil filled dampers were in almost universal use, though Renault ran a gas filled de Carbon unit and in 1983 McLaren forged an exclusive Formula One liaison with longtime Porsche supplier Bilstein, getting special lightweight gas dampers produced on its behalf. Always the damper was run with a coaxial titanium or steel spring. Suspension links and anti-roll bars were fashioned from steel, carrying steel or magnesium uprights in which live steel axles ran in large diameter low friction bearings. Driveshafts were similarly of steel and Lobro steel c.v. joints were widely employed. Teams produced their own rack and pinion steering or worked with renowned UK specialist Jack Knight.

It was normal for the left and right suspension linkages to be connected by a short anti-roll bar. Such a bar controls roll in conjunction with the roll resistance of the springs. However, Brabham had dispensed with the rear bar. As the bar helps transfer load from inner to outer wheel under cornering, dispensing with it should in theory leave the inner wheel more heavily loaded, to the benefit of mechanical grip and traction.

As we have noted, traction is a major consideration with high power to weight ratios. If the inner wheel is less heavily loaded (as on slower corners) and the differential is not constrained a lot of torque can be wasted in tyre smoke for torque follows the path of least resistance. Hewland gearbox users usually specified a Salisbury type limited slip differential. This used multi disc clutches to inhibit the action of the differential. As the speed of the half shaft increased above that of the differential case there was increasing pressure on the discs up to the limit at which the speed of the half shaft could not increase further relative to the case. The Salisbury clutch pack was simple and its characteristics could be easily varied by altering the way in which the clutches were packed. It was progressive in its action and was reckoned to be easy to drive.

Tyrrell had developed its own clutch pack differential in the days when Hewland runners used the ZF cam and pawl while Ferrari had developed its own differential for use with its transverse transmission. The shafts of its gearbox lay across the car and were turned at 70% of engine speed by spiral bevel gears. When launched in '75 there was a claim of a 20% better power flow than a longitudinal gearbox, as employed by Hewland. The British company's classic behind- the -differential five speed 'box for Formula One use was the FG which had been derived by crossing the FT200 Formula Two model introduced in '67 with the heavy '66 DG300 Formula One model that in turn had been derived from a big banger sportscar model. Born in '68, the FG400 had undergone subtle modifications through FGA to FGB specification: introduced in '79 the FGB was stronger and narrower, with better c.w.p. lubrication, but was significantly heavier.

The Hewland FG 'boxes had been developed with the intention of the magnesium main case (incorporating the gear case and c.w.p./ differential housing) acting as a structural chassis member. However, during the wing car era teams had started producing their own slimmer bespoke cases and often their own bellhousing cum spacer incorporating the oil tank. The oil tank was positioned immediately behind the clutch, a longer gearbox input shaft running through a sleeve in the integral tank. The clutch release mechanism was buried inside the bellhousing with the slave cylinder in unit with the release bearing and concentric with the input shaft. The oil tank carried 10 litres or more and had a header tank bolted to the top of it.

The transaxle case had become an integral part of the chassis design

and the typical bespoke transaxle was tall but narrow leaving room for wider diffuser ramps. Constructionally the most important consideration was that it should minimise the inevitable distortion which occurs as a result of the transmission of high torque levels. If the gear housing distorted significantly the gears would not mesh properly and the 'box would fail. Forming the bellhousing structure integrally with the main gearbox case produced a stiffer structure. Brabham pioneered such a practice with its transaxle, which also had only one differential access plate.

Large torque, small clutch

Regardless of transaxle, the early Eighties Grand Prix car was equipped with an AP Racing 7 1/4 inch twin plate clutch, as used in conjunction with the Cosworth engine through the Seventies. It was a diaphragm spring unit with gear driven pressure plates. Sandwiched between the flywheel and the dished end cover carrying the diaphragm spring was a steel adapter ring with teeth cut into its inner surface. Those teeth meshed with teeth around the circumference of each steel pressure plate. The cover and adapter ring were attached to a steel flywheel, initially by six bolts. Typically the flywheel was no larger than the outside diameter of the adapter ring - 213mm. (just under 8 1/2 inches).

The steel flywheel and intermediate and main pressure plates worked in conjunction with steel driven plates onto which a bronze based friction material was sintered. The two driven plates were rigidly attached to hubs splined to the gearbox input shaft. The flywheel weighed around 2kg., the basic Cosworth clutch 4.15kg. With its early turbocar, Renault carried a heavier triple plate version but never found it necessary to run at a meeting. However, with increasing turbo torque the twin plate clutch's pressure plates started to distort in the face of the enormous heat generated at the start. In response, AP thickened up the pressure plates, increasing the weight to 4.45kg. Four cylinder turbo engines, thanks to greater vibration and harsher power characteristics, started to crack the adapter ring, and with centrifugal force that, if unchecked would lead to a dramatic burst. The problem was overcome through a 12 bolt fixing - the title winning '83 Brabham ran with an AP 7 1/4 inch twin plate clutch attached by 12 bolts. The continuing success of the unit was indicative of the excellence of the specialist engineering which lay behind the rise of the turbocharged Grand Prix car. ∎

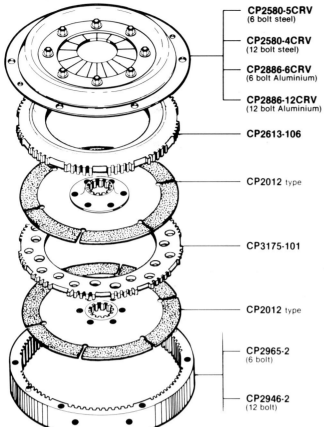

- CP2580-5CRV (6 bolt steel)
- CP2580-4CRV (12 bolt steel)
- CP2886-6CRV (6 bolt Aluminium)
- CP2886-12CRV (12 bolt Aluminium)
- CP2613-106
- CP2012 type
- CP3175-101
- CP2012 type
- CP2965-2 (6 bolt)
- CP2946-2 (12 bolt)

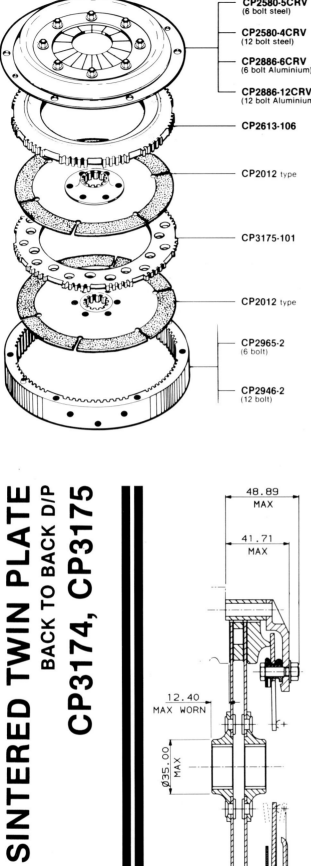

SINTERED TWIN PLATE
BACK TO BACK D/P
CP3174, CP3175

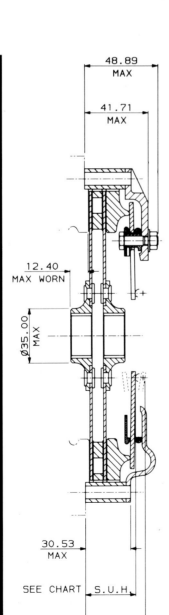

48.89 MAX

41.71 MAX

12.40 MAX WORN

Ø35.00 MAX

30.53 MAX

SEE CHART   S.U.H

40.44
MAX FULLY WORN

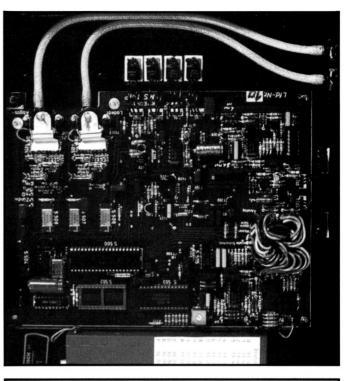

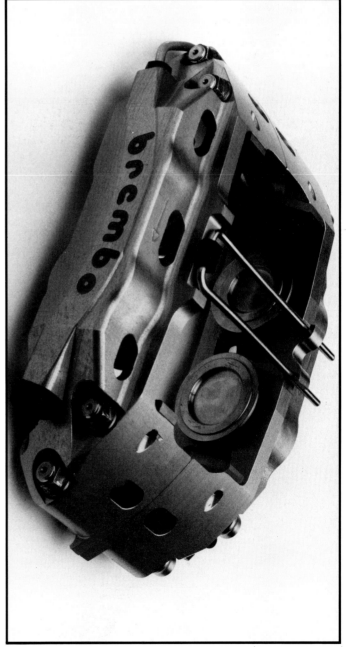

POWER STRUGGLES

Trends '84-'87:
Development of
the Mid Eighties
Grand Prix car

The Eighties four valve race engine was a highly efficient pump. With a tolerant fuel and precise control of ignition and injection to push up the detonation threshold, allowing a very high compression ratio to be run, together with adequate charge cooling, it could produce four times its normally aspirated output on four times the inlet manifold pressure.

As we have noted, the superseded 3.0 litre Formula One engine produced in the region of 175b.h.p. per litre: a comparable 1.5 litre engine would offer 262.5b.h.p. at atmospheric pressure (1 bar absolute at sea level) with power increasing as a function of boost. At 2.0 bar absolute 525b.h.p. (the 3.0 litre engine's output); at 3.0 bar 787.5b.h.p.; at 4.0 bar 1050b.h.p... on an idealised linear scale.

In 1987 pumping a genuine (twin pop-off valve controlled) 4.0 bar Cosworth managed to extract over 1000b.h.p. It was running a toluene- based fuel, a highly sophisticated engine management system and an undisclosed compression ratio: at least 8.0:1 and almost certainly higher. Adequate charge cooling was ensured by very careful attention to the aerodynamics of the Benetton chassis it ran in, water sprayed aftercoolers having been outlawed for the final season of high boost.

That late-season qualifying performance was arguably the most impressive power per litre per bar manifold pressure realised over the period 1984 - '87. Others had earlier gone into four figures running 4.5 bar and beyond, up to 5.5 bar in the case of BMW. BMW had exceeded 4.5 bar and 1000b.h.p. first, in late '84, and with continuing fuel, engine management and turbocharger development saw that record 5.5 bar flash reading, again in a Benetton chassis, worth 1443.75b.h.p. on the idealised linear scale and rated "over 1300b.h.p". In the circumstances there had to be a loss of efficiency causing a drop off from the linear scale. Charge temperature was higher than ideal at such a high boost level (in spite of an elaborate water spray) and the rugged in line four's compression ratio (always a good barometer of turbocharged engine development) was "only" 7.5:1...

The pioneer of fuel technology and digital electronic engine control, BMW ran a 7.5:1 compression ratio throughout the '84 - '87 period both in qualifying and on race day. In '84, the only V6 rival to race 7.5:1 was the Porsche/TAG engine which burned doctored Avgas and exploited a fully electronic version of the Bosch Motronic engine management system used by BMW. With its higher pressure system ensuring better atomisation and with more advanced fuel, BMW had the more powerful engine and it ran a higher race boost on 220 litres. BMW engine chief Paul Rosche says his engine exploited as much as 3.9 bar on race day towards the end of '84, whereas Porsche/TAG will not confess to more than "3.2 bar" and "750b.h.p." for its first World Championship winning season.

Race boost and power estimates over the years '84 - '87 are clouded by conflicting claims. All we know with certainty is that with the development of toluene-based fuel (as exploited, for example, by Porsche/TAG from mid '85) average race power was at least 800b.h.p. That figure was offered by Porsche/TAG for '85, while Ferrari revealed a figure of 880b.h.p. for the same season pumping as much as 3.8 bar through its V6, which was running on a 7.0:1 compression ratio (and was running out of development potential). In '86 Honda set the race pace with manifold pressures exceeding 4.0 bar despite 195 litres, running an undisclosed compression ratio and feeding over 900b.h.p. to the rear wheels.

If snowballing development of fuel, digital control and turbochargers had charted new territory in terms of the power it was possible to extract, clearly it had also made possible impressive strides in specific fuel consumption. For example, Ferrari announced that for the first time in 1987 it had achieved a figure under 200gms. per h.p. per hour. As we have seen, prior to 1984 fuel consumption had been of lesser concern and, indeed, running rich offered greater performance through offsetting the higher stress of higher boost. That stress, mainly thermodynamic, became of paramount concern under the fuel restrictions of '84 - '87.

It took a lot of electronic and mechanical development work, generous engine cooling provision and generous aftercooling provision merely to make the engine and turbocharger survive. To win it was necessary to extract the maximum amount of potential heat energy from a limited capacity fuel tank and to turn as much of that as possible into useful work at the crankshaft. That implied running right on the verge of detonation without actually suffering piston crown (or turbine) melt down.

As we have noted, digital control was essential in this respect, consequently it was important to have the right deal with an engine management specialist. If Porsche/TAG and BMW were off to a good start with Bosch, then Renault, Ferrari and Honda had some catching up to do. While BMW exploited the superior atomisation of electro- mechanical injection, Renault, like Porsche, wanted the superior control of a low pressure system. Alas, Renault's in house (Renix) answer to Bosch Motronic (which employed Marelli Weber solenoid injectors) was not ready to race until almost the end of the '84 season.

Ferrari had waited until mid '84 before receiving a workable (read noise immune) low pressure system from fellow Fiat Group members Marelli Weber. The Italian alliance had a good relationship with Hart but towards the end of '83 Hart had perceived that it would be unlikely to get the emerging equipment and had turned to ERA, a two man company run by ex-Lucas employees Brian Mason and Bill Gibson. Mason and Gibson came up with a low pressure system using Bosch injectors and a lot of initiative. It was ready in time for Monaco putting the Renix delay in perspective.

Like Renault and Ferrari, Honda produced an in house low pressure system. Motori Moderni gratefully accepted whatever Ferrari had cast off while Alfa Romeo and Zakspeed were eventually supplied by Bosch with a low pressure four cylinder system. Cosworth received a system devised by Motorola - Ford USA's electronics wing - using Marelli Weber injectors.

All the aforementioned were full engine management systems with coordinated ignition control. Often the low pressure systems ran two or more injectors per cylinder to inject a greater amount of fuel in a given period of time. Otherwise the computer timed injection pulse might get 'tripped up' by the valve. In truth, the injectors supplied by Bosch and Marelli Weber simply did not have a large enough nozzle to meet the requirements of a mid Eighties Grand Prix engine. The situation was worse for the four cylinder engine with its larger capacity per cylinder: Hart ran four injectors per cylinder.

Seeking the superior atomisation of electro-mechanical injection for '84 (running pump fuel), Brian Hart had tried developing a Lucas- Ferrari type system similarly based on Lucas' classic mechanical injection. However, he couldn't get an adequate servo motor to operate the Lucas metering cam, given the response time required and the vibration of a four cylinder engine. The Lucas-Ferrari system won at Zolder in '84 before it was finally pensioned off: the last win for a V6 engine without fully electronic injection.

Though the superb atomisation of high pressure electro-mechanical injection remained an impossible ideal, fuel company research allowed the production of toluene based fuel which atomised extremely well from low pressure, fully electronic systems. Whereas Bosch ran 5.0 bar pressure in its Motronic system, Marelli Weber's own system was claimed to run at over 10 bar.

Interestingly, Bosch had on offer direct injection as used widely in the Fifties (for example, by the Mercedes Grand Prix car). There were, however, no takers.

Everyone had problems keeping the ECU comfortable and the system free from 'spikes'. There were the inevitable headaches of heat and vibration. The secrets of a successful engine management system were still the noise immunity of the hardware and the sophistication (and freedom from bugs) of the software. The rest was down to patient mapping; exhaustive dyno work which the smaller operations simply could not afford. The aim was always to ensure accurate fuelling under all conditions, especially transient ones. By '87 the Porsche/TAG engine had every single r.p.m. mapped. The Motori Moderni V6 was light years from that ideal...

Given fuel rationing precise injection control was essential and engineers talked in terms of balancing air pressure and fuel droplet size. Fuel was, of course, an area of important co-operation between engine manufacturer and supplier. Essentially, Mobil looked after Honda and in '87 Cosworth (which had previously run BP); Winterschall looked after BMW, Zakspeed and likely Hart ("source undisclosed"); AGIP looked after Ferrari, Alfa Romeo and Motori Moderni; Elf, Renault; Shell, Porsche/TAG. However, as we have noted, there were important differences between pump petrol (run only by the rabbits of '84), doctored Avgas and toluene based 'rocket fuel'.

Chemical fuels containing 80% toluene registered 102 octane on low speed test rigs but behaved like a far higher octane brew in the turbo engine. Partly through speeding up the rate of flame spread (slowed by high boost) to beat the onset of detonation. Toluene had been known at Indy since the mid Sixties when Ford found that diluting the regular Speedway methanol with 20% toluene cut fuel consumption 24% for only a 2% power loss. Toluene (the second T in TNT) is an aromatic hydrocarbon which means it is closely related to benzene (it is otherwise known as methyl benzene). Benzene has a greater heat content per unit volume than pump petrol and offers a higher resistance to detonation.

In other words, toluene based fuel was denser and less heat intolerant than pump petrol and it behaved differently in the high boost turbo engine. It atomised well and burned very well needing little ignition advance. It offered power without effort. So it was that the fuel chemist was able to produce a legal liquid generating significantly more heat energy than pump petrol, having an extremely high resistance to detonation with greater density. Fuel was rationed by volume, irrespective of weight. The density of pump petrol is around 0.70 - 0.78: Elf admitted 0.87 for its heavy toluene based '86 fuel. It produced 300,000 litres for the season to service six cars. In some instances different fuels were supplied for racing and qualifying.

Shell claimed to have a unique 'combustion stimulant' which gave a higher initial speed to the flame front, promoting a more rapid and more even combustion. It also boasted that its '84 fuel (in fact, doctored Avgas) would not wax when chilled - a problem that Elf ran into early in the season. Both Shell and Elf had immediately responded to the 220 litre ration by chilling (from a norm of 10 degrees centigrade) to as low as -50 degrees to cram more into the 220 litre tank. It was reckoned that a 1% reduction in volume was achieved for every 10 degrees drop in temperature. Since the chilled fuel was denser, the engine could be run leaner but, of course, as soon as it was in the tank it started warming up again: some of the potential gain could bubble through the breather...

Elf's problem was such that the Renault cars had to install heaters in the fuel line. In contrast, Porsche's Motronic system was programmed to work well with Shell's cold brew. Although BMW tended to shun chilled fuel, most other parties regularly prepared it in '84. Thereafter the regulations demanded a minimum temperature of -10 degrees centigrade.

Winterschall and Mobil led the way into 'rocket fuel' followed by Shell and AGIP with Elf lagging somewhat - significantly for Renault. Interestingly, the under-privileged rabbits could calculate to run out of fuel before the allotted race distance, safe in the inevitability of being lapped by the leaders! The density of rocket fuel added a significant weight penalty to the overall package - even a 195 litre tankful weighed over 200kg. On slow circuits fuel efficient cars had the option of running less fuel (perhaps 180 litres as, for example, Prost ran at Monaco in '85) along with less boost, saving weight and brakes while running softer tyres. Not only slow circuits could be easy on fuel - Spa was kind on consumption, for

Honda V6 - rear shot of the most consistently successful mid Eighties engine.
A front view of the same unit appears in colour on page 14.

example, as the cars kept up momentum through the sweeps. Imola was a another matter...

Overall, the competitive toluene fuelled engine developed an average race power in excess of 900b.h.p. on 195 litres, as we have noted. That implied good (engine and charge) cooling, good fuelling, an efficient combustion chamber shape and very precise ignition timing. In '86 Renault introduced improved ignition control through elimination of the distributor. Each plug had a tiny in built HT coil, allowing direct control by the ECU. The idea was followed, in '87, by both Honda and Ferrari.

Control of the ignition point was one crucial consideration in the avoidance of detonation, one crucial consideration contributing to the compression ratio escalation. But there was no one single factor that allowed Honda to set the toluene fuelled pace in late '85 through '86 and much of '87. Rival engineers do not believe there was anything 'trick' about the Honda engine. As with the Porsche/TAG before it, the entire engine system was correct and was part of a highly competitive car package. Williams, as McLaren, deserve much credit in getting that package right, but in this era the winning edge was engine rather than chassis performance. Honda had sufficiently intense on going engine and turbo development, first class fuel and excellent engine control. It had learned how to atomise its fuel well despite employing fully electronic injection (and would not admit the fuel pressure its in house system ran).

In '86 Renault came close to matching Honda race power with its ultimate engine, the EF15C. In the opinion of Renault engine chief Bernard Dudot, Honda's edge was simply that it was able to run just a fraction closer to the verge of detonation. "They had good experience of control of detonation - all aspects, combustion chamber design, air intake, fuel, electronic control and so forth. Perhaps Honda was a little closer on each point..."

Qualifying was a different matter as fuel gushed through lower compression engines, lowering peak temperatures. Boost attainment rather than detonation avoidance was the name of the game. BMW outstripped Porsche then Renault had the edge on Honda in those heady qualifying battles before the 4.0 bar limit of '87. As we have seen, even at a genuine 4.0 bar qualifying power could be nudged above 1000b.h.p. And in '87 some engines were coaxed to run at more than 4.0 bar. With a carefully located single pop off

valve merely an irritating leak in a heavily boosted system as much as 4.4 bar could be felt in the manifold. The key was in the location of the valve. It was possible to position it over a venturi in the charge plumbing system. Air gained speed through the venturi losing pressure. Either side of the venturi the flow was correct and the pressure was higher.

The Qualifying Power King in the days of unlimited boost, BMW appears to have run 3.8/3.9 bar as a race average throughout the '84 - '87 period, exploiting as much as 890b.h.p. and working hard to maintain power in the face of the cut to 195 litres for '86. The four cylinder engine from Munich could not accept more than 11,500 r.p.m. and 7.5:1 and lost out heavily in '87 as V6 rivals exploited higher revs and higher compression ratios to overcome the 4.0 bar restriction. Since power is a function of load and speed, higher revs could help compensate for lost boost. By '86 V6 engines could scream to 13,000r.p.m.; higher in the case of the Renault engine which was equipped with a pneumatic rather than a coil spring valve closing mechanism.

Whereas running higher revs compromised consumption, running a higher compression ratio produced more power from a given amount of fuel. A relatively high compression ratio had been one of the secrets of the success of the Porsche/TAG engine in '84. By '86 7.5:1 was the norm for a V6 engine and towards the end of the season Porsche/TAG, Cosworth (and doubtless Honda) were running 8.0:1. Ferrari caught up with the new engine it produced for '87 - when even higher geometric ratios were seen. The effective compression ratio was nearer 24:1 than 12:1. Compression ratio increases had followed fuel development. On rocket fuel, with sophisticated engine management, by '87 the piston had come so far up the bore the leading V6 units were starting to run "like an atmospheric engine", according to one insider...

One important characteristic of those high compression engines was a small bore: 82mm. or less was the order of the day. Consequently, six was the right number of cylinders. In theory a four cylinder engine, having less rings, camshafts and valve springs to drive enjoyed less frictional loss but that advantage was "academic", according to Hart. It also offered lower surface to volume ratio for the combustion chamber so less heat was lost to coolant but again that was of academic interest. The crucial consideration was the size of a piston crown. A smaller crown meant a shorter travel for the flame front and reduced the heat path from crown centre to cylinder wall.

29

Honda started out with an extremely short stroke six having a 90mm. bore, fractionally larger than the BMW four. Like Renault (originally running 86mm.) it switched to the region of 80mm. to challenge Porsche/TAG's later generation engine which had an 82mm. bore. In '85 Cosworth designed the new Ford six with a bore under 80mm.

BMW had to run a four cylinder engine for marketing reasons while Hart and Zakspeed ran four cylinders for logistical reasons. At 88mm. Hart had a smaller bore than BMW and Zakspeed yet developed an 86mm. derivative with much promise. Given sufficient resources both Hart and Zakspeed would have switched to brand new sixes. Alfa Romeo designed a four cylinder with a 92mm. bore in '83 - and aborted its pre-race development programme early in '87...

The four cylinder engine, with its single turbo, offered superior torque but "light switch" power - for example, the BMW engine tripled its output from 6000 - 9000r.p.m. BMW naturally continued to run a 12 bolt clutch and Honda and Renault joined it in '86 along with Cosworth while Porsche joined the club in '87 (and Ferrari continued to rely upon six bolts and a crankshaft damper).

Initially only BMW and Honda ran cast iron blocks, everyone else ran wet Nikasil liners (or in Ferrari's case, its own alternative) in an alloy block. As we have seen, that was the optimum solution but as boost increased so did the loadings and the ruggedness of an iron block became reassuring: 1000b.h.p. was pushing Ferrari's six year old alloy block (originally designed for two thirds of that output) a little too far. Porsche/TAG didn't ever reach four figures while Renault somehow got away with over 1100b.h.p. coursing through the new alloy casting it phased in during '83. Cosworth employed a very special casting process to produce an alloy engine with the strength of an iron engine. Ferrari turned to iron for '87, employing advanced materials technology to check the weight penalty.

Honda was the only engine manufacturer not to employ Mahle pistons (though there was no standard Mahle piston). Honda insisted its pace making engine had metal pistons. Iron on iron is a good combination with a high resistance to detonation, and Honda might have gone that route exploiting modern casting techniques and high grade irons to overcome the traditional weight handicap. The more exotic beryllium - lighter and more heat resistant than aluminium - is another possibility.

Engine manufacturers investigated nickel plating aluminium pistons and the possibilities of ceramics. A purely ceramic piston wouldn't work with a metal bore but ceramic material could have been sprayed onto the crown or ceramic fibres could have provided local reinforcement. However, pushed too far ceramic material will shatter. There is no evidence to suggest that either nickel or ceramic experiments paid off. Certainly, the oil gallery cooled aluminium piston stood up to the hammering given to its crown in the face of effective compression ratios at least as high as 24:1. And ceramic valves were not necessary in the face of the intense heat. In fact, as toluene based fuel jacked up power temperatures actually fell.

Aside from the piston, the most vulnerable components were the valve seats and the turbine wheel. Stellite valve seats became common in '84. Stellite is a class of extremely hard alloys. A ceramic turbine wheel was employed in a Garrett turbo tested but not raced by Renault in '86. However, towards the end of '87 Ferrari raced a Garrett turbo having a silicon nitride ceramic coating for its rotor assembly.

The ceramic turbo was part of a general R&D programme by Garrett targeted towards ceramics in road car turbos. The idea was to reduce rotational inertia by saving weight and to maintain a very close tip clearance under high temperature conditions while increasing the ultimate temperature resistance to harness more energy. Using the latest silicon nitride ceramic material Garrett reckoned to reduce the weight of the rotor assembly by 50% and to provide thermal resistance up to 1300 degrees centigrade. Renault raced Garrett turbos employing special steels to the same end, also having compressor wheels machined from a solid billet of aluminium. Honda admits that IHI supplied turbine wheels of Inconel, an ultra high temperature alloy that is very hard to work.

Close development work with a turbo manufacturer was essential. Lean running gave turbochargers a hard time and BMW had many problems with the big KKK turbo it employed in '84. The most dramatic example was Brands Hatch, where turbo failure stopped Piquet's challenge to Lauda. BMW subsequently switched

to Garrett, which was bad news for Zakspeed as single turbo development work understandably fell off. Zakspeed was eventually able to follow it into the Garrett camp, as was Alfa Romeo. Garrett, of course, already supplied twin turbos for Renault and later added Cosworth and Ferrari. Hart continued with Holset while Porsche/TAG and Motori Moderni continued with twin KKK turbos. Before switching to Garrett mid way through '86, Ferrari had made an unsuccessful pitch for IHI turbos: IHI's deal with Honda was exclusive. IHI, like Garrett, developed a ceramic turbine.

In mid '85 Porsche got tailor made mirror image units to match the slightly different exhaust systems either side of the block. Mirror image units subsequently became commonplace. Turbo development in the mid Eighties was such that by '85, as we have seen, maximum available boost had gone up up by around 50% from the 3.5 bar witnessed in '83, compressor outputs assisted a little by periscope intakes. These upset chassis aerodynamics but became a feature of most cars (and made it impossible to accurately measure ultimate b.h.p. on a dyno, even if there had been the capacity so to do). Equally as impressive was the fact that turbocharger and engine management systems development had drastically cut turbo lag. In mid '87 Cosworth produced a very sophisticated device to enhance compressor performance and found it had made lag virtually undetectable on the ECU log!

Two stage turbocharging, whereby the exhaust gas passes from high pressure to low pressure turbine while the charge air travels in the other direction, promised significantly higher boost and was tested by both Ferrari and Renault. Alas, there was insufficient time for this exciting development to surface.

As early as '85 it had become feasible to run without wastegates: the balance of gas flows then provided the ideal running condition. The compressor could not pass any more air, while the turbine could not pass any more gas. The turbine was, of course, running right at its limit: on the verge of overspeed (explosion) and melt down! Inevitably, power delivery was rather sudden, and race engines were always equipped with wastegates and were set up for a more subtle spread of power.

There was still (usually) an important choice between a larger turbo and more power and a smaller turbo and less lag. For example, the '85 Toleman was a very capable chassis and its driver, Fabi, was very sensitive. The chassis could get its power down earlier than certain Hart equipped rivals allowing Fabi to enjoy a larger turbo by driving around the inherent throttle lag. Senna was another sensitive driver - he honed the technique, widely imitated, of judiciously juggling with the throttle while cornering to sustain turbine momentum. By playing with the throttle on the run up to the apex Senna not only kept his turbos well spooled up but actually managed to achieve higher flash boost readings.

Clearly the four cylinder engine with single turbo was generally at somewhat of a disadvantage compared to a twin turbo six and both Hart and Alfa Romeo developed split port blocks with each cylinder's two exhaust outlets fed to a different turbocharger. Neither twin turbo engine raced, both programmes prematurely curtailed. Another behind-the-scenes development was variable geometry scroll (VGS) turbines employing a ring of adjustable vanes around the turbine wheel to increase gas speed as engine speed fell off. Honda track tested IHI VGS turbines and a water cooled turbocharger. It also introduced a device to by-pass air from the aftercooler, sending it direct from compressor to plenum chamber under certain conditions of temperature and pressure for faster response.

The concept of giving compressor inlet air a pre swirl was embraced by Renault through its DPV - Dispositive Prarotation Variable - device, which employed variable incidence vanes both to provide a pre-swirl and to cut off the air supply when the throttle was closed. That left the compressor in a partial vacuum helping to maintain its momentum. However, as the DPV's many vanes were in an annular ring with a circumferential feed, incoming air had to take a somewhat convoluted path to the compressor eye which cost a little pressure. Renault kept faith with the system, while the aforementioned (secret) compressor performance enhancer Cosworth introduced in '87 was reckoned to cost no pressure drop.

An increasing feature in the mid Eighties was electronic wastegate control. For example, BMW and Porsche each developed a system whereby the wastegate was regulated by the ECU according to a control curve that plotted the desired relationship between revs and boost pressure. Invariably, however, the driver was in overall control of boost and had a three (sometimes more) position switch to play with according to tactics and his fuel position. The calculation of fuel consumed was via a straightforward logging of the time solenoid operated injectors were open and a radio blip from the pits could signal the completion of each lap, allowing the ECU to calculate laps left at existing rate of progress. The driver could then compare that to the actual number of laps remaining as signalled (or radioed) by the pits. Honda had a four position boost switch: fuel saver - low race boost - high race boost - a bonus 100 b.h.p.; it was integrated very sensitively into the management system, resetting the entire engine map.

Of course, driving technique was important in the conservation of fuel - for example, a driver running into trouble could consider the options of changing gear a few hundred revs earlier, lifting off earlier approaching corners, cornering in a higher gear and downchanging direct from top to the required cog. Driving smoothly and keeping tyres in good shape was of crucial importance. Tyre scrub cost fuel and consumption markedly worsened as tyres went off - to the extent that a time consuming tyre stop could represent a useful fuel saving. Consideration of fuel consumption saw a move towards six-speed gearboxes and put more emphasis upon the reduction of aerodynamic drag.

It was very subtle: for qualifying, larger brake ducts could improve braking and pod-mounted winglets could add useful downforce but those bonuses were likely offset by additional fuel consumption on race day. Drag was caused by the wheels, the wings, the fuselage shape and cooling flows and there was an important trade off to be made between more cooler area for more power and better reliability and less cooler area for less drag. One useful item that found increasingly widespread adoption was the oil heat exchanger plumbed into the water radiator system. The heat exchanger called for more water in the system but reduced the size of the bellhousing oil tank, saved some weight and reduced drag.

Running an engine in the open could make a significant difference to water and charge temperatures but the aerodynamicist wanted a clean airflow to the rear wing and few cars were run without an engine shroud. The least drag was attained by venting sidepod mounted coolers out through the engine bay, the wake behind the car drawing hot air from the tail. However, for satisfactory temperatures invariably it was necessary to provide an additional escape route.

The pattern established in '83 was for V6 cars to run top vented water radiators ahead of engine bay vented aftercoolers. In '85 Ferrari, Renault and Lotus introduced alternative side vented pods and by '87 side venting had replaced top venting as the regular option. The side vented pod was longer and lower and consequently tended to reduce drag. However, one body of opinion had it that the top vented pod created more downforce by throwing air towards the rear wing. Another body of opinion had it that the side vented pod created more downforce by clearing the flow to the rear wing. As with most aspects of race car aerodynamics: take the opposite to one theory and you have another perfectly valid theory...

The mid Eighties saw refinement of the full length diffuser underwing, which all cars had adopted by '87. However, those talented designers Gordon Murray and Rory Byrne had not applied the full length diffuser to the four cylinder engined chassis they had produced over the years '84-'86. Murray continued to maintain that a full length diffuser needed exhaust activation and further developed his combination of flip ups and distinctive rear shroud while Byrne evolved a unique package that set a small low mounted wing in tandem with the flip ups.

Byrne created a certain amount of excitement in '85 with a vee-shaped, snowplough-like step, 25mm. deep, ahead of his flat bottom area. In crude terms, this cut the air as a ship's prow cuts water, throwing it away from the underbody region. By this stage everyone was aware of the importance of discouraging air from flowing under the car to help reduce pressure: Murray, for example, ran a vee-shaped nose skirt. Within 12 months of the appearance of the 'stepped monocoque' Byrne had found "a better way to achieve the same thing" (which, understandably, he was not prepared to discuss) so it was obsolete.

It was important not only to discourage air from flowing under the car but also to control the flow to the diffuser. For example, the

shape of the leading edge of the pod floor was a crucial consideration, as was the shape of the lower corners of the monocoque at either edge of the flat bottom. Again, it was very subtle; theorizing would be dangerous. It is probable that even aerodynamic brake ducts and front wheel turning vanes significantly influenced the operation of the underwing.

The aerodynamic brake duct appeared in '85: it was a duct that shrouded much of the wheel rim and, according to brake engineers, was designed for its external rather than its internal shape. It cleaned up the airflow behind the front wings smoothing it around the inside of the wheel, reducing turbulence. That in turn clearly influenced the air flows to the underwing, the rear wing and the coolers. The aerodynamic duct was effectively outlawed for '86 by a new regulation. Brake ducts were required to keep within an imaginary box extending 140mm. above and below wheel axis, 120mm. inwards from the rim and as far forwards as the tyre.

Before it was outlawed, the aerodynamic duct was typically intended to work in conjunction with a front wheel turning vane. A curved vertical vane situated immediately behind the tyre this appeared simply to split the air circulating around the tyre from the flow down the side of the car. It was a device introduced by Lotus designer Gerard Ducarouge at Rio in '85. Ducarouge will only say that his vanes: "Changed the regime of flow around the turning front wheels and on the side of the car". Of course, it was more complex than that might suggest. For a start the vanes had to remain immobile whereas the front wheels moved.

Ducarouge admits the vanes only worked in certain circumstances, increasing drag (significantly cutting top speed) and (surprisingly) reducing cooling efficiency while increasing downforce. In race car aerodynamics, everything on the car interacts with everthing else in a very subtle way. Moving airflows cannot be seen and teams were understandably secretive so one can but speculate...

Ducarouge introduced both turning vanes and pod mounted winglets at Rio, the latter helping compensate for the loss of endplate mounted winglets. For '85 the regulations demanded a maximum width of 1000mm. above rear wheel height. Overall it emerged that the most efficient rear and underwing solution was a one or two tier wing above a full length diffuser, working in conjunction with a pronounced bottleneck rear plan. In essence this was, of course, the solution anticipated by John Barnard. However, the bulbous dorsum of Barnard's MP4, thought to help lower its drag co-efficient, was out of keeping with mid Eighties trends. With 195 litre tanks rear cowls were slimmed and there emerged a trend for reclining the driver to achieve a lower dorsal cross-section (taken to extremes by the lay-down BMW-Brabham BT55). Mass airflow to the rear wing was all-important.

The two tier rear wing with the second tier at rear deck height or thereabouts was introduced by Byrne in '85. By '87 there was a growing tendency for cars to run two tier rear wings even on fast circuits. Endplates were deep, extending down to the diffuser, under which were often vertical fins which acted as flow correctors and separators. Typically, the '87 car ran a single tier front wing with deep endplates (designed to act as nose skirts) having their rear edges contoured as closely as possible to the adjacent front tyre edge. At that point was the lip of the regulation size brake duct, curving around the tyre sidewall which it fed off while helping to smooth flow with its external surface. Between the wheels, Benetton narrowed the monocoque in the pedal box area by locating the dampers above the driver's feet achieving, according to Byrne, "a significant aerodynamic gain".

Ahead, the nose was often shaped as a deep prow to help deflect air from the underbody region, while further back the leading edge of the sidepod floor was typically upswept to help accelerate air towards the diffuser. By '87 engineers were able to offer around 25% as the proportion of total downforce produced by a full length, twin exhaust blown underwing. Cars were run low, a trend accelerated by Lotus in '85, regularly rubbing titanium skids screwed into the base of the transaxle case (titanium offers outstanding heat and fatigue resistance). A spectacular shower of sparks charted progress. Running low reduced under car turbulence, reducing drag and lowering and improving the efficiency of the diffuser. It also lowered the front wing and its endplates, increasing front end downforce. It also lowered the centre of gravity.

The mid Eighties Grand Prix car was extremely sensitive to pitch and ride height. It was necessary not only to run it low but as far as

Details of the McLaren MP4/2C - the ultimate development by John Barnard of his trendsetting flat bottom, turbo engined chassis designed back in 1983.

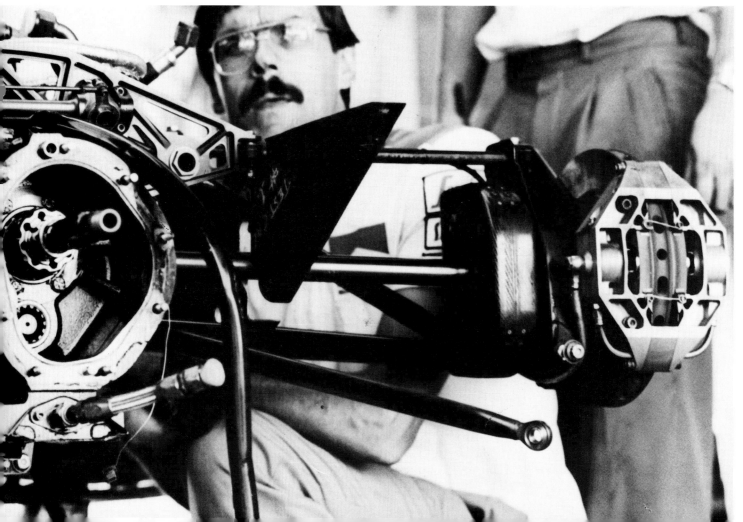

possible at a consistent attitude. The attitude of the car under all conditions was found to be crucially important. Downforce was focussed front and rear rather than more uniformly spread as in the wing car era and a 4mm. alteration in ride height at either end could be worth over 50kg. downforce. Clearly, it was vital to minimise pitch changes. This called for stiff springing, particularly at the front end to keep the rise and fall of the less heavily weighted nose under control. At the rear softer springing was to the benefit of traction and helped protect undersized rear tyres.

In '86 Lotus employed a hydraulically operated lowering system to help maintain ride height as the fuel load lightened while Ligier experimented with a Citroen based hydro-pneumatic self levelling suspension system. 1987 brought 'active suspension'. With conventional suspension ride height had always been a compromise as it varied with speed: low speed meant a higher than ideal ride height, ride height having to be adequate at high speed. And bumps would unsettle ride height. By way of contrast, micro processor controlled active suspension could in theory maintain an ideal ride height at all times.

Lotus' active system controlled ride height and springing: a variable resistance hydraulic jack - known as the 'activator' - fully determined wheel movement at each corner. The activator's movement was in turn determined by an electronically operated 'Moog' hydraulic servo valve which responded to input signals from the micro processor. The processor took readings from a wide variety of sensors monitoring chassis behaviour and compared that information to a pre-set programme, dictating wheel movement accordingly. Clearly, the system offered vast potential but it was immensely complex, and was heavy.

Williams devised a more simple system which, in effect, was a computer controlled ride height levelling system. Influenced by the Citroen system, it effectively lengthened and shortened the damper unit, gas filled spheres working in conjunction with a hydraulic jack at each corner. Mean jack height was dictated by servo valves controlled by the central processor. The processor took less inputs than Lotus' equivalent and the system was lighter being less complex. Lotus admitted its system was perhaps over-complex for Formula One needs and in one short season clearly did not have time to fully exploit its awesome potential.

The influence of pitch and ride height was, of course, yet another tricky factor to grapple with in the wind tunnel. Almost all teams gained access to rolling road tunnels. Alas, it was not possible to simulate the effect of exhaust activation in the tunnel. Another drawback was size: the largest models that could be accommodated by available tunnels were 40%. The larger the model, the greater the accuracy.

Brabham developed a full sized rolling road tunnel in conjunction with Southampton University but as it was only suitable for lightweight models it could only be used effectively for detail design work. The '87 season witnessed the opening of a 50% tunnel by March Engineering at Bicester and Lotus was able to test its 40% model in that facility, as well as in the 'Honda' tunnel at Imperial College. The 40% Imperial College tunnel was sponsored by Honda and was only available to Lotus and Williams. Other teams had to use the London institution's regular 25% rolling road tunnel. MIRA also offered a 25% tunnel, as did Dallara in Italy, while more satisfactory 33/35% tunnels were available at Cranfield Institute of Technology and Southampton University for those teams without private facilities. McLaren set up a deal with the National Maritime Institute (33.3%), Benetton with the Royal Military College at Shrivenham (25%) while Ferrari and Brabham built in house 35% tunnels which came on stream in '86 and '87 respectively.

By '87 much of the downforce lost through the flat bottom ruling had been regained: lateral forces were beginning to approach those of the ground effect era. And weight distribution was tending towards the 42 - 58 seen during that period, traction less of a problem with increasing downforce. However, traction remained of great concern due to tyre sizes and was a particular headache on street circuits where corners were tight and downforce was low. Weight distribution and aerodynamics remained primary concerns of the mid Eighties chassis engineer. Ferrari concentrated upon weight distribution in '84, producing a short wheelbase car with low moment of polar inertia. It found more benefit lengthening the wheelbase for aerodynamic gain and it's '87 upswing was as much due to its new tunnel as to its new engine.

If wind tunnel modelling was the key to successful chassis design, the design process itself was often eased somewhat thanks to computerisation. Williams made one of the most ambitious uses of Computer Aided Design (CAD) putting the giant General Electric Company of America's 'Calma' system to its toughest ever test. The system allowed the Williams design office to draw and stress test all chassis components on screen working in three dimensions. Team Director Frank Williams reckoned it was: "In effect, building complete cars in the drawing office".

The Calma system comprised three software packages: GEOMOD for conceptual three-dimensional modelling, DDM for detail design and draughting and Supertab for F.E.M. Williams reckoned it allowed it to do two weeks traditional engineering in one day. It could do plans more quickly and more easily and it could work to much finer tolerances and save valuable kilograms. Williams offered the example of the engine shroud for the FW11: designing with Calma's assistance gave the team the confidence to allow less engine clearance to the benefit of aerodynamics.

The F.E.M. facility was, of course, of major importance given the universal adoption of advanced composite tubs in the mid Eighties. The typical monocoque set carbon fibre and Kevlar skins over an aluminium honeycomb core. Nomex honeycomb only tended to be preferred in '84 in the fuel tank region where it helped insulate chilled fuel against heat. A general trend was towards the tub forming the cockpit coaming, in the manner pioneered by Brunner. With his RAM 03 design Brunner introduced the idea of setting notches in the lower half of each tank flank (below pod height) to sink coolers closer to the car's centreline thereby narrowing pod width. Byrne championed this concept and, as we have noted, also pinched the '87 Benetton monocoque between the front wheels for aerodynamic gain.

The majority of teams developed the facility to produce plastic monocoques in house. Indeed, Tyrrell clung to aluminium outer skinning until such a facility was available. Facilities ranged from the large autoclave operated by Ferrari to the oven and vacuum bag employed by Benetton. Notable outside suppliers of composite tubs (other than Hercules) were the French military equipment manufacturer MOC (Renault/AGS) and race car specialist Advanced Composite Technology (ACT) of Derby. Roger Sloman's ACT concern supplied tubs to Alfa Romeo, Ligier and Arrows.

Increasingly designers felt able to abandon metal bulkheads, and seamless shells (into which the bulkheads were threaded from either end) became as popular as split shells. Arguably the most advanced monocoques were those formed as a single shell with integral front and rear bulkheads, less floor panel. Such a tub was manufactured upside down and the floor was bonded in place after insertion of the inner bulkheads through the missing flat bottom. For maximum rigidity the cockpit opening was small and the gap through which the bulkheads were inserted did not fill the entire floor area, leaving a stiffening ledge.

Floor accessed monocoques were developed by the likes of Williams, Ferrari and Brabham. Teams refused to quote figures for torsional rigidity but *Racecar Engineering* was able to establish that the realistic target had become twice the 7500ft.lbs. per degree recorded by a typical aluminium honeycomb monocoque. Looking at it another way, the 2500ft. lbs. per degree of Chapman's pioneering monocoque could be improved upon sixfold!

There is no doubt that good mid Eighties monocoques were extremely good in terms of impact resistance but there were some instances of poor design, including Renault's '84 tub which suffered wishbone penetration on more than one occasion.

One driver was killed during the '84 - '87 period, de Angelis, but he perished through suffocation, trapped in a burning car after a high speed crash, rather than through any weakness of the Brabham monocoque. Regulation changes saw pedal box lengths re-specified for '84 while a requirement for a crash tested nose box was introduced the following year. Aluminium honeycomb proved a satisfactory material. Few cars kept the driver's feet behind the front wheel axis and the requirement for box members either side of the driver cell tended to be ignored, composite skins over honeycomb effectively replacing the boxes that had characterised Chapman's original aluminium tub.

With the monocoque approaching the stiffness of the engine and transaxle, engine mounts had become potential weak points in the chassis package. Honda and Renault found it necessary to improve upon their upper tub links, both adopting the familiar, ingenious Cosworth cam cover plate system. For his '87 Cosworth turbo car

Byrne designed a transaxle case which flared to meet the rear of each cam cover allowing the use of plates at both ends and producing a notably stiff chassis structure.

Integral bespoke transaxle cases, running from engine to end cover, became standard chassis members and were generally produced in magnesium. However, Minardi employed MSR, a magnesium based material with the strength of aluminium which allowed 4mm. rather than 7mm. walls. Split or integral, the transaxle case had become the universal location for the oil tank and invariably incorporated bespoke suspension mounts, setting upright spring/damper units either side.

While tension /compression link suspension supported by an integral case became fashionable, in '84 McLaren and Williams both ran rocker arm rear suspension. There was a suggestion that in McLaren's case the compliance of the rockers worked with the Michelin tyres it exploited so well. Lotus's rival Goodyear shod car ran a combined pull rod and rocker rear suspension system. Clearly, attacking the spring/damper unit from both ends altered the ratio of wheel to spring movement but this was not proved advantageous. Subsequently Osella and Minardi adopted the concept, though both teams' systems had disappeared by '87.

Up front straightforward tension/compression link suspension remained the fashion with dampers generally located upright either side of the pedal box. However, in '87 both Benetton and Ligier put the damper units above the driver's feet for a narrower pedal box. Ligier put all the inboard suspension members and the steering rack on the scuttle and thus eliminated holes in the side of the pedal box.

Gas dampers as pioneered by de Carbon and Bilstein (run by Renault and McLaren, respectively) became sought after items. Williams came to an arrangement with the Penske Indy Car team whereby it got Monroe gas dampers that had been developed specifically for Penske. These had a remote cylinder to enable easy pressure adjustment.

As we have seen, Brabham traditionally ran without a rear anti roll bar, Murray designing geometry to compensate. In contrast, Byrne ran a very thick rear bar on each of his competitive mid Eighties designs. Having moved to McLaren Murray frequently took the rear bar off the MP4/3. Indeed, by '87 many other teams were regularly running without a rear bar. One design engineer walked down the dummy grid at Rio in '87 to check the state of play and found at least half of the cars running without a rear bar.

Interestingly, in '86 Ferrari introduced aluminium ribbed carbon fibre wishbone arms. Earlier, Barnard had started a trend by incorporating the outer c.v. joint with the rear hub, switching to expensive ball bearings and machining the outer track into the hub. This made for a lighter, more rigid assembly which had a longer life.

Wheels were increasingly one piece magnesium, Speedline developing a Dymag-type item in '86 to save a little weight. OZ, new a company formed by ex-Speedline employees, and Fondmetal, also Italian, came into the picture, each supplying a number of teams including, for the former, Lotus and, for the latter, Williams.

Tyres continued to be undersize thanks to FISA regulations and Goodyear was able to report that: "the attempt to slow the cars by reducing the power transmitted to the ground worked very well". Tyre stops were common throughout the period. The classic tyre man's success was Berger's '86 Mexican victory, his BMW/Mader-Benetton's performance aided mightily by Pirelli longevity. However, Pirelli also recorded the worst tyre performance of the period: in the wet at Estoril in '85 the majority of its runners had to throw in the towel. Poor tyre construction was to blame. However, Pirelli made marked improvement from '84 until it quit at the end of '86 with just two wins to its credit. In '84 it had no leading team but in '85 took on Brabham then the improving Toleman operation. Murray reckons that Brabham's switch to Pirelli "threw the '85 season away", though he says that over the second half of the year the Italian company did produce some competitive rubber following the introduction of more satisfactory constructions. One such new construction enabled Brabham to give Pirelli its first win of the modern era, at Paul Ricard in '85. Alas, in '86 neither Brabham nor Benetton (nee Toleman) was a consistent front runner.

Following Michelin's withdrawal at the end of the '84 season, Goodyear snapped up McLaren to add to Lotus, Ferrari and Williams and it cleaned up against Pirelli, taking 30 victories over the '85/'86 period. However, Akron had been less competitive in

'84 as it switched from crossply to radial technology. It won only on the rough surfaces at Zolder and Dallas while, with both McLaren and Brabham on board, Michelin dominated. However, Goodyear's transition was relatively painless and while Michelin generally had a superior tyre Goodyear was not far behind and would doubtless have been a match for the radial pioneer, had battle continued in '85. As it was there were only two companies left to fight it out, Toleman failing to entice either Bridgestone or Yokohama to enter the fray after finding itself beached through Michelin's withdrawal.

In general terms, Pirelli commented that the main problem facing tyre companies in the mid Eighties was one of loading: as flat bottom loadings were concentrated at two points life had become more difficult for the tyre engineer. Development Chief Mezzannotte told *Autosport*: "Our tyres had to run between roughly 70 degrees and 100 degrees centigrade - run them too cold and you'd get graining, where the surface would literally rub off, and - remembering that the tread compound is really a very high density liquid - if you ran them too hot the surface would literally boil and this would cause blistering.

"You had to take all sorts of things into account to keep within the temperature range. The compound itself, of course, and then the surface, the weather, the circuit... We had three main tyres of tyre, for high (up to 220k.p.h.), medium (200k.p.h.) and low (160k.p.h.) speed circuits. For Silverstone we used a hard compound, for Monaco a soft one. Possibly the most difficult circuits were the slow ones with smooth asphalt, such as Rio. It was noticeable at Rio in '87 that tyre changes were required because of tread degradation and not wear: it was both smooth and slow, so tyres couldn't reach their working temperature so easily".

Nevertheless, the single tyre agreement for '87 worked well. Goodyear produced a specific tyre for each circuit at its Akron, USA base and the onus was on the chassis engineer to get the most from the available rubber, rather than for tyre companies to assist one or more favoured teams. There were few complaints about the quality of rubber supplied by Goodyear thanks to its long experience of Grand Prix requirements. Indeed, qualifying and race records fell in spite of standard rubber. The only possible complaint was that the single tyre agreement somewhat obscured the advantage of Lotus' active suspension, perhaps checking a revolution in chassis design.

A revolution that looked to be just around the corner was semi automatic transmission: both McLaren and Ferrari had 'shiftless' gearboxes in behind the scenes development. Neither surfaced: the overriding concern, as with tyres, was keeping well proven technology up to spiralling engine performance. Almost all cars ran the traditional longitudinal Hewland gearbox outboard and the FGB gradually gave way to the heavier DGB. Many teams modified DGB internals to save weight. Often teams strove to produce a six-speed gearbox at no weight penalty. Brabham introduced a seven speed transverse Weismann gearbox with its BT55 'lay down' special in recognition of the narrow BMW power band. The Weismann gearbox featured a unique quick-shift mechanism that did away with the usual spring-loaded plungers (and was kept a closely guarded secret).

A number of teams produced their own strengthened crown wheels and there was a certain amount of dissent at the rule of the Salisbury- type differential. Brabham and Ferrari both ran the narrower ZF cam and pawl as did Lotus on street circuits, while Benetton introduced a unique Quaife diff having worm gears and using the frictional force generated by the gears against the casing to bias the torque.

Earlier, at Monaco in '84, McLaren had introduced the Torsen worm gear diff. Like the Quaife diff, this exploited principle that a worm can drive a wheel but a wheel cannot drive a worm. However, the Torsen applied this principle to bias torque. Produced by the Gleason Gear Works of Rochester, New York, it was claimed to improve both handling and traction and was certainly useful in the wet, offering improved drivability.

Not surprisingly given McLaren's success, almost every team experimented with the Torsen diff but by '87 apparently all but McLaren had abandoned it (and Salisbury still reigned supreme). The Torsen was a heavy diff with small gears relative to the available torque and it needed a lot of development work to help it survive the rigours of mid Eighties Grand Prix racing. Engineer Carletti tested the Torsen with both Ferrari and Renault. He says that a driver could detect a difference if told a Torsen diff had been fitted but otherwise would be unaware of its presence. And no clear advantage was revealed by the stop watch.

A "huge advantage" according to Ducarouge was the deployment of carbon-carbon discs by rivals Murray and Barnard throughout '84. McLaren did it most thoroughly, running ventilated SEP discs everywhere, even on street circuits. The challenge had been overcoming the limited cooling rate: previously it had been impossible to get rid of all the heat on heavy braking circuits. Running carbon-carbon discs too hot led to a soft pedal and oxidisation of the material which would consequently wear out very quickly. Making carbon-carbon brakes work on all circuits was a revolution.

The big advantage of carbon-carbon discs was not so much in weight reduction as in braking performance. Leading runners could reach 540kg. with iron discs and the unsprung weight gain was only a marginal performance factor. As we have seen, carbon-carbon discs had a far higher co-efficient of friction (0.5 mu versus 0.3) offering lower pedal effort yet significantly greater deceleration.

Most teams (including Lotus) toyed with carbon-carbon in '84 but only McLaren and Brabham had sufficient experience to run them regularly. Significantly, both had developed their own calipers specifically for the new material. Lotus, for example, was not ready to properly exploit carbon-carbon until it had its own design Brembo manufactured calipers, late in the season. Typically, Lotus was supplied by McLaren partner SEP (which had asked to be known as Carbone Industrie in the mid Eighties). Renault, Ferrari, Alfa Romeo, RAM and Osella were other teams which bought CI discs in '84, while Hitco supplied Brabham and, via AP Racing, Williams. CI's ventilated disc was clearly superior and both Brabham and Williams subsequently moved to the French camp. In '85 CI was effectively the monopoly supplier of carbon-carbon discs.

AP was keen to get in on the carbon-carbon game and had come to a manufacturing agreement with Hitco. Initially it received the 0.7" thick solid discs Brabham ran but it was clear that CI-style 1" thick ventilated items were required. AP lost '85 to CI while such discs were developed but in '86 entered the field as supplier to Arrows, Tyrrell and Zakspeed.

By '87 it had been established that CI discs were more suited to turbo cars while AP/Hitco discs were ideal for the atmospheric runners. The difference was in the material. Hitco's material was more stable: it had a higher co-efficient of friction cold and increased its co-efficient more gently than the CI disc. CI material was poor when cold and increased its mu value violently, though it ultimately attained a higher value. Hitco discs were easier to drive with better response giving the driver more confidence. They were adequate for turbo cars but more experienced drivers preferred the marginally higher performance of CI carbon-carbon given plenty of turbo power to put heat into the disc. In '87 CI introduced an 0.9" thick disc having less mass in an attempt to improve the rate of temperature rise (and steady the cooling rate).

Cooling continued to be a headache for both CI and AP on street circuits where frequently in '85 teams had switched back to iron discs. Indeed, CI had found consumption of discs higher than anticipated which had led to a mid season shortage.

AP Racing Services Engineer Steve Bryan says that operating temperatures on carbon-carbon could become so high that the pad and disc wear rate was unacceptable, though the brakes continued to operate properly (so long as there was some friction material left). Perhaps the worst case was at Adelaide where as late as '87 discs actually wore away. At the other end of the spectrum, says Bryan, were circuits such as Rio and the Osterreichring where discs and pads would be in a perfect condition at the end of the race.

Bryan notes that the '86/7 restrictions on brake duct size did not create a problem: "those enormous ducts were really aerodynamic aids and did not always work well as a brake duct". Bryan explains that the design of the upright was as important as the sheer size of the duct. In that respect the arrival of carbon-carbon had changed designers thinking. "Up to the early Eighties teams designed a car then bolted on the brakes. The brakes were an afterthought. With the advent of carbon-carbon designers had to contemplate brake cooling in the design of uprights and the overall aerodynamics of the car. They had to get cooling right to get the brakes to work properly; of necessity it had become an early design factor".

Carbon-carbon was a good friction material: the problem was adapting the rest of the system to work with it, in particular the calipers. As we have noted, come '84 and AP and Brembo were both supplying four pot calipers for Formula One use, these designed primarily for the cast iron discs employed by the majority of runners. AP, however, had dropped its lightweight '83 'sphericone' disc, having found that with its small mass it cooled so rapidly as to cause extremes of temperature fluctuation. The face of the disc would be hot while the core would be cold setting up stresses that had led to disc cracking as cars got quicker. Consequently AP had re-introduced a heavier, older-style curved vane '3099' disc for '84: "a good, reliable disc", according to Bryan. It had thick vanes and tended to run hot but its temperature didn't fluctuate as much. It was used in 1" and heavier but longer lasting 1.1" guises until finally phased out by carbon-carbon. The last win on iron discs was Rosberg at Adelaide in '85. By '86 almost all teams were running carbon-carbon on the vast majority of circuits.

The ultimate lightweight four pot caliper for iron brakes was that introduced by AP early in '84: having titanium pistons and bolts and a magnesium inner half it weighed a mere 2.1kg. (3.0kg. complete with Ferodo DS11 pads). The rival Brembo caliper employed aluminium for both halves and weighed 0.2kg. more with pads. Magnesium was unsuitable for use with carbon-carbon brakes as there was much more radiated heat and caliper body temperature increased to around 300 degrees centigrade, at which point magnesium loses strength. AP switched back to all aluminium calipers with O-ring seals on the pistons to help protect the fluid from the heat.

With carbon-carbon discs increasingly widespread in use AP switched for '86 to a caliper machined from a solid billet of aluminium. There were two major advantages, Bryan explains. It was possible to use a grade of aluminium better suited to the high temperature. And machining from solid allowed AP to do away with the central joint: bolting two halves together had called for a thicker caliper and given the limited space within the 13" rim this had blocked attempts to put insulation between the caliper and the disc. The machined from solid integral caliper was stiffer and lighter and carried heat insulation inserts. The caliper had also grown wider to help keep the sides away from the heat source. AP adopted the concept of smaller bore pistons at the leading edge to help combat taper wear. Taper wear was caused by a tendency for the surface of the semi-molten pad to migrate: staggered piston sizes cured it. Pistons continued to be of titanium.

While the majority of teams ran AP or rival Brembo four pot calipers McLaren continued with its own twin two pot items. The twin two pot system was heavier but as it gripped the disc both sides it put less strain on the wheel bearing and in theory a smaller bearing could be employed. Throughout, McLaren calipers were machined from a solid billet of aluminium and were of a complex design with aluminium cylinders and a titanium bridge and incorporated some clever ideas to protect against the heat. Apart from McLaren and Brabham, Renault also produced its own calipers.

In '86 Ferrari and Ligier occasionally ran a Brembo 'shuttle valve' system which helped circulate fluid to avoid heat build up. It was a complicated system with separate inward and outward fluid lines for each caliper. The drawback was that there was more to go wrong, and valve failure could spell total brake failure.

Another interesting development was the re-introduction of the twin disc system, tried by Girling in the early Seventies. With the arrival of carbon-carbon discs the concept of two floating discs looked more practical and it was re-introduced by AP, partly to help offset the superior ultimate performance of CI discs. The two discs were operated by a single piston on the inside of the caliper so there was no fluid on the outside, helping overcome the heat problem. And the altered ratio between master cylinder and piston provided much reduced pedal travel.

The AP system provided superior braking performance. However, the main problem was cooling the outer disc. A fundamental duct and upright redesign was required and with the CI single disc an easy alternative and upcoming power restrictions there was little incentive for a team to carry it through. Says Bryan: "the '88 regulations finished off the twin disc project".

The AP twin disc system was run by Williams and Tyrrell in '86 but was only raced once, by Mansell at Rio where he lasted less than a lap, tangling with Senna. Thereafter the system tended to be used only in qualifying and it faded from the Williams camp in view of the World Championship situation. Tyrrell revived it, using it in qualifying around mid season and Lotus and Arrows tried it in testing, yet the project kept getting shelved. Bryan reflects: "We never really got a successful looking system. Cooling the outer disc remained a problem, and the project was unfinished..."

Reduction in power, however, offered to highlight the value of another application of carbon-carbon: as a clutch material, on all friction faces. The traditional AP 7 1/4 inch clutch continued to hold sway until 1987 when Honda switched to a 5 1/2 inch triple plate AP clutch and Tilton pioneered the carbon-carbon clutch. Prior to that, Honda had switched to the heavy duty (ie., having thickened pressure plates and sometimes Nimonic linings) 12-bolt 7 1/4 inch clutch run by four cylinder runners BMW, Hart and Zakspeed. Cosworth and Renault also joined the heavy duty 12-bolt clan while Ferrari continued with a standard 6-bolt clutch, as did Porsche until '87, when it, too, became a convert to 12-bolts.

AP 7 1/4 inch clutch development saw some cross-drilling of the internal pressure plate and, for '85, a change from pressed steel to aluminium cover to produce a lighter version of the 'heavy duty' clutch. In '86 the company was honoured by the British Design Council with an Award in recognition of the excellence of the design of the classic 7 1/4 inch clutch. The lightest turbo version was then 3.85kg. and turbo cars always ran steel flywheels. Experiments with titanium had failed as sintered metal couldn't be run against it untreated and no satisfactory treatment could be found. There seemed the possibility of plating the titanium face but all platings were found to reduce the co-efficient of friction. Renault had persevered longest, until '85.

The idea of using a smaller flywheel with a 5 1/2 inch clutch came from Honda, via Ron Tauranac's Honda-Ralt Formula Two car. The available AP 5 1/2 inch item was driven by six lugs rather than a toothed adapter ring. In theory its size allowed a lower crankshaft axis but Honda did not take advantage of that. Together with a suitably sized flywheel, it offered less mass and that mass was concentrated nearer to the centre so there was less inertia: the main gain. The reduction in inertia offered superior engine response and better acceleration. However in view of the smaller effective radius of the clutch it was necessary to increase the spring load and to run a third and perhaps a fourth plate to get adequate torque capacity. Early experiments were with a quadruple plate version but by early '87 AP had developed a triple plate example with a new spring and this had a new cover machined from a solid bar of aluminium. Given the 4.0 bar limit it worked just fine and Honda bought sufficient to service its 60 engines for Williams and Lotus.

Tyrrell adopted a 5 1/2 inch clutch for its '87 atmospheric Cosworth engine and other teams were supplied for test purposes only: this was still a development item. "We were loath to write off the 7 1/4 inch clutch", recalls Bryan, explaining that AP was interested primarily in reliability. "We proceeded cautiously. The 7 1/4 inch clutch had been developed with gear drive and there was no reason to change, particularly in view of the engine vibrations that had called for the 12 bolt clutch. The lug drive clutch was heavily stressed where the lug joined the cover, especially with the tall lugs on the three and four plate versions. The lugs had to transmit heavy torque and at first we were not certain that the clutch would hold together".

Bryan explains that the lug drive offered certain advantages. It was a little lighter, ran cooler and, the main advantage, it didn't trap dust and other debris as the clutch wore, unlike the toothed adapter ring. The 4.0 bar limit allowed the lug driven 5 1/2 inch triple plate clutch to work whereas further unrestrained engine development might well have led to a 'super heavy duty' triple plate 7 1/4 inch clutch. One particular bonus of lug drive at this time was that it allowed easier machining of the plates: an important consideration in view of the inevitable arrival of carbon-carbon, which is difficult to work.

Exactly the same material exploited so well for brake discs promised to produce a better, far lighter clutch. However, AP had found little success converting a regular 7 1/4 inch clutch to Hitco carbon-carbon plates back in the Cosworth era. The DFV clutch had very thin pressure plates and it was not practical to make carbon-carbon plates as thin. Consequently it had been necessary to produce a single plate clutch and that didn't work. It was tried by Williams and Tyrrell in the early Eighties and led to AP suggesting that Hitco should improve its low temperature co-efficient of friction, the clutch slipping badly when cold.

Faced with a growing batch of turbo cars AP understandably had to concentrate upon development of the traditional 7 1/4 inch clutch. During '84 AP engineer John Lindo moved to Tilton Engineering Inc., the California based racing equipment supplier run by McLane "Mac" Tilton which was a AP's major West Coast distributor. Away from the Formula One rat race, Lindo was able to properly develop a carbon-carbon clutch. Tilton says: "I introduced Hitco (a fellow Californian company) to AP. They came to an agreement for brake and clutch development but the first AP carbon-carbon clutch failed and further development was abandoned. Hitco was disappointed and got in touch with me. I had recently hired John Lindo and he took on the project".

Lindo's first carbon-carbon clutch ran in a heavy American stock car and it worked. Tilton had discovered only a small input of heat was sufficient to double the co-efficient of friction while Hitco had found a solution to the low temperature friction problem. It had developed material with stable friction properties at temperatures as low as 212 degrees centigrade. A conventional clutch had a mu of around 0.3. Tilton's carbon-carbon clutch had a static value of 0.2 which rapidly rose to 0.4.

By '86 the Tilton clutch was running in a wide variety of American road racing cars and at the end of the year it signed a formal agreement with Hitco to produce carbon-carbon race clutches from blanks supplied by the local company. The early Tilton clutches resembled AP 7 1/4 inch units (not surprisingly, given Lindo's background). However, in January '87 Lotus asked for a 5 1/2 inch lug driven clutch to replace its regular Honda-supplied AP item.

Tilton reflects: "Honda was furnishing Lotus so it had no direct relationship with AP. Lotus felt that the carbon-carbon clutch was overdue". Of course, the team was eager to explore any route to weight saving to offset the burden of its active suspension system. Intensive work produced a prototype by March '87. Essentially, this appears to have been a converted (early-style) four plate AP lug drive clutch, the four conventional plates replaced by three Hitco carbon-carbon plates. Weight plummeted from 3.6kg. to 1.5kg. Further development led to a clutch which was good enough to claim pole at Monaco, then win Detroit. That, says Tilton: "Made AP a little upset". It was the end of his days as a major customer of the British company.

Tilton says Senna often raced a metal clutch as he found carbon-carbon insufficiently aggressive at the start. In contrast, Alboreto and Berger found carbon-carbon "too aggressive". Ferrari ran a 7 1/4 inch twin plate Tilton clutch from Monaco to Mexico after which it came off in the light of a problem with the vibration damper. The damper manufacturer blamed the reduced mass on the end of the crankshaft and Tilton missed out on two further wins...

Tilton points to a number of advantages for the carbon-carbon clutch, not least significantly reduced weight and inertia and he says even more mass was saved in the flywheel, which could be aluminium, than in the clutch itself. However, marginal engine performance and fuel economy gains were obscured by the very high output of mid Eighties turbo engines. Tilton offers that carbon-carbon plates wouldn't warp so released cleanly and that they dampened vibrations. After initial burnishing wear rate fell rapidly and the clutch would last far longer. It also withstood starts better and could be slipped intentionally without damage, making up for having the wrong gear as when baulked in a slow corner. Up to a point heat was beneficial to the carbon-carbon clutch, increasing rather than decreasing the co-efficient of friction.

AP introduced its own carbon-carbon clutch in '87, stirred by Tilton's progress, using material supplied by CI. The French company could sell discs and pads direct to teams but did not have the infrastructure to manufacture and service clutch units (which were not solely of carbon-carbon). The first CI material carbon-carbon clutch had been produced independently by McLaren in '85, was a converted 7 1/4 AP clutch only used in the team's test programme. AP came straight in with a 5 1/2 inch lug drive clutch, initially four plate. It worked out of the box in a Williams chassis and AP found that it could take the fourth plate out. It first performed in public in the Honda-Williams at Monza, where it won. Thereafter it was generally used in qualifying and both Lotus and Ferrari were supplied with development units. Says Bryan: "our conventional clutches had developed so far that it was almost as simple as putting carbon-carbon plates in the '87 spec. 5 1/2 inch lug driven clutch". ■

ALFA ROMEO

Autodelta SpA
Via Enrico Fermi, 7
20019 Settimo Milanese
Italy

The mid Eighties saw the Alfa Romeo V8 the only survivor of the renowned Italian school of intricate eight and twelve cylinder racing engines, and increasingly stringent fuel consumption dictates had effectively strangled it. Whether from Alfa Romeo, Ferrari or Maserati, Italy's multi-cylinder jewels had seemingly always been powerful yet thirsty and the 1980-conceived 890T was no exception. It was a characteristic quite unsuited to the 1984 instigated fuel factor, a factor undreamt of when design began.

Renault's turbocharged success of the late Seventies prompted both Ferrari and Alfa Romeo to follow suit. But whereas Ferrari started in 1979 and had its blown V6 racing by 1981, Alfa Romeo didn't start until 1980 and took three years to achieve a state of race-readiness.

In 1980 Alfa Romeo was represented in Formula One by the Milan-based Autodelta concern, its official competition wing since 1966. Autodelta had been founded in 1963 by former Ferrari Technical Director Carlo Chiti and Alfa Romeo agent Ludovico Chizzola and Chiti remained at its helm as it became an offshoot of a marque with a proud Grand Prix racing tradition. Chiti oversaw the creation of 90 degree V8 and 180 degree V12 engines, both of which saw service as 3.0 litre Grand Prix power plants in English chassis as Autodelta concentrated on sports and saloon car racing. However, in 1978 Chiti designed a 90 degree V12 as a power plant for both Brabham and Autodelta Formula One cars, the latter making its entrance in 1979.

The turbo engine go-ahead was given at the end of '79, an understandably lean year for the new World Championship effort as Autodelta struggled to find its feet. Chiti says he opted for eight cylinders as the best compromise between power potential and considerations of complexity and dependability. His was only the second clean-sheet-of-paper design for a 1.5 litre Formula One turbo engine (following Ferrari) and at the time many engineers were of the opinion that (given unlimited fuel) eight cylinders offered greater potential than four (BMW) or six (Ferrari, Renault).

Chiti's previous experience of forced induction had been the production of a turbocharged version of his 180 degree V12 for sportscar racing. That had entailed reducing its capacity to the maximum permissible under Group 6 regulations, 2140cc. The capacity per cylinder had then been similar to that for a 1.5 litre eight cylinder engine but Chiti says the old blown unit in no way influenced the new.

The 890T was designed by Chiti and three assistants over the first half of 1980 and the prototype was unveiled at the mid September Italian Grand Prix in which the turbo-Ferrari made its public track debut. Whereas the six cylinder Ferrari was a 120 degree unit with exhausts and either Comprex supercharger or twin turbos within its wide vee, Chiti's offering was a traditional 90 degree Italian race engine with a KKK turbocharger set either side of the crankcase, Renault fashion.

Chiti's new baby was designed for high revs with dimensions of 94mm. x 43.5mm. (a stroke:bore ratio of 0.588:1) and on a 7.0:1 compression ratio was rated at 550b.h.p./11,600r.p.m., but had yet to run in anger. It wasn't intended to race until the latter half of '81, the 90 degree V12 still a competitive proposition. In the meantime Alfa Romeo division Spica would develop a suitable fuel injection system. As a stop gap measure the engine was run on carbs - 1 per cylinder! Track testing, still on carbs didn't begin until June '81, the belt driven alloy unit then running in an old 'muletta' chassis. By this stage Alfa Romeo had decided that its new Avio turbo division should supply the turbos. It was the spring of '82 before the V8 was ready to run with Spica mechanical injection and Avio turbos and (thanks partly to a summer of race shunts), it was the autumn of '82 before it nestled in a chassis based on the contemporary 182 model.

The 182T was only just finished in time for a short demonstration run at the Italian Grand Prix and was not slated to race until the following season. For 1983, Chiti quoted 620b.h.p./11,000 r.p.m., with a rev limit of 12,500 and a consumption of 240gms. fuel per b.h.p. compared to 220gms. per b.h.p. for the superseded, 85b.h.p. less powerful atmospheric V12. The 182T was equipped with the largest permissible 250 litre fuel tank and employed air/air after-coolers.

For 1983 Alfa Romeo entered into an agreement with Euroracing to run its Formula One team, leaving Autodelta as engine supplier. Euroracing was a similarly Marlboro sponsored formula car team based in a Milan suburb and run by one time mechanic Giampaolo Pavanello. Using Alfa Romeo engines it had broken a Toyota stranglehold on Formula Three, winning the European Championship three consecutive years, 1980 - '82. For its big step it moved to a new, purpose-designed factory in Senago, Milan and increased its staff from 10 to 40, taking on many ex-Autodelta chassis men, including 182 designer Gerard Ducarouge.

Ducarouge had been with Autodelta since mid '81 and had engineered some very effective carbon fibre/Kevlar cars propelled by the V12, which was reckoned to be the most powerful of all 3.0 litre engines. However, the 535b.h.p. power pack had been typically thirsty and concrete results had been few. On the one hand, farming out the race team to leave Autodelta to concentrate upon development of the turbo engine could be seen as a positive step to try to improve matters; on the other hand reducing Autodelta's competition activities (which included axing all interests other than Formula One) was a commercial expediency for Alfa Romeo.

For '83 Ducarouge produced an evolution of the prototype turbo car adapted to flat bottom specification, the 183T which was to be driven by Cesaris and Baldi. Ten AGIP-fuelled engines were available initially, with a 20-strong batch planned. Winter testing was promising but the season kicked off with two unimpressive races followed by the infamous empty fire extinguisher bottle incident during qualifying at Paul Ricard for which Ducarouge was forced to carry the can.

The departure of Ducarouge left the team an all-Italian affair with engineering headed by Luigi Marmiroli. He saw the 183T regularly qualify in the top 10, in spite of high boost often cracking the Avio turbos, and Cesaris convincingly led the Francorchamps race before a wheel change was fumbled. Chiti says there was nothing inherently wrong with the V8 engine in '83, but emphasises that the Avio turbos, forced onto him by "in house politics" were "a big problem".

Revised heads and turbos were introduced during the season, the latter at Hockenheim where Cesaris was third fastest and second in the race, highly relieved to have finished as ominous noises were coming from over his shoulder. It was reckoned that the competitive drive had consumed over 300 litres. The final highlight of 1983 was another morale boosting second place in South Africa, but more than high morale would be needed in the face of a 220 litre race ration...

During '83 Alfa Romeo, clearly inspired by BMW's success, had charted a four cylinder future, and had secured a promise of Bosch engine management technology. The plan was for electronic injection to keep the V8 alive for another season, with a computer controlled in line four testing, to come on stream for 1985.

890T
90 degree V8

74 x 43.5mm./ 1496.7cc.
2 Avio turbochargers
Aluminium block and heads
Nikasil wet aluminium liners
5 main bearings, plain
Steel crankshaft, 4 pins
Titanium con rods
Mahle light alloy pistons
Goetze rings
4 o.h.c., belt driven
4 valves/cylinder, 1 plug
Valve sizes undisclosed
Included valve angle undisclosed
Marelli ignition
Spica injection
Compression ratio 7.0:1
Maximum r.p.m. 12,500
180kg. including turbos and wastegates

August 1995

To Whom it may concern - Mr Paul Chandler.

Prestige Technical is a company whose principle business is the supply and maintenance of office equipment and as stationery suppliers. Our clients include several newspapers including the Daily Telegraph and Guardian.

Mr Chandler worked for us initially freelance and then full time for almost seven years leaving in December 1993. His responsibilities were to attend to call outs and to carry out remedial works on site when practical. Our contracts covered several hundred desktop machines and Paul demonstrated his competence and common sense in keeping workshop recalls to a satisfactory level. Paul attended several manufacturer's courses and obtained the relevant certification on each occasion though his grasp of fundamentals was good enough for him to diagnose and repair machines he was not familiar with.

Paul's attitude to work was very good. He was punctual yet frequently prepared to work out of hours when need arose. He maintained his cheery disposition when working under pressure and had a good relationship with our customers and thus promoted sales.

I would endorse Paul's candidature for any similar position and would be happy to elaborate any points on request.

Yours Faithfully

Jack Brittin
Director

PRESTIGE TECHNICAL SERVICES LTD.
22 FINCHLEY ROAD
ST. JOHNS WOOD
LONDON NW8 6EB
TELEPHONE: 0171 483 1763
FACSIMILE: 0171 586 5635

Registered Office: 1033a Finchley Road London NW11 9ES
Registered No. 3089013   V.A.T. No. 663 0131 71

Cheever gives the Alfa Romeo-Euroracing 890T-184T its head at Rio; alas
the new Euroracing driver suffered a spate of engine detonations...

The 890T was a conventional four valve turbocharged V8 race engine, running a typical compression ratio on mechanical injection. Whereas it carried conventional Nikasil liners, the similarly alloy in line 4 under development was based around a linerless block with integral head, Hart 415T-style. As the 890T had been, the coming 415T was a clean sheet of paper design, and it was the first in line 4 designed to be run fully stressed. Like the 890T, it was belt driven, and featured a low crank axis for a low centre of gravity. However, in the face of the new fuel ration, the large piston crown of the four cylinder heir looked inappropriate, its cylinder dimensions being 92 x 56.4mm, compared to an 89mm. bore for BMW and an 88mm. bore for Hart.

Compared to the 890T, the 415T was perceived as lighter and less complex: it was reckoned that it could save 30kg. and would take literally half the time to strip and rebuild, with less parts to go wrong. However, it was some while before it would be ready to track test, and at the start of 1984 Autodelta did not have electronically controlled injection for either it, or the 890T. The only new features for the V8 were revised Dinoplex ignition and new cam profiles. It was shown with weight saving carbon fibre heads and sump, but come the races, there was no sign of these.

The promise of injection control had encouraged Cheever and Patrese to assume cockpit duties, while Michelin and Marlboro had given way to Goodyear and Benetton. AGIP continued to supply fuel: similar to that used by Ferrari. Euroracing's challenger for the new season was a fresh design, the 184T, penned by Mario Tolentino. Technical Director Marmiroli race engineered

Cheever's example while Gustav Brunner, who had moved from ATS in February, took care of Patrese's machine. It was March before the car had run, leaving time for only a short shakedown on Alfa Romeo's Balocco test track before Rio. Cheever had praised the handling at Balocco but was less impressed by his Rio experience, endlessly detonating engines...

Without micro processor control the detonation threshold was low, and in '84 the 890T couldn't safely be boosted high enough for competitive qualifying, or race, pace. Avio's qualifying turbo was inadequate and a long drawn out attempt to engineer a high compression qualifying engine was only moderately productive. Cheever recalls that just one stayed together, offering a useful 5m.p.h. top speed improvement. Lacking power and with questionable aerodynamics, the 890T-184T demonstrated a fundamental lack of straightline speed: flat out it tended to hit a brick wall, and on occasion it found Cosworth-Tyrrell speed hard to match!

Early on the model dipped into the top 10 qualifiers with Patrese seventh at Zolder and Cheever eighth at Imola, but thereafter it was outside (with Cheever missing the 20-car Monaco cut) until its rear end aerodynamics were modified, in time for Monza. That improvement saw Alfa Romeo outqualify Ferrari - but claiming only ninth and tenth places, the best that the revised car would achieve.

The sad fact is that throughout '84 the Alfa Romeo V8 tended to detonate on qualifying boost then run dry on race day as meeting after meeting passed without any sign of the fruits of the Bosch programme. Qualifying boost was theoretically 3.8 bar, with 3.0 bar race boost but Chiti says that in '84 the boost was often wound down as low as 2.2/2.3 bar - less than 600b.h.p. - to try to survive the distance on 220 litres. Electronic control for the Spica metering unit was developed in conjunction with the local Nord Electronics concern, and was tried at Brands Hatch and Hockenheim, without success.

Although Cheever bagged fourth at Rio, he was a lap in arrears, and while Patrese similarly managed fourth at Kyalami, he had insufficient fuel to finish the lap by which the race had been shortened. Neither had been a significant factor in the race. At Imola Cheever ran short two laps from the finish, while at Montreal, heading for points he fell dry a full seven laps adrift... Fuel consumption was a headache everywhere, though Patrese managed to splutter home one lap down at Monza and at the Nurburgring to added another five points to the team's unimpressive '84 total. The only inspiring race was Detroit, where rival cars started with far less than 220 litres on board. Full to the brim, much hope was pinned on the 184Ts, and Cheever was lying a splendid third when an aftercooler split.

In North America there had been a new face in the Euroracing pit, that of former Lancia race/rally engineer Gianni Tonti. According to Cheever: "the hierarchy of the State owned company felt a shake up was needed, and found very little resistance from the team or the drivers..." Chiti had been shuffled into a desk job and a number of engineers had been approached, apparently among them Porsche engine designer Hans Mezger. With Tonti effectively taking over the reigns of the Formula One engine programme, Chiti moved on in October, forming Motori Moderni. While his new company produced a V6 engine, Tonti oversaw continuing development of the Autodelta in line four.

Sources close to Autodelta say that it was fundamental problems rather than any shortage of cash that postponed the debut of the in line four from the start of the 1985 season. In fact, Autodelta didn't even have Bosch injection ready for Rio '85, though it did now have effective electronic control for the Spica system (based on an analogue ECU and a servo motor to adjust the metering cam) produced by Jofa, which was reckoned to improve fuel consumption by 8.5 - 10%. And at last the handicap of home brewed turbos was overcome, through a switch to KKK. With a few modifications, the V8 had now been coaxed to run to 12,700r.p.m. in qualifying and KKK supplied specific qualifying turbos, but there would still be many turbo and engine failures to handicap the effort. By the end of '85 Cheever reckoned to have suffered over 50 engine detonations testing and racing the V8...

Both Cheever and Patrese stayed put for '85, along with Goodyear and Benetton. However, their race engineers were missing. The previous autumn Marmiroli had moved to Lamborghini, then Brunner had gone off to design a new Hart-RAM. Pavanello's head hunting had secured the services of Toleman engineer John Gentry and he had penned an evolutionary 185T chassis, only to abruptly leave at Christmas bound for Renault. In his absence Tolentino became Technical Director and engineered Cheever's car while Maurizio Colombo (son of the legendary engineer) ran Patrese's mount.

The early season races were no more inspiring than '84 had been but Imola brought long awaited Bosch injection control equipment. The system supplied was based on BMW's electro-mechanical Motronic equipment (doubled up), but was apparently generation or so behind. However, it provided better calibration than the Jofa system, further improving fuel consumption and throttle response, if doing nothing for top end power. With Bosch electro-mechanical injection the V8, still AGIP fuelled, still qualified at 3.8 bar and raced at 3.0 bar, was officially rated over 800b.h.p. Properly sorted, it was a revelation at Monaco, Patrese setting second fastest time in first qualifying before slipping to 12th, while Cheever moved up to fourth place. Alas, an early alternator problem cost him the advantage of that grid position.

Montreal and Detroit weren't quite so impressive but, away from power circuits, a top 10 grid position was a realistic target once more and Cheever set third fastest race lap at Montreal (knocking on the door of the top six when he retired), sixth fastest at Detroit. With the return to fast tracks the 185T was at sea. Partly due to the lack of top end power, partly due to poor chassis performance - the drivers told of lack of grip and unpredictable handling. Cheever tried an old 184T at Silverstone and it was an improvement, so two 184T based cars were run from the 'Ring onwards. Nevertheless, the Alfa Romeo- Euroracings remained mid field runners, as they had been since Ricard, only twice scraping into the top 10 qualifying positions, at the Nurburgring (ninth) and the Osterreichring (tenth).

In 1985 Euroracing failed to score any points. With its chassis designer elsewhere and its engine, even with electronic injection, something of a dinosaur, it had excuses for lack of pace but endless race retirements were less easy to explain, although to be fair a good number were down to engine or turbo failure. In any case for 1986 both Alfa Romeo and Benetton resolved to put their resources elsewhere. The four cylinder engine having been run on the bench

since the summer of '85, Alfa Romeo entered into serious negotiations with Benetton and the clothing manufacturer's second team, Toleman in an effort to find a good home for it.

Based on autumn '85 bench tests the Tonti-developed in line four was reckoned to offer marginally more power than the Motronic V8 for a given boost level and less fuel consumption for a given power level. On 3.6 - 3.8 bar, in October an Autodelta engineer quoted the author power as 780b.h.p. - 820b.h.p., with a 5 - 7% consumption improvement. An important factor in that was said to be the use of Porsche-type fully fully electronic injection with co-ordinated ignition.

The fully stressed 415T was intended to be practical from a chassis designer's point of view - and Toleman's Rory Byrne had shown a remarkable aptitude for producing effective four cylinder cars. Toleman looked very seriously at it but, having been bought outright by Benetton at the end of the season, the team plumped for an offer of proven BMW fours.

Although it had withdrawn its support from Euroracing, Alfa Romeo continued to run Autodelta under the Alfa Corse banner into 1986 with a bench and track test programme for the in line four. Test driver Giorgio Francia started lapping Balocco with the 415/85T installed in a modified 185T chassis in May and in July it was announced that the Ligier team would race the unit the following season. Alfa Romeo had offered a favourable deal to supply over 20 engines for the French two car operation, along with full engineering support.

At this stage, blown by a single KKK turbocharger and with two injectors per cylinder the unit was officially rated at 830b.h.p./10,500r.p.m. on 3.8 bar, with a maximum r.p.m. of 11,500, and a potential 1200b.h.p. qualifying output. In September, Ligier driver Arnoux sampled the test hack and was said to be: "very satisfied" with the engine's performance.

In the face of the 4.0 bar restriction for '87, Tonti's team developed a double-turbo installation. Each cylinder's two exhaust ports fed a different manifold, one for each of two Garrett turbos which sat side by side to the left of the block. The two turbos shared a single wastegate and blew into the same aftercooler. The installation gave the 415T an official 4.0 bar output of 900b.h.p./10,500r.p.m. on a 7.5:1 compression ratio.

To accommodate the twin turbo set up various revisions were

By 1984 the 890T was the last survivor of the classic Italian school of V8 and V12 Grand Prix engines. Note single Marelli distributor for all eight cylinders.

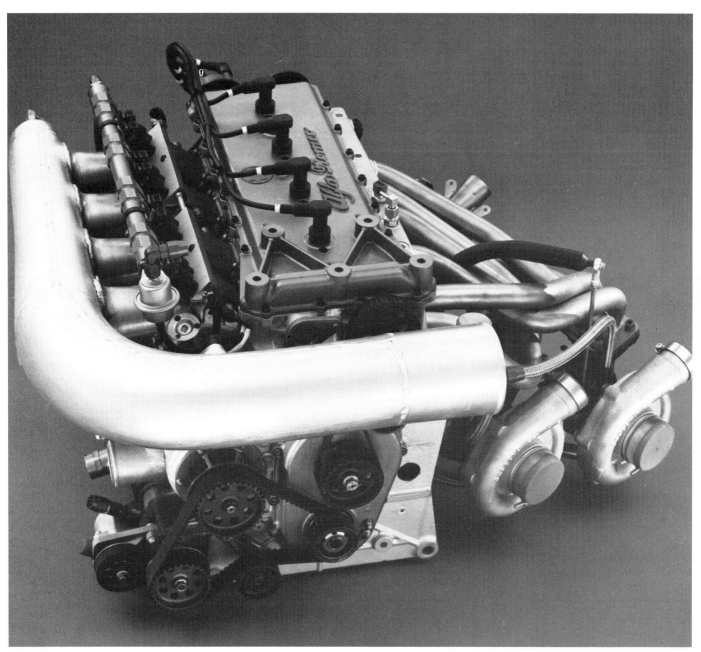

The ultimate version of the 1983 - conceived in line four cylinder had low pressure Bosch Motronic injection and twin Garrett turbochargers.

required to the original Ligier chassis design, and this delayed launched of the Alfa Romeo-Ligier JS29 until late January. At this juncture Arnoux was the only confirmed driver, due to uncertainty over the fitness of '86 partner Laffite, still recovering from an '86 mid-season injury. Arnoux debuted the car at Paul Ricard and pronounced the engine "powerful but suffering poor low speed response". Response was improved through fitting smaller turbos, but top speed was then inadequate.

Testing continued in public at Jerez in mid February, where after only ten laps Arnoux lost rear brakes and wrote off the prototype. While other teams lapped Rio towards the end of the month, Ligier went to Monza, and during this test agreement was struck for Ghinzani - a renowned test driver favoured by Alfa Romeo - to drive the second car. In mid March Ghinzani drove a 415/85T-JS29 at Imola and lapped less than two seconds slower than Alboreto's new Ferrari before hitting turbo problems. The entire batch of turbos suffered from a manufacturing fault, delaying progress by one week and ruling out any question of attendance at the final Rio test.

Arnoux drove again when testing resumed at Imola and on the evening of Thursday the 26th, two weeks before the start of Rio qualifying, he said on Italian TV: "the situation is disastrous - the engine constantly has problems...it seems as though we break a piston or turbo every lap we do..." He also expressed dissatisfaction over the Alfa Corse representation at Imola. The following

morning Alfa Romeo issued a statement saying that it had cancelled its agreement with Ligier as Arnoux's behaviour had contravened a clause "charging the Ligier team and its drivers with the responsibility for the development of Alfa's 'image' through F1 racing..."

Alfa Romeo was now owned by the Fiat Group and apparently Group policy was that Ferrari should be its sole Grand Prix representative, with Alfa Romeo concentrating upon production car racing, Lancia upon rallying. Certainly, while a four cylinder engine had looked good in '83, it didn't seem such a wise choice in the face of the 4.0 bar restriction, and the 415T's public track appearances suggested that Alfa Romeo had a lot of work ahead of it - with no longer any possible long term reward. Faced with a threat of legal action by Guy Ligier, the Group offered to supply ten engines and two engineers for the first two races, but the irate team owner refused to pay the price of keeping the affair out of court. Ghinzani expressed horror at his teammate's comments, saying "it is quite normal for new engines to be unreliable, but I think the four cylinder is basically good". That belief would not be put to the test.

Although Fiat withdrew the Alfa Romeo name from Grand Prix racing the turbocharged V8 continued to see service as an Osella engine. Osella Squadra Corse based near Turin was run by Vincenzo ('Enzo') Osella, an enthusiast whose wallet didn't match his Grand Prix aspirations. Nevertheless, year after year he managed to survive on the proverbial shoestring. A one time builder, Osella had been introduced to the sport by Carlo Abarth and had ended up taking over the assets of Abarth's famous tuning/race business in the early Seventies. Over the latter half of the decade he contested the European Formula Two Championship, never on a big budget, and in 1979 his driver Cheever won the most races.

Osella moved into Grand Prix racing in 1980 and ran a succession of Cosworth cars until, for 1983, Alfa Romeo offered him the V12 made redundant by its move to turbocharging. This didn't raise his underfinanced team from also-ran status but Alfa Romeo kept faith with it and supplied the V8 engine for 1984, along with a certain amount of technical support. It even donated an old carbon fibre/Kevlar monocoque as the basis of Osella chassis engineer Guiseppe Petrotta's first turbo car, the FA1-F model, which was somewhat overweight at around 600kg.

The plan was to run regular driver Ghinzani throughout the year, with a second Pirelli shod FA1-F in selected races for Gartner. Imola was targeted for the debut of the first Osella-tub FA1-F but it was called for somewhat sooner. Following a fruitless Rio debut, Ghinzani qualified one position higher at Kyalami, 20th, then crashed in the warm up. For reasons unknown, he went off at high speed and struck a bank with sufficient force to rip the car in two, and was lucky to escape with light burns and a damaged hand. Less than three weeks later he was back in action at Zolder in FA1-F 02, which was some 10kg. lighter. The FA1-F 02 had a home produced monocoque but drew heavily upon the original Alfa Romeo design as the team lacked experience of advanced composites.

Gartner joined the team for Imola where he drove an old V12 machine and pushed Ghinzani's ignition-troubled V8 car off the grid! Gartner rejoined to drive an FA1-F from Brands Hatch onwards, the Osella-tub model making a total of 20 starts in 1984, Ghinzani even qualifying for Monaco, unlike Cheever. However, that was only one of three occasions on which Osella scraped into the top 20 qualifiers. Nevertheless, on two occasions the team scored points, Ghinzani coming home fifth, two laps down at Dallas, then Gartner doing the same thing at Monza. Ghinzani should have led Gartner over the line but had spluttered out of fuel...

In the course of the '84 season, Ghinzani noted that the Osella team had become, in his estimation, more serious, more professional. Alas, it failed to sustain the level of financial support needed to build on its progress. Petrotta says he had drawings and a wind tunnel model for a fresh chassis completed by October, but that the financial situation was such that he had to leave them in the cupboard. Osella turned up at Rio in '85 with Ghinzani its sole driver and no sign of a new car. And when a new model did appear,

at Imola, it was a budget compromised modification of the FA1-F, untested and strictly one-off. The FA1-G was a little lighter than its predecessor but was still hopelessly overweight and without even Jofa control its mechanically injected V8 was thirsty and underpowered. "In 1984 we were close to Alfa Romeo, but after there was less support", a team member reflected.

With a diminished budget, Osella was inevitably an also ran and midway through the season Ghinzani had to be bundled out to make way for Rothengatter, a driver who could bring sufficient funds to allow the team to survive to the end of the year. Things were so bad that when Rothengatter had a dramatic spin in the course of failing to qualify for Brands Hatch one could but sympathise - the FA1-G couldn't get Pirelli tyres developed for 1000b.h.p. turbo cars up to working temperature!

Predictably, like Ghinzani before him, Rothengatter failed either to qualify in the top 20 (aside from the 20-car Kyalami field) or to accumulate any World Championship points. Nevertheless, Enzo Osella didn't give up. He figured that as long as he clung to a Grand Prix programme there was always the chance of decent sponsorship turning up. And winter developments suggested the finance might be raised to switch to Motori Moderni power for '86. Petrotta started work on the FA1-H to accept the V6 engine - but due to shortage of funds had to produce an evolution of the existing car rather than a much needed new design. And it couldn't be readied before Imola.

Osella was able to return to a two car team for '86, Ghinzani rejoining to be partnered by Danner. Alfa Romeo offered to loan its V8 as a stop gap, the team running it in a modified FA1-F and the FA1-G. Alas, when the prototype FA1-H arrived at Imola its engine bay was empty - Osella couldn't firm up the finance to pay Motori Moderni. Thankfully, Alfa Romeo came to the rescue again, generously allowing the team to retain its engines until the end of the season, and continuing to provide a spares lifeline.

Having given Osella access to KKK turbos towards the end of '85, in mid '86 Alfa Romeo made the Jofa control system available, this a vain attempt to try to contest 195 litre races with unsophisticated, essentially '84-spec units. Those engines weren't adequate to keep Osella off the back row of the grid. Indeed, the team couldn't afford to do too many qualifying laps, for fear of non starting through

Osella began its Alfa Romeo turbo engine adventure with a modified 1983 Euroracing chassis which, at Kyalami, ended its career like this...

mechanical mishap! So desperate was Osella's plight, sometimes it couldn't find the cash to avail itself of the Alfa Romeo spares supply. Personnel had been cut back, and Osella was the only team to still rebuild engines in the paddock...

Danner's budget gave him access to the FA1-H, converted to accept the familiar, uncompetitive Alfa Romeo engine. After struggling with it at Francorchamps, in Montreal he understandably went over to take up the offer of a vacant Arrows seat. Only to be shoved back into the slow machine by the team boss, who couldn't afford to break his contractual obligation to FOCA. Thereafter, the '86 car was driven by Berg, who wrote it off at Brands Hatch and continued with the modified FA1-F, other than at Monza where Caffi took over the drive for financial reasons. Of course, neither the FA1-H nor the older cars, with or without electro-mechanical injection, offered a realistic chance of collecting points in '86 - Osella's best result was 11th for Ghinzani at the Osterreichring, four laps down. Merely to finish was an achievement.

At the end of the year, Petrotta accepted a job at Alfa Romeo, never having been able to turn all his ideas from drawings into metal and plastics. However, Osella secured a small amount of backing for '87. Ignazio Lunetta succeeded Petrotta as Technical Director and was able to put a new design in hand, and was even able to undertake a certain amount of wind tunnel and later track testing, something unheard of since '84. Previously Osella had been forced to copy other teams' underbody profiles, now it could devise its own, Lunetta confided.

Lunetta's FA1-I was a significant evolution of the FA1-H incorporating substantial modifications, and paring weight down to almost 540kg, in spite of cast iron discs - carbon-carbon discs had disappeared after '84. The problem remained in the engine bay, though: Osella still couldn't afford the switch to Motori Moderni. Thankfully, Alfa Romeo agreed to sell him the V8s and parts he held, on condition the marque's name was removed from the cam covers. Officially, the V8 became an 'Osella'. The team had half a dozen examples, and the parts to produce a couple more. For spares it went directly to Alfa Romeo suppliers, or fabricated its

own, or recycled. Osella was renowned as an engine wizard...

The antiquated Osella V8 retained Jofa controlled Spica injection and Marelli Dinoplex ignition. Osella introduced a modified engine at Paul Ricard. He altered the plenum chamber and intake trumpets, repositioning the injectors, worked on the camshafts and valves and even produced new pistons. He acquired a choice of two KKK turbo sizes but high boost - and the engine was designed to be wound up to 3.8 bar in qualifying - tended to crack the turbos. Worse, it was found that high boost would sometimes crack the crankshaft. The determined engineer also came across a valve seat headache.

Osella rated 'his' V8 turbo engine at 780b.h.p./11,500r.p.m. on 3.8 bar, and reckoned to race it at around 730b.h.p./11,000r.p.m. on 3.5 bar (the maximum that had been used for qualifying in '86). It was far from competitive, and the chassis improvements were masked. Initially only one 'I' model was produced for regular driver Caffi, a Formula One rookie. A second example arrived towards the end of the season - it took so long to build as the same dozen mechanics were employed both on car build and the race programme.

Car development was frustrated by engine headaches: "the car was always doing one or two laps, then stopping", Lunetta reflects. When it was running properly in qualifying, Caffi generally managed to scrape into the top 20 qualifiers, ahead of the 3.5 litre 'atmos'. The highlight of the season was Monaco, where lack of power was less of an embarrassment: Caffi qualified 16th, and he moved into the top 10 at one third race distance when the electrics failed. Engine and transmission problems were common, and three times from 14 starts Caffi ran short of fuel many miles from the flag. On 10 other occasions his car broke, while at Rio he retired, exhausted! He failed to qualify after troubled sessions at Jerez and Adelaide. Forini raced a second entry at Monza and Estoril, and likewise failed to qualify in Spain, his final appearance for the team. He, too failed to post a finish in his older (FA1-G) chassis, as did Tarquini who had a one off outing in an ancient FA1-F at Imola.

Osella certainly was operating on the proverbial shoestring, with no real hope of success. However, the participation of the enthusiastic engineer was admired by all those believing Grand Prix racing should be primarily be a sport.

Mechanically injected 890T nestles in the back of a 1984 built Osella FA1-F chassis, pictured here still in active service in 1986.

EURORACING 184T

Advanced Composite Technology carbon fibre/Kevlar monocoque
Stressed engine
Push rod front suspension, pull rod rear - Koni dampers
Speedline aluminium and magnesium rims
Brembo cast iron discs, outboard
Single Brembo four pot calipers - Ferodo pads
Kevlar bodywork
2 IPRA water radiators - 2 IPRA oil radiators
2 Secan air:air aftercoolers
AP twin plate clutch
Hewland/Euroracing five-speed gearbox - Salisbury diff
220 litre ATL fuel cell - 10 litre oil tank
Nippon battery - Bosch instruments
2720mm. wheelbase; 1780mm. front track, 1680mm. rear
552kg.

The 184 was an evolution from Ducarouge's '83 car which had hidden a tub made in the UK by Roger Sloman's Derby-based A.C.T. concern under locally produced composite bodywork, had squatted on rocker arm suspension, and had weighed 560kg. For the new car, Tolentino drew a smaller, 220 litre tank monocoque to form the shape of the front half of the fuselage and introduced tension link suspension. Designed to suit Goodyear crossplies rather than Michelin radials, the new suspension was tried on a converted 183T in the January Rio tyre test while the '84 tub was under production in the UK.

Wind tunnel tests were carried out using the Pininfarina 100% fixed floor facility, and the sculpturing of the new aluminium honeycomb sandwich monocoque was reminiscent of the 183T's shape but extended above the tank to form a distinctive roll pyramid and elegantly tapered to a much narrower nose. Its converging snout extended well beyond the pedal bulkhead to carry the front wing post. The 184T carried only the tip of a nose cone, though a flared extension back from that covered a cutout in the snout which provided awkward access to the upright front dampers, located between the pedal and dash bulkheads. With the switch to push rod front suspension the front track was narrowed by 40mm.

Behind the aerodynamic monocoque's roll pyramid a bulbous fairing concealed the engine and blended into a flat tail deck which bridged the gap between the wheels and extended back to the rear wing's gearbox-mounted central post. The wide deck continued the lie of the pod lids aft of top vents for the water radiators, the new car refining a rear end and cooler layout established by Ducarouge. The radiators still sloped upwards and forwards ahead of upright engine bay vented aftercoolers which flanked the rear bulkhead. The oil radiators were now set flush into the slab-sided pods' straight walls, just ahead of the rear wheels. A little further forward were oval shaped ducts to collect air for the turbos.

The Euroracing-produced magnesium transaxle case carrying the new pull rod suspension contained the same Hewland-derived, Euroracing five-speed gearbox and the newcomer retained 183T wheelbase and rear track dimensions. Behind the oil tank in the bellhousing, a tank for water injection sat over the gearbox (each aftercooler neatly incorporated a tank for a water spray in the leading edge of its casing). Significantly, the 184T did not sport the full length diffuser tunnels that had risen behind the driveshafts, under the even longer, similarly all-enclosing rear deck of the superseded model.

Running on cast iron brakes, but with a lighter monocoque and less Kevlar panels, the 184T was reckoned to be 8kg. closer to the weight limit than its predecessor. Having its first run at Balocco in March, there was little chance to learn about the new model prior to Rio. Only two examples were ready for the start of the season; a tension link 183T was required as spare car until Zolder. There a fuel consumption read out was incorporated, to tell the drivers the worst. One means of tackling the car's excessive thirst was development of a six speed gearbox, and this was introduced at Imola.

At Dijon the 184T trio sported slightly longer pods housing larger water radiators while at Montreal the pods were further modified with higher reaching leading edges to improve cooling and 'sharks fins' ahead of the rear wheels. Such alterations did nothing for the lack of straightline speed so in the summer Tolentino went modelling in Dallara's 25% moving floor wind tunnel. The idea was to develop a McLaren-type bottleneck rear plan. The tail could be narrowed only a little between the wheels, and this was done. The net gain, according to Cheever, was around 3m.p.h. on top speed.

Since Hockenheim the team had drawn on a fourth 184T chassis and for winter testing a 'TB' conversion was produced, having the push rod rear suspension developed for the 185T derivative. Thus modified, with the rear bodywork cut away behind the engine and snorkel turbo intakes, the model reappeared at '85 Silverstone, going on to supersede the 185T. Come Monza, even the spare car was a 184TB. Here the model's aerodynamics were modified with a switch to side-vented pods that blended into a narrow tail. There was also a lower dorsum, thanks to relocation of the ECU from the top of the tank, while the car adopted front wheel turning vanes.

EURORACING 185T

Monofrini carbon fibre/Kevlar monocoque
Stressed engine
Pull rod front suspension, push rod rear - Koni dampers
Speedline aluminium and magnesium rims
Brembo cast iron discs, outboard
Single Brembo four pot calipers - Ferodo pads
Carbon fibre/Kevlar bodywork
2 IPRA combined water/oil radiators
2 Secan air:air aftercoolers
AP twin plate clutch
Hewland/Euroracing six-speed gearbox - Salisbury diff
220 litre ATL fuel cell - 10 litre oil tank
Nippon battery - Bosch instruments
2800mm. wheelbase; 1800mm. front track, 1620mm. rear
555kg.

185T designer Gentry stayed at Euroracing for less than two months, just long enough to pen an evolution of the existing car with Toleman inspired push rod rear suspension. However, while the rear went push rod, the front went pull rod, unlike the interim 184TB which, harmoniously, found itself with push rods at both ends. Gentry's push rod system placed the spring/dampers side by side, transversely, lying almost horizontally above the diff housing. The car retained the familiar transaxle case, with a choice of five or six speeds.

The other major novelty of the 185T was an aluminium honeycomb monocoque produced locally, in Milan by the aerospace company that had previously supplied Euroracing's Kevlar/Nomex body panels. It was broadly similar in shape to the superseded item, but had a tubular roll hoop, and a detachable nose box to meet the new nose box test requirement. Its scuttle was lower and flatter and, in the interests of saving weight and improving rigidity, the carbon fibre/Kevlar weave was different.

The evolutionary car's aerodynamics were developed from further work on 25% models in the Dallara tunnel. While the front end shape was only subtly revised, and the sidepods were still top vented (although reaching further forward and higher to contain larger coolers), the tail treatment was new. The pods pinched in behind the aftercoolers to envelop the turbo installations and the engine bay shroud finished at the bellhousing, leaving the transaxle and suspension exposed. However, the underbody continued between the wheels with proper diffuser tunnels into which the exhausts exited.

Running on a slightly wider track and 80mm. longer wheelbase, the 185T was first aired at Balocco in February, then had a shakedown Imola in March, only a fortnight before Rio. For the first race there were two examples, with a 184TB as spare car. Estoril saw revised front suspension geometry and new locating points for the rear dampers. The pod top vents were higher and further back, but while this improved hot air extraction it hurt the flow to the rear wing. To further improve cooling, there was a cutout in each pod side panel by Imola.

A third 185T was introduced at Imola, but the 184TB was retained to allow the team to field two Motronic and two Jofa cars on this occasion. At Monte Carlo the 185T trio appeared on distinctive red and yellow wheels. The yellow rims were spun aluminium, the red centres were cast and the manufacturer was OZ, a relatively new Italian company formed by ex-Speedline personnel.

Between the American street circuits and the faster European venues the underbody was shortened to save weight and gain revs and snorkel air intakes were introduced, all to no avail. With the prompt switch to the 184TB model, only three Monofrini chassis cars were ever completed. Over the course of the season the team continued to use only five speeds at races, but toyed with the Torsen differential.

LIGIER JS29

Advanced Composite Technology carbon fibre/Kevlar monocoque
Stressed engine
Push rod front and rear suspension - Koni dampers
Fondmetal magnesium rims
SEP carbon-carbon discs, outboard
Single Brembo four pot calipers - SEP pads
Carbon fibre/Kevlar bodywork
1 Chausson water radiator - 1 Secan oil heat exchanger
1 Secan air:air aftercooler
AP twin plate clutch
Hewland/Ligier five-speed gearbox - Salisbury diff
195 litre ATL fuel cell - 12 litre oil tank
Yuasa battery - Contactless instruments
2835mm. wheelbase; 1790mm. front track, 1665mm. rear
540kg.

Tetu's team had a clean sheet of paper for its switch to Alfa Romeo power, after years of modifying an original Renault design. Both the monocoque and transaxle case were freshly drawn and the team claimed that only the gearbox internals and wheel hubs were adopted from the superseded JS27. The monocoque, again with an aluminium honeycomb core, and the only sub-contracted fabrication, was of a new concept, having its upper portion shrouded and carrying its inboard suspension components - spring/dampers, push rod rockers and anti roll bar - on rather than under the scuttle. This eased access and eliminated holes from the sides of the tub, improving safety. And as the dampers ran side by side longitudinally along an almost flat scuttle, the layout enabled the nose to be narrower than that of the JS27, while retaining similar pedal box dimensions.

Located on the dash bulkhead, each damper was worked by a crank pivoted atop the rear of the pedal box. A link ran forward from each crank (either side of a central hole providing access to the pedals) to the roll bar, which was mounted atop the front bulkhead. The tub incorporated aluminium and titanium reinforcements on the scuttle and the forward bulkheads where the suspension components located, and on the rear bulkhead at the engine pick ups.

In addition to base mounting points, the stressed engine's supports included a horizontal plate reaching from its flat cam cover to a point on either side of the rear bulkhead, towards the top of the tank. The in line four saved 15kg. over

Ligier's regular Renault V6 so, having started with a clean sheet of paper getting weight down to 540kg. was not a problem. The new transaxle mated directly to the 415T and its compact design provided an integral bellhousing and diff housing, the former naturally incorporating the oil tank. Designed by Michel Beaujon with the co-operation of Glaenzer-Spicer, it provided all mounts for the revised push rod suspension.

Behind a fully detachable nose cone, a single shroud concealed the upper portion of the monocoque, the engine and the transaxle, and formed the pod lids and side panels. Conventionally, the aftercooler sat in the left-hand pod with the water radiator opposite, while the oil heat exchanger was positioned alongside the block, opposite the twin turbo installation. The pods were top vented through unusual slatted apertures and careful packaging of engine ancillaries allowed tight waisting, a narrow tail fairing running through the rear suspension. However, the sleek lines of the central fuselage were broken on the right by a bulge to accommodate the plenum chamber, on the left by a mirror image scoop which fed the two compressors.

The car carried a diffuser and a two tier rear wing. The left-hand diffuser tunnel was blown by the exhaust, for the first time at Ricard in late January. The prototype JS29 was written off at Estoril: it was followed by three further Alfa Romeo chassis, all of which, unraced, were converted to BMW JS29B spec.
• Ligier JS29B appears on page 64.

OSELLA FA1-F

Composite Material Aeronautic carbon fibre/Kevlar monocoque
Stressed engine
Push rod front suspension, pull rod rear - Koni dampers
Fondmetal magnesium rims
SEP carbon-carbon discs, outboard
Single Brembo four pot calipers - Ferodo pads
Kevlar/g.r.p. bodywork
2 IPRA combined water/oil radiators
2 Secan air:air aftercoolers
AP twin plate clutch
Hewland five-speed gearbox - Salisbury diff
220 litre Pirelli fuel cell - 8 litre oil tank
Marelli battery - VDO instruments
2720mm. wheelbase; 1750mm. front track, 1700mm. rear
570kg.

Due to a lack of experience in carbon fibre technology, Osella based the design of its first composite car on the '83 Euroracing chassis raced at Rio and destroyed at Kyalami. That was an example which had been converted by Osella to tension link suspension and Petrotta retained a push rod system for his C.M.A. produced monocoque (the first from the aerospace specialist) and devised a Hewland-based transaxle similarly to carry pull rod rear suspension. C.M.A. was based near Novara and was known in Formula One for Renault and Ligier bodywork. Its monocoque employed carbon fibre outer skins, aluminium honeycomb and carbon/Kevlar inner skins.

Emphasising its 183T design base, the Osella was the last Grand Prix car without its oil tank set into the bellhousing - it carried its oil immediately ahead of the engine in a recess in the tank moulding. The transaxle was based on the DGB, with Osella side-plates. The gearbox supported

the rear wing post. While the general layout, including cooler arrangement, and the overall shape of the Italian-manufactured car followed 183T practice, the engine bay shrouding was cropped to leave the transaxle and rear suspension exposed and the pods were modelled after the 184T.

Like the 183T, the FA1-F had an integrated cover for the fuselage, including pods: the style favoured by Ducarouge. This g.r.p.-based shroud incorporated a familiar Alfa Romeo wedge nose. Indeed, the car was essentially an adaptation of the 183T design with monocoque made at home rather than in the UK. The 183T chassis Osella ran at Rio and Kyalami had incorporated most of the FA1-F design features and had been dubbed FA1-F 01. It had made its first run at Balocco in March '84 and had been intended to serve until Imola. Osella had only the first C.M.A. chassis (02) until Monte Carlo, where 03 made its entrance, while 04 was ready

for Gartner at Brands Hatch.

The three C.M.A. chassis cars were reckoned to be around 10kg. lighter than the modified 183T thanks to a lighter tub (with composite rather than aluminium front, bulkheads) and lighter bodywork. Pininfarina full scale wind tunnel research on 01 prior to South Africa had led to a long or short nose option and the fairing-in of the transaxle, but there was no proper diffuser. Osella retained Sergio Beccio as aerodynamic consultant, the Italian also working with Abarth.

The FA1-F's suspension geometry was revised during the Atlantic crossing and for Hockenheim a 35mm. spacer lengthened the wheelbase from its Alfa Romeo inheritance. Back in Germany at the 'Ring, Ghinzani's mount (03) sported new pinched-in rear bodywork - as close as Petrotta could get to a bottleneck plan tail without a longed-for all-Osella design.

Without the funds for that design, Osella arrived at Rio in '85 with two FA1-F models, untested over the off-season. Chassis 03 was unchanged, while 04 had a wider front track and was dubbed FA1-G 01 for carnet reasons. After the introduction of the real FA1-G at Imola, 01 continued to play a spare car role, and was raced by Rothengatter at Monza and Francorchamps. It continued to see service in 1986, alongside the one-off FA1-G (the two car team not running a spare) until the FA1-H was ready, then re-appeared after that '86 model was written off, seeing the year out. In '87 FA1-F 02 reappeared, the oldest C.M.A. monocoque car dusted off for Tarquini to race at Imola.

OSELLA FA1-G

Composite Material Aeronautic carbon fibre/Kevlar monocoque
Stressed engine
Push rod front and rear suspension - Koni dampers
Fondmetal magnesium rims
Brembo cast iron discs, outboard
Single Brembo four pot calipers - Ferodo pads
Kevlar/g.r.p. bodywork
2 IPRA combined water/oil radiators
2 Secan air:air aftercoolers
AP twin plate clutch
Hewland five-speed gearbox - Salisbury diff
220 litre Pirelli fuel cell - 8 litre oil tank
Marelli battery - VDO instruments
2830mm. wheelbase; 1800mm. front track, 1620mm. rear
580kg.

The FA1-G was an evolution of the FA1-F differing mainly in terms of aerodynamics, though the team's budget had not run to any wind tunnel work. And, frustrating for Petrotta, it could not incorporate all his ideas - it had to be an adaptation of the existing car rather than a much needed fresh design, with modifications strictly limited by financial considerations.

The one-off FA1-G model had a widened front track and a wheelbase lengthened from the modified FA1-F's 2755mm., with a revised transaxle carrying new push rod rear suspension

of conventional design. The monocoque was from the regular mould, with detachable nose box as per the '85 test requirement. However, the cooler arrangement was new, with side vented radiators in re-profiled, closed lid pods. The pods were tightly pinched behind the engine bay vented aftercoolers to blend into a bottleneck plan tail, under which was a short diffuser, blown by the exhaust. Again, the upper fuselage shroud and pod lids were moulded in one piece, while the lengthened pod side panels were formed with the extended Kevlar underbody.

Due to its shortage of funds, Osella ran its cars on cast iron discs in '85 and the new model, debuted at Imola, was reckoned to be 10kg. lighter than the older design. At Silverstone it appeared with shortened, lower drag diffuser, while the Osterreichring saw revised front suspension geometry, Monza revised rear geometry.

The FA1-G continued to see service throughout '86 as a race car and throughout '87 as a spare car. At '86 Hockenheim it appeared with a combined pull rod and rocker arm rear suspension devised for the FA1-H and it continued with this through '87. It was raced twice in '87, by Forini.

OSELLA FA1-H

Composite Material Aeronautic carbon fibre/Kevlar monocoque
Stressed engine
Push rod front suspension, pull rod and rocker rear - Koni dampers
Fondmetal magnesium rims
Brembo cast iron discs, outboard
Single Brembo four pot calipers - Ferodo pads
Kevlar/g.r.p. bodywork
2 IPRA combined water/oil radiators
2 Secan air:air aftercoolers
AP twin plate clutch
Hewland five-speed gearbox - Salisbury diff
195 litre Pirelli fuel cell - 10 litre oil tank
Marelli battery - VDO instruments
2860mm. wheelbase; 1800mm. front track, 1672mm. rear
565kg.

Although developments over the winter of '85/86 put a switch to Motori Moderni engines on the agenda, Osella wasn't able to give Petrotta a long-overdue clean sheet of paper. Nevertheless, there would be a revised model for the V6 engine, lighter and with improved weight distribution and a new rear suspension. Petrotta wanted to change the monocoque design, but says that

would have been too expensive. Thus, the one-off FA1-H tub came from the FA1-F/G mould, with the top of the tank cut down in the light of the 195 litre fuel cell, enhancing air flow to the rear wing. Otherwise, the aerodynamics were familiar, the team still not having been able to afford wind tunnel work.

To alter the weight distribution, Petrotta lengthened the wheelbase by 30mm. and relocated the oil tank in an Osella-produced bellhousing, and he changed the engine mounting system in the process of adapting from Motori Moderni back to Alfa Romeo. His new rear suspension was reminiscent of Ducarouge's '84 Lotus system, a combination of rocker and pull rod attacking the spring/damper unit from both ends. This gave him a preferred relationship between wheel and spring movement.

The FA1-H, featuring snorkel turbo intakes, was run at Francorchamps after a short Misano shakedown, but was not raced until Montreal due to its lack of sorting. That left it only three races before it was written off.

OSELLA FA1-I

Composite Material Aeronautic carbon fibre/Kevlar monocoque
Stressed engine
Push rod front suspension, pull rod rear - Koni dampers
Fondmetal magnesium rims
Brembo cast iron discs, outboard
Single Brembo four pot calipers - Ferodo pads
Carbon fibre bodywork
2 IPRA water radiators - 2 Secan oil heat exchangers
2 Secan air:air aftercoolers
AP twin plate clutch
Hewland five-speed gearbox - Salisbury diff
195 litre ATL fuel cell - 5 litre oil tank
Marelli battery - Contactless instruments
2800mm. wheelbase; 1800mm. front track, 1670mm. rear
542kg.

Moving over from Osella's customer sports-racer programme, Lunetta started work on the FA1-I in December '86 with three specific targets for improvement: aerodynamics, rear suspension and weight. As we have seen, the FA1-G and -H models were evolutions of the -F badly compromised by budget, and shaped without the benefit of wind tunnel testing. Now, for the first time since early '84, Osella could afford to hire tunnel time and Lunetta and Beccio worked on 25% models in Dallara's moving floor facility.

Like Petrotta before him, Lunetta didn't have a free hand, having to employ the existing monocoque mould which restricted aerodynamic options. Thus, the FA1-I emerged with a similar overall shape to the previous cars, with the transaxle exposed and, for the first time with an underbody based on more than intuition and pit lane observation. While the profile of the underbody and the influence of pitch were confirmed at Dallara, in March the finished car was put into the Pininfarina fixed floor facility to check the body shape and wing configuration.

Initially, the FA1-I was a one-off, the spare car being the FA1-G with -H rear suspension. That suspension was abandoned for the new car, Lunetta returning to a conventional pull rod system. He says Petrotta favoured little wheel movement and that caused wheelspin. Lunetta returned to "normal suspension movement" and saved the drag of the rocker arm. He also widened the track slightly for better airflow, and employed more rear wheel offset. The new suspension was mounted on new, purpose designed, Osella bellhousing and side-plates.

Lunetta retained the familiar front suspension, employing steel rather than electron uprights and modifying the geometry for less camber change (hence less pitch change) and lighter steering. The monocoque was modified with a new engine mounting, putting the Osella V8 closer to the rear bulkhead to shorten the wheelbase. Lunetta considered the 60mm. longer wheelbase of the FA1-H excessive.

Weight was saved wherever possible, by many small improvements through the car and by lighter aftercoolers, by switching to oil heat exchangers, and by carbon fibre bodywork. Lunetta claimed his car rolled out at 542kg, in spite of having to retain cast iron discs. It was tested at Misano and Imola prior to Rio and ran the '87 season, with a second example arriving at Estoril.

Chassis development was frustrated by endless engine problems. The model regularly ran a two tier rear wing and following further Dallara tunnel work in July the underbody and wings were modified, the fruits seen at Hockenheim. There were small suspension revisions at Monaco (rear) and Detroit (front). At Adelaide the car appeared with an interesting aerodynamic tweak: a pipe ran from the underwing to a point in the exhaust system at which there was a vacuum. The exhaust thus sucked turbulent air from the diffuser: an ingenious idea of dubious legality.

BMW Motorsport GmbH
Preussenstrasse 45
8000 Munich 40
Germany

Basis of arguably the most powerful Grand Prix engine ever, BMW's in line four cylinder engine was of considerable vintage. And the Barvarian wizard who coaxed over 1250b.h.p. from the old iron lump, Paul Rosche, had been a member of its design team a quarter of a century earlier. Thanks to an aptitude for mathematics, Rosche had been the camshaft specialist of a group working under Technical Director Alex von Falkenhausen. That group's brief from the fresh management team that swept into an ailing BMW at the end of the Fifties had been to produce a sophisticated four cylinder engine for a new sporting saloon.

Contemporary practice favoured pushrods and a three bearing crank. Von Falkenhausen opted for a chain driven s.o.h.c. and a five bearing steel crank running in a deep iron monobloc which extended down from the deck to well below crank axis, forming a rigid beam structure well capable of handling future power increases. The initial 1500cc engine produced 80b.h.p.; a substantial figure for an early Sixties saloon. Larger displacements, up to 2.0 litres followed as, in the mid Sixties, did a racing programme. A European Touring Car Championship race winning version of 1964 produced twice the original output from 1800cc.

Saloon successes flowed in and thoughts turned to formula car racing following a successful experiment with an unusual Apfelbeck four valve head that had inlet and exhaust valves diametrically opposed and radially disposed, and operated by double rockers. BMW went Formula Two racing with a 1600cc Lucas injected Apfelbeck engine that produced a highly promising 225b.h.p. at 10,500r.p.m. Alas, it was heavy and lacked the torque and the reliability to win. Rosche points to three major drawbacks of the design: while the head formed an ideal combustion chamber roof, the piston crown shape was disadvantageous; the incoming charge air didn't assist exhaust gas scavenging; additionally, the double rockers were prone to flex.

In 1969 an 'M12' derivative with upright but still diametrically opposed valves and three plugs per cylinder, producing 220b.h.p. at 10,500r.p.m., took Hahne to the runner up slot in the ungraded drivers' championship. In 1970 came the M12/2 with conventional four valve head. The 'compromise' head had allowed bigger inlet valves for extra top end power but additional air friction in the inlet tracts was at the expense of torque.

Following a short absence from official competition activity (during which Rosche helped driver Dieter Quester run an 'underground' effort from a small Munich garage), came a 2.0 litre M12 for the increased displacement Formula Two of 1973, again with conventional four valve head, and only a single plug. Rosche explains that, "running over 10,000r.p.m., three plugs gave the 1.6 litre engine more top end power: an extra 5 - 10b.h.p. Running below 10,000r.p.m., for the 2.0 litre version there was no difference". The M12/6 and its derivative, the M12/7 introduced in 1974 took the BMW-March works team to victory in 67 of 142 Formula

Two races contested over the years 1973-83.

When BMW Motorsport GmbH was founded in 1973 its 2.0 litre Formula Two engine was rated 275b.h.p./8,500r.p.m.: by 1983 Technical Director Rosche's ultimate development of the M12/7 was producing 312 - 315b.h.p./10,000r.p.m., with maximum revs of 10,250 and a dyno 'high' of 321b.h.p.. The classic Formula Two power plant featured a gear driven alloy head with a 40 degree included valve angle. Each camshaft ran in five bearings and was enclosed by its own slim casing, so that the four plugs nestled in a deep vee. The inlet cam was on the right and drove a Kugelfischer metering unit while a Bosch distributor ran directly off the exhaust cam.

Inside the stock five bearing monobloc was a nitrided steel crank turned by Mahle valve clearance notched flat top, three ring pistons via titanium con rods. The stroke was 80mm., while the bore was 89.2mm. and an 11.0:1 compression ratio was run. At its outset, the BMW Motorsport contender had brushed aside Ford's Cosworth BDG and alloy Hart BDA engines, reaching 300b.h.p. by the middle of the decade. Following the admission of pure racing engines, it had shared spoils with Renault's two-season wonder V6 then, in the early Eighties, with the Hart in line four and Honda V6 - all its sparring partners purpose designed alloy units. Its career was ended only by the demands of a Formula One turbo programme.

The idea of turbocharging was an old one in Munich. Just after Christmas 1968 von Falkenhausen had told Rosche and colleagues of his plan to turbocharge the contemporary 2.0 litre saloon racer. Its two valve four cylinder engine was duly given a single KKK turbocharger and lowered compression ratio and 2.2 bar lifted power from 200 to over 275b.h.p. There was no aftercooler and, never properly developed thanks to a swift outlawing of turbos, the engine often detonated, yet the car hung together to win four E.T.C.C. races. BMW had started knowing nothing of turbocharging, and its pioneering work had been assisted by Swiss engineering genius Michael May on a consultancy basis. Other than for BMW's work, turbocharging was unknown in road racing. However, its exploitation was continued, first in Can Am, then in prototype racing by Porsche.

The mid Seventies brought silhouette racing, and from Stuttgart a twin turbo Porsche 911 lookalike, the 935. BMW countered with a twin turbo derivative of its six cylinder CSL saloon racer, a project sub-contracted to Schnitzer. The base CSL racer had an M12/7-style head (though chain driven) on a 3.5 litre straight six block and was good for around 475b.h.p. A 3.2 litre version blown by KKK turbos to 2.3 bar was rated 750b.h.p. Alas, neither was this BMW turbo engine fully developed as the CSL had become an obsolete model. However, in 1977 BMW Motorsport developed a turbocharged four cylinder 320i lookalike in conjunction with McLaren Engines of Detroit, USA, primarily for IMSA silhouette competition.

The IMSA 320i carried a 2.0 litre M12 series engine blown by a single Garrett turbo. Codenamed M12/9, it drew heavily upon the Indy turbo experience of McLaren engineer Gary Knudsen and featured American pistons (TRW) and con rods (Carello) as well as an American turbo. Blown to 2.3 bar it was reckoned to produce 550b.h.p. Although at a disadvantage against larger capacity Porsche 935s, it won the July 1977 Road Atlanta IMSA GT race. Late in the year a sister car surfaced in Europe, run by English tuner John Nicholson. However, the Atlantic crossing was not successful, poorer octane fuel blamed for loss of reliability.

While Nicholson was grappling with the problem of running the fire-breathing 2.0 litre in long distance races, German tuner Schnitzer was running his own turbocharged 1.4 litre M12/7 derivative in the 2.0 litre category of national sprint races with a fair amount of success. BMW Motorsport had its own 1.4 litre turbo on the dyno, coded M12/12 and equipped with a single KKK turbo. The idea was to produce a batch of turbo cars for the 1979 German silhouette series. Alas, the series organisers hastily weighted the dice in favour of atmospheric 2.0 litre cars. All was not lost. From the outset, Rosche admits he had produced a 60mm. stroke crank, was well as the standard 56mm. version. The 1.5 derivative was to be coded M12/13...

Formula One wasn't a new idea in Munich, either. Upon his retirement in 1975, von Falkenhausen had put forward a proposal for an eight cylinder, 3.0 litre Formula One boxer engine which found some favour. But it was a time of flux for BMW Motorsport.

The organisation was growing fast under the direction of Jochen Neerpasch and had found itself faced with a choice for the late Seventies of Formula One or its own 400-off 'production' racer, the M1. The BMW board favoured the anti-Porsche 935 weapon and Lamborghini was duly charged with production of the mid engine, 3.5 litre six cylinder M1's homologation quantity.

Sadly, financial problems down at the Modena company delayed the project, and in any case silhouette racing flopped. Undeterred, Neerpasch cleverly devised the 'Procar' concept of a high profile, Grand Prix meeting orientated M1 series. Consequently, 1979 saw the ultimate in one make racing: 475b.h.p. mid engined supercars dicing in front of Grand Prix crowds, with the participation of Grand Prix drivers. BMW was now part of the Formula One scene, after all.

While the M1 was entertaining, the Renault turbo car started winning. At the same time the exploratory 1.4 litre turbo was running well. Fitted with a 3D metering cam (as used by Renault) to adjust its mechanical injection according to boost pressure as well as throttle opening, and Bosch CD ignition with fixed timing, at around 2.6 bar it gave 550b.h.p./10,500r.p.m. Pushed to 2.8bar and beyond, it proved capable of handling over 600b.h.p. Neerpasch told Lauda about it. Eager for a new challenge, Lauda was keen to drive a BMW-McLaren in 1980, and Marlboro was prepared to back it. Neerpasch put it to the board, but hadn't played the political game well enough: the answer was 'nein'. Shortly afterwards Lauda abruptly quit Formula One and Neerpasch went off to head Talbot's new, Grand Prix aspiring competition department.

Neerpasch had arranged for BMW Motorsport know how to be sold to Talbot: Rosche's emerging turbo engine would be given a Talbot badge and raced by Ligier on behalf of the French marque. Supported by two members of the main board, Sales Director Hans-Erdmann Schonbeck and development chief Dr. Karlheinz Radermacher, Neerpasch's successor Dieter Stappert and Rosche protested that the production basis of the engine was reason enough for BMW to invest in its own race programme. The support of the sales and marketing and Press/PR departments was important here: this time the main board said 'yah!'

Although talks continued with Talbot on the basis of the French company entering 'BMW-Talbot' cars, on April 24 1980 it was officially announced that BMW would equip Brabham with the M12/13. Blown by a single KKK turbo, the M12/7 based unit was officially rated at 550b.h.p./9,500r.p.m. at a conservative 2.3 bar. However, it had only just started bench testing.

Brabham was to be supplied with the engine free of charge, the team chosen as an ideal partner. It was a strong force in Grand Prix racing, and was noted for innovation. And ever since Bernie Ecclestone had bought the Motor Racing Developments company from Ron Tauranac in 1972, he had shown a willingness to experiment with alternatives to the ubiquitous Cosworth DFV - first the Weslake V12, then the Alfa Romeo V12, now the BMW turbo.

Throughout most of the Ecclestone era Brabham's chief designer had been Gordon Murray, and it was from his fertile mind that much of the team's inventivness sprung. Murray was the pioneer of pull rod suspension, bespoke transaxle cases and carbon-carbon discs, and was among the first to properly exploit underbody aerodynamics and the use of advanced composites in chassis construction. He had also produced the controversial Brabham fan car.

So Brabham had the expertise, and had the right attitude to the challenge of developing a new turbo engine (the awesome magnitude of which had been demonstrated by Renault). Track testing got underway in late 1980 with a Brabham BT49 wing car converted from fully stressed Cosworth-Ford to unstressed BMW, turbo system and all. Both parties were set for a long hard slog and a proper chassis for the M12/13 engine, the BT50 wasn't produced until mid 1981. The BT50 was a development of the contemporary Cosworth car with bigger fuel cell and slightly longer wheelbase and carried engine telemetry equipment, allowing Rosche's team to sit in a receiver van and monitor the engine while the car was on the move. Telemetry was developed as a spin off from electromechanical injection, which Bosch pioneered for BMW's use in Formula One, using an analogue-based system.

Early on, the BT50 was taken to Donington to adjust its electronics and the test went so well that it appeared soon afterwards in qualifying at Silverstone, where it proved high on top speed and cut a lap quick enough for the second row in Piquet's hands. However, it wasn't quicker than Piquet's regular Cosworth car and the Brazilian was able to win the 1981 World Championship without once resorting to turbo power. The original plan had been to start racing the turbo at Monza, but that had been shelved so as not to jeopardise Piquet's strong position by using unproven equipment. Nevertheless, the writing was on the wall for atmospheric engines and Piquet was determined to help develop the BT50 to a high state.

Alas, problems were rife - the new electronics largely to blame, Rosche recalls. Kyalami in January approached faster than the development programme could cope and, under pressure from the BMW board for concrete results from its big, two year investment, 'M Power' made its entrance in South Africa on mechanical injection. The high altitude of the Kyalami circuit favoured turbos and Piquet and teammate Patrese were second and fourth in qualifying, up with the Renault and Ferrari V6 turbos (and with Piquet over two seconds clear of the fastest Cosworth car). Alas, Piquet made a poor start and subsequently spun out, while Patrese retired due to a failed turbo.

With the analogue-based injection control troublesome, Brabham reverted to Cosworth power, joining in with the controversial use of a large water tank ostensibly for brake cooling. Piquet won the Brazilian Grand Prix on the road after a late stop for water, only to be disqualified as his car, allegedly, hadn't conformed with the minimum weight ruling throughout the race. The upshot was that the majority of FOCA stalwarts (among whom only Brabham had a turbo deal) boycotted Imola, round four of the 1982 World Championship.

Having abandoned the BMW engine since Kyalami, and having become embroiled in a fight with FISA, Ecclestone hadn't endeared himself to the BMW board. A week prior to the next Grand Prix at Zolder he faced a public ultimatum from Munich: 'field two BT50s at Zolder or we shall terminate our association'.

Piquet and Patrese qualified the BMW cars just inside the top ten and although Patrese spun out this time, Piquet finished fifth. Thereafter, Piquet persevered with the turbo car while Patrese reverted to Cosworth power - and won straight away, at Monte Carlo. Piquet's gearbox failed in Monaco then in first qualifying at Detroit the engine blew in the race car while the T car refused to run cleanly - Piquet was off the grid. With second qualifying washed out, there was no race for him.

Rosche recalls that "50% of the electronic boxes at Detroit were no good!" In the few days prior to Montreal qualifying: "we worked to make four good boxes from eight". Murray wanted to give the World Champion one BMW and one Cosworth car for Montreal but Stappert insisted he stick to the two BMW machines. The race car misfired in first qualifying but this time the T car ran sweetly. One decent ECU made all the difference, transforming the engine from 'undrivable' to smooth and progressive. Piquet qualified fourth fastest, up with the Renault and Ferrari turbo cars.

Come the race and he quickly dispatched them, going on to win round seven of the 1982 World Championship.

Over the remainder of the season both Brabhams were BMW powered and Murray devised the pit stop tactic whereby the cars could run hard on soft tyres and a light fuel load, hopefully building up a sufficient lead to allow for replenishment. However, it wasn't until the fourth attempt that either car lasted long enough to make the planned stop. The engine was still bugged by problems with its electronics and Montreal remained the high of 1982. In the light of the problems Bosch had commenced work on a digital-based control system, and this was readied for 1983. At the same time, Rosche revised the turbo system layout and repositioned certain ancillaries to allow Murray to produce a more effective ground effect chassis, the BT51. Then came the bombshell that even FOCA boss Ecclestone hadn't anticipated - 1983 Formula One cars would be flat bottomed. The BT51 was stillborn.

Murray rush-produced the BT52, a dart-shaped car without conventional sidepods, the coolers fanning out either side of the engine. With that layout, a long wheelbase, the driver sitting well back and a heavy engine, the rearward weight bias was pronounced. Faced with a loss of aerodynamic grip and increasing power Murray put the emphasis on traction. The static weight distribution was in the region of 35 - 65, compared to 42 - 58 for a typical wing car.

In 1983 the digital-controlled M12/13 started racing at around 2.9 bar, producing in the region of 640b.h.p. on a 6.7:1 compression ratio, and was pushed to over 700b.h.p. in qualifying. The four cylinder engine's single turbo was hard worked and a pits cooling blower was introduced to help its bearings. Qualifying also saw the use of a water spray onto the aftercooler.

Rosche tried water injection on the dyno but found it more beneficial to concentrate upon fuel. Zandvoort, round 12, was the turning point. BMW had commissioned fuel from BASF subsidiary Winterschall to replace its regular doctored Avgas, and Rosche says that improved fuel and a bigger turbo released more race and qualifying power. Consequently, Piquet could come out of the shadows and grapple with Renault and Ferrari in qualifying, and at Monza he took his first pole of the season.

Although overshadowed in qualifying for much of the season, Piquet had usually been a factor on race day. He had won the Rio opener with ease, then had suffered a rare off day at Long Beach. Thereafter, as a rule the BMW-Brabham had either been the class of the field, or second only to Prost's Renault. However, small, infuriating problems had left Piquet's pickings as three seconds, a third and two fourths prior to Zandvoort. He languished 14 points behind Prost. Piquet and Prost tangled at Zandvoort but thereafter, with the improved BMW engine raced as high as 3.4 bar, producing almost 750b.h.p., there was no stopping Piquet. Prost could not respond as Piquet strode ahead of him to claim the world title, the first for a stock block propelled driver since 1967. And one that BMW salesmen could exploit to great effect.

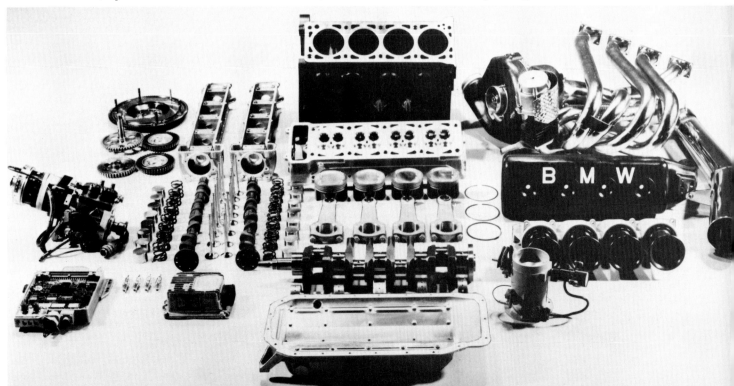

M12/13
in line 4

89.2 x 60.0mm./ 1499cc.
1 KKK turbocharger
Iron block, aluminium head
Linerless
5 main bearings, plain
Steel crankshaft, 4 pins
Titanium con rods
Mahle light alloy pistons
Goetze rings
2 o.h.c., gear driven
4 valves/cylinder, 1 plug
35.5mm. inlet valve, 30.2mm. exhaust
40 degree included valve angle
Bosch ignition
Kugelfischer injection
Bosch engine management system
Compression ratio 7.5:1
Maximum r.p.m. 11,500
160kg.

The iron block designed by von Falkenhausen in 1959 was still in series production in 1984, powering the 316, 318 and 518 saloons and BMW Motorsport used essentially 'stock' blocks, treated via a heat and chemical process to relieve inherent stresses. During the Formula Two days the company had sometimes instead employed well run in (around 100,000km.) examples. As in those days, the stabilized block had its internal walls machined smooth to assist oil return, while surplus ribs and water channels on the inlet side were machined off, to save around 7kg. New for '84 were some detail modifications to strengthen the area around the main bearing caps.

The deep iron monobloc was closed by the aluminium M12/7 type head secured by five pairs of studs, and by a shallow magnesium sump pan. Each of the crankshaft's five bearings was retained by a two-bolt cap. Conveniently, the standard production journal diameter of 48mm. could be employed, the plain bearings supplied by Glyco. The shaft itself, other than for the 60mm. rather than 80mm. stroke, was still the regular Formula Two forged item with deep nitriding, in which the oilways had been modified for greater oil circulation. It was a typical 'mirror image' in line four shaft, with extended balancing webs to reduce bearing and crankcase loads.

At the front end a rubber crank seal was incorporated in the block, while at the rear a seal was retained by a small bolt-on aluminium casting. The main timing gear was carried at the front end as a push fit, secured by circlip, while at the rear a 12-bolt 7 1/4 inch clutch was carried by a suitably small steel flywheel bolted to a crankshaft flange by eight high tensile steel bolts.

The con rod journals retained the same 45mm. diameter as the production 'shaft, and again plain Glyco shells were employed. The H- section rods, 153.6mm. long, were milled and turned from a titanium forging and were shot peened for strength. The big end caps were secured by two titanium bolts with steel nuts. At the other end, a hollow steel gudgeon was fully floating and was retained by Rosan-type nuts rather than conventional circlips. The three ring Mahle pistons were of a 'semi-slipper' form, with short thrust pads integral with the crown. Each weighed little more than one third of a kilogram, complete with gudgeon pin. A vast piston stock was held, allowing a piston to be selected for a precise fit in each bore. The bores, machined directly into the cast iron block, were very precisely honed.

Rosche denies that the M12/13 engine was ever run with Nikasil coated bores or conventional Nikasil liners, as alleged by some of his rivals, saying that coated bores were "not necessary". Piston cooling was taken care of by a simple spray to the underside of the crown, the piston not of the oil gallery type.

The conventional steel valves and bronze-based valve seats and guides of the M12/7 head had been changed to cope with the heat, new exhaust valves being nimonic, seats, beryllium bronze. Conventional double springs and sintered steel bucket tappets were retained, with shims inside the buckets for clearance adjustment. Although the head carried a single, central plug, provision had originally been made in the M12/7 head for three plugs as in earlier engines and the turbo engine had been tested with three plugs on the dyno. However, with the right quality of fuel one plug was found to be sufficient.

The head carried a cast magnesium manifold which housed four throttle butterflies, operated by a single shaft which was in communication with a butterfly at the compressor inlet. Earlier versions of the M12/13 engine had run only a single butterfly at the compressor inlet, the single butterfly system found to offer more power - though Rosche notes that it made leaving the pits, "a big problem", due to poor idle and low speed characteristics. The five butterfly system offered improved response, and the relationship between the opening of the single large and four small butterflies was important in that respect. Rosche says he tried a DPV-style device on the dyno, but that it was "never a success".

The head was sealed to the block by a regular gasket and carried alloy cam carriers, located by studs which projected up through the caps for the five camshaft bearings. Again, plain Glyco bearings were employed. Naturally, the hardened steel camshafts were profiled specifically for the turbo engine. Each had its own magnesium cover that proudly bore the legend 'BMW M Power'.

Timing adjustment was available through movement of the drive gear in relation to the shaft. Those gears were rubber mounted and acted, in effect as vibration dampers for the engine. Driven through a train of three intermediate gears, they rotated in the same direction as the engine. The intermediate gears ran on

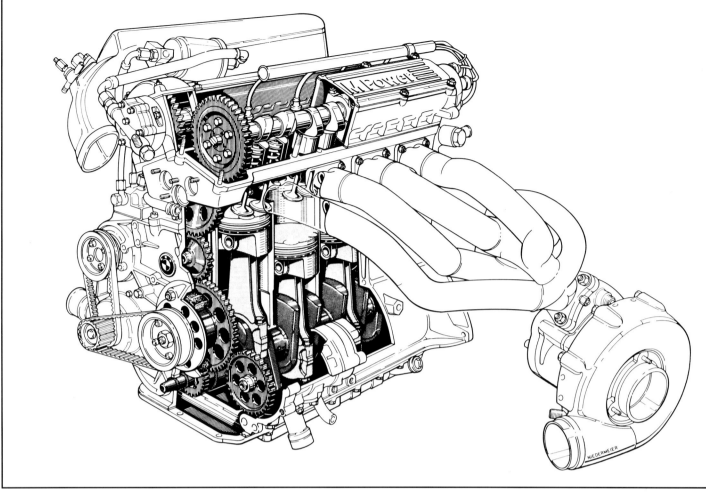

needle roller bearings, the uppermost one carried by the head, the others by a thick aluminium plate bolted to the front of the block. This wide plate carried oil pumps to the left, acted as an oil gallery and also carried water pumps and metering unit to the right. The timing drive was concealed by an alloy casting, which incorporated the alternator housing. The alternator was driven directly off the lowermost intermediate gear and a drive was passed through it to an external ancillary drive pulley.

The external pulley drove the water pump pulley to the right via a short belt, and that pulley in turn drove the metering unit pulley above it, again via a short belt. The oil pumps were driven by an internal gear, off the lowermost intermediate gear. The engine was equipped with two Zebra water pumps, a Lenz oil pressure pump and four scavenge pumps.

The pressure pump fed through a filter screwed into the plate at the front of the block to the distribution gallery within. Early turbo experience had revealed a problem of blow by blocking the return of oil from head to sump. Consequently of the four scavenge pumps, one was to service the head. Another looked after the turbo, while the sump was drained via two longitudinal channels above which were oil/air separator plates.

Fuel was supplied by a Lucas mechanical pump driven directly off the front of the inlet camshaft. This fed the Kugelfischer metering unit via a filter, the plunger-type unit in turn continuously supplying four injectors screwed into the carbon fibre plenum chamber, one directly above each inlet trumpet. As we have noted, from the outset the metering cam had been servo controlled. For 1984 Rosche retained the digital ECU proven in '83, this taking information from sensors for the position of the butterflies, engine speed, boost pressure, charge temperature, water temperature and fuel temperature. It controlled the metering cam, the CD ignition system and the wastegate, regulating wastegate opening according to a consideration of the relationship between boost pressure and engine revs. However, ultimate boost control was in the hands of the driver.

The distributor was mounted on the rear of the exhaust cam and fed 10mm. Bosch plugs. The exhaust plumbing was in stainless steel and the four pipes fed into a twin entry 'biflux' turbine housing according to firing order: 1/4 - 2/3. The turbo shaft's axis was at right angles to the crank axis and the wastegate was tucked alongside the turbo.

Planned race boost was 2.9 - 3.3 bar: 640 - 750b.h.p., with the power band running from 8,500-10,500r.p.m. Maximum race

Performance of the 1984 M12/13 engine was improved by the incorporation of an oil cooler in the nose of the Brabham BT53 chassis, as from Montreal.

r.p.m. was 11,000. BMW's all-important 102 octane brew - one of its keys to success in '83 - continued to be brewed by BASF subsidiary Winterschall, a chemicals company based near Osnabruck in Northern Germany. A Bosch software programme calculated fuel consumption from the information handled by the ECU. Careful calibration on the basis of practice results was required: the method could not be as precise as measuring the opening time of solenoid-activated injectors. A new-for-'84 cockpit read out advised the driver of the number of laps that should be available from the remaining fuel, which he then compared to the number of laps to run, as signalled by the pits.

The '84 M12/13 was fitted to a 220 litre tank evolution of the BT52, the BT53, with bigger, sidepod housed coolers and more sophisticated aerodynamics. The '52 had been produced in a rush and the '53 benefited in particular from a certain amount of wind tunnel work. It likewise ran on Hitco carbon-carbon discs, Murray considering Brabham's lead in this field to be an important advantage. The two Michelin shod BT53s were driven by Piquet and one of the Fabi brothers, Corrado acting as understudy for Teo who had certain clashing American commitments.

Rosche denies that he ever produced specific qualifying engines. However, the rugged old iron block took high boost well and a larger turbo was available for qualifying. In '84 the combination of Piquet and the M Power Brabham was more successful than any other in the quest for pole, nine times in all. Qualifying power was quoted officially as "850b.h.p.", but by the end of '84 boost was nudging 5.0 bar and Rosche admits that power was then in excess of 1000b.h.p. Almost certainly, M qualifying Power was the first to reach four figures. The water spray onto the aftercooler was essential in keeping charge temperature under control as boost soared.

Race day was a different matter altogether. BMW had under estimated the amount of power that would be required to be competitive under the new conditions. Race boost, 3.3 bar from the outset, had to be significantly increased over the season, reaching 3.8/3.9 bar: far in excess of 720b.h.p. (the official power figure at 10,500r.p.m. on 3.1 bar, with 52m.kg. torque at 8,500r.p.m.). Higher boost, with no longer fuel to spare to assist cooling, led to a strain on parts, in particular the turbo.

Early on there was a problem of sub-standard components, the first six races witnessing a succession of engine failures as a consequence. Motorsport had found itself overstretched as a host of problems came at once and its quality control department was too small to cope. Most failures were blamed on parts from outside suppliers, BMW confessing only to incorrectly machined big end bolts which failed at Zolder in spectacular fashion: Piquet coasted to a smoky halt with the block ripped asunder. And that after a bad fuel batch had detonated over half a dozen engines over the weekend.

However, the most common problem was failure of the highly stressed single turbo. Rosche admits that as power climbed over the period '83 - '84, the turbo supplied by KKK was pushed to its limits in terms of turbine operating temperature and revs. Montreal, round seven, saw the BT53 boast an extra, nose mounted oil radiator which Rosche confesses was "very important - in '84 everything was too hot..."

Piquet won Montreal, then repeated the feat at Detroit. Rosche had, of course, prepared specific street race engines. The second half of the season saw retention of the nose radiator but there were no more wins. However, Piquet had a fuel-efficient engine and could turn the boost high enough to challenge the dominating Porsche-TAG McLarens everywhere, if he still hadn't the stamina to beat them.

Significantly, the six cylinder rival enjoyed more efficient aerodynamics - this was particularly noticeable at the sweeping Osterreichring, where the MP4 chassis required less road, enjoying greater grip. Consequently, Piquet had to drive harder, to the detriment of tyres, fuel consumption and chassis reliability. And neither chassis, nor engine, nor turbo reliability was good.

The BMW propelled car proved difficult to get off the line but once underway its acceleration was blistering. And, on balance, its electro-mechanical injection system was highly effective. Chilling fuel was a low priority, and was undertaken only spasmodically, and only in Europe. The fuel consumption read-out was "never terribly accurate", according to Murray, yet BMW didn't face the sort of late- race consumption dramas Renault suffered. Murray considered 1984: "the most competitive year I'd ever had in Grand Prix racing - the car was quick everywhere. Overall, it was the most competitive car, but we didn't get the results we deserved. Engine and turbo reliability had disappeared, and turbo failures were rife".

Rosche reflects: "we had no problem on 220 litres, and had more power than the Porsche engine, but lost half a dozen races through turbo failure. The turbo was the biggest problem". While he was running, Piquet was a real menace to the McLaren drivers and he led 243 laps of '84, in comparison to 347 for Prost and 165 for Lauda. Alas, he added only a second, a third and a sixth to his two wins, collecting 29 points whereas both McLaren drivers, for whom he was the most serious rival, amassed over 70.

While Motorsport was fettling 25 highly potent 'development' engines for Brabham in '84, down in Switzerland Heini Mader was looking after 24 more conservative 'standard' engines for ATS and Arrows, these teams reputedly paying DM180,000 per leased M12/13. Mader's newly opened Geneva factory was supplied with the parts to rebuild the engines (eight per car) every 600km., and to update as Motorsport deemed appropriate.

ATS, British based but German owned, had been supplied directly by Motorsport in '83. The one car team was run by ATS wheels boss Hans Gunter Schmid, who on occasion acted as both team manager and race engineer. Austrian designer/engineer Gustav Brunner had come and gone three times, though in making more than one visit he wasn't emulated by any of the autocratic Schmid's various team managers. Brunner's first visit had been made in 1978, when the operation was relatively new to Grand Prix racing having bought the resources of the wound up Penske operation. Brunner developed an effective BMW-Maurer Formula Two car between ATS spells, returning for the third time to design the car that took Schmid from Cosworth to BMW power.

With his D6 design, Brunner pioneered the concept of sculpturing the monocoque to form the shape of the cockpit coaming and the Goodyear shod creation added to his growing reputation by regularly qualifying in the top 10 in BMW protege Winkelhock's hands. Alas, not once did it stay around long enough to collect points...

Brunner followed the D6 with the evolutionary D7, to be Pirelli shod and Shell fuelled. However, he left for Euroracing before seeing it run. Schmid instructed Team Manager Paul Owens to expand his duties to encompass those of engineer. He too resigned before the '84 season got underway. So it was that Winkelhock found himself with Schmid as both engineer and team manager at Rio...

As the prototype D7 had been finished late in the day, Winkelhock concentrated on an updated D6 at Rio, only to be disqualified after a minor infringement of track regulations erupted into a major row between his team manager and the organisers! The D7 came on stream at Kyalami and Stefan Fober was appointed engineer, under Schmidt's 'guidance'. Having built a second D7, the team expanded to run it for Berger, a more recent BMW protege, at the Osterreichring. Winkelhock had the audacity to protest - the team was so short of resources that he even had to share a gearbox with the newcomer in qualifying! Nevertheless, Berger came back at Monza and as at the Osterreichring Winkelhock found himself sidelined by gearbox breakage in the warm up. Thereafter Winkelhock's outspoken criticism was answered: by his own expulsion.

By this stage BMW had announced that Schmid's contract would not be renewed. Of Winkelhock's 11 starts, only the first three had been from the grid top 10 (the highlight; sixth at Zolder) and he hadn't scored a single point, normally retiring. Berger finished sixth at Monza, but as he wasn't a registered driver he didn't qualify for a point. As in '83, ATS's World Championship participation had been pointless. To be fair, it should be noted that the Mader engines leased by both ATS and Arrows had to be run conservatively throughout the weekend, in deference to budgetry considerations. Neither operation could afford to risk high boost, and both lacked qualifying turbos. By the end of the season BMW was using more power on race day than the Mader teams qualified with. Both second division cars carried a significant weight penalty and ATS was further disadvantaged by running Pirelli's '84 offering, which was usually inferior to that of Michelin and Goodyear.

Running on Goodyear, Arrows was a newcomer to the BMW camp. Its deal had been late in completion, and it had to wait until mid season for sufficient engines to be available to run both its entries on M Power. Nevertheless, going turbo was a welcome break: after coming so close to winning its second ever Grand Prix, at Kyalami in 1978, the team's six year affair with the Cosworth engine had been one of constant setback. A splinter group from the Shadow team, its very competitive, rush-built first car had been shot down by Shadow boss Don Nichols on a copyright claim, and also in its first year its financier had been locked up for alleged currency irregularities. Thereafter, backers of various sorts had come and gone, and the Jackie Oliver run, Milton Keynes based two car operation had always operated on a modest budget.

Founder designer Tony Southgate had left abruptly at the end of 1980, leaving founder draughtsman Dave Wass Technical Director. Wass had soon found himself struggling with uncompetitive Pirelli radials. However, his flat bottom offering had been Goodyear shod and had proved a competent design, to the extent that Arrows had beaten Tyrrell and Toleman to the BMW contract. The deal was for two years, backing came primarily from Barclay cigarettes and the drivers were Boutsen and Surer (though it was Detroit that first saw both in BMW cars).

The Wass designed BMW-Arrows D7 wasn't ready until Zolder. It was a straightforward evolution of the aluminium honeycomb monocoque Cosworth D6, overweight, with an inherited wheelbase that proved too short, and proven suspension that couldn't cope with the new application. Worse, its aerodynamics proved inadequate and torsional rigidity had been badly compromised by lack of a fully stressed engine. The engine situation allowed very little testing over the first half of the season and a lengthened wheelbase (pushing the engine forward from the diff, to the detriment of traction) and compromise modified suspension and aerodynamics didn't enable the adapted Cosworth design to break into the top 10 qualifiers. Some improvement was evident by August, but only at the Osterreichring did the model collect points, Boutsen and Surer taking fifth and sixth places, a lap down. Arrows needed a purpose-designed turbo chassis.

Brabham also needed a new element in its package: Ecclestone neatly anticipated Michelin's withdrawal in signing on to help develop Pirelli radials in the summer. Pirelli testing began in September on the Nurburgring and an 'interim' version of the BT53 was constructed to carry on the work in the Southern hemisphere over the closed season. Seemingly endless lappery at Kyalami gave the relatively inexperienced tyre manufacturer a chance to develop a better race tyre, and gave Rosche's team an ideal opportunity to work on engine durability.

For 1985 the M12/13 turbo system was more tightly packaged with lower plenum chamber and a revised exhaust layout to lower the turbo and wastegate, tucking them well into the side of the block, the compressor facing forward. Murray produced a revised car, the BT54, with improved aerodynamics and even longer wheelbase through a longer transaxle. As more downforce was found from the underbody, the centre of pressure moved forward and traction was less of a problem, so the centre of gravity could be shifted forward. Cooling improvements, the product of over 10,000 miles running by the interim machine at Kyalami, then a further developed example in the February Rio test, were, according to Rosche, the key to improved engine performance. Internally, the M12/13 featured only a new exhaust camshaft, but the better cooling offered by the '85 aftercooler/radiator package was "a big step forward".

Brabham found a new backer in the Italian Benedetti company, but the Italian driving connection was lost in favour of rich French rookie Hesnault. He did not get to grips with the narrow power band and the difficult handling posed by early Pirelli tyres and was replaced by Surer after only four races. This season Motorsport again provided a 25-strong M12/13 pool and, officially, power was

Installation of the M12/13 in the 1984 BT53 chassis : aftercooler on the left, combined water/oil radiator on the right. Note neat charge plumbing.

quoted as "800b.h.p." in race trim, with "950b.h.p." available for qualifying. Throughout qualifying power was in four figures and Rosche says 5.3/5.4 bar was seen on occasion, representing short bursts of 1150 - 1200b.h.p. Awesome high boost runs by howling, ground quaking BT54s were characterised by a vast, hazy plume of brown gas reaching high into the air as fuel gushed through the engine flinging out unburned hydrocarbons and a vast quantity of water was sprayed through the aftercooler, turning to steam. But brute power wasn't enough.

Over the first half of the season the BMW-Brabham pole quest was disadvantaged by poor Pirelli qualifying tyres. That was understandable, given that winter work had concentrated on development of a good race tyre. Twice in early races a Renault-Ligier stole the prime Pirelli grid slot, probably due to the excessive weight of the French car. For Brabham, poor turn in and frequent locking of front brakes were evidence of insufficiently heated front tyres. Yet Pirelli race rubber also posed headaches.

Pirelli's race tyre worked well in the heat of Rio (only for differential failure to cause Piquet an early exit) but did not work again until new, stiffer sidewall fronts were run on a hot, abrasive Ricard circuit. Meantime, low track temperatures, low grip surfaces and low speed (low downforce) circuits all caused headaches. Just prior to Ricard, the BT54 was tested at Silverstone with a lead weighted nosecone! Murray recalls: "Early in '85 there were big discrepancies in tyre temperatures. For the first half of the season we were floundering. We tried altering the weight distribution to get more heat into the fronts. But in '83 we had run a lot less weight on the front and hadn't had a problem..."

Between Rio and Ricard, race power had to be compromised to tyre life. The nadir of Pirelli performance came at Estoril, where all its cars were undrivable on its wet weather offering. However, the same tread pattern in a softer compound subsequently proved acceptable. On dry roads, lack of grip left Piquet struggling to get into the grid top 10 and out of the picture on race day - until Ricard, which, Murray reflects, "was night and day": Piquet qualified fifth

and went on to win.

Immediately after its Ricard boost, Pirelli produced a qualifier that let Piquet in on the battle for pole at Silverstone. However, it was the low powered Hart-Toleman that gave Pirelli its first ever pole position, in freak circumstances at the Nurburgring. From the latter half of the season Piquet claimed but one pole position, though the BMW-Brabham could be counted on to be in the top six slots. On race days there was no repeat of Ricard. Second at Monza following the introduction of another new tyre was the only other podium position: this year, even with the improved Pirelli race tyres, Piquet wasn't a major factor.

Murray considers the tyres Pirelli produced for the second half of the season to have been good, and regrets that the earlier tyre problems had "thrown the season away". He accepts Piquet's reckoning that the exhaustive off season tyre and engine testing had been at the expense of chassis development, and admits that the BT54 did suffer a degree of high speed rear end instability, while pointing out that it was difficult to separate chassis from tyre problems. However, he did feel that the BT52/53/54 chassis series was nearing the end of its development potential.

"We tried for the whole year, and couldn't find more downforce. We needed a 10% bigger wing but the greater depth of such a wing would have 'hidden' it behind the rear deck". It was a fundamental problem of the height of the engine package. In view of that Murray concentrated hard on the genesis of a radical replacement with a lay down engine. This season, well designed V6 engined cars demonstrated markedly superior aerodynamic grip. Again, the sweeps of the Osterreichring provided a good measure of that: in qualifying, Piquet slammed through a speed trap on the fastest part of the course at 341k.p.h., Prost at only 309k.p.h., yet the Porsche/TAG-McLaren driver wrapped up pole...

And this year, from mid season, there were three extremely

1985 M12/13 with turbo rotor axis north/south - compressor feed is down from a duct alongside the driver's shoulder. The engine produced over 1100 b.h.p.

The '85 M12/13 in the Brabham BT54 chassis. The car had extremely long sidepods and generous cooler provision. Oil radiator is alongside the engine rather than in the nose.

effective V6 packages, the others the Honda-Williams and Renault-Lotus. The (similarly iron block) Japanese V6 came on strongly with brute qualifying power to rival BMW - something in excess of 1100 b.h.p. - and a wider power band, while the French alloy V6 also reached four figure horsepower.

Inferior aerodynamics naturally compromised race day performances, too. Overall, the BMW engine package was more reliable this year, but wasn't wholly dependable, and nor was Brabham's transmission. The most positive aspect of the season, other than Pirelli's eventual improvement, was Motorsport's switch to Garrett, another step taken at Ricard. Following the problems experienced with KKK's offering, BMW had eventually managed to conclude a contract whereby it paid the American company to develop special turbos for its use.

The Mader engines supplied to Arrows continued throughout with KKK, this year Arrows benefiting from more appropriate turbine and compressor sizes for its needs. In May Arrows tried an IHI turbo in a private test. The team had retained its Barclay backing and Boutsen, who was joined by Berger. They were equipped with the much needed no compromise turbo car. The A8 was lighter (it was claimed to be right on the weight limit) with a plastic tub, longer, lower tank, longer wheelbase, a more rigid engine mounting and properly conceived aerodynamics.

The A8 was ready in time for pre-season testing and proved quick out of the box: it was quickest in the Imola general test using a loaned works engine. The car wasn't so impressive with Mader engines installed but at Imola both examples made the grid top 10, Boutsen exploiting his Goodyear tyres outqualify Piquet, a feat he repeated at Monaco and Montreal. Thereafter, top 10 appearances were limited to three per driver and Boutsen's number five slot at Imola remained the season's qualifying high.

Imola was also the scene of Arrows' only podium finish, Boutsen a somewhat fortunate second. Generally, the A8 was a midfield runner, and an inconsistent one at that. It was short on testing through budget constraints and had to undergo significant modifications to tackle a lack of grip in fast corners and improve traction including, in mid season, a yet more rigid engine mounting.

Overall, Arrows didn't perform as well as BMW might have expected it to and Benetton (nee Toleman) became favourite for the Mader deal for '86. However, Benetton, like Brabham, ran on Pirelli tyres and Arrows' continuing Akron supply was an important factor in its eventual retention of its Swiss-fettled engines, alongside Benetton. Berger moved over to Benetton and Surer came back into the fold, de Angelis and Patrese having signed to drive the radical new Brabham.

There were no lay down engines for Mader, who continued with '85 works specification (7.5:1 c.r./11,500 r.p.m.) M12/13 units carrying Garrett turbos, his pool expanded to 40 to service four cars. Whereas the Mader teams had previously leased their engines, there was now a straight rental agreement, the charge to equip two cars for the season reputedly $3 million.

Having retained its backers, Arrows enjoyed improved funding but continued to race its A8 model while awaiting a new 195 litre tank chassis with gearbox ahead of the differential. That ambitious design was developed in conjunction with British Aerospace and a strike at British Aerospace's Manchester plant allowed the first half of '86 to slip by without any sign of it. Having been handicapped by the ageing, 220 litre tank A8 design, Boutsen was relieved to get his hands on the prototype A9 soon after Brands Hatch, at which stage the team hadn't qualified better than 12th, and hadn't scored a single point. Surer was in hospital recovering from a severe rallying accident immediately prior to the North American trip, and Danner had taken his place.

The A9's unusual gearbox location and a long wheelbase endowed it with a favourably long span between upright BMW and rear wing without unduly compromising weight distribution. However, there wasn't time to sort the car properly prior to Hockenheim and the gearbox proved troublesome on its debut. The single entry for Boutsen was subsequently converted to accept a conventional A8 rear end for Hungary and, while better, again proved disappointing. It lacked grip, oversteering excessively, and remained insensitive to chassis set-up alterations.

Creator Wass had taken leave and wasn't recalled: Gordon Coppuck came in on a freelance basis to engineer Austria, Italy and Portugal as a favour to old friend Boutsen. The A9 was given a final fling at the Osterreichring, then Coppuck confirmed an unacceptable lack of torsional rigidity, measuring 50% less than the A8. The team concentrated upon the older model for the balance of the season, a season badly compromised by the heavy diversion of resources to an unproductive new design. A season that brought only one point, for Danner, three laps down in an A8 on the Osterrichring.

Benetton made much better use of Mader's upright engines. The team's switch from Hart engines had given it an estimated 20% increase in race power, almost 50% increase in qualifying power. It had also put up the cost of a season but Benetton took care of that, exercising its option to buy the operation outright. Thus it was that on January 1 1986 Benetton Formula Ltd came into being with Luciano Benetton as Chairman and Davido Paolini as Managing Director. On a stronger financial base the Witney team's workforce expanded to 70 and Peter Collins, Team Manager since mid '85 and Technical Director Rory Byrne shared day to day running.

Starting late, having been forced to await confirmation of the BMW deal, Byrne's technical team produced a brand new car for the Mader prepared engine; a careful evolution from a good handling Hart machine. The Hart car had enjoyed a classic 40 - 60 weight distribution: Byrne encouraged the rearward weight shift inherent in a switch from alloy to iron block for improved traction in acknowledgement of the extra power, though going nowhere near the 35 - 65 of earlier Brabhams. He retained his favoured 106 inch wheelbase and further improved the effective aerodynamics of the superseded Hart design.

The first example of the Pirelli shod B186 to be campaigned by Berger and Fabi was ready for the Rio test but the build programme was too late for comfort. Nevertheless, in the Rio race Fabi was fastest on the main straight and, even if the model didn't feature in the top ten qualifiers, Fabi clocked second quickest race lap. From Spain the car was a regular top ten qualifier, though Berger was somewhat lucky to collect third at Imola for the first rostrum finish. However, his front row start at Francorchamps was no fluke - properly sorted, on power circuits the B186 had emerged as a real force.

Byrne's Hart-Toleman had been noted for fine aerodynamics,

with high speed cornering its forte. Its BMW propelled replacement was a whole new ball game with its rearward weight bias and more brutal power, but the extra power was put to good use once the team had learnt how to come to terms with it. That challenge had been eased through Pirelli's enthusiastic co-operation: from early on it had been clear to Pirelli that Brabham was a deep trouble. Indeed, by Francorchamps its was clear that the BMW-Benetton was an all round more effective package than the BMW-Brabham, in particular exploiting the acceleration that the troubled lay down car so badly lacked.

Benetton, then, rather than Brabham benefited from Pirelli's valuable '85 experience. The B186 started at Rio 25kg. overweight but, says Byrne, "a lot of hard work reduced that - at the end we were close to 540kg." Byrne admits that less than satisfactory handling led to a revised rear suspension first seen at Hockenheim. For the high speed European circuits Byrne had an improved aerodynamic package and Benetton livery went well to the fore at Hockenheim, the Osterreichring and Monza. In Germany, Berger set fastest race lap, then in Austria the team tried a larger qualifying turbo which didn't work, yet still buttoned up the front row. The cars majestically led one - two until Fabi bounced over a kerb and buzzed his engine, then Berger's battery failed due to porosity in a connection between a plate and terminal...

If the Osterreichring speed was proof of the excellence of Byrne's aerodynamics, another illustration came in Italy where Berger used the big turbo and sky high boost to clock the fastest ever Formula One speed - 218.238m.p.h. Byrne says: "Mader did a lot of development work on the qualifying set up. At Monza we saw a 5.5 bar flash reading - Mader estimated that was worth over 1300b.h.p. Qualifying boost was regularly 5.3 bar, with a charge temperature of 45 degrees. We pumped a lot of water onto the intercooler - we had 20 jets, spraying about three litres of water per lap!"

Byrne reports that race boost on 195 litres was generally around 3.7 bar, representing something in the region of 850b.h.p. After the splendid performance in Austria came Berger, Benetton and Mader's first Grand Prix win in Mexico, the result greatly aided by Pirelli longevity Alas, overall reliability was poor with a total of only six points finishes netting the poor score of 19. Retirements were generally down to either engine (mostly ancillaries) or transmission failure, with half a dozen of the latter, including a strange c.w.p. failure in Hungary, a broken gear selector finger and failed rear wheel drive pegs.

During the course of the season the injectors were relocated in the inlet manifold from the plenum chamber (following the lead of the lay down engine) which overcame an engine cut out problem and, according to Rosche, offered better response and 7 - 8% better fuel consumption, if less top end power. At the end of the season all Mader's Motorsport equipment, every last nut and bolt, was taken back to Munich, BMW having announced that it would not continue in Formula One in 1987. However, before the year was out the remaining 38 upright engines, and parts for a dozen or so more, were back in Switzerland, the rights to the upright M12/13 unit having been bought by computer leasing company Megatron.

Megatron was a Michigan based operation which boss John Schmidt had sold to the United States Fidelity & Guaranty (USF&G) insurance company in 1984, Schmidt taking a seat on the USF&G board while remaining Chairman of Megatron. Spurred by his enthusiasm, USF&G had lent increasing support to Arrows through '86 and had agreed to underwrite its 1987 season. The upright M12/13 was badged as a 'Megatron' and was prepared by Mader for Arrows' exclusive use.

Ligier's sudden loss of Alfa Romeo engines at the end of March gave USF&G an aspiring customer for Megatron engines. Guy Ligier refused to consider moving down to the normally aspirated class and Renault made it clear that a reversion to its retired engine was out of the question - that left Megatron, Motori Moderni and Porsche-TAG as possibilities. TAG's Mansour Ojjeh offered a deal but could not supply until August, while Ligier didn't feel that the MM6VTC was adequately competitive. He ordered that the work to convert the JS29 Alfa Romeo chassis to accept a Megatron engine commence without delay, while he worked out a deal with Schmidt, and sought to finance it. Schmidt saw co-operation with Ligier as potentially profitable for both parties, provided Mader could cope.

The conversion job wasn't straightforward, and as the Alfa Romeo engines were to have been supplied at a favourable rate

Ligier had a good deal of extra finance to find. However, sponsors Gitanes and Loto were state owned concerns and in '85 the Government had promised to fund Ligier's expensive Renault deal for three years. Ligier was a close friend of President Mitterand and was eventually able to extract sufficient extra finance to satisfy Schmidt. The deal that saved his beached team was concluded in late April and on May 1 Ligier had two Megatron cars at San Marino, following a hectic month's toil in the factory. However, with a taller, heavier engine that had to be supported by A-frames the 'JS29B' was overweight, had less than ideal weight distribution and had a higher engine cowl which disrupted its aerodynamics.

Neither of the two chassis on hand had run prior to official practice and on Friday Ghinzani's car broke a front wishbone, the shunt sidelining it. Another converted tub was rushed from Vichy, arriving just before untimed practice on Saturday and this was built up in time for Ghinzani to qualify, both cars having been fitted with reinforced wishbones. Alas, during the race morning warm up Arnoux' monocoque lost its right front lower wishbone leg, putting the Frenchman, who had qualified 14th fastest one second adrift of the Arrows, out of the race. Ghinzani found his hastily built car handling so badly that he withdrew after only seven laps...

It was the start of a very trying season for the late-starting Ligier team. At Francorchamps Arnoux collected a point, but he was two laps down. The car was plainly uncompetitive, woefully short of grip. Having seen neither driver break into the top 20 qualifiers at Monaco, Ligier flew back to Vichy in a huff taking Michel Tetu, instructing the designer to work night and day to produce a revamped car in time for the French Grand Prix, one month hence. While Arnoux and Ghinzani again qualified outside the top 20 at Detroit, Tetu worked on a 'JS29C' package, using the St Cyr 100% fixed floor tunnel to verify aerodynamic changes and having Schlesser to undertake the first proper track tests of the BMW/Megatron programme.

The converted JS29Cs seen at Ricard were 25kg. lighter, with improved aerodynamics and better weight distribution. However, the still badly compromised model was never better than a mid grid qualifier, its highest position 12th at Hockenheim, while there were only half a dozen finishes from 19 starts, after Francorchamps always outside the points and two or three laps down. Engine failures and ignition troubles were rife. Having committed his team to a normally aspirated future with Judd engines in mid season, Ligier was vocal in his condemnation of Mader reliability.

Mader ran short of engines for Ligier at the Osterreichring and at the end of season events outside Europe. However, during the course of the season some additional blocks had been supplied by BMW to help support his four car effort, and the Geneva-based Austrian engineer had taken on extra staff to help cope. However, it was a disappointing season for the upright M12/13, penalised harder than the higher revving vee sixes by the 4.0 bar limit and no longer the most powerful engine on the World Championship trail.

Arrows had started out with high hopes, its USF&G backing providing its best ever budget and allowing it to increase its workforce and open its own composite production facility. FORCE aerodynamicist Ross Brawn had been recruited to design an all new car, and the A10 was ready to run in mid March, allowing a certain amount of pre-season testing. Warwick and Cheever were the drivers for Brawn's tidy, FORCE- influenced car, which was expected to qualify comfortably within the top ten and to collect points on a regular basis.

It didn't work out that way. Only on six occasions did Arrows appear in the top 10 qualifiers, and only at Monaco and Detroit was the marque higher than the fifth row, Cheever hauling his A10 around sixth quickest at both street circuits. And there were only half a dozen points scoring finishes, with no rostrum appearance for either driver. The A10 was a mid field runner, and an unreliable one at that, with engine failures rife and poor fuel efficiency. As early as Monaco, Mader had complained that its coolers were too small. Nevertheless, and in spite of the departure of Schmidt from the USF&G group, the Megatron programme was scheduled to continue in 1988, unlike the BMW Motorsport programme...

ARROWS A7

Arrows aluminium and carbon fibre monocoque
Semi-stressed engine
Pull rod front suspension, rocker arm rear - Koni dampers
Dymag magnesium rims
AP cast iron discs, outboard
Single Brembo four pot calipers front - Ferodo pads
Twin AP two pot calipers rear - Ferodo pads
Kevlar/g.r.p. bodywork
1 Behr combined water/oil radiator
1 Behr air:air aftercooler
AP twin plate clutch
Hewland/Arrows six-speed gearbox - Salisbury diff
220 litre ATL fuel cell - 7 litre oil tank
Yuasa battery - VDO instruments
2640mm. wheelbase; 1727mm. front track, 1626mm. rear
565kg.

Hastily conceived, the A7 was an adaptation of Arrows' existing, competitive Cosworth car. That in turn had been based on Wass' A5 design of 1982, which had been heavily influenced by the Williams FW08, and similarly featured a relatively short wheelbase and an aluminium honeycomb monocoque. The A7's 220 litre tank monocoque was stiffened and lightened by a carbon fibre inner skin for the driver cell. The structure incorporated a boxy tank (topped by an unusual four prong roll hoop) and a wedge-shaped nose box. With high trapezoidal scuttle, its angular form was in the interests of rigidity. Compared to a state of the art black tub, Wass did not consider his design was necessarily lacking in torsional rigidity, but admitted to a weight penalty.

From the A6, the short wheelbase BMW-Arrows inherited well proven conventional pull rod front suspension, rocker arm rear. Typically, the rocker pivots were supported by substantial aluminium plate yokes straddling Arrows' magnesium transaxle case. The Hewland/Salis-

bury equipped transaxle incorporated the oil tank in the bellhousing, picked up a conventional steel support frame for the Mader BMW and supported the rear wing's central post. The front wings were carried by the integral nose box.

The overall shape of the A7 was similar to that of the dumpy A6, modified at the rear to accommodate the in line four and its ancillaries. The nose was of a wide wedge shape and the nose box fairing reached back to conceal the angular scuttle, while the slab sides of the tub were left exposed. The top of the tank and all but the tip of the roll bar were concealed by a fairing that blended into a separate engine cowl, and formed a pronounced hump. The typically rounded engine cowl flared out at its base to form closed pod lids.

Housing coolers that sloped upwards either side of the tank, the rear vented pods were short and boxy, stopping well before the rear wheels. On the right the gap between the side panel and the wheel was bridged by a small additional oil cooler, on the left the equivalent gap left room for a compressor intake funnel. The engine and turbo system package was as standard for ATS. The transaxle was left unshrouded, and the underbody similarly stopped short at the bellhousing.

Shaken-down at Donington in April, the prototype A7 was shipped to Dijon for further testing prior to its Zolder race debut. Two chassis were

ready for Zolder but a lack of engines saw only one race. Although the team had sufficient engines to race both from Dallas, it did so without an A7 T car until Hockenheim. A fourth A7 appeared following damage to chassis 2 at Zandvoort.

Imola saw an early switch to twin AP two pot calipers at both ends and the team subsequently played with both AP and Brembo two and four pot calipers. Early problems included rear tyres blistering and poor traction. Wass responded with a wider rear track for Monaco, while Montreal saw rear suspension reinforcement links to combat sag under power.

By the start of the North American tour rear end aerodynamics had been revised. As early as Dijon the roll hoop cowl had been dispensed with, then for Monaco the engine cover and rear of the pod tops had been cropped somewhat to improve cooling. Detroit saw the wheelbase lengthened by a 100mm. bellhousing spacer with the pod side panels curved inwards at the rear. Lengthening the wheelbase improved the overall weight distribution but pushing weight forward from the rear wheels did nothing to assist the ever present traction problem.

Detroit also saw revised front suspension geometry, while Brands Hatch brought a modified rear suspension - a combination of rocker and pull rod. In addition, there was a revised engine cowl and an umbrella-like shroud for the transaxle to help clean airflow to the rear wing.

ARROWS A8

Advanced Composite Technology carbon fibre/Kevlar monocoque
Semi-stressed engine
Push rod front and rear suspension - Koni dampers
Dymag magnesium rims
SEP carbon-carbon discs, outboard
Single AP four pot calipers - SEP pads
Carbon fibre/Kevlar bodywork
1 Unipart combined water/oil radiator
1 Behr air:air aftercooler
AP twin plate clutch
Hewland/Arrows six-speed gearbox - Salisbury diff
220 litre ATL fuel cell - 9 litre oil tank
Varley battery - VDO instruments
2750mm. wheelbase; 1800mm. front track, 1650mm. rear
540kg.

Wass' uncompromised turbo car was based around a brand new monocoque, entirely skinned in carbon fibre and Kevlar and having a longer fuel tank to provide a wheelbase similar to that of the modified A7 without recourse to a bellhousing spacer, and to lower the centre of gravity. The car also benefited from an improved engine mounting, and was more rigid and lighter than its predecessor - equipped with SEP discs, it was reckoned to be right on the weight limit. It had purpose-designed suspension front and rear and considerably revised aerodynamics following model tests in the Imperial College

25% rolling road tunnel.

The monocoque was shaped to form the cockpit coaming and a hood over the fuel tank that blended into an integral roll pyramid. It was constructed from upper and lower sections produced by A.C.T. Wass located aluminium panels between the two bulkheads supporting the front suspension, to assist the mandatory crash-test-proven nose box in the absorption of frontal impact.

Stiffer engine support was provided by wider based steel A-frames, picked up by Arrows' regular magnesium transaxle case. Wass reck-

oned he had found an extra 75% rigidity in engine mounting, confessing that rigidity had originally been lost through the switch to Munich power. He switched from pull to push rod suspension seeking extra scope in terms of geometry and at the rear looked for improved wheel control under acceleration with the c.v. joint outside the upright and the lower wishbone mounts at halfshaft height. This called for an unusual upright with the caliper underslung. Inboard, new transaxle pick ups were supplemented by short fabricated yokes over the case.

New, longer coolers stood on edge lengthwise

and were splayed outwards alongside the tank within short, boxy engine bay vented pods. The lower half of each side panel was formed with the undertray and that on the left-hand side reached no further than the engine, cut away to expose the turbo. Arrows didn't have the turbo tucked as closely to the block as Brabham and this year had the shaft axis at an acute angle rather than at right angles to crankshaft axis. Thus, a slight inward sweep to the end of the side panel directed air into the compressor funnel and the main exhaust pipe had an almost straight route, and was fed into the left-hand tunnel of a diffuser that ran either side of the gearbox.

A single fairing provided a rounded engine cowl and splayed to form closed pod lids, on both sides extending as far as the bellhousing (leaving the transaxle exposed). The cooling benefit from having the turbo in the open air and the tail unshrouded was considered more important than bottleneck-plan streamlining. At the other end, a wide wedge nose concealed the detachable nose box; reminiscent of the A7. The front wing post was carried by the nose box, while the rear wing sat on a typical centre post.

The prototype A8 missed the February Rio test but, having been aired at a damp Donington that month, then at a similarly moist Paul Ricard, it

made the March session. Chassis 2 was introduced at the subsequent Imola general test, while three cars were on hand for the first race. A Rio fire delaminated the monocoque of chassis 2 so chassis 4, with wider rear track and more rigid monocoque was introduced at Estoril. Subsequently, all cars had a wider rear track for improved traction. Monaco saw revised rear suspension geometry, while Francorchamps brought a wider front track.

For the Atlantic crossing there was improved structural rigidity thanks to stiffer engine and rear suspension mounts. Further strengthening of the engine mounts was evident at Paul Ricard, where a 50mm. bellhousing spacer was tried but quickly rejected. Wind tunnel testing saw revised rear wings (a choice of one or two tier) and, from Hockenheim, double front wheel turning vanes.

A fifth chassis was introduced at the Osterreichring with the monocoque modified in the cockpit area, and subsequently chassis 3 was pensioned off. A new chassis was produced for 1986, and comparative wheelbase tests led to the adoption of a 50mm. spacer for the new season. However, with spacer and wheel vanes the model proved slower at Imola the second time around, so these items became optional. At Brands Hatch chassis 4 became the second write-off.

After the unsuccessful introduction of the A9 (which just missed Brands Hatch) and Wass' departure, Coppuck modified the suspension geometry, at the rear for Monza and the front for Estoril and introduced a new underbody, a new rear wing and single front wheel turning vanes.

ARROWS A9

Advanced Composite Technology carbon fibre/Kevlar monocoque
Semi-stressed engine
Push rod front and rear suspension - Koni dampers
Dymag magnesium rims
SEP carbon-carbon discs, outboard
Single AP four pot calipers - SEP pads
Carbon fibre bodywork
1 Behr combined water/oil radiator
1 Behr air:air aftercooler
AP twin plate clutch
Hewland/Arrows six-speed gearbox - Salisbury diff
195 litre ATL fuel cell - 7 litre oil tank
Varley battery - VDO instruments
2921mm. wheelbase; 1822mm. front track, 1676mm. rear
540kg.

Given a free hand to progress from the A8 to a 195 litre tank machine, Wass responded with the concept of an inboard gearbox - primarily for aerodynamic reasons. Traditionally an inboard gearbox had been employed specifically to minimise the moment of polar inertia - concentrating mass towards the centre of gravity reduces the 'dumb bell effect' - a prime example being the Porsche 908/3 Targa Florio special, designed to be as agile as possible. Wass reckoned that an inboard gearbox would allow him to produce a well balanced long wheelbase chassis, with good torsional rigidity afforded by the unconventional transaxle layout, and with scope for cleaner airflow around the back of the car thanks to a longer span between engine installation and rear wheel axis (from which wing overhang is determined). Wass plumped for a wheelbase 100mm. longer than that of the A8, with the gearbox location providing improved weight distribution.

Studies of scale models at Imperial College, and of a full sized mock up at MIRA produced a shape that benefited rear airflow but one drawback of the location of the gearbox was lack of accessibility. To help overcome that, Wass designed the transaxle and rear suspension as one quickly detachable module, employing dry-break fluid couplings. It was calculated that the

time penalty for ratio changes would be only 20 minutes. The gearbox itself, an adapted DGB, was located within the oil tank, sealed inside its own pod. Careful attention to lubrication suggested that there would be no danger of high transmission temperature.

In addition to a complex new transaxle, Wass penned a brand new monocoque, using the facilities of British Aerospace. The hi tech company offered CAD facilities and advanced composite expertise and production capability. However, a prolonged strike at the company's Wythenshawe, Manchester plant delayed production of the car and in the event the first tub was produced by A.C.T. It was a one piece moulding with three aluminium bulkheads inserted to enhance rigidity, and it was significantly lighter than the A8 tub.

Lower than the A8, the A9's monocoque similarly formed the cockpit coaming, with steeply sloping arched scuttle reaching higher than the top of the 195 litre tank, which was flat and was capped by a roll hoop and a detachable head rest fairing. Long coolers, as in the A8, were set on edge lengthwise and splayed out alongside the tank and a portion of the cockpit. The front half of each cooler vented through slats in the pod side panel (parallel to the tank), the remaining hot air escaping through the engine bay. Along-

side the engine, the side panels swept inwards to meet the new transaxle at the rear suspension. The pods and engine were covered by a shroud that extended the ridge formed by the horizontal tank top over the block, then swept down to provide a hood for the transaxle. The turbo intake was a NACA duct in an otherwise closed pod lid. The overall impression was of a well packaged, well streamlined rear end.

The new transaxle case, running from engine to c.w.p. housing, was split vertically for access. It picked up the usual engine support frames and provided all the supports for the rear suspension, with an outrigger behind to carry the upright dampers and the rear wing post. The rear wing was two tier, with endplates extending down to meet a full length diffuser. The front wings sat either side of a chisel nose and the model carried Arrows' usual double front wheel turning vanes.

The prototype first turned its wheels at Silverstone soon after the British Grand Prix and was promptly dispatched to Hockenheim as Boutsen's race car. The meeting had to be approached as a test session and the gearbox proved troublesome. In response, a conventional rear end was grafted on for the Hungaroring and the car remained in that configuration through its short, sad career.

ARROWS A10

Arrows carbon fibre/Kevlar monocoque
Semi-stressed engine
Push rod front and rear suspension - Koni dampers
Dymag magnesium rims
AP carbon-carbon discs, outboard
Single AP four pot calipers - AP pads
Carbon fibre/Kevlar bodywork
1 Secan water radiator - 1 Secan oil heat exchanger
1 Secan air:air aftercooler
AP twin plate clutch
Hewland/Arrows six-speed gearbox - Salisbury diff
195 litre ATL fuel cell - 7 litre oil tank
Sonnenschein battery - Stack & Contactless instruments
2743mm. wheelbase; 1803mm. front track, 1626mm. rear
548kg.

The first car designed by Brawn represented a fresh approach for Arrows in the wake of the A9 disaster, and was produced upon a stronger financial base. Inevitably somewhat influenced by the FORCE cars that Brawn had worked with, the A10 was based around Arrows' first in house monocoque, which had an aluminium honeycomb core. The A10 also featured a new transaxle case (with DGB gearbox internals once more) that was designed in conjunction with the team's own strengthened sump, allowing a lighter engine cradle. Each side a simple V-frame linked the push rod rocker mount on the transaxle to

two points on the outer edge of the rear bulkhead (with, on the left the exhaust manifold bent awkwardly under the horizontal upper arm).

The monocoque formed the cockpit coaming and tank shroud, and the height of the central fuselage was kept relatively low with a fairly reclined driving position ahead of a squat tank that was topped by a high roll hoop. Echoing FORCE practice, the A10 had a low and unusually long, flat and wide dorsum formed by its fuel tank and engine shroud. After clearing the cam covers, the engine shroud swept down behind the block to blend into the tail deck, while the pod side panels swept inwards either side of the engine and extended through the suspension in regular (though not pronounced) bottleneck plan style. However, the neat rear end form was spoiled on the right by a necessarily prominent bulge to accommodate the plenum chamber. A full length diffuser swept up under the rear suspension, with a central post supported, two tier rear wing above.

The pods contained coolers that slanted upwards lengthwise alongside the fuel tank. The pod lids were stepped with the drop from the higher forward portion forming a vent for the upper region of the cooler, the lower region venting through the fully enclosed engine bay. The compressor inlet faced forward and was fed from a duct in the side panel.

Equipped with Hitco produced carbon-carbon brakes, the A10 first ran at Donington in mid March, prior to the Rio test. SEP discs were tried at Imola and minor cooling revisions were seen at Francorchamps, Detroit and Ricard. A periscope compressor intake was introduced at the Osterreichring, and was run for two races. Five models were produced over the season, of which one was written off at Mexico.

ATS D7

Keller Luft und Raumfahrt Technik carbon fibre monocoque
Semi-stressed engine
Pull rod front and rear suspension - Koni dampers
ATS aluminium and magnesium rims
AP cast iron discs, outboard
Single AP four pot calipers - Ferodo pads
Carbon fibre/Kevlar bodywork
1 Behr combined water/oil radiator
1 Behr air:air aftercooler
AP twin plate clutch
Hewland/ATS five-speed gearbox - Salisbury diff
220 litre ATL fuel cell - 12 litre oil tank
Yuasa battery - VDO instruments
2642mm. wheelbase; 1753mm. front track, 1626mm. rear
554kg.

Although it had a brand new monocoque with integral roll pyramid the D7 was essentially a refined D6, adapted to Pirelli radials. Consequently, from the front bulkhead to the top of the tank the central fuselage was, in Brunner's pioneering style, shaped by an exposed monocoque, and the new car retained the basic form of the old, with arched scuttle and slab cockpit sides. Aside from the nose cone, the only bodywork was a combined engine and pod cover, the pod side panels being formed with the undertray.

The rear cover fitted around the engine so tightly that the top of the plenum chamber with its four injectors had to be left exposed, as did some exhaust pipework on the other side. The snug cover sloped down from the roll pyramid, over the back of the tank and the block, to wrap around the top of a cylindrical bellhousing oil tank. The pods were top vented and the rear

bodywork was pinched in as tightly as possible around the rear wheels, though extending no further than the bellhousing. The waisting left the turbo completely exposed.

Naturally, the coolers slanted upwards, and ahead of the top vent aperture the pod lid was well raked, McLaren style. The rear wing was carried on a central post from the gearbox, while underneath was short, full width diffuser which swept up abruptly behind the suspension. The front wings were moulded with the nose cone, projecting slightly ahead of it, and were adjustable only via trim tabs.

The shape of the A7 was a product of Brunner's intuition - as in the design of the D6 and his competitive Maurer Formula Two cars, he had no access to wind tunnel test facilities. The car's suspension featured regular pull rod systems, with geometry revised from the crossply shod D6 to suit radials. The rear suspension was hung on ATS' own transaxle case, while the engine was supported by regular A- frames.

Initially, the D7 was a one-off model, and it was first run at the Rio Grand Prix meeting. First raced at Kyalami, it was revamped for Zolder by Fober. An 80mm. wheelbase spacer pushed the rear wing back, improving the air flow, helping tackle excessive oversteer, as was a wider track and modified suspension geometry. To improve cooling an additional oil radiator was set (vertically) in the taper of the right-hand pod wall. Subsequently, weight was trimmed wherever possible, but the team could not afford carbon-carbon discs and the originally quoted weight had been on the optimistic side.

A second example of the D7 was not ready until the British Grand Prix. It had a longer, lower fuel tank providing a wheelbase 100mm. longer than Brunner's original. Lacking a shakedown, it was not raced before Hockenheim.

BENETTON B186

Benetton carbon fibre/Kevlar monocoque
Semi-stressed engine
Pull rod front suspension, push rod rear - Koni dampers
Dymag magnesium rims
SEP carbon-carbon discs, outboard
Single Brembo front, AP rear, four pot calipers - SEP pads
Carbon fibre/Kevlar bodywork
1 Secan water radiator - 1 Serck/Benetton oil heat exchanger
1 Secan air:air aftercooler
AP twin plate clutch
Hewland/Benetton six-speed gearbox - Quaife diff
195 litre Marston fuel cell - 9 litre oil tank
Hitachi battery - Yamaha instruments
2692mm. wheelbase; 1816mm. front track, 1682mm. rear
548kg.

Although evolved from his good handling Hart-Toleman, Byrne's BMW car differed in certain fundamental respects - components were laid out differently, and were new productions: only the pedals and wheel nuts were interchangeable. Work couldn't start until the final week of October '85 due to the late completion of the BMW deal, the aim to improve on an already very effective four cylinder aerodynamic package, while coping with heavier, more powerful engine.

A key development was use of the scope af-

forded by the smaller fuel cell capacity to provide a recess in either side of the tank; the lower half of the monocoque tapered to a mere 200mm. width at the rear bulkhead. This enabled the coolers, still standing on edge lengthwise and splaying outwards from the sides of the tank, to be sunk inwards, closer to the car's centreline, leaving less obtrusive pods to the benefit of rear end airflow.

Weight was a problem thanks to the switch to an iron block. Lighter coolers and the adoption of carbon-carbon discs helped save kilos on the chassis but the overall weight was initially

565kg. More weight under the engine cowl shifted the centre of gravity rearwards and this was accepted as beneficial in the interest of improved traction. The wheelbase remained identical to that of the superseded car.

The BMW engine, while supported by A-frames, was bolted directly to the T-shaped rear bulkhead via alloy blocks. Byrne says the BMW engine was more difficult to install, with narrower based mountings. The monocoque was a stiffer evolution of the TG185 tub, the team's first in house composite production. Again the tub shaped the central fuselage, with a well arched scuttle and integral roll pyramid, and it carried a familiar pull rod front suspension, the suspension front and rear cleaned up aerodynamically.

Carrying mounts for the push rod rear suspension, the integral transaxle case, produced by Kent Aerospace Castings to Benetton's design, was revised, and was slimmer. Modified DGB rather than FGB gearbox internals were employed, with the option of five or six speeds. Interestingly, Byrne switched from Salisbury to Quaife diff: although this looked like a Torsen, incorporating worm gears, it was fundamentally

different in operation, using friction force generated by the gears against the casing to bias the torques. The team had an exclusive agreement to run the Quaife in Formula One in 1986.

If the chassis structure was a straightforward evolution from that of the TG185, the aerodynamic package was only superficially similar. The nose was far narrower and, with the sunken coolers, the rear end treatment was new. However, the B186 inherited the TG185's novel wing and underwing characteristics, with fanned front wings, stepped monocoque below, and short diffuser upsweeps with a small wing profile mounted in tandem. The flip ups were again either side of the bellhousing, with the wing profile behind being the low set third tier of the rear wing. The exhaust was blown into the left-hand flip up.

The B186 featured remodelled pods with side panels which bulged out from a narrow inlet then tapered inwards as a series of louvres which followed the run of the cooler. Thus, all but a small rear portion of each cooler was side rather than tail vented. Interestingly, the flat, closed pod lids did not follow the tapering side panels but were overhung, forming a prominent ledge ahead of each rear wheel. Moulded with the pod lids, the engine-cum-transaxle shroud just cleared the M12/13, and was symmetrical in the sense that the plenum bulge was echoed by a scoop on the left to collect air for the forward facing compressor.

With stronger team backing, Byrne could afford to run carbon-carbon discs everywhere, and was happy with AP rear calipers, other than for Monaco. The prototype B186 briefly debuted at Silverstone in February, having been completed just in time for shipment to the Rio test. The Rio race saw three examples ready, chassis 2 adapted to suit Berger's long legs while Fabi's race car was number 3. That was written off at Montreal, where Berger was given chassis 5. Fabi used Berger's old car until Ricard, where chassis 6 was ready for him. The last of the batch was number 7, supplied for Berger from Estoril. By that stage weight was approaching 540kg.

Early development, as Byrne's team finished its late initial build programme and started to get to grips with M power, saw new rear suspension pick up points for Jerez followed by a further revised rear suspension at Imola, but Byrne considers neither development particularly significant. At Monaco the team was requested by FISA to take flex out of its front wing endplates. Byrne says, "FISA saw a damaged endplate. There was no endplate trickery: our endplates never moved in relation to the rest of the chassis". Ricard brought a more efficient Secan oil heat exchanger while at Hockenhiem there was an important rear suspension revision. For the faster circuits there was a revised aerodynamic package, and in mid season the car lost its distinctive monocoque step: "we found a better way of achieving the same objective, so it was obsolete".

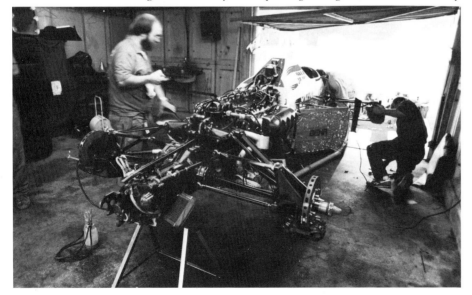

BRABHAM BT53

Brabham carbon fibre and aluminium monocoque
Semi-stressed engine
Push rod front and rear suspension - Koni dampers
Momo magnesium rims
Hitco carbon-carbon discs, outboard
Single Girling four pot calipers - Hitco pads
Kevlar/g.r.p. bodywork
1 Unipart water radiator - 1 Serck oil radiator
1 Behr air:air aftercooler
AP twin plate clutch
Hewland/Brabham six-speed gearbox - ZF diff
220 litre ATL fuel cell - 12 litre oil tank
Yuasa battery - Contactless instruments
2934mm. wheelbase; 1702mm. front track, 1626mm. rear
540kg.

Murray considers the BT53 a straightforward development of the World Championship winning BT52. In the light of a 60% cut in downforce, increasing turbo power and the on/off nature of the BMW power, that car had put emphasis on traction and had shunned conventional sidepods for an arrow shaped planform with the arrow's head formed by delta- shaped front wings, its tail by an unusual cooler arrangement, the upright cooling surfaces raked out either side of the engine. The car had enjoyed a long wheelbase with the driver sitting well back, emphasising the rearward weight bias. And its rear suspension had been designed to work without an anti roll bar.

The basic philosophy of the BT52 was retained by the BT53, which introduced short sidepods to house larger coolers, and won more downforce from its underbody. Thus, the centre of gravity and the centre of pressure moved forward together. The rush-built BT52 had lacked serious wind tunnel research: working primarily with the Southampton University 33.3% rolling road Murray found useful underbody downforce, and improved the lift:drag ratio, in spite of the larger cooler area. However, he could not get a proper diffuser to work without exhaust activation, and without a long diffuser a true bottleneck rear planform did not prove advantageous. The new car retained short flip ups under a wide rear deck. It had a bigger tank than the superseded pit stop special and this extended the wheelbase by 60mm. Still, however, the weight bias was to the rear, in the interests of traction, the static distribution nearer 36 - 64 than 40 - 60.

The BT53 was based on the same, unique chassis construction as its predecessor, with a front suspension module detachable from a combined plastic and metal tub. The module was a boxy magnesium casting that bolted to the front bulkhead and carried the upright front dampers, the push rod rockers, the mounts for the upper wishbone and the forward leg of the lower wishbone, the anti roll bar and the steering rack. It also carried a deformable aluminium nose box (anticipating '85 regulations) and the brake and clutch pedals, which passed through the frame-structure front bulkhead when it was bolted in place. The modular construction eased maintenance.

Murray was safety conscious, and reluctant to adopt an entirely 'plastic' tub: "it was purely caution", says the carbon fibre pioneer. Prior to production of the BT52, he had crash tested a BT49 at BMW, and as a consequence had introduced Kevlar to complement carbon fibre, while continuing to shun honeycomb, using carbon fibre/Kevlar as black aluminium. The BT53's main bulkheads were machined from solid aluminium and aluminium sheet was wrapped around them to form the lower half of the tub "purely for 'crash-ability'". The tub was completed by complex carbon fibre/Kevlar mouldings from Brabham's own autoclave, forming the tank and roll hoop, the seat back and cockpit interior and the scuttle. The semi-stressed engine assembly bolted on via an aluminium front plate.

The engine was supported by regular A-frames, picked up by Brabham's bespoke integral magnesium transaxle case, which was notably slim and was internally ribbed to leave a smooth exterior and accessed the diff via a single detachable sideplate. The dampers sat upright either side of the oil tank and the push rod rockers and upper wishbones articulated on a common pin, supported by an aluminium bracket. The gearbox internals were repackaged FGB with some Getrag gears, while the diff was a ZF cam and pawl modified by Brabham.

Brabham uniquely used Hitco discs in '84, together with modified Girling calipers, this system developed over a number of years. Murray had started working with Hitco in 1980 and had run Girling calipers since the early Seventies. Girling finished in racing in 1980 and Brabham bought its entire stock, having found its open bridge four pot items to be well suited to carbon-carbon discs. The uprights were magnesium, and each rear upright carried a hydraulic jack. The wheels were Brabham designed and Momo produced: one piece magnesium items, they were reckoned to be stronger yet quite possibly lighter than Dymags.

The coolers were positioned longitudinally and sloped upwards (aftercooler on the left, water ahead of oil cooler on the right) but were engine bay rather than top vented. The pod side panels swept inwards around the rear wheels, but the effect was 'Thermos flask' rather than 'Coke bottle' in plan. The flat top pods and the undertray stopped short at the differential. The rear wing, mounted on a central, gearbox supported post, was single tier, while the front wings were two-tier. The main, delta-plan element was not adjustable, being moulded with a detachable, pointed nose fairing. A single fairing covered the rest of the fuselage, with a prominent bulge on the right of a tight fitting asymmetrical engine cover concealing the plenum chamber. The turbo was fed from a duct in the side of the left- hand pod and a grill was provided in the deck above to assist hot air extraction.

The prototype BT53 was in fact a modified BT52 - the BT52D - which tested at Paul Ricard in February '84, then at Kyalami. Three brand new BT53s were present for the Rio race and in view of the heat an extra oil cooler was mounted piggy back on the existing cooler and a vent was cut in the pod lid above it. At Kyalami crude ducting was used to feed cooling air to the turbo.

Cooling and aerodynamic revisions were seen on a car tested at Snetterton, Murray "never really happy with the original packaging for complex reasons". Reshaped rear bodywork appeared at Monaco: the rear portion of each pod side panel was reshaped, and was vented to assist hot air extraction. Rosche's street race engine's longer inlet trumpets pushed the plenum through the engine cowl.

The nose oil radiator first seen at Montreal was carried by the aluminium nose box. A larger, ungainly looking version was tried in the searing heat of Dallas but was rejected as it caused excessive understeer. Instead, the car was equipped with a small additional cooler attached to the side of the tub at the entrance to the left- hand pod, while retaining the 'Montreal' cooler.

Brands Hatch witnessed the 53B, derived from the modified car seen earlier at Snetterton. Remodelled pods accommodating more compact, more steeply raked coolers, revised underbody and revamped rear suspension were the key modifications. The B spec had worked well both in the wind tunnel and in more recent Snetterton testing but the car wouldn't heat its tyres at Brands Hatch and the new package was abandoned for the race. Nevertheless, following further wind tunnel work "some details" from the B spec underbody and suspension revisions were adopted for the balance of the season.

At the Estoril finale Brabham abandoned Hitco discs for more common SEP items for "political reasons". By that stage six monocoques had been utilised by the race and test teams, the latter using the BT52D, dubbed BT53-1. Tubs were regularly checked, and were retired once any loss of torsional rigidity was detected.

BRABHAM BT54

Brabham carbon fibre and aluminium monocoque
Semi-stressed engine
Push rod front and rear suspension - Koni dampers
Momo magnesium rims
SEP carbon-carbon discs, outboard
Single Girling four pot calipers - SEP pads
Kevlar/g.r.p. bodywork
1 Unipart water radiator - 1 Unipart oil radiator
1 Behr air:air aftercooler
AP twin plate clutch
Hewland/Brabham six-speed gearbox - ZF diff
220 litre ATL fuel cell - 12 litre oil tank
Yuasa battery - Contactless instruments
3023mm. wheelbase; 1753mm. front track, 1651mm. rear
540kg.

The BT54 was a logical evolution of the Michelin shod BT53 via the 'interim' BT53 Pirelli test cars, an example seen at the second, March '85 Rio test having sported the longer wheelbase and longer pods characteristic of the new model. Murray had been able to devote more time to wind tunnel testing, still using the Southampton University rolling road, though improvement was through refinement of the basic package rather than any fundamental revision.

A longer transaxle case lengthened the wheelbase by 100mm. between the bellhousing and main case which pushed the rear wing back into cleaner air and put more weight on the front wheels. While the centre of gravity moved forwards, so did the centre of pressure, thanks to pods that reached as far forward as the dash bulkhead, extending the underbody plan area. With the centre of pressure further forward, less front wing was required, cutting down drag and improving the airflow to the pods.

The BT54 dispensed with the nose oil radiator,

introducing a new cooler arrangement. Both pods were engine bay vented. In the left-hand pod a new Behr aftercooler was positioned vertically alongside the fuel tank and was raked across the tunnel while in the right-hand pod the water radiator was raked from the horizontal, as was the oil radiator behind it, again the front portion of the pod alongside the cockpit remaining empty. With the revised turbo system, air was channelled to the forward facing compressor inlet from an aperture alongside the driver's left shoulder, the upper portion of the ducting recessed into the fuel tank moulding. The higher collection point promised to collect less dirt. A small duct in the pod side panel collected turbo cooling air, and again there was a heat extraction grill above, in the pod lid.

The form of the central fuselage and the rear end treatment was little changed, the lower plenum chamber allowing a slightly less obtrusive engine cowl. The Brabham was now one of very few cars without a full length diffuser.

Murray could still not get a full length diffuser to work better than a short flip up without exhaust activation.

The gearbox was a beefed-up FGB with a revised lubrication system. The tub and front suspension module were new productions but alterations were of detail design only, while the suspension was modified only in geometry. The car continued to shun a rear anti roll bar.

Three BT54 chassis were readied for Rio, where Piquet raced the T car, 02, and damaged it, confining it to a role as wind tunnel test car. Subsequently, a further six chassis were constructed over the course of the season and one was burned out in testing at the Nurburgring while another had suspect handling and was consequently pensioned off early.

Imola saw lengthened rear bodywork and a longer chord rear wing while winglets were added to the sidepods, just ahead of the rear wheels, at the aborted Francorchamps meeting. Controversially, at the Nurburgring the aftercooler was fitted with driver-operated blinds that blanked off a portion of the cooler area. Winterschall race fuel was proving critical to intake temperature and the blind was designed to control that. Murray insisted the blind was part of the engine but FISA deemed it a moveable aerodynamic device and it was subsequently removed.

Echoing Toleman's stepped monocoque, the BT54 appeared with a carbon fibre air-deflector nose skirt late in the season. The model reappeared at Brands Hatch in 1986 in the light of problems with the BT55: chassis 9 was removed from the Donington Museum and dusted down. The experiment was inconclusive and, with no further upright engines available, was not repeated.

LIGIER JS29B

Basic specification as per JS29, except:
Semi-stressed engine
Sonnenschein battery
575kg.

The BMW-Megatron engine's extra height and length, its need to be run semi-stressed, a 20mm. higher crank axis and the differences in general layout compared to the purpose designed Alfa Romeo package presented a headache for Tetu's design team. Adaptation of the JS29 was reckoned to have involved 136 drawings, 10 new composite mouldings, 30 new forgings, no less than 1000 new parts from the machine shop and 20,000 man hours. Other than for engine installation the monocoque design (and front suspension) remained unaltered, but the conversion work necessitated shipping tubs back to manufacturer Advanced Composite Technology in Derby for rear end modification. Additionally, the transaxle had to be modified to accept the higher input shaft, while the iron block and its cradle represented a significant weight penalty.

The special strengthened sump which Arrows' A10 design benefited from was an Arrows rather than a Megatron part and the JS29B carried its M12/13 in conventional steel A-frames. The overall weight handicap was reckoned to be 35kg. and both weight distribution and aerodynamics were upset, the rear bodywork having to be modified to accept a bulkier engine package at the expense of airflow to the rear wing. However, the general aerodynamics, the cooler installation and the rear suspension remained unaltered.

Following the Imola shunts, Arnoux' ill-fated race car, 04, was replaced at Francorchamps by a new chassis, 05, with a modified engine cowl shape. It also enjoyed a stiffer monocoque. This and the remaining previously converted cars, 02

and 03, featured reinforced front suspension mounts, at the cost of 2.5kg. excess weight. At Detroit the cars appeared with revised pod ducting aimed at improving the flow over the lid.

Major modification on the aerodynamic front was completed in time for the home race at Ricard. Smaller, lighter coolers were repositioned on edge lengthwise and splayed away from the tank to allow side venting and both the pods and rear cowl were reshaped by the new, still integral chassis shroud. The new side vented pods were shorter and the turbo intake was set into the lid of the left-hand pod as the engine cover was re-profiled. There was also a reshaped nose cone and modified diffuser to complete the 'JS29C' aerodynamic revamp. In addition, weight was saved throughout the chassis, a total of some 25kg., and weight distribution was improved, making the car a little less tail heavy. The three existing race cars were converted.

Hockenheim saw a small additional weight saving while there was a larger oil cooler for Hungary. A fifth chassis was introduced at Jerez with revised front suspension, the wishbones angled to shift the front wheels back to revise weight distribution.

M12/13/1 in line 4

Basic specification as per upright version.

Gordon Murray's first project after joining Brabham in 1970 was an Indy Car with a lay-down Offenhauser in line four. Although unexploited since the advent of the mid engine era, the lay-down concept was well known at 'The Brickyard', having formed the basis of the later front engined Roadsters.

Frank Kurtis invented the Roadster in the early Fifties, canting his Offenhauser in line four over to the right by 36 degrees, its prop shaft running to the left of an off-centre seating position. At a stroke Kurtis had lowered the centre of gravity and reduced frontal area - his was the car to beat...

In 1957 Quinn Epperly responded with an engine canted over by 72 degrees, having revised the oil system with a new sump casting, plus a new cam box to handle the larger volume of oil in the top end. It was worth the effort, the even lower centre of gravity, even smaller frontal area 'Belond Exhaust Special' built by Epperly winning the 500 miles in '57 and '58. The lay-down concept was applied by Colin Chapman to his Coventry Climax in line four propelled '58 Grand Prix car but he ran into oil circulation problems.

Come the mid engine era and vee-engined cars ruled - until turbocharging was pioneered at Indianapolis to give the traditional Offenhauser in line four a new lease of life. If, in theory a lay-down installation offered many advantages, the obstacle now was the off-centre crank axis, given that the engine mass could not be offset. However, Californian transmission specialist Pete Weismann offered an inboard gearbox that would divert an off-centre drive to a central differential.

Weismann's transmission had its two parallel gear shafts set transversely and one behind the other, rather than set longitudinally and one directly above the other as in the case of the Hewland gearbox. Having the inboard-mounted shafts parallel to the rear axle line allowed the conventional, hypoid c.w.p. to be replaced by a pair of spur gears. The straight cut ring gear carrying the differential meshed with a straight cut pinion positioned mid way along the nearer of the two transverse shafts. Ahead, the parallel sister shaft was driven by a bevel gear on its right-hand end. That gear meshed with a bevel gear on the end of a short input shaft which came at a right-angles to the gear shafts, extending back from the offset clutch.

Working with Weismann, Murray recalls that he did "a fair amount of work" on the lay-down Brabham project and that he found it "very feasible". Nevertheless, for various (non-technical) reasons the Brabham lay-down Indy Car adventure fizzled out at the drawing board stage. Nevertheless, Weismann's lay-down transmission package was subsequently exploited by Roman Slobodynskyj - just as the turbo Offenhauser was swamped by the turbocharged Cosworth DFX.

Weismann subsequently produced versions of his transverse gearbox for conventional, centre drive cars, reversing and increasing in size the input bevel gear so that it meshed with a drive bevel positioned directly behind, rather than alongside, the gearbox. The Weismann gearbox was used by a number of American race cars, and a version was produced for the Cosworth/Ford-Brabham of 1980 with five speeds packed onto very short gear shafts to keep the width as low as possible in the interest of rear airflow.

Brabham concentrated upon a Hewland-based longitudinal outboard gearbox through the early Eighties, employing Weismann's assistance in development. However, with the switch to an in line four engine Weismann reckoned the time was ripe to take a fresh look at his lay-down package. In 1984 he had his son

rework a 1/25th scale Tamiya plastic kit of the M12/13-BT50 to set the engine at 72 degrees from the vertical, illustrating the advantages to all at Brabham and BMW.

Murray was, of course, aware of the potential, and had previously considered canting the BMW block. He recalls: "Piquet had long kept on about the idea of a reclined driving position, but given the engine height there was no point in lowering the driver and the fuel tank". He explains that lowering only the cockpit coaming and tank implied an extra long wheelbase, causing extra weight for only a marginal reduction in centre of gravity height and little aerodynamic gain.

Canting the BMW engine over just a little was no help - it was not possible to tilt both the intrusive plenum chamber and the cam boxes out of sight without going to 72 degrees from the vertical: a full lay-down engine with an offset crank. Such a solution significantly lowered the centre of gravity and opened up a route to major aerodynamic improvement. Given that the BT52/53/54 series was running out of development potential, Murray put his weight behind a proposal to BMW for lay-down works engines.

Murray recalls that he first suggested the idea to Rosche at the '85 pre-season Rio test, and that, while Rosche agreed it was feasible, it represented a big investment for BMW and consequently the company, "needed quite a lot of pushing". However, as Murray saw it: "without doing something, 1986 was looking bleak. At the time we built the BT54 we knew we couldn't find any more downforce..."

It was eventually agreed that Motorsport would supply 30 new engines (M12/13/1-1 - M12/13/1-30) with the block tilted 72 degrees left from the vertical so that the exhaust ports fed downwards and the clutch would be offset to the right. Rosche says the only significant modification required to allow the block to be tilted was to the left corner of the flywheel area, but that some other modifications were made to lighten the casting. However, the machining was basically the same as for the upright engine. Around 100 fresh blocks were cast.

The M12/13/1 engine had modified scavenge channels in its sump and was fitted with oil gallery pistons. Otherwise, Rosche confirms, it was to standard 'upright' specification, and it retained the regular 7.5:1 compression ratio. Designed to meet a chassis engineer's brief, it was very tidily packaged in a BMW engine cradle of which the rear plate incorporated a portion of the charge plumbing. The plenum chamber was now to be found on top of the unit in a central position, while the underneath location of the exhaust ports necessitated a sharp bend in the manifold. The turbo and aftercooler remained on the left, with the compressor inlet facing forwards.

Race power was officially quoted at 850b.h.p., with qualifying potential admitted as in excess of 1000b.h.p. However, the engine still had the narrow power band of 8,500 - 11,000r.p.m., with its output virtually tripling from 6,500r.p.m.! On the dyno there was no difference in performance between the regular upright engine and the prototype lay-down engine. Work on the M12/13/1 project had commenced in August '85 and the first was running on the dyno just before Christmas.

With the commitment to a lay-down engine Murray had started exploring chassis possibilities. He boldly decided to get everything as low as possible, including reclining the driver to a degree unheard of since the low power, low 'g' 1.5 litre cars of the Sixties. He could then enjoy a very low centre of gravity and a 10% reduction of frontal area, as well as a better air flow to the rear wing: the key gain. Another bonus was a smaller moment of polar inertia through the placement of the gearbox between the engine and the differential. That location, the layout of the gearbox, the length of the low tank and the situation of the driver, keeping his feet behind the front wheel axis, left the BT55 with an even longer wheelbase than Murray's previous long wheelbase specials, albeit with less weight over the rear wheels. With increasing downforce weight distribution was moving ever closer to the classic 40 - 60 split; a far cry from the 35 - 65 of the BT52.

Murray stresses that the saving in the height of the fuselage was primarily in the interest of enhanced flow to the rear wing, though a 10% reduction in frontal area was not insignificant. It was not greater than 10% as the car naturally retained the regulation one metre maximum to the top of its regulation one metre wide rear wing. The cross-sectional area reduction was to be found in a bigger gap between the underside of the single tier wing and the

rear deck, either side of the smaller shadow projected by a lower headrest/roll bar.

Far more important was the fact that a radically slimmed central fuselage left the rear wing in much cleaner air: early tests revealed a 30% gain in downforce. It was a major leap. The increased download together with a lower centre of gravity promised far more grip while an improved lift:drag ratio thanks to a more efficient rear wing and the reduced frontal area would assist fuel efficiency.

The Weismann gearbox' transverse shafts were made long enough to carry seven speeds, Murray prepared to trade additional gear shifting for closer matching to the BMW engine's tight power band. It was not necessary to make the transaxle slim since it sat behind a wide engine package. Its spur rather than hypoid final drive avoided the heavy side loadings of the conventional c.w.p., and in theory the transverse layout promised to sap less power.

The transaxle case was drawn to meet Brabham's chassis requirements by Murray's assistant David North, who traded plans by fax with Weismann in the States. Weismann was based in Los Angeles, where he ran the show with wife Michelle: she managed and machined while he drew. Whereas previously gearboxes had been overhauled as part of the regular chassis rebuild process, now a specific Weismann service facility was set up within the Brabham factory.

In the midst of the BT55's evolution Piquet announced that he was to defect to Williams, Ecclestone having refused to up his retainer. That came as a shock to both BMW and Pirelli, for whom the Brazilian had been a worthy development driver. Ecclestone approached Lauda who admitted he was intrigued by the radical new car. It was not to be: Piquet and Surer were replaced by Patrese and de Angelis. Prior to the introduction of the BT55 the new drivers tried a BT54 at Estoril and reported more power than the vee engines they had left behind, if over a narrower band. Murray remarked that the team had been rejuvenated by the break up of a partnership that had gone stale.

Principal sponsor Olivetti unveiled the BT55 on January 20, claiming that it had taken 732 working drawings, 117,000 man-hours and an investment of £6,800,000 to produce. In retrospect, everyone involved with the project agrees that the radical car had arrived too late. For example, the winter build phase had rushed ahead of transmission development; this, according to Weismann, was due to late delivery of an engine mock up, and he anticipated early transmission headaches. For his part, Rosche says: "everything was too late - the gearbox was very late. We wanted to run earlier but it wasn't possible - the gearbox wasn't ready".

The greatest worry during the design phase concerned the driving position: if the drivers couldn't adapt to the car the entire concept would have been wasted. Thankfully, the first, short test at an icy Donington confirmed that the drivers could cope, as Piquet had predicted. A second, more extensive but largely washed out test at Estoril confirmed impressive cornering power but, Rosche recalls: "the gearbox kept breaking and the only thing we could see was that the oil and water temperatures were very high..."

Rio confirmed the worst. Rosche got an oil temperature reading of 128 degrees - the top of his scale. He suspects it might have gone as high as 150 degrees. Water temperature and charge temperature were also too high. The car was designed to be engine bay vented but the vacuum in its wake was insufficient to extract all the hot air. The entire cooling system had to be revised: engine bay venting was supplemented by side venting, reducing downforce, and the oil and charge coolers had to be moved forward, compromising the weight distribution. There was also an undependable transmission to contend with, and the Brazilian Grand Prix was only a week or so away...

As a race car, the BT55 was a failure. Throughout the season it suffered a fundamental lack of acceleration. Properly sorted, it would corner quickly and would eventually reach a high top speed, but it wouldn't pull strongly from low to high speed. Rosche's abiding memory is of "lots of wheelspin". Murray says: "it came out of corners and just stopped!" He adds that the BT54 had pulled from 2.0 to 5.0 bar in around 2.5 seconds, while early in the season the BT55 took almost three times as long. With longer

Brabham BT55 unclothed (left). This shows the car in its original guise, prior to the extensive cooling modifications necessary in the light of track testing.

inlet trumpets and a revised exhaust system, that was improved, but Murray insists: "the engine never picked up properly out of corners". The Rio test modifications lengthened already long charge plumbing and Murray reflects that, "in later tests, we found it had made no difference to response - the basic engine response was so poor!".

Lack of traction was certainly a failing of the BT55, and was down to the dynamics of its weight distribution. The Rio test modifications had taken 2% off the rear, leaving the car with a 41 - 59 static distribution, and that caused a traction problem, given a very long wheelbase and a low centre of gravity, both of which discourage weight transfer. The lack of weight transfer provided "great braking", Murray explains, "with all four wheels sharing the load". But as little weight went forward under braking, so little weight went backwards under acceleration and traction was poor. Additionally, Murray believes the engine suffered poor pick up due to a scavenging problem.

Murray reckons the lay-down engine didn't scavenge properly on right hand corners, the oil in the crankcase mounting to a level at which the crank was thrashing around in it to the detriment of power output. He says "The car generated 30 - 50% higher oil temperature than the BT54 all year - we never could explain that. It needed a huge amount of oil cooling". He points to an earlier engine he experienced which had a scavenge problem and ran hot. Rosche, however, says: "We made many tests to see if there was a scavenging problem, and never found one. I don't think there was a problem".

Murray reflects: "There were a lot of unsolved mysteries with the BT55". He points to the engine's poor pick up, and to the fact that it wouldn't run as high qualifying boost as the upright engine. The BT55 worked well at the Osterreichring, for example, Patrese fastest through the speed trap and fourth on the grid; his best position of the season. But the upright engined, similarly Pirelli shod BMW- Benetton was only a fraction slower through the trap, and sat on the front row. Murray reckons the BT55 was cornering faster but was only running 4.9 bar boost whereas the B186 was accelerating faster and was pumping 5.3 bar. Rosche admits that boost had been constricted by the charge pipe incorporated in the engine cradle prior to Hungary. However, thereafter the integral pipe was by-passed and with the same turbo the BT55 should have enjoyed the same boost...

Both Murray and Rosche agree that the project lacked development time. Murray reflects: "In retrospect, given the resources we had, it was too big a step in the time available. We needed six months development prior to the first race".

Steady progress was seen from the shambolic Rio test to the point at which Patrese was able to qualify sixth for Monaco. From Estoril the car ran the longer (street circuit standard) inlet trumpets for better torque and response which, Murray says: "made the car more drivable and only upset the aerodynamics a little". Monaco brought the revised exhaust: "That improved pick up a lot, it had been a disaster before..." The Principality also saw certain elements repositioned to put more weight on the rear, to the benefit of traction.

Immediately after the encouragement of Monaco came tragedy at Ricard. As de Angelis took the flat out Verrerie esses his car got out of control and, having vaulted the armco, it came to rest upside down, trapping its driver. Although, thanks to the inherent strength of the chassis, de Angelis' injuries were light, fire starved him of oxygen. The team took his death very hard and Murray opted to miss the following race.

Over the summer the BT55 development programme lost momentum as the team found itself torn by internal strife. Technical decisions became political battles. For example, Murray wanted a shorter transaxle case between engine and differential to push weight back - perfectly feasible, given the possibility of rolling the pinion shaft up around the parallel transverse sister shaft. Instead, the team shortened the wheelbase experimentally by cutting a section from the tank. Murray could see no logic in taking length out of the chassis right at the centre of gravity, and the experiment was not a success.

Brabham had taken on an over-ambitious project, and the team did not have the resources to cope with its difficult season. According to Murray, the project deteriorated amidst: "Bad politics - so many people putting there noses in and nothing logical being done. Energy was put into the wrong things. The way the team had operated for 15 years broke down..." He often had to take a back seat as others meddled in his domain. By the end of the season he had left, and he went on to replace Barnard as Technical Director at McLaren International.

After Monaco the BT55 did not appear in the top six qualifiers once more until the Osterreichring. Warwick had the second drive from Montreal and generally it was a struggle to make the grid top 10. Warwick re-joined his former race engineer John Gentry, who had moved from the now defunct Renault team towards the end of '85. He was the sole BT55 runner at Brands Hatch, an old BT54 sitting in the next pit. Patrese suffered a mysterious lack of straight-line speed from the dusted off upright engined car yet lap times were equal. Murray asserts: "The underlying problem was an engine problem - the lay-down engine never approached the upright engine. The BT54 was cornering slower but accelerating faster..."

Motorsport was not prepared to furnish an upright engine supply, so the experiment could not be repeated. Throughout the year lay-down engine reliability was poor; there were a dozen failures from 29 starts. And the BT55 only scored points twice, Patrese running home sixth on each occasion. In contrast, Benetton won the Mexican Grand Prix...

During the course of the troubled season, BMW looked seriously at running its own, in house team using a chassis produced by old partner March and possibly designed by Barnard. However, as March boss Robin Herd studied a proposal in June, the marque announced that it was to quit Formula One from the end of the year. Nevertheless, Ecclestone held BMW to his supply contract for '87. However, his attempt to revert to upright engines was rebuffed - the stock was sold to Megatron.

Reversion to the upright engine was one of the contentious issues

1987 Brabham BT56 was less radical than the low line BT55 (pictured left alongside the superseded BT54 of '85). BT56 was an adaptation of an upright engine design.

that had divided the team during the summer of '86. Early on Murray had instructed North to draw up a repackaged BT55 to tackle the traction problem. June found the plans on North's drawing board those of an upright engined machine. This was now North's own project, reporting directly to Ecclestone.

North believed the lay-down engine to be unduly handicapped by its apparent lack of performance and the need for extra oil cooler surface area and drew an upright engined car with bottleneck plan tail and full length diffuser which he considered "not a lot worse" than the modified BT55 in terms of aerodynamic efficiency. He figured the existing transaxle for the upright package to be perfectly good, whereas he accepted that the lay-down transaxle needed repackaging into a shorter case: a substantial undertaking. Consequently, his BT56 had a BT54 power-train, and soon the older car was in action again, at Brands Hatch.

North says that while Patrese found going back to the upright driving position less comfortable, he also found it more 'aggressive'. His upright engined car featured a semi-reclined driving position: the driver's head was raised around 50mm. Consequently, the fuel tank could be a little higher, and thus shorter while the driver's feet were further forward, allowing the chassis a more conventional wheelbase. North planned to alter the method of monocoque construction and with a taller, narrower tub incorporating a smaller cockpit opening reckoned he would gain torsional rigidity over the BT55. However, Murray refutes suggestions that the BT55 had insufficient rigidity and points out that it was stiffer than the BT54, which in turn had been stiffer than his previous, highly successful designs.

After Murray left, North became, in effect, Chief Designer, though Ecclestone did not formally appoint either a Technical Director or a Chief Designer. Work on the BT56 was shared by North, Gentry, Sergio Rinland who had moved from Williams in mid season and John Baldwin from the FORCE team. Ecclestone had bought the assets of the defunct FORCE operation, including wind tunnel models and underwing moulds for a full-length diffuser chassis.

It was November before the design team was instructed to convert the conventional, upright engined chassis laid out by North to accept the lay-down powertrain, and the final go-ahead for a 1987 race programme was not given until December 10. The biggest panic was repackaging the transaxle to provide the shorter span between engine and differential that Murray had wanted. In the light of the BT55 experience the BT56 boasted large top vented coolers and it came out with a 40 - 60 static weight distribution which in conjunction with a significantly shorter wheelbase transformed the traction problem. However, the team still suspected an engine scavenging problem.

The engine had been developed to accept fully electronic injection, using the same basic control system, which offered improved response and a more effective rev limiter. Rosche says that with the Weismann 'box, it had been all too easy for the drivers to exceed 11,500r.p.m., the limiter too slow in cutting off the fuel supply to avoid damage. The problem was the time it took for the servo motor to wind the cam down to zero: with fully electronic injection the solenoid operation was instantly cut.

Other than for electronic injection and a repackaged turbo system (with new position for the turbo and aftercooler and revised exhaust) the '87 M12/13/1 was unchanged, still retaining a 7.5:1 compression ratio, according to Rosche. He says higher ratios had been tried on the dyno, without success. '86/'87 winter work had concentrated upon adapting to the pop-off valve. Clearly a four cylinder engine was harder hit by the 4.0 bar restriction than a six as it lacked revs: power is function of revs and boost. In '86 the Porsche/TAG engine had qualified at less than 4.0 bar whereas the BMW engine had raced at around 4.0 bar...

Patrese was retained for the new season, partnered by de Cesaris whose recruitment brought a certain amount of financial assistance, Ecclestone now lacking a major sponsor. Brabham was no longer a top team with substantial backing and a real chance of winning races, and as its owner became ever more heavily involved in the administration of international motor racing there were suggestions that he was looking to sell it. Asked in mid season if this was so by journalist Edouard Seidler, Ecclestone would only reply, "I am an entrepreneur, anything I have is for sale". He told Seidler that he hadn't looked for a sponsor for '87, saying: "I don't like to sell something by deceiving people. We had a bad year last year. This year our chassis is very good but the engine is bad".

Rosche opinions that in '87, the four cylinder engine was at a significant disadvantage against a six for the first time. Lack of revs was the problem. To give it any sort of chance, the M12/13/1 had to be raced at 3.9 bar, which put it squarely in the area in which the pop-off started to come into play - the level at which any given valve operated was inexact. Patrese reckoned that for '87 there had been a small improvement in the engine, at high revs, but was critical of its response and low speed torque. After Rio his car was converted back to electro-mechanical injection in the interest of improved fuel economy, both cars running high pressure injection from Monaco onwards.

Rosche says the valves maintaining fuel pressure at 5.0 bar were inconsistent and that the significantly lower pressure (as against 40.0 bar) meant a longer injection period, with more fuel going through on valve overlap. Of course, a four cylinder engine requires more fuel per cylinder than a six cylinder engine, and BMW "lacked time to develop 100% the low pressure system", which was beneficial at small throttle openings.

Patrese generally managed to break into the top 10 qualifiers, ahead of the Megatron-badged M12/13 runners, but the highest grid position achieved by either driver was seventh, which Patrese managed twice, de Cesaris once. On race day the '87 BMW-Brabham only looked really strong at Imola, where Patrese challenged for the runner up spot before coasting to a halt with four laps to run. North says: "The BT56 had good aerodynamics and good traction. It was a stiff chassis and only needed a good set up and a decent engine. The engine went well at Imola..."

The following race at Francorchamps saw de Cesaris' low pressure injection equipped BT56 run out of fuel just over a lap short. Nevertheless, there were few finishers and de Cesaris collected third place - the highlight of the season until Patrese repeated the result at Mexico.

Shortly after Francorchamps North had quit, moving to Ralt to draw its 1988 Formula 3000 car before rejoining Murray at McLaren. Gentry left the same day, going back to Benetton and leaving Rinland and Baldwin to race-engineer the rest of the season. Mexico was significant for team morale, as shortly beforehand news had come through that it wasn't to be wound up, as had been feared, though its short term future was apparently to be tied to silhouette as much as Grand Prix racing.

Once again, Ecclestone didn't have a fully competitive package to sell to a potential Formula One sponsor, the tally from '87 only three points finishes. Engine and transmission failures had been rife and it was sad to see how far the combination of major manufacturer and specialist team that had won the 1983 World Championship had been knocked off its pedestal. Having jumped ship at the right time, Piquet had meanwhile sailed to another World Championship...

BRABHAM BT55

Brabham carbon fibre/Kevlar monocoque
Semi-stressed engine
Pull rod front suspension, push rod rear - Koni dampers
Momo magnesium rims
SEP carbon-carbon discs, outboard
Single Brabham four pot calipers - SEP pads
Carbon fibre/Kevlar bodywork
1 Llanelli water radiator - 1 Llanelli oil radiator
1 Behr air:air aftercooler
AP twin plate clutch
Weismann/Brabham seven-speed gearbox - ZF diff
195 litre ATL fuel cell - 12 litre oil tank
Yuasa battery - Contactless instruments
3048mm. wheelbase; 1700mm. front track, 1600mm. rear
560kg.

North began drawing the radical lowline BT55 under Murray's direction in May '85 and the first wooden mock up was ready in June, Piquet sitting in it to get a feel for the viability of the proposed driving position. It included a near-horizontal steering wheel (London bus driver style), allowed via a gearbox in the steering linkage, but a second mock up standardised conventional steering. Every panel had been adjustable on the first mock up - the second was a lot closer to the definitive article.

Meanwhile a great deal of work was going into the evolution of an in house production technique for a seamless plastic monocoque, which Murray admits added quite a bit of time to development. He was not prepared to abandon the traditional aluminium lower section for any form of two piece bonded shell. The alternative was to fit bulkheads in from either end of a seamless tube, having sent someone inside the low shell on a trolley to lay up the inner skin. The skins were carbon fibre and Kevlar over a Nomex honeycomb core. This being Murray's first application of plastic over honeycomb, the honeycomb was notably thick, while the bulkheads were again machined from solid aluminium items. The first tub produced had to be scrapped as it was less stiff than the BT54 in the dashboard area. To overcome that it was necessary to slightly raise the scuttle, to enable the dash bulkhead to provide an adequate bridge section.

While the radical BT55 was a brand new car in all respects - "only the wheels" were interchangeable with the BT54 - a few aspects of the design were familiar. At the front a bolt on casting was still employed to carry the front suspension, which was pull rod to minimise the cross sectional area of the module. However, the pedals were now located inside the module. The cockpit was unusually shallow and seated in it the driver had his helmet some 15% lower than normal and his chin tucked against his chest.

Ahead of the driver the scuttle tapered to meet the suspension module, while the rest of the tub was slab sided and was dominated by a uniquely long, low fuel tank. Running the length of the square shouldered tank was a narrow, square cut central ridge, its top (carrying the roll hoop at the front) horizontal and less than two thirds of a metre from the ground. The inverted-T tank cross section matched the reduced height cross section of the lay-down BMW.

Behind the in line four in its carefully designed cradle (which incorporated the usual A-frames), the new transaxle case contained the oil tank and carried the push rod operated dampers behind the central diff housing on an outrigger. The outrigger incorporated two crossplates to carry the push rod rockers and to provide wishbone supports, the forward legs of the wishbones picking up on the inboard gearbox main case. The upper wishbones were of unequal reach, the left-hand wishbone's pick up further ahead on the asymmetric transaxle case. This did not,

TERRY
FARRELL
&
COMPANY

ARCHITECTS · PLANNERS · DESIGNERS

BC/085.PER/ls   24 March 1989

To whom it may concern

Dear Sirs

PAUL CHANDLER

During the period March 1982 to December 1985, Paul was employed by Conran
Associates Ltd. as House Manager. He reported to me in my position as Finance
Director responsible for all administration and financial matters.

His duties were wide ranging and included:-

(a)   provision of building maintenance, decoration and security including
        organising and supervising external contractors;

(b)   managing incoming and outgoing mail and deliveries including sorting,
        distribution and transmission of both UK and overseas post often using
        couriers and special delivery services;

(c)   management of conference and meeting rooms including provision of
        projection equipment and other presentation aids;

(d)   Purchasing and controlling stationery, furniture and drawing office
        supplies;

(e)   provision and maintenance of office equipment such as dyeline and PMT
        machines, photocopiers, telex, typewriters, wordprocessors, etc.

The role required dealing with the needs of a busy multidisciplinary design
practice some 200 strong, often on an urgent basis whilst still carrying out
the more routine tasks of building and office management.

Paul carried out his duties effectively and responsibly. His ability to
respond quickly and recognise priorities was much appreciated as was his
willingness to do that little bit extra to ensure everything worked smoothly.
He responded well to all levels of staff and built strong working
relationships with managers as well as more junior staff. He brought to the
role a sensible, organised attitude but was sufficiently competent to remain
flexible to changing needs.

I would not hesitate in recommending Paul for a similar administrative
position and will be happy to provide a personal reference if requested.

Yours sincerely

Brian Chantler
Financial Controller

TERRY FARRELL & COMPANY LIMITED
THE OLD AEROWORKS
17 HATTON STREET, LONDON NW8 8PL
Tel: 01 258 3433 *Fax:* 01 723 7059

Directors: Terry Farrell OBE MRTPI FCSD RIBA, John Chatwin Dip Arch RIBA, Ashok Tendle BE(Civil) MIE(Ind). Registered in England number 2042783. Registered Office Walgate House, 25 Church Street, Basingstoke RG21 1QQ

however, affect geometry. As usual for Brabham, the BT55 carried no rear anti roll bar.

Power transmission was from a clutch approximately 300mm. off the central axis and the transverse Weismann gearbox featured a unique, quick action shift mechanism which did away with the usual spring- loaded plungers. The gate pattern put reverse top left, in front of first, leaving a straight through movement from sixth to seventh. The seven gears were accessed via a plate on the left of the case, just ahead of the upper wishbone mount.

A single tier rear wing was supported by the transaxle outrigger, while the nosebox carried two-element front wings. The nosebox and scuttle were concealed by a front shroud which tapered to a deep prow and set a long, sunken-bullet shaped windscreen fairing ahead of the steering wheel. The long side pods came up to the height of the cockpit walls, yet were some 40mm. lower than the BT54's pods. The pods ran from dash level to the rear suspension, the coolers venting back through the suspension to leave a sealed tunnel either side of the cockpit, tank and drivetrain. The pods were waisted modestly at the rear, producing a typically understated bottleneck plan to work in conjunction with the usual flip up. As usual the aerodynamics were modelled using the Southampton University 33.3% rolling road facility.

The turbo and aftercooler nestled in the lefthand pod, the cooler running lengthwise along the pod, slanted upwards. Long and narrow and extending the length of the tank, it called for an extraordinary length of charge plumbing. The turbo was fed from a NACA duct set in the pod lid. Adopting a similar stance, a slightly shorter water radiator sat opposite the aftercooler, with a smaller oil radiator behind it, raked in tandem.

Long detachable lids closed the pods and formed a wide flat deck either side of the narrow central ridge of the tank and the plenum chamber. The deck swept gently down at the rear. The tank ridge and plenum chamber were hidden by a slim dorsal cowl that ran back from the base of the roll bar, then swept down behind the engine to meet the diff housing under the rear wing. The detachable dorsal cowl sat only 660mm. above ground level, gaining 230mm. over the height of the BT54 fuselage. The bodywork had carbon fibre outer skins, Kevlar inner, sandwiching Nomex honeycomb.

Around 20kg. overweight, the prototype BT55 emerged at Donington on a damp January day, sporting winglets on its low slung pods. For the first proper test at Estoril, commencing late in the month, a small lip was added to the windscreen

to reduce wind buffeting and the gear lever position was modified. Weismann was able to take safeguards out of the gear linkage as they were only slowing changes.

Front wheel turning vanes were fitted for the February Rio test but there was little time for chassis set up due to the severe overheating experienced. The pod inlets were widened and holes were cut and patched up again in the side panels and lids. Top venting was tried for the front portion of the aftercooler without sufficient temperature reduction, so it was relocated. It was stood on edge lengthwise further forward in the pod, splayed away from the tub to allow side venting. The letters LIV were cut out of the word OLIVETTI which stretched down the side panel.

In the right hand pod the radiators were transposed and at the front the tunnel was split vertically, with the oil radiator stood on edge and splayed across the outer channel to side vent

while the water radiator, fed from the inner channel, remained upward slanted and rear vented. This cooling arrangement, with a more effective aftercooler fitted and the intake as large as possible, was standardised for the race cars.

For Rio a larger gearbox oil cooler was fitted and modifications to the bevel input drive - a stiffer bearing housing, improved lubrication and modified gears - improved gearbox strength. Parts had been rush-produced both by Weismann and, at BMW's request, by German helicopter company Renk but only the Weismann parts were employed.

Rio saw a small pyramid extension to the front roll hoop keep the car within FISA regulations. A second rear wing tier, like the turning vanes and winglets was now an occasional fitting. A larger aftercooler was incorporated from Estoril, and longer inlet trumpets pushed the plenum chamber through the dorsal cowl. The fuel system was also revised.

Following back to back tests against a BT54 at

Imola, the rear suspension rocker ratio was revised to help traction, this development seen at the Imola race. At Monaco the cars appeared with certain components relocated to shift weight - moved forward through the cooler repackaging - rearwards. The turbo and aftercooler were moved back in the left pod and the fire extinguisher was taken from under the driver's knees to put weight into the opposite pod. Moving the aftercooler rearwards shortened the charge plumbing, which was theoretically to the benefit of engine response.

For Montreal revised rear suspension pushed the wheels forward 25mm., putting yet more weight onto them, but Murray reflects that: "The original cooling modifications had destroyed the weight distribution and aerodynamics - nothing we did to the chassis made any difference".

At this stage testing saw a revised cooling layout, and also the short wheelbase version with 75mm. missing from the tank. It was not a Murray directed development and made no difference. Hockenheim saw a flatter rear deck to increase pod exit area, while a revised tank hood for the Hungaroring concealed the roll hoop. At the Osterreichring the brake calipers were fitted with twin coils that projected into the air stream to cool the fluid while in Mexico calipers with extra cooling fins were introduced. Meanwhile, Monza had seen revised front suspension geometry for better turn in. The final innovation was a snorkel air scoop for the turbo, first seen in Mexico.

Mexico introduced the eighth BT55 chassis. Of the first three race cars, 2 had been written off following the Ricard tragedy while 3 and 4 had seen service until the autumn. Chassis 5 had been introduced at Monaco only be be written off after that race in testing, so 6 had been new for Montreal. Chassis 7 had been introduced at Monza to replace 4, while chassis 8 then pensioned off 3.

BRABHAM BT56

Brabham carbon fibre/Kevlar monocoque
Semi-stressed engine
Pull rod front suspension, push rod rear - Koni dampers
Momo magnesium rims
SEP carbon-carbon discs, outboard
Single Brabham four pot calipers - SEP pads
Carbon fibre/Kevlar bodywork
1 Llanelli water radiator - 1 Llanelli oil radiator
1 Behr air:air aftercooler
AP twin plate clutch
Weismann/Brabham six-speed gearbox - ZF diff
195 litre ATL fuel cell - 12 litre oil tank
Sonnenschein battery - Contactless instruments
2800mm. wheelbase; 1803mm. front track, 1676mm. rear
555kg.

As we have seen, the BT56 was a conversion of an upright-engined design by North to accept the lay-down engine, with a shortened transaxle. The transaxle was converted by Baldwin, and in view of the 4.0 bar limit it was felt expedient to remove one speed, saving weight. However, as the pinion shaft was rolled up around its sister

shaft it was necessary to introduce a more complex dry sump lubrication system with an extra scavenge pump, which offset the weight gain.

The new tub was detailed by Rinland who had experience of the contemporary Williams design, from which it was not far removed. It was produced as a single shell forming the cockpit

coaming and tank shroud with the floor pan bonded in. The front and rear bulkheads were composite and were integral. It was narrow, leaving scope for wide pods, and located fuel in a cell which extended up behind the driver's headrest, helping keep the tank short. It had an aluminium honeycomb core, composite bulk-

heads throughout and with its high sides and narrow cockpit opening was reckoned to be exceptionally rigid.

Gone was the front suspension module favoured by Murray: the front end was of conventional layout with the dampers located under the scuttle, and the front bulkhead was located 25mm. ahead of the front wheel axis. The rear end layout again put the dampers on an outrigger behind the diff housing but with the transaxle case having been narrowed the upper wishbones were of equal length base. The forward arm of the right-hand lower wishbone passed through a window in the case to mount within.

The suspension was new front and rear and the front dampers were mounted on 'roller tracks',

as previously seen on the BT48. The pull rod acted directly upon a pin at the base of the spring/damper unit, this pin following a curved track which described the arc that would be allowed by the normal inboard rocker arm. As usual, the rear suspension was designed to work without an anti roll bar. With the take-over of FORCE, Brabham switched to THL2-type rear uprights having the outer c.v. joint buried within.

Aerodynamically, the BT56 retained a traditional Brabham-style front end allied to a typical vee six rear end, a narrow dorsum curving down from the driver's headrest over the engine bay to blend into a bottleneck plan tail. Thanks to the lay-down package, the waisting wasn't particularly tight but the dorsum was very slim. The tail fairing fully enclosed the transaxle, extending as far as the central post supporting a two tier rear wing.

A full-length diffuser was carried, the wing and underwing profiles developed from the models and moulds acquired from FORCE. Consequently there was a lot of similarity to the profiles seen on the upright- engined Arrows A10 penned by FORCE aerodynamicist Ross Brawn. Wind tunnel modelling, as usual, was carried out at Southampton, though Brabham was close to opening an in-house rolling road facility. A full sized mock up was checked in the BMW fixed floor tunnel.

The BT56 set its coolers upward slanted lengthwise either side of the tank, the span reaching alongside the cockpit. As usual the aftercooler was on the left, with a combined oil and water radiator sitting on the other side. An oil heat exchanger was not considered advisable given oil temperatures seen in '86. A fashionable side vented layout was shunned as the team sought plenty of cooler area to serve the lay-down engine: the coolers were part top, part engine bay vented, the upper region of the cooler venting though the gap left at the step in a split-level pod lid. The lower, rear portion of the lid was formed

with the engine shroud, the forward portion with the side panel. The forward facing turbo was fed from an oval duct in the adjacent side panel.

The BT56 rolled out at similar weight to the BT55: 10/20kg. too heavy. However, its weight distribution was a more satisfactory 40 - 60, with a short enough wheelbase to encourage adequate weight transfer for good traction. It first ran on a damp Donington circuit in March, prior to the Rio test. Thanks to the lessons learned with the BT55 it did not require substantial revision through the season. A periscope compressor intake was introduced at Hockenheim, where a fourth chassis was added to the original trio. In the absence of Murray and North, the team toyed with a rear anti roll bar on occasion.

COSWORTH/FORD

**Cosworth Engineering
St. James Mill Road
Northampton
England**

It was something Keith Duckworth had to do rather than wanted to do. Given an option, the creator of the legendary 3.0 litre Cosworth Ford DFV engine would have contentedly pursued development of his masterpiece on through the Eighties. Indeed, he had begged the rule makers for a workable equivalence between blown and unblown engines as soon as the turbos had started to rise.

Duckworth lobbied for a fuel flow regulator rather than any displacement limits, with the flow rate set low enough to peg power around 500/550b.h.p. (a realistic DFV output). He set about development of a suitable metering device and in 1980 FOCA hardliners proposed to adopt it as the basis of their threatened breakaway 'World Series'. However, as a consequence of the subsequent 'Concorde Agreement' which buried the hatchet between FOCA and FISA, the Eighties would belong to 1.5 litre turbo engines as championed by the major manufacturers that had supported FISA through the wrangling. Nevertheless, Duckworth was keen to support those teams which had to struggle on with his increasingly outgunned V8.

The ageing Cosworth was strong enough in '81 and '82 to power Piquet then Rosberg to the World title, but by the end of '82 it was clear that a lightweight car with a sophisticated chassis was no longer sufficient to stem the turbo tide, particularly as ground effect technology, so skilfully used to advantage by the Cosworth underdogs, was to be outlawed for '83. By then the leading Cosworth teams of '81/'82 - Williams, Brabham, Lotus and McLaren - had all managed to book space in the turbo camp. Undaunted, Duckworth had instigated a major development programme for an engine that in 1982 had notched up its 150th Grand Prix win.

Cosworth's 1983 short stroke DFY offered a useful extra 25b.h.p. but that became insignificant in the face of the progress made by turbo engines exploiting advanced fuel. Nevertheless, even before the development engine's mid season introduction, McLaren had notched up win 151 at Long Beach, and then the modestly funded Tyrrell team used the good old DFV to win Detroit. Tyrrell was left as Cosworth's sole '84 foothold, aside from a short lived stop-gap supply for Arrows and a one-race fill-in for Spirit. It was a Tyrrell team woefully short of finance, with two rookie drivers; a team hopelessly outclassed except on tight street circuits, but the only team due to benefit from the 195 litre fuel ration originally scheduled by FISA for 1985.

The exclusion of the Tyrrell team from the 1984 World Championship, in the face of alleged technical infringements, removed the only obstacle to a postponement of the 195 litre ration and ended the 3.0 litre era. To stay in the game Duckworth had to build a turbo engine. That much had been evident for some while, and the image boost to be gained from the development of a successful turbo unit could but assist a company that increasingly lived on contract engineering work. The problem was one of finance. Would Ford again foot the bill?

Ford had already decided that a Formula One turbo engine could offer it positive performance-with-economy publicity and research benefits. But did those benefits justify the expenditure? Turbo Formula One was a whole new type of investment for Detroit. Although it had long been heavily involved in motorsport, Ford hadn't previously made a major commitment to Grand Prix racing - the Cosworth DFV had been a relatively low budget gamble by its British subsidiary. The classic engine's successor would have to be heavily funded in the face of the uncharted potential of turbo technology and the big budget pioneering work being undertaken by other giants of the automotive world. Early in '84 FISA President Balestre visited Detroit and reassured Ford's policy makers that any turbo engine investment would remain valid to the end of the decade and Detroit motorsport boss Mike Kranefuss hatched a Five Year Plan: two years research followed by three years on track.

Although Kranefuss' Dearborn, Detroit based Special Vehicle Operations (SVO) did not have the resources to produce an engine in house, Ford USA could and would develop the all-important electronic engine control. For the mechanicals, Cosworth was a natural choice, to Zakspeed's disappointment. Cosworth had been founded with the support of Ford, the major manufacturer giving access to its Anglia 105E engine prior to the official launch. That was 1959: over the intervening quarter century Cosworth had grown from strength to strength, largely with Ford supported engines. The only novelty of the new project was that Cosworth would have to work closely with Motorola, Detroit's Electronic Engine Development (EED) Department.

Cosworth set out by evaluating a 1.5 litre turbocharged derivative of its well proven in line four cylinder 'BD' (Belt Driven) series which stemmed from the renowned 'BDA' of 1968. Interestingly, that original engine was, in essence, a marriage of Ford Kent crossflow stock block and Cosworth 'FVA' type head, the gear driven Four Valve A (FVA) unit being the starting point for the Double Four Valve (DFV) engine. However, by the mid Eighties the heart of the successful BD series was a proven alloy block.

Ford had seen BMW's success with what, ostentatiously, was a "production" engine and, from a marketing point of view, was keen to investigate the feasibility of a similar project. Viewers of the splendid television documentary 'Turbo' in which Patrick Uden followed the birth of the new Cosworth Ford for Britain's Channel Four saw the first test of the projected in-line engine.

A modified BD series 1600cc block, reduced to 1497cc via a short crank, was pressurised by an industrial compressor to 3.0 bar (2.0 bar gauge boost). Taken to 11,000r.p.m. it abruptly stopped. Internal damage was rife and the block was distorted. Five further such failures were incurred over the following three weeks, and the root cause was traced to vibration at the crankshaft. While for International Rallying a 1.8 litre 'BDT' could offer a reliable and competitive 470b.h.p. running 2.0 bar, and while atmospheric BD series engines had been coaxed to run safely over 11,000r.p.m., the loadings had become too high. "On pump fuel it might have been possible", Geoff Goddard reflects.

With 'rocket fuel' a fact of life, the only practical response for Duckworth and Chief Racing Engine Designer Goddard was a clean sheet of paper. The original contract had recognised the need for flexibility and, as a natural progression, in September '84 Ford gave the green light for an all new engine. Cosworth had a completely free hand: apart from Detroit developed electronics, Ford insisted only upon designing the logo for the cam covers. Within 12 short months a compact 120 degree V6, dubbed the 'TEC Turbo' by Ford, was ready to take its turn on the Cosworth dyno. "A true Cosworth engine", Goddard notes: "compact, light and powerful".

TEC TURBO 120 degree V6

Bore and stroke undisclosed/ 1497cc.
2 Garrett turbochargers
Aluminium block and heads
Nikasil wet aluminium liners
4 main bearings, plain
Steel crankshaft, 3 pins
Titanium con rods
Mahle light alloy pistons
Goetze rings
4 o.h.c., chain driven
4 valves/cylinder, 1 plug
Valve sizes undisclosed
40 degree included valve angle
Marelli ignition
Weber injection
Ford engine management system
Compression ratio 7.0:1
Maximum r.p.m. 10,500
128kg.

When Keith Duckworth first put pen to paper, six cylinders were employed by the majority of successful engines and Duckworth reasoned that by joining the club Cosworth was least likely to find itself out in the cold through regulation changes. The 80 degree V6 Porsche/TAG engine was the one to beat. Its designer Hans Mezger had been instructed to produce a unit with a maximum of 90 degrees between cylinder banks, less if possible in the light of 'wing car' chassis considerations. Duckworth didn't have the constraint imposed by ground effect tunnels thanks to the flat bottom ruling of '83 and opted for a a squat 120 degree configuration.

The relatively wide vee angle not only made for a compact and strong package but left plenty of space between the cylinder banks. That was important, as Cosworth intended to pioneer compound turbocharging. "We started out with the idea of some very exotic compounding systems", Goddard could admit, though the various plans had to remain secret. Renault, Ferrari and others had experimented with relatively straightforward two stage turbocharging: compounding, as it is normally understood, goes further than that, implying a mechanical connection between the engine and the turbo system to feed any surplus of power developed by the turbine over the compressor back to the output shaft, thereby significantly improving the overall thermal efficiency of the engine. Cosworth had space to package a complex compounding installation within its wide angle vee - conventional V6 engined cars would not have found space given the constraints of a reasonable chassis layout.

In the short term, Cosworth had no team with which to discuss a compounding installation and its cooling requirements and opted to begin development with a conventional single stage twin turbo system. Nevertheless, the 120 degree vee angle was advantageous, providing a low centre of gravity and allowing an unobtrusive engine shroud, ensuring a good airflow to the rear wing. A 180 degree vee would be even better in those respects, "but the heads would be wrongly situated for the chassis designer", God-

dard points out.

The 120 degree V6 was the smallest practical package, offering the least and lowest-located mass. Further, whereas the classic Cosworth V8 had been a "bone shaker" with its flat plane crank, the 120 degree six configuration was inherently much better balanced - "very smooth... and you can make a lovely little engine out of it".

Goddard confirms that at this stage it wasn't clear whether or not maximum capacity would be reduced to 1200cc. for '86, FISA threatening such a curb, along with further fuel restrictions. Consequently, he and Duckworth laid out their original sums for both 1200cc and 1500cc options, considering the merits of various bore and stroke combinations. Ford asked them not to reveal their final 1500cc choice, though the bore was known to be less than 80mm. for a very small piston crown. From the available evidence *Racecar Engineering* contributor Enrico Benzing calculated 78mm. x 52.18mm.

The Cosworth engine was kept as compact as possible "with no wasted space", Goddard points out. With the narrow bores necessary to keep piston crown temperature under control, and little length added by a novel chain drive at the front, the tidy unit measured no more than 510mm. high and 450mm. long. The exhaust and turbos were, of course, on the outside, and the space within the vee, between plenum chambers, was used to house the spark box and Ford EED's ECU.

The heart of the new engine was an aluminium monobloc (with detachable heads) that extended well below crank axis. Plain bearings were supplied by Vandervell and the main bearing caps were formed within buttresses across the lower half of the crankcase, located both by bolts and interference fit (the walls of the block had to be jacked apart to allow installation or removal). In addition to the normal, vertical main bearing cap bolts, the buttresses held horizontal cross bolts spreading the bottom end loads and producing a structure well capable of handling immense loading.

The top end was similarly designed to be robust. Above the conventional Nikasil liners, sealed by O rings the head and cam carrier was a single alloy casting bolted to the block by four pairs of angled studs. The axis of a conventional, vertical head bolt tends to align with the camshaft above - hence the separate cam carrier on the DFV engine. Angling the bolts inwards (in opposite manner to the valve stems) not only cleared the camshafts but also took the stud into the block at an angle. Each pair of opposite studs squeezed the block at the top of the bore, increasing strength where gas pressure is highest.

From the head, oil was returned to scavenge via external oilways. To understand why external oilways were employed, it is necessary to appreciate a fundamental principle of Cosworth race engine design. Cosworth primarily considers not stress, but strain. It was known, and accepted that the alloy DFV block weaved 22 thou'. Goddard gives the graphic example of a con rod: "there are 12 tons going down a rod, so it gets slightly shorter. Then seven tons go up the rod, so it gets slightly longer".

All the mechanicals are affected. Big ends change shape, while a head moves up something like 11 thou' - "so there is no chance of a head gasket working, so we don't have a gasket!" Goddard explains: "The whole engine is designed as an elastic device".

Given this philosophy, clearly an aluminium structure is preferred over the rigidity of iron. In fact, Cosworth had developed a very special aluminium foundry at Wocester and was able to produce an aluminium block which was stronger than a regular cast iron block. In a conventional foundry the molten aluminium is poured into a mould, the pouring process causing porosity, weakening the casting. Cosworth acquired a French produced inductive pump developed for the nuclear industry. This pumped the molten metal up into the mould, causing only "micro porosity", according to Goddard. As a consequence, the process was virtually die casting in a sand mould, allowing Cosworth to "cast exactly what we draw", while achieving a strength better than many irons.

The new V6 engine was all alloy, apart from the cam covers which were of magnesium and, as with the DFV, were of sufficient strength to accept chassis pick ups. All chassis loads were fed into the fully stressed engine via the head and the lower crankcase, which was attached to the base of the block via studs. The crank was around 25mm. lower set than that of the DFV. The nitrided steel item was naturally produced in house and, short and compact, featured only two extended, counterbalance webs, one at either

Cosworth V6 nestling in the FORCE chassis, with the EEC IV box
relocated atop the tank. A cutaway of the TEC-THL1 appears on page 26.

end. Of course, there was no question of any need for a vibration damper.

The camshaft drive was taken off the nose of the crank. Surprisingly, Cosworth's mid Eighties design was not gear driven in the manner of the FVA and DFV, nor was it belt driven. It was felt that the fact that belts operate in torsion could affect timing accuracy. For the first time since the mid Sixties Repco V8 and Ferrari and BRM V12 engines that the DFV had so ruthlessly swept aside, a Grand Prix engine's valve gear was chain driven. A gear either side of a helical cut take off at the front of the crank provided the half speed reduction and drove its respective bank via a short chain.

Goddard notes that "all cam drives (gear, belt and chain) work, and all cam drives fail! You have to try to do it well and make it survive..." Chains were compact - no wider than gears - light and introduced some damping. Compared to gears, chains were "simpler and equally as effective". The twin chain arrangement made for smaller chain sprockets and shorter, more stable chains, while the system offered less inertia than a train of gears, though gears were attractive in other respects. In the end it was almost a case of flipping a coin...

Toothed belts were visible on the outside of the timing cover, one either side driven by an extension from the respective half speed helical. Each belt reached down and across to drive ancillaries tucked under the neighbouring cylinder bank, either side of the block. Positioning belt driven pumps thus was good packaging and was, of course, the widely imitated DFV practice.

The drive on the left-hand side doubled revolutions back to engine speed to power the water pump and behind it the oil pressure pump and alternator. The oil pump actually sat within the alternator, its filter coaxial with the alternator drive shaft, and separating the two items. The right-hand belt drove three oil scavenge pumps (two for the sump, one for the turbo) and a centrifugal oil/air separator at cam speed.

Driving H-section, steel con rods through steel gudgeon pins, the flat top, valve clearance notched three ring pistons were, of course, oil cooled, incorporating oil galleries. However, Cosworth employed a unique, secret, method of feeding the oil to the piston. It initially employed Mahle manufactured pistons, but planned to produce in house. Cosworth had already produced its own pistons to run in the Nikasil linered DFV engines. It made almost everything in house, including the steel camshafts.

The head was, says Goddard, "a typical Cosworth design" and the valve angle was (by coincidence) that of the FVA - wider than that of the DFV as keeping the valves well apart allowed more

scope for valve cooling, a crucial consideration for an engine that would have to face extremes of exhaust valve temperature. As with cylinder dimensions, Ford would not divulge valve sizes. We do know that the valves were as large as would comfortably fit. The valves seats and guides were of a bronze-based material, as usual, and Schmitthelm supplied the springs. The engine was reckoned to take around 120 hours to rebuild.

Detroit plumped for American turbos, turning to Garrett. Of course, Garrett had a special relationship with Renault. Cosworth became a development partner with Garrett, giving standard Garrett Formula One turbos its own "embellishments". The company had considered producing its own turbos but had found the timescale impractical. Interestingly, it brought in an ex-Holset turbo engineer to run its turbocharger department.

While Detroit specified American turbos, its electronics boffins worked with Italian ignition and injection systems, Marelli-Weber supplying its capacitor discharge 'Raceplex' ignition and solenoid-operated injectors. Cosworth had built a good relationship with Marelli-Weber through a Ford road car project and the deal for race engine parts was built on the back of that.

There was an ignition pick up on the front of the crank for crank speed and position and another on the back of the left-hand inlet camshaft for spark phasing, while the Marelli distributor was driven off, and mounted on the back of the right-hand inlet camshaft. Since Weber's injectors (like those from Bosch) were too small to meet the needs of a 1500cc turbocharged race engine, two were fitted for each cylinder. Fuel was supplied via Cosworth's own fuel pump and pressure regulator system. Given the quality of fuel that would be available for the engine, Goddard does not feel that a high pressure electro- mechanical injection system would have provided an advantage in terms of superior atomisation: "... fuel company research had overcome the problem..."

Cosworth laid down the criteria that the Detroit developed engine management system had to meet. The system was based on Motorola's regular road car 'EEC IV' system, claimed to be the most advanced in the world, and controlled ignition timing and injection timing and duration, and was designed so that it could also regulate an electronically controlled wastegate, if required so to do. EEC IV was a very powerful, very sophisticated and very complex system. At the time the American auto industry led the world in the exploitation of engine management systems and Motorola produced both hardware and software, making its own chips. The company was expert in condensing electronics, allowing faster, more advanced processing.

EEC-IV was based on a 16 bit microprocessor fed information from a host of sensors. Detroit emphasised its relationship to regular production car equipment and much publicity was given, for example, to the fact that a standard production car throttle sensor and air temperature probe were used, part numbers intact. However, the EEC-IV's packaging was certainly a whole new ball game thanks to the unfriendly environment of a race car, and the Motorola boffins had to learn to work in a much hotter kitchen...

The prototype engine having been completed in mid '85, the original aim was to start track testing at the end of the season, soon after the Australian Grand Prix. In the event, the TEC Turbo was confined to the dyno until February 1986, problems sorting its advanced electronics to blame. Northampton and Detroit ran parallel dyno programmes. New to racing, Detroit appeared to have under estimated the task. Goddard notes that EEC IV was "a fine system, but it needed a lot of development". The challenge was to ensure accurate fuelling at all times.

If it took longer than anticipated, eventually an effective race engine control system emerged, one which Ford claimed was more sophisticated than Porsche/TAG's proven Bosch Motronic equipment. Cosworth did not ask EEC IV to control boost, leaving that in the hands of the driver. However, the ECU was programmed to calculate fuel consumption (from the time the injectors were open), and received a signal at the completion of each lap. If properly calibrated, the reading it then gave the driver on the dash board indicated how much faster or slower he should drive the last lap to finish, as a percentage. Minus 100% indicated he would fail to start the lap! The idea was to try to determine in advance a boost level at which the driver should be able to drive the race flat out and leave the fine tuning to him.

Mapping was the most important aspect of engine development up until mid February 1986. The process produced a relatively "coarse" map, with which the TEC Turbo made its long awaited track debut on February 20 1986 at Ford UK's Boreham test track, in the back of a Goodyear shod, BP fuelled FORCE chassis. The engine was subsequently shown to the press at the Geneva Motor Show. Ford's stated long term aim was to productionize it, DFV style but in 1986 it was to be for the exclusive use of Carl Haas' young Formula One operation.

Ford's deal with a team had been left until May '85, when there was a meeting between Haas, Kranefuss, James L. Dutt and Don Petersen. Kranefuss and Ford Chairman Petersen were attracted by Haas' fine reputation in American racing, the substantial backing Dutt's giant Beatrice corporation was giving him, and by potential spin off business opportunities - in particular with Beatrice subsidiary Avis. The deal was done at the highest level, between Petersen and fellow Chairman of the Board Dutt. It was ironic, then, that almost as the Cosworth engine was being bolted into the back of the purpose designed, Lola badged but FORCE designed and built chassis, Beatrice should ditch Dutt and pull out of racing. However, the buy-out clause of Haas' sponsorship contract was sufficiently lucrative to keep 'Team Haas USA' and its Heathrow, England based car construction company FORCE (Formula One Race Car Engineering Ltd) in business, and Beatrice had stayed around long enough to keep the coveted Ford deal from the claws of an envious Formula One establishment...

Haas had worked for the 'Blue Oval' marque in a lowly capacity as a lad. Now as a successful Chicago businessman and racing entrepreneur he carried the responsibility for putting its new era DFV on the road. Haas' team had shown potential using Hart engines in '85. Managed by McLaren's pre-Ron Dennis bosses Teddy Meyer and Tyler Alexander, its car was engineered by Neil Oatley with assistance from John Baldwin and aerodynamicist Ross Brawn. Expanded to field two entries over a full season after an initial part-season as a one car operation, Team Haas USA/FORCE was expected by Ford to show strongly. The deal anticipated a three year collaboration, but exclusivity was to be related to the performance of Haas' equipe. It had also anticipated testing to start in November, and for the engine to be raced from Rio '86.

Ford couldn't make it and Haas used a stop-gap Hart supply. It was Imola before the Cosworth engine was ready to race, and at that stage there was equipment for only one car. At least by Imola the EEC IV's data logging facility was operational. At first this only recorded minimum and maximum values, but in time it would provide continuous monitoring on a time basis, giving the reading for each parameter (revs, boost, etc) at any given point on any particular lap.

The men whose work came under scrutiny, Jones and Tambay, had been enthusiastic from the word go, in spite of a 10,500r.p.m.

rev limit and a maximum of 2.5 bar. After only a dozen or so laps each of bumpy Boreham they had said that the V6 felt tractable and easy to drive, and that they would gladly race it at Rio, given the option. However, it was Monaco, in mid May, before the Cosworth engine equipped two cars, and at that stage the project was admitted to be 10 weeks behind schedule.

Serious track testing had commenced early in March at Paul Ricard, the two engines produced for the occasion including the Geneva Show unit, reclaimed after Press Day. Cosworth was building race engines, not show engines and was still assembling a fleet to use for the endless mapping process, in addition to those required for the track programme. There had been one instance of block cracking - after 23 hours 45 minutes of dyno running. The cure was simply altering the radius of an oil hole. Very few problems occurred on the dyno in these early days.

At Paul Ricard, one engine was run over 500km., the other over a Grand Prix distance, without serious mishap. Thereafter, revs and boost had carefully increased to the 11,000r.p.m./3.6 bar race and qualifying maximum for Imola, the engine retaining its original 7.0:1 compression ratio; it was running on doctored Avgas at this stage, rather than 'rocket fuel'. Duckworth took a cautious approach, anxious to avoid wasteful engine failures and keen to develop a broad power band for good driveability ahead of outright power.

Come Imola, and only three engines were on hand, for logistical reasons, the sensible plan to run only one car at this stage. It had been decided to develop a reduced size EEC-IV 'black box', and to move it from its position within the vee to a fuel tank top location as electro-magnetic fields from the engine had been playing havoc with the operation of the processor. However, this change was not effected until Monaco, where five engines were available to service two cars.

The 'Lola' THL2 model was a logical development of its good handling Hart predecessor and the smooth power delivery of its V6 engine helped alleviate the unsettling pitch changes which had bugged the THL1. The Ford-FORCE/Lola was more responsive, and with power progressive throughout the rev range the well balanced car would shine in the wet and on slow circuits. However, initially, the Cosworth was reckoned to be weaker than the Hart on acceleration, short of punch, and ran out of steam at the top end.

Soon up to 3.8 bar, Goddard reckons that Cosworth started out around Hart power, then strode ahead. The introduction of 'rocket fuel' in mid season was the key that unlocked the door. The engine was run to 4.0 bar without significant gain, and 11,000r.p.m. remained the usual rev limit, attempts at higher revs unproductive. However, the compression ratio was increased, matching fuel improvement. The first step was made at Brands Hatch, with a 7.5:1 compression ratio. Alas, there was a cooling problem, which FORCE blames upon local overheating within the engine and which called for larger coolers, first available for Monza.

Monza saw a prototype engine having new pistons and a high compression ratio, which would appear to have been 8.0:1. Properly tuned into 'rocket fuel', Goddard says: "the difference now was that 750b.h.p. was the minimum, rather than the maximum power!" On the regular engine Monza terminal speeds were poor, but Tambay tried the prototype high compression unit in the warm up and his speed trap readings soared. The 8.0:1 engine reappeared at Adelaide, where three examples were available.

Throughout, head and camshafts had remained the same - it was simply a question of the piston coming up the bore. Continual mapping had refined the map, concentrating on filling in the bottom end and transient conditions. The intention had always

TEC Turbo in the Benetton B187 chassis. The transaxle picks up on the back of the cam cover, helping form a very rigid chassis structure.

been to create a straight line power curve and that had been achieved: it could be drawn with a ruler. At Adelaide, Cosworth reckons it had an engine producing in excess of 1000b.h.p. on little over 4.0 bar, with a maximum of 12,000r.p.m.- and more revs and boost available beyond these "sensible limits".

Qualifying engines hadn't been produced as a matter of policy; the car hadn't given Jones and Tambay the chance of a good grid position on anything like a power circuit. And, although the engine had demonstrated good stamina, endless gremlins had cost potential points finishes. No engine had been lost and 20 examples had been produced, with sufficient parts to create five more. Generally, FORCE had six or seven engines on hand.

For FORCE, the campaign had started undramatically, Jones clocking 17th quickest time on the second of three hot laps in first qualifying at Imola, in spite of a slight oil leak and a caliper fouling the rim. The same engine was left in for second qualifying when a cracked exhaust manifold left the Cosworth/Ford-FORCE to line up 21st on the grid. Jones characteristically charged through to ninth place, only for a broken gear linkage to drop him out of contention. At Monaco Tambay qualified eighth, while at Francorchamps he was 10th quickest, fastest through Eau Rouge and fifth quickest in the race morning warm up.

A high speed shunt at Montreal caused by a cracked wishbone mount letting go left Tambay with bruised ribs and Cheever subbed for Detroit, qualifying 10th and running in the top 10 until wheel pegs broke. Tambay bounced back to run in the top 10 at Ricard, only for a brake caliper to leak. That sort of gremlin was all too common. Oatley comments: " silly things went wrong on the chassis. We also had silly things go wrong on the engine, but always in qualifying rather than during a race..."

At Brands Hatch Tambay looked set for one point, a lap adrift, when his gearbox failed, while both Tambay and Jones qualified in the top 10 at the Hungaroring, a lack of qualifying power no embarrassment on the slippery new circuit. Tambay managed the team's best grid position, sixth, but again chassis gremlins cost Team Haas USA a World Championship score. However, points came at the Osterreichring: Jones finished fourth, albeit two laps adrift, while Tambay finished fifth. At Monza Jones picked up the final '86 point for the team, while in Mexico Tambay managed eighth on the grid, the final performance of any note.

During the season intra-team politics hadn't impressed Ford, the problem a clash of personalities between Jones and Meyer. Oatley had worked with Jones at Williams and ran his car while Meyer steered clear of the Australian, running Tambay's car. Mid season Haas won a mega-buck struggle with the Kraco Indy Car team for the services of star March CART engineer Adrian Newey and he engineered Tambay's car from Paul Ricard. At Hockenheim Haas commenced negotiations with Ecclestone with a view to selling the team as he had no sponsor lined up for '87.

Ecclestone was clearly attracted by the Ford engine and Ford indicated that it would consent to a transfer of team ownership. However, Haas appeared to start having second thoughs, while Ford was becoming increasingly concerned about the future of its engine. In October Kranefuss came out and said that the programme had cost more than originally anticipated, while ruling out the vast expenditure that would be necessary to beat Honda in '87, given the limited life of the TEC Turbo. FISA's 3.5 litre cause had made a mockery of Detroit's long term aim.

Right at the end of the season it was announced that Ecclestone had bought the assets of Haas' operation. However, Ford had terminated Haas' three year engine deal so there were no Ford engines for Brabham. Meanwhile, Newey and Alexander moved sideways to the Newman/Haas Indy Car team, while Oatley went off to McLaren, Brawn to Arrows, Baldwin to Brabham.

Happily, that wasn't the end of the road for the TEC Turbo V6 as Benetton stepped in to lease engines while Ford sponsored Cosworth to develop a 3.5 litre DFV replacement. Clearly, after working with an inexperienced team riddled by politics, Cosworth was happy to co- operate with the longer established, fast rising operation. For Benetton it was the third make of engine in as many years, and designer Rory Byrne produced yet another fresh and innovative design to maximise the potential of the compact engine. Boutsen and Fabi were signed to handle the B187 and fast Rio testing times suggested that Byrne had produced another fine chassis to follow his Grand Prix winning BMW-Benetton. Cosworth provided 22 engines, rebuilding from the existing stock,

and neatly accommodated its pop-off valves in the vee. Claimed 4.0 bar horsepower was 900b.h.p. at 11,500r.p.m. on a 7.5:1 compression ratio. Of course, in practice, everything was a little higher than that, other than boost. With two pop-offs, Cosworth would have found it hard to play 'beat the pop-off', in any case. As we have seen, essentially engine development had followed fuel availability and as the compression ratio had gone up a four figure output had been "easily achieved" without going far over 4.0 bar. For '87, Mobil rather than BP supplied the necessary 'rocket fuel' and the compression ratio almost certainly rose above 8.0:1. Consequently, the engine was now more vulnerable, and could be lost through a missed shift...

Fabi was fastest of all in the Rio test immediately preceding the opening race, and both cars qualified in the top six, if not on the front row. There was further evidence of competitive speed at Imola with Fabi qualifying fourth again, and setting fastest race lap, but at Francorchamps and Monte Carlo the Benettons sank into mid field. And prior to Ford's important 'home' race the only points were two taken by Boutsen at Rio, the cars suffering an equal share of engine, turbo and transmission failures. On the transmission front, the weakness was in the Lobro c.v. joints employed by the team. The same joints had been used without problem in '86 and Byrne suggests the '87 Goodyear rubber probably had a higher tractive capacity. However, there were also some quality control problems.

Detroit brought a new turbo package to provide a smoother power delivery. Goddard gives lie to the popular belief that Cosworth employed its own version of DPV. Unlike DPV (the Renault Sport licensed device) Cosworth's compressor performance-enhancer did not cause the pressure of the incoming air to drop. Needless to say, Cosworth kept its intriguing device secret. In conjunction with "turbo development", it made throttle lag: "virtually unmeasureable", none appearing on the ECU log! With the new system, Benetton was in the hunt again, and thereafter at least one B187 would qualify in the top six on all but two occasions, and only once was either car outside the top 10 qualifiers. However, not once did the strictly 4.0 bar team make the front row, and on only four occasions did it appear again on the second row.

Benetton was hot on the heels of the fast boys, not setting the qualifying pace. But chasing grid glory was still of secondary importance to Ford. Alas, race finishes were few and disappointing: only at the Osterreichring did a Benetton driver stand on the rostrum, and it took Senna's disqualification at Adelaide to give the team two third places. With the team fabricating c.v. parts in house, the transmission weakness was cured around mid season, though not before Fabi had finished Ricard on one driven wheel. Engine reliability improved with new specification fuel introduced at the Osterreichring. Nevertheless, Benetton's disappointing total of points finishes was 11 from 32 starts. If after Detroit the reliability record was a little better, problems, often niggling little ones, continued to be rife and only at late season races did the Ford race challenge look really strong.

Towards the end of the '87 season Cosworth was running a "very high" compression ratio and Goddard estimates that the V6 had "just crept above" Honda race power. He reckons that Honda was running in the region of mid-900b.h.p., and confesses that Cosworth eventually got "on the fringe of 1000b.h.p." in race trim. Byrne says that qualifying power at Suzuka was a shade over 1000b.h.p., the team running on the edge of 4.0 bar. Bore and valve sizes remained as at the outset, and neither sodium filled nor Nimonic valves had been found necessary - as the power had been jacked up, on 'rocket fuel' temperatures actually fell! At the same time, Motorola and Cosworth were improving the EEC IV management system, providing accurate fuelling over a wider range of conditions - the engine map was getting more refined as time went on. Goddard reckons: "BMW had been running (computer control) five years, yet Ford went ahead in two".

He considers: "it took a year to knit together, but towards the end of '87 Benetton was deserving of a place on the rostrum". Indeed, Boutsen looked a good bet to win in Mexico until a gremlin in his ECU switched the engine off. Alas, in '87 the very capable combination of Cosworth and Benetton failed to reap the reward of its obvious potential. And having killed off the 'Cosworth Formula', FISA changed the Grand Prix formula again, just as the paragon of race engine design and development was ready to move in for another term of office.

BENETTON B187

Although it bore a family resemblance to the BMW-Benetton, the Ford- Benetton was far from an adaptation of an existing four cylinder concept. Byrne retained his preferred wheelbase and continued to employ push rod suspension operation but, other than for a characteristic style, there design similarities ended. The B187 was a fresh and original concept, intended to fully exploit the potential of Duckworth's uniquely compact, fully stressed vee six.

The new, longer transaxle case was typical of Byrne's approach. It flared prominently upward and outward from the bellhousing to reach over to the back of the cam boxes, so as to provide for a chassis link at the rear as well as the front of each cam cover. Loads were thus fed from the

transmission through the cam covers to the monocoque, producing a very rigid structure, and providing an important torsional gain over the four cylinder predecessors. Further, space found between the bellhousing (as usual carrying the oil tank) and the integral main case was used to provide recesses for the dampers, sinking them close to the centreline, either side of a tunnel that had only to be wide enough to take the power shaft.

The Benetton monocoque was engineered after the team's earlier tubs and again formed the cockpit coaming and a roll pyramid. However, while reminiscent of the BMW car's form, its flanks were smoothly squeezed in at the pedal box, Byrne thus adventurously reducing the width of the fuselage between the wheels for improved airflow. To allow for such beneficial sculpturing (which wouldn't have been possible given a traditional metal skin) the dampers were located atop the pedal box, running across the tub, side by side but compartmentalised by a three-row scuttle bulkhead. Byrne says that a significant aerodynamic gain was acheived.

The rear bulkhead was shaped after the engine's front elevation outline and was consequently of approximate T-shape, with the tank having a low set recess in each flank. Those recesses accomodated oil radiators, tucking them inboard of similarly upright and forward facing aftercoolers. While, in flanking the rear bulkhead, the aftercoolers were conventionally positioned, they were unusually thick and low, only reaching half pod height. The pods were split horizontally, with the upper tunnel housing a thick, low profile water radiator that was similarly forward facing, but sat closer to the front.

The thickness, and the height and positioning of the coolers recognised the ban on water sprayed aftercoolers (which called for a larger

matrix) and Byrne's desire to avoid top or side venting to minimise drag. All six coolers were engine bay vented, the oil radiator flow exiting under the respective cylinder bank. However, louvres were cut in the side panels along the water radiator exit channel to assist hot air extraction. The side panels were cut away behind the turbos, helping air extraction, while the pod lids blended into a low set deck that shrouded the squat engine and the transaxle, small humps clearing the plenum chambers. Air was ducted to the compressors from scoops either side of a short tank cowl that sloped down from the roll pyramid to blend into the unusual, bottleneck plan rear deck.

Byrne's creative fuselage form was headed by a characteristic front wing package, while at the rear a conventional exhaust blown diffuser rose under a two tier, central post supported wing. The brand new, integral transaxle case essentially inherited internals from the BMW car. The team now exclusively used AP calipers.

Although the Ford deal hadn't been confirmed until late October, the prototype B187 was systems-checked at Donington in late February, prior to the Rio test - where a rear rocker failure caused a shunt that pushed a wheel into the monocoque, prematurely ending the exercise. With 01 written off, three further chassis were readied for the Brazilian Grand Prix, and during the course of the season an additional four tubs were phased into the programme. There was only one other write off - chassis 8 in Mexico.

There were no major modifications during the season. The rear suspension geometry was changed for the French Grand Prix providing "a small improvement in handling" and, as usual, there was a "high speed" aerodynamic package, which was introduced at Silverstone. Basically, this consisted of a revised rear wing and diffuser.

Benetton carbon fibre/Kevlar monocoque
Stressed engine
Push rod front and rear suspension - Koni dampers
Dymag magnesium rims
SEP carbon-carbon discs, outboard
Single AP four pot calipers - SEP pads
Carbon fibre/Kevlar bodywork
2 Secan water radiators - 2 Secan oil radiators
2 Secan air:air aftercoolers
AP twin plate clutch
Hewland/Benetton six-speed gearbox - Quaife diff
195 litre ATL fuel cell - 9 litre oil tank
2 Hitachi batteries - Yamaha instruments
2692mm. wheelbase; 1861mm. front track, 1682mm. rear
540kg.

FORCE/LOLA THL2

FORCE carbon fibre monocoque
Stressed engine
Push rod front and rear suspension - Koni dampers
Dymag magnesium rims
SEP carbon-carbon discs, outboard
Single AP four pot calipers - SEP pads
Carbon fibre bodywork
2 Secan water radiators - 1 Secan oil heat exchanger
2 Secan air:air aftercoolers
AP twin plate clutch
Hewland/FORCE six-speed gearbox - Salisbury diff
195 litre ATL fuel cell - 9 litre oil tank
Gates battery - VDO instruments
2794mm. wheelbase; 1803mm. front track, 1626mm. rear
540kg.

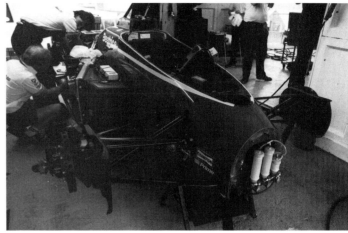

For its new venture FORCE had first constructed an 'interim' Cosworth/Ford test chassis on a THL1 base, but that had never run in its intended guise. Consequently, from the outset the Cosworth/Ford- FORCE was a no compromise machine, taking full advantage of the shorter, lower, fully stressed V6 block and smaller, 195 litre fuel cell. Although very much an evolution of the short lived Hart car, and generally echoing its design, the newcomer, based around a fresh in house monocoque and transaxle case, shared few components.

While the stressed engine allowed a revised rear chassis, the THL2's monocoque was of familiar pattern and construction. However, in addition to a slighlty shorter tank, it boasted taller cockpit flanks for improved rigidity, while a radius was given to each side's bottom corner for aerodynamic reasons. In principle, front and rear suspension were carried over, with alterations to geometry and with improved rigidity. With the shorter tank and block there was extra length in a new FORCE magnesium transaxle case to maintain the THL1's wheelbase. The effect of the situation of the light V6 plus an amount of component relocation put 0.5% more weight on the rear wheels, while the new layout reduced the variation between full and empty tank weight distribution.

The longer transaxle (carrying familiar internals) left scope for slightly tighter rear waisting. Naturally, the THL2's rear canopy was lower

and slimmer, and its pods and tail deck were 40mm. lower. As was regular V6 practice, each pod housed a water radiator and an aftercooler, and these were set on edge lengthwise and, end to end, were angled across the pod as the THL1's single cooler had been. The forward positioned radiators were side vented while the aftercoolers vented through the engine bay, with the oil heat exchanger positioned alongside the aftercooler in the right-hand pod. The intake for each turbo was a NACA duct set into the pod lid.

Other than for dorsum and tail treatment, and for details of air inlets and outlets, to the eye there was no difference between the two models FORCE lined up in the Imola pit lane. However, the THL2 offered a cleaner airflow to the rear wing and while it had the same underwing, a new treatment for the sidepod leading edge helped reduce pitch sensitivity. The prototype had first run at Boreham, having been completed only the night before the TEC Turbo's baptism, and had subsequently been shaken down at Snetterton in Norfolk, late in February. After Paul Ricard in early March, further testing had been carried out at Silverstone and Imola.

Chassis 001 (T-car) and 003 were used at Imola, with 002 added at Monaco, where the prototype was written off. 002 was written off in Montreal,

taking chassis production to five. Chassis modifications were few, prior to Monza, where larger coolers were adopted. At Monza there was also revised suspension geometry: "a comprehensive change", says Oatley, offering anti dive and squat as part of the general car development programme. Testing had revealed the benefit of a longer wheelbase, with a 50mm. spacer between the engine and transaxle. This put 0.5 - 1.0% more weight on the front, reduced pitch changes and improved drivability. It was adopted for Mexico. During the season the team had toyed with the Torsen differential, running it in selected races.

By Ingegnere Enrico Benzing

Scuderia Ferrari SpA
Via Ascari 55
41053 Maranello
Modena, Italy

In the Eighties Formula One shot ahead with far advanced technical achievements and an engine which displayed first class operating characteristics in one successful season could even appear outdated the following year. The excellent 120 degree V6 Ferrari engine, created in 1980 to open a new era of turbocharging (the engineers at Maranello the first to follow Renault's belief in it) experienced this more than once in its long development cycle. So much so that at the end of 1983 it had to be 80% redesigned.

Why is it, one might wonder, that in other periods in the history of technology-based competition, there have been machines able to stay at the forefront for longer? The answer is in the development process itself: the turbocharged engine opened up wide prospects, to make possible spectacular progress to great power. The 580b.h.p. of the original 120 degree V6 led to a level of 1000b.h.p. in not much more than five years of resolute research. Such increase explains why a structure planned for a particular power range has to be relentlessly revised. It happens especially if other programmes are developed, with new solutions to test out, and all the more urgently if cut-throat competition is involved and other major motor manufacturers enter the field.

Thus, 1984 had been planned by Ing. Enzo Ferrari with the following main objectives: the 126 C4, the new weapon, had to be a logical evolution of the 126 C3 - a particularly well developed car - marking a clear turning point in chassis design and the increase of engine power. The Chief Design Engineer of the time, Ing. Mauro Forghieri noted that the first stage of 1984 season would bring five races on tracks with average lap speeds under or around 200k.p.h. and consequently planned a suitable chassis, with modification to come for the faster tracks in the later stage of the season. Forghieri opted for a lighter, more compact and more responsive car. The prescription included a short wheelbase and a high concentration of mass towards the centre of gravity, Forghieri insisting on the transversal gearbox ahead of the differential, moving the air:air aftercoolers further back, and obtaining a front:rear weight distribution of 42:58.

In terms of weight reduction, 6% was taken off the bodywork, 10% off the engine and 8% off the transaxle. Weight has always been a delicate subject at Ferrari: even during highly competitive seasons (such as 1982 and 1983) there had been a few kilograms excess, which had been offset by higher engine power. This time the Ferrari engineers firmly intended to reach the 540kg. minimum, and succeeded in so doing, at least for the initial stage of the project.

In addition, as regards the main technical considerations, there was the question of aerodynamic efficiency and the resurgence of ground effect, in spite of the flat bottom ruling of 1983. Italian designers had too often neglected this essential aspect of Formula One, and as late as 1979, during the age of the 'wing car', Ferrari had gained a world title without high values of negative lift. Enzo

Ferrari himself, at the time said of his 312T4: "it is not a ground effect car, nor is it even half a wing car". It was only in 1982 that Ferrari reached for the first time a high degree of downforce.

In order to account for aerodynamic development the whole general formulation of the flat bottom Ferrari had to be changed, starting with the engine and transaxle which, with the wide angle vee, had awkward dimensions, particularly if one wanted to persevere with the transverse gearbox. Realistic judgements were made: there was neither time to redesign the engine and transmission from top to bottom, nor to venture into intense aerodynamic research (at the time Ferrari had not completed its own wind tunnel) so it was decided to enhance the qualities of the existing engine (with further increases in performance) through an arrow-shaped car of reduced plan area, suitable for more sinuous tracks. Only the external airflows were taken into account from the point of view of aerodynamics; however, Ferrari designers had been the first to sport winglets on the rear wing endplates, to take fullest advantage of the 1400mm. width allowance ahead of the rear axle line.

In short, at the beginning of 1984, Ferrari's Engineering School, although it had already planned a considerable number of development programmes for the long term, preferred to concentrate its capabilities upon the short term. Thus, there were a number of engine modifications: weight reduction for each component; reduction of overall dimensions; modifications to the cylinder bores and to cooling passages and improvement in combustion chamber design, towards higher thermodynamic efficiency on the basis of four years turbo experience and in view of the tougher restrictions for fuel consumption and development of engine electronics.

The '126' 120 degree V6 (126 indicating, with the first two figures the vee angle, in tens, and with the third, the number of cylinders) had a well developed structure, an 81mm. bore and a 48.4mm. stroke, a short crankshaft, a torsional vibration damper and good general characteristics thanks to the positioning of the turbochargers within the vee. Its general design had not previously been questioned. Now the primary aim was to reduce the height of the block, and it was redesigned, still in aluminium, with pressed in liners of the same material having special chrome-plating treatments. It was a suitable opportunity also to strengthen the block. The heads were also revised, with the combustion chambers altered to suit the new anti-knock levels offered by the new fuels which were on their way; the so called 'heavy fuels', with fewer volatile components, a wide use of aromatics and olefines and a specific gravity of around 0.8kg per litre, compared to 0.74kg. per litre for pump petrol. Experience suggested that adjustments should also be made to inlet and exhaust systems, leading to a distinctive layout of one tract for each valve, to increase the number of pulsations; however, this solution had to be abandoned for manufacturing reasons.

The most significant innovation from the technical point of view came from the fully electronic injection system, which met with serious reliability problems to start with but would eventually supersede the Lucas-Ferrari electro-mechanical system. In this respect, we ought to point out that the Maranello engineers had a guiding role. In fact, we might consider that the turbo engine owes each of its astonishing developments to electronics, initially helping overcome the throttle lag characteristic of the early Renault engines. Electronic control had first appeared on the V6 Ferrari - a five parameter system - and it was a truly effective solution to which other engine builders resorted. Ferrari's exploitation of water injection (following an aeronautic practice which dated back to the age of piston engines) succeeded in producing good results thanks to the same electronic controls. To be precise, it was not so much a question of water injection, as of emulsion, with an apparatus devised by AGIP and called *Emulsistem*, which was only abandoned following the development of advanced fuels.

1984 was a year of breakthrough, with the first use of solenoid-operated injectors. Fully electronic injection was ideal for fuel consumption control: the micro-processor was able to calculate with precision outputs which could occur within limits of 0.6 to 0.7 milliseconds. This development was down to Weber and Marelli, two giants of Italian motor components industries and fellow members of the Fiat Group, with Ferrari. The name of Weber was famous for specialisation over decades in the manufacture of fuel systems, from carburettors to fuel injection, while Marelli was a company devoted to electrical parts, which for some while had turned to electrical components for motor vehicles ('autronics'). Marelli Weber achieved considerable progress in anticipating German and Japanese specialists, but there were some problems, and in particular there was a discrepancy between the quality of the system and its ability to face up to the enormous thermal shocks and vibrating stresses incurred.

With his usual shrewdness, Enzo Ferrari said: "it was like one of those old-fashioned marriages, arranged by great families: each of the two parties thought the dowry of the other was really considerable. Then they realised they had a lot less in common, but they worked as hard as they could and finally reached the target".

In the light of injection developments, the following factors ought to be considered: the the change over from one to two injectors per cylinder, in order to ensure the best metering, shared out within a maximum of 3 milliseconds per cycle; the operation of the first injector at low revs and the intervention of the second only at higher r.p.m., the sequential function offering higher flexibility; an operating pressure higher than 10 bar; the positioning of the injectors ahead of the slide valves; the introduction of a new design and materials for the injector itself.

Amidst the technical difficulties, the C4 engine stood up in best Italian tradition, and in 1984 would give a good account of itself generally, as we shall see when tracing its development.

126 C4
120 degree V6

81 x 48.4mm / 1496.4cc
2 KKK turbochargers
Aluminium block and heads
Aluminium wet liners
4 main bearings, plain
Steel crankshaft, 3 pins
Titanium con rods
Mahle light alloy pistons
Goetze rings
4 o.h.c., gear driven
4 valves/ cylinder, 1 plug
Valve sizes undisclosed
38 degree included valve angle
Marelli ignition
Lucas-Ferrari injection
Compression ratio 6.7:1
Maximum r.p.m. 11,000
151.8kg.

Within its classical build, the fourth generation 120 degree V6 engine was undoubtedly the richest in internal improvements, which could be noted only with difficulty externally but which played a major role in general performance. At base there was still an aluminium block with unchanged bore and stroke, but what had changed radically was the basic structure, with its dimensions and sectional design, as well as the streamlining of major components in order to produce considerable improvements in efficiency; that is in frictional resistance.

In redesigning the base engine the main objectives were strengthening, and weight and size reduction. The mere lowering by 20mm. in cross section of the cylinder block indicated the extent of the operation, involving the whole inlet and cooling systems, and contributing to the reduction by a few millimetres of the height of the cars' centre of gravity. The engine weight came down from 168kg. for the 1983 version, which in turn was a reduction from 177kg. for the original engine. It ought to be emphasised that we are talking about the complete weight of the engine, with all components in working order. In specific terms, this means an envisaged power to weight ratio between 0.23 and 0.18kg. per b.h.p.

The block carried cylinder liners in aluminium with special chrome- based treatments to match the usual Mahle Nikasil cylinders. The aluminium heads, with new red-coloured cam covers, were redesigned in the area of fluid-dynamics: ie, all the gas tracts as well as the combustion chamber, aimed at further increases in volumetric efficiency and thermodynamics.

Timing was still by gear driven twin overhead camshafts and the relatively low valve angle of 38 degrees remained. There was a special steel crankshaft running in four plain bearings, driven by titanium con rods (paired on each pin) of modified design.

Supercharging was obtained by two KKK turbochargers mounted within the vee, with the wastegate in the same area. The fuel system was the fruit of continual evolution, and in 1983 featured electro-mechanical injection having a Lucas mechanical metering unit controlled by a servo motor. Experimentation then began with fully electronic Marelli Weber equipment, initially involving AGIP *Emulsistem*. Ignition was by an electronic system with one 10mm. plug per cylinder, controlled by the ECU, the complete computerisation of the system requiring a very sophisticated set up to achieve the right torque distribution and a noticeable reduction in fuel consumption, given the 220 litre race ration.

At the launch of this edition of the 120 degree V6, which took place on February 16, 1984 at the Fiorano test track, the manufacturer was more than usually generous in supplying information relating to performance, supplying even typical power and torque curves, something he had not done for many years. The quoted output was 660b.h.p. at 11,000r.p.m. as against 600b.h.p. at 10,500r.p.m. for the '83 version, with the compression ratio 6.7:1 as before. But even as these figures were announced, higher performance was being registered on the test bench, and this would become evident during the year.

Highly competitive on its first appearance at Rio, the fourth generation 120 degree V6 focused the technicians' attention to the problem of fuel supply. The new fully electronic Marelli Weber equipment was fitted only to Alboreto's car (second fastest) and brought into the open all the operational problems, requiring a comparison between two versions, one having the solenoid activated injectors pointing downwards (that is, in the direction of the airflow), the other with the injectors pointing upstream. The use of only one injector per cylinder (as tested since 1983) did not provide good fuel metering over 9000r.p.m. and a step forward was the use of twin injectors for each inlet tract, which offered perfect fuelling at low revs and the necessary increase in the high r.p.m. band (near maximum power and within a 2000r.p.m. range). The downstream injectors immediately prevailed, becoming definitive.

However, testing the equipment, which was fitted to both cars for Kyalami, became difficult and complicated, giving rise to a number of setbacks. These concerned the wiring system as well as the ECU, the sensors and the solenoids. At Kyalami compressor air scoops were first used. They had a considerable influence on subsequent engine performance gains. A pause for reflection was required for the fully-electronic injection: the 120 degree V6 went back to the Lucas-Ferrari system on the occasion of the Belgian Grand Prix, displaying its strong qualities at Zolder. Alboreto and Arnoux were on the front row and came home first and third respectively. In this event, split and crossed exhaust pipes were

Alboreto, the Ferrari 126 C4 and Mauro Forghieri. The renowned engineer's short wheelbase machine is pictured below in action at Brands Hatch.

used for the first time, on Alboreto's car. A pipe was taken from each of the two valves of each cylinder, to double the number of pulses on each turbine: a very original, and certainly favourable solution, which must be credited to Ing. Forghieri. It was thought to be the most important factor in the general engine development; only later was it possible to better evaluate its importance, which was of a more specific benefit.

The other side of the coin, as far as the split exhausts was concerned, was a difficultly in construction of the winding, spa-

ghetti-like pipes, as well as the choice of material and almost impossible welding. At Imola, Alboreto's engine started to show the strain of a severe race, although he played a leading role to the end. The exhaust pipe fatigue problem also extended to Arnoux's car, which gained second place.

It was clear from the results of the San Marino Grand Prix that the leading position of Porsche/TAG-McLaren in terms of the relationship between fuel consumption and race power had been consolidated. The Ferrari engine lagged behind, and fuel consumption was a real problem on faster and more demanding circuits. It is true, however, that Ferrari remained competitive on slow circuits, using small turbos to spread power over a wider r.p.m. range. But Alboreto's accident in the rain at Monte Carlo and his broken heat exchanger at Detroit, and another exhaust failure there for Arnoux prevented proof of that, and the favourable opportunity of Dallas was also missed, with Alboreto out again. However, the spectacular come-back of Arnoux, from last to second position, spoke in favour of Ferrari potential.

What is remarkable from the point of view of engine design is that since the Grand Prix of Detroit the fully-electronic injection had come back into operation. It again allowed for comparison between the two different positions of the injectors. During the brief interlude, the engineers had carried out a large number of tests and had made improvements to the whole system, and added new control boxes at Dallas.

For the plus-200k.p.h. circuits, from Brands Hatch, the 126 C4 engine was able to exploit in excess of 700b.h.p., and the chassis required cooling modifications. The lateral and vertical water radiators were replaced by longitudinal and sloping coolers. Even when the aerodynamically-modified 'M2' version arrived, during tests for the Italian Grand Prix, the engine did not require significant modification. The aftercoolers were rotated through 90 degrees from the Nurburgring and further control boxes with new wiring were introduced in Portugal. Here Ferrari reached the season's peak, with more than 730b.h.p. race power and 820b.h.p. in qualifying: specific power equal to 488 and 548b.h.p. per litre on 3.6 and 4.2 bar respectively. Pressure had risen from 3.2 bar (race)/

3.7 bar (qualifying) early in the season.

Overall, the 126 C4 did not disappoint on slow circuits, although good opportunities had been lost through various setbacks. The Goodyear-shod C4 only started from pole at Zolder; however, 21 of 32 starts were from the grid top 10. There were no less than 15 points finishes, including half a dozen rostrum finishes apart from Alboreto's Belgian win; following second for Arnoux at Imola and Dallas, Alboreto took second place at Monza and the Nurburgring. However, various mid season problems had brought about the exit of a Ing. Forghieri, who had been in the limelight for 20 years, and had produced the parallel planning of the 'M' version, better suited to fast circuits. This was a period which could be concluded with some satisfaction from the point of view of engine design. It had pushed the engineers towards ambitious ideas, thinking about two-stage turbocharging and VGS turbines. However, these were solutions which would stay in the designers drawers, especially after the exit of Forghieri.

The fifth generation 120 degree V6 was revealed on February 16, 1985. In altered turbo positioning it was most striking. The name was also altered, and with the figure 156, Ferrari went back to the old definition of cubic capacity, expressed in hundreds of cubic centimetres, plus the number of cylinders. The reason that led to the new position for the turbochargers was attributed mainly to car installation requirements, rather than for considerations of engine functioning. The constraints of a new rear fuselage shape inspired by the McLaren MP4/2, following work started with the M2, made it necessary to relocate the turbos from their situation within the vee, to a more conventional six-cylinder layout, either side of the block. The modification allowed the ECU to be carried in the vee, which was advantageous from the point of view of cooling and accessibility.

This turning point in location of the turbochargers (still KKK, with variants in size and rotor features) involved a redesign of the cylinder heads, with the inlet inside rather than outside the vee. In the revision of the head, the opportunity was taken to add improvements to the timing system (mainly in terms of valve control). The rationalisation in design of the entire drivetrain assembly was

Ferrari's 120 degree V6 uniquely positioned its turbochargers (twin KKK units) within the vee in 1984. Fully electronic injection was new for the first season of fuel rationing.

remarkable, and included a new oil tank in a revised transaxle case. The Marelli Weber electronic injection system marked other improvements, and the double injectors now pointed downwards towards butterfly rather than slide valves. The bore and stroke dimensions were left unchanged and the crank gear was left substantially unmodified.

Looking at details, great care was devoted to the new plenum chambers, separate for each cylinder bank and within the vee. Due to the new turbo position, it was no longer possible to continue with the split and crossed exhaust pipe layout; but in any case new criteria had been adopted for general engine function in the search of greater performance.

Right from the launch of the 156/85, it was clear that Ferrari had taken a step up. The compression ratio was increased from 6.7:1 to 7.0:1: always a very significant index of turbocharging progress. As regards power output, Enzo Ferrari changed his policy in this exciting phase of development: he himself was amazed by the fast escalation and started to declare each year the highest value reached the previous season. Thus, declaring 780b.h.p. at 11,000r.p.m. on a pressure of 3.5 - 3.6 bar, he implicitly confirmed the 1984 levels, as an average of race and qualifying performance.

Once again, the engine lived its racing year as a strong performer, from a debut of pole position in Rio (and eight laps for Alboreto at the head of that race). The 1985 regulations forbade fuel chilling and this created an advantage for the Ferrari engine, which had hardly ever worked using that expedient. However, water injection had been employed in certain circumstances and *Emulsistem* continued to be used with the 1985 engine, but only early in the season: subsequently it was pensioned off for good. This was due to its 15kg. weight penalty, and progress made with fuel technology and electronic injection.

The 156/85 looked competitive in both qualifying guise - compared to the powerful presences of Honda, Renault and BMW - and in racing conditions, where the Porsche/TAG continued its relentless ascent towards the highest efficiency, with the absolutely lowest specific consumption. On 'power circuits' where acceleration is a key factor, results were good. After second places at Rio, Estoril and Monte Carlo, came victory for Alboreto in Canada, followed home by Johansson. This put the Italian driver at the head of the World Championship, and emphasised the good qualities of the 156. Included in this promising period was provisional pole position for the aborted Belgian Grand Prix. For that missed confrontation (which might have influenced the destiny of the championship), Ferrari had prepared more efficient engines, with considerable lubrication improvements (along with new oil). Modifications were made to the crank and, above all, the electronic injection programme was marked by a considerable jump in quality. Of all the modifications mentioned, a revised scavenge pump

Johansson, the Ferrari 156/85 and Ing Tomaini who race engineered the team after Forghieri's sideways move. Note high damper access plates characteristic of this later '85 monocoque.

After the blow of '85, a Renault Sport engineer was brought in to head the engine team: Jean-Jacques His. It was decided to change the turbo supply, gradually moving to the more promising Garrett product. 1986 was to be the last year for the 120 degree V6 and even its code name was simplified, to F1-86. Taking into account that failures had been mainly caused by the chassis, no important modifications were made to the drivetrain: the biggest innovation would come in 1987, with a new 90 degree V6.

1986 was a very frustrating season, although good engine performance was achieved. The compression ratio had been further increased to 7.5:1 and race power was officially 850b.h.p. at 11,500r.p.m., on 3.8 bar, with 4.6 bar for qualifying. Once again the levels reached the previous season had been confirmed. Speculation revolved around what the adaptation to the 195 litre ration involved. In this respect, the progress achieved with the digital electronic injection had been substantial: new solenoid-operated valves to encourage fuel economy in the transitional r.p.m. range; fewer oscillating masses, with more suitable design and materials; reduced fuel input timing, in operation for up to 0.6 milliseconds;

Ferrari 156/85 had turbochargers relocated either side of the block in conventional fashion. Note Raceplex spark box between plenum chambers.

system had the greatest impact on future development.

Basing ourselves upon complicated calculations to take into account the aerodynamics of the car and the speed developed (as registered by Olivetti Data Processing) it was possible to assign an average value of 795b.h.p. to the 156/85 engine over the early phase of the season. At Francorchamps this rose to 810b.h.p. and the qualifying peak reached 950b.h.p. Examining the slower circuits: the general performance was good, but engine failures emerged with a return to faster circuits (at Ricard), after reaching for the first time, and unequivocally, a qualifying record of 1000b.h.p. A rapid modification of the engine followed and a race power of 840b.h.p. was achieved in time for Silverstone.

There was drama for the engineers: on the Ferrari side, errors in injection programming were reported. From the opposition came an increase of 400r.p.m., achieved by the Porsche/TAG engine. We had to await the German Grand Prix at the Nurburgring for a further trial. Alboreto took a striking victory. He had up to 880b.h.p. available in race trim. This was the last success of long and brilliant career for the 120 degree V6 engine. Immediately afterwards it reached its limits for consumption and reliability, and also chassis efficiency fell short of the required standard.

How Ferrari so dramatically lost competitiveness remained a mystery for the Maranello engineers: in Austria Alboreto was caught by Prost at the head of the world championship, and he was beaten following engine failures (Zandvoort and Monza), clutch failure (Francorchamps), turbine failure (Brands Hatch and Kyalami) and gearbox failure (Adelaide). Overall, Ferrari, running Johansson rather than Arnoux alongside Alboreto ever since Estoril, made 19 of 32 starts from the grid top ten and scored points on 18 occasions, including 10 rostrum finishes (with second for Johansson both at Montreal and Detroit). Alboreto's runner-up position in the World Championship was a very respectable result, but complete success had been expected from the 156/85 Ferrari and therefore the defeat brought controversy.

The relationship with KKK was criticised: the turbos, instead of improving showed signs of frailty. This led to direct modifications in Italy to the bearings and lubrication circuit. Dissatisfaction also emerged as regards the electronics, and there was some reorganisation within the Engineering Department. The biggest blame was thrown on the chassis, to the total bewilderment of the specialists.

running pressure higher than 10 bar; sequential phased ignition with better programming flexibility, due to more sophisticated circuitry; cut-off system, to increase fuel-economy in delivery; more accurate airflow measurement, with a speed-density sensor. Achieving 210gms. per h.p. per hour as a specific consumption was mainly due to this hi-tech development work.

It is amazing to think of the amount of work involved to improve the engine, without evident change in external appearance, except for the considerable modification of the turbos. From the Belgian Grand Prix, Garrett turbos were used, while KKK continued to be employed in qualifying up until the British Grand Prix. In the case of the Canadian Grand Prix, the track conditions did not allow full exploitation of the maximum power. There were also complications with new exhausts. The first difference noticed with the Garrett turbos concerned reliability, and to achieve full reliability some special constructions were required, as well as a change in the electronic control. A concerted effort achieved the necessary modifications in time for the German Grand Prix.

According to our calculations effected during the first few races of the year (a complete disaster from the point of view of reliability), up to Monaco, the average race power remained as 830b.h.p.: 20b.h.p. below the original estimate. From Francorchamps, higher

performance came into action with a jump to 890b.h.p., with a maximum torque of about 58kg./m. at 8,000r.p.m. In qualifying 1000b.h.p. was regularly achieved, as was shown by the fantastic terminal speeds reached at Ricard - up to 342.2k.p.h., which was achieved from 1070b.h.p. Alas, the power potential was not fully exploited, due to lack of chassis reliability. It only resulted in a best of second place for Alboreto, one lap behind, in Australia. In total there were only five rostrum finishes in 11 point scoring drives, and of 32 starts only 15 were from the grid top 10, none from pole.

During the early phase of the season the Ferrari engineers devoted themselves mainly to modification of the cylinder heads, altering the combustion chamber and gas passages. On the occasion of the San Marino Grand Prix new exhausts were seen, and the next step, in Canada, was to feed three exhaust pipes and the wastegate pipe onto the underwing. A lot of work was put into new butterfly valves ahead of the turbos to reduce lag. Towards the end of the season, further adjustments were made to the electronics, to allow control of the wastegate. From the Osterreichring, new turbo casings appeared and on the occasion of the home Grand Prix the cooling system was modified, with improved aftercoolers. Most of these modifications anticipated further improvements planned for 1987, for which year there appeared to be great promise.

F1-87
90 degree V6

81 x 48.4mm./ 1496.4mm
2 Garrett turbochargers
Cast iron block with aluminium heads
Linerless
4 main bearings, plain
Steel crankshaft, 3 pins
Titanium con rods
Mahle light alloy pistons
Goetze rings
4 o.h.c., gear driven
4 valves/cylinder, 1 plug
Valve sizes undisclosed
32 degree included valve angle
Marelli ignition
Weber injection
Marelli/Weber engine management system
Compression ratio 8:1
Maximum r.p.m. 11,500
150kg.

The definite change of course in engine design in 1987 included cylinder configuration, and involved a number of other important innovations as regards design and materials. Ferrari required a Formula One engine with a stronger block and smaller transverse dimension. The first official appearance of the brand new 'F1-87' was at Imola on March 16 1987 for a test in anticipation of a Brazilian Grand Prix debut. However, the engine had already undergone circuit tests at Fiorano, while the chassis had been shown back in September 1986.

Originally the designers considered a vee angle slightly narrower than 90 degrees, but the long experience gained by Chief Engineer His at Renault finally dictated 90 degrees (which offers more balancing difficulties than 120 degrees for a six cylinder engine). The 120 degree engine's bore and stroke were retained, and the engine construction was revised around these basic dimensions. Structural requirements were catered for by a change to a linerless cast iron block: with the performance reached by turbo engines (in excess of 1000b.h.p.) causing very high internal pressures, and massive forces acting on the crank assembly, it was very difficult to maintain the required stiffness in an aluminium base, without resorting to weights and dimensions which would no longer have justified this type of material. Besides, notable progress had been made in metallurgy in the development of a special cast iron alloy with some very interesting opportunities. This work involved the Teksid company within the Fiat Group, which had developed some very advanced casting techniques. That is why the excellent design engineer Renzetti was called in to participate in the project: Renzetti had been responsible for the development of the Fiat FIRE engine: a hi-tech engine with a resemblance to the sort of block envisaged in terms of materials.

For the Ferrari engineers, the main objective was to plan a strong

engine block that would avoid distortion of the main bearings. Fears regarding excessive weight of the cast iron component were overcome through the fineness of design, with thin walls and perfect structural dimensions. The end result was so good that the total weight figure was slightly improved over the superseded alloy engine. A novelty was the move of the timing gear from the rear to a more conventional front position, with an included valve angle of 32 degrees. The crank retained a familiar vibration damper.

The entire technical formulation of the F1-87 was aimed at the highest thermodynamic efficiency. With due pride, Enzo Ferrari wanted to make clear at the launch the important achievement of his engine development team in for the first time achieving a specific consumption of under 200 gms. per h.p. per hour, reaching the value of 198 gms. This was considered essential, given the maximum tank capacity of 195 litres and the new 4.0 bar limit.

A contributory factor was an improvement in the digital electronics, with further modifications to the injectors and an operating pressure considerably higher than 10 bar. An important step was made with a new Marelli static ignition, providing a coil for each of the six plugs. Near the plugs was a three-point connector which carried current to the coil, placed in the well. The system was very reliable, minimised hi tension voltage leakage and, from the point of view of electronic control, enabled a valuable optimisation of the ignition for each cylinder, with instant correction.

As usual, one looks at the compression ratio in order to understand the range of performance increase: with the F1-87 it rises from 7.5:1 to 8.0:1 for a stated power of 880b.h.p. at 11,500r.p.m.; equal to a specific power of 588b.h.p. per litre.

In the new chassis, the engine was matched with a longitudinal gearbox, ending a long standing practice of setting a transverse

gearbox ahead of the rear axle. Remarkable development brought the new engine to the top of the Formula One tree within only seven months of development, going from the initial placings (Berger fourth at Rio, Alboreto third at Imola) to the victories in Japan and Australia. The most surprising aspect is that no striking engine modification was made from the first to the last race of the season, except for the routine variations in turbocharger. This means both that the 90 degree iron block engine was well produced and came out of an excellently formulated project, and that in this development phase of the turbo engine all the mechanical refinements had reached their peak and the highest performance levels were achieved only through electronic fuel control, ignition control and general turbo function.

The F1-87 chassis had been designed by Harvey Postlethwaite and newcomer Gustav Brunner, with finalisation of specification approved by newly arrived Technical Director John Barnard. Undoubtedly, the chassis matched the best ever encountered in the years immediately preceding, due to the arrival of Barnard and the commencement of operation of the Ferrari wind tunnel. These factors made for good overall success after two years of failures. But when an engine makes such significant advance as to reach the levels of the established best engines from Honda and Porsche, special credit is due.

The engine made a preview with modified injection and a split plenum chamber, but from the first race a single chamber was fitted to allow just one pop-off valve to be fitted. Thereafter, no external modification was made. Internally, there was a slight alteration to the combustion chambers and inlet tracts from Francorchamps.

Although the quoted power was 880b.h.p. at 11,500r.p.m., the output looked less in early races. We devoted ourself to the usual calculations taking into account the aerodynamic characteristics of the car and its speed range; the system well tested over a number of years. From the first significant study at Imola we calculated 874b.h.p. in qualifying and 791b.h.p. race power. When Chief Engineer His saw this his only comment was: "C'est bon".

Subsequently came improvement at Francorchamps and Ricard, (while the slow circuits saw a resort to smaller turbos). Calculations relevant to the faster tracks showed 909-910b.h.p. at a maximum pressure of 4.0 bar, with 846-861b.h.p. at 3.71-3.78 bar race boost. The values increased at the German Grand Prix (to 932b.h.p. and 867b.h.p., respectively) and the Hungarian Grand Prix, where 950b.h.p. was reached during qualifying, 900b.h.p. during the race. Meanwhile, turbos utilising new materials had arrived and, above all, it was possible for the first time for the Ferrari engineers to surpass 4.0 bar by a few tenths, reaching levels of 4.1 and 4.2 bar, as Honda had been doing from the start of the season.

The die was cast and thereafter the Ferrari F1-87 was highly competitive. Over the season as a whole Ferrari made all but one of its 32 starts from the grid top 10, while the second half of the season saw three poles: Berger at Estoril, Suzuka and Adelaide. As regards the engine everything was left unchanged, apart from intense research work into the fuel system configuration and electronic controls. New inputs were incorporated for the ECU: pressure sensors outside the compressors (at the Osterreichring) and a rev counter on the large turbos tested in Mexico.

During hurried turbo development, Ferrari had gone through the experience of Estoril; Berger, after taking pole position, missing victory by the skin of his teeth. New turbo equipment was supplied by Garrett as only left-hand units, as there had not been time to complete construction of left and right-hand versions. Ferrari compensated for the counter-rotation with the construction of different exhaust systems: a fast adaptation which produced good results. The new turbos had rotors with a silicon nitride ceramic coating and notably emphasised the lightness of their rotating parts and their low friction bearings. The contribution was considerable, as regards performance and reliability, as a record on the test track and the two victories of Berger showed.

At his customary press conference in December 1987, Enzo Ferrari did not fail to emphasise the merits of such advanced progress in engine design, and confirmed: "It is true that we faced the last competitions of the year with 910-920b.h.p., and we ended up qualifying at 960b.h.p." But he was already urging his engineers to develop the 1988 version of the 90 degree V6, with new heads and an r.p.m. increase to face the 2.5 bar limit. Thus the Ferrari Engine Development Department proceeds tirelessly on the path of progress, and faces up to the most advanced technology.

FERRARI 126 C4

Ferrari carbon fibre/Kevlar monocoque
Stressed engine
Pull rod front and rear suspension' - Koni dampers
Speedline aluminium and magnesium rims
Brembo cast iron discs, outboard
Single Brembo four pot calipers - Ferodo pads
Carbon fibre/Kevlar bodywork
2 IPRA combined water/oil radiators
2 Behr air:air aftercoolers
AP twin plate clutch
Ferrari five-speed gearbox - ZF diff
220 litre fuel cell - 12 litre oil tank
Yuasa battery - Borletti instruments
2600mm. wheelbase; 1786mm. front track, 1665mm. rear
540kg.

Conceptually, the 126 C4 was a logical evolution of the C3, retaining a similar arrow-shaped planform. Indeed, the arrow-shape was further emphasised thus avoiding from the outset any aerodynamic research into the restoration of ground effect; Ferrari was concentrating upon the external airflow.

The main objective was to obtain, for the first time, considerable overall lightness, with chassis characteristics particularly well suited to the most sinuous circuits: short wheelbase (at 2.6 metres, the shortest of any in Formula One at the time); concentration of mass towards the centre of gravity; rearward cooler location and 42 - 58 front:rear weight distribution.

The monocoque again was formed in-house from composite materials with a significant innovation in that the shell was produced as upper and lower halves bonded together. This allowed the height to be lowered by 25mm., reducing the

centre of gravity by a similar amount, along with a weight reduction of 2.5kg. For a tub normally weighing 40kg., this represented a reduction of more than 6%, while the development of composite technology had led to a noteable improvement in rigidity.

As regards general layout, redesigned water/oil radiators were fitted either side of the tank, upright and raked rearwards following the plan of the leading edge of the arrow's tail. The aftercoolers were positioned behind, similarly upright and set into the short pods' side panels which extended straight back as far as the rear tyre.

The fuel tank shroud was lower and after the first run the engine bay was left uncloaked to improve the efficiency of the rear wing, which was mounted on a central post. The wing carried winglets ahead of the rear wheel axis, taking advantage of the more generous 1400mm. width prescription. Introduced by Ferrari in 1983, this pioneering idea was copied by almost all 1984 cars.

In the demanding weight reduction programme which brought the C4 to 540kg., the reductions of 10% in engine weight and 8% in transaxle weight should be noted. The transaxle was redesigned but retained a transverse five-speed gearbox within the wheelbase. The braking system was also renewed, with four new ventilated special cast-iron discs and single four pot calipers from Brembo. Right from the Brazilian Grand Prix, tests began with SEP carbon-carbon discs.

Kyalami saw a modified rear wing with the central post replaced by a transverse pole between endplates. Dissatisfaction with the C4 on faster circuits produced substantial development in two phases. The first phase was seen at Brands Hatch. Long sidepods were fitted with longitudinally-tilted, top vented water/oil radiators, the location of the aftercoolers remaining unchanged. The second, and more important, phase was seen in the form of the M2 version (M for modified) which was first produced at the official trials for the Austrian Grand Prix (running only one lap, while the other cars were trying out an elongated wheelbase). It was subsequently seen at the Italian Grand Prix, but did not race until the Nurburgring, where Alboreto took an encouraging second place.

With the M2 aerodynamic development concerned itself with ground effect, following a tentative step at Dijon, where the spare car was fitted with a short diffuser either side of the gearbox. The M2 featured a wheelbase lengthened by 127mm. (to 2727mm.) thanks to a spacer between engine and transaxle and a redesigned version of the push-rod rear suspension that had been introduced earlier. Additionally, the sidepods were revised, with the radiators moved forwards and the aftercoolers rotated through 90 degrees. This made space for a redesign of the rear bodywork, McLaren-style. The increase in weight was more than offset by an overall improvement in car performance. Three of the seven C4 chassis (071-077) produced were modified.

FERRARI 156/ 85

Ferrari carbon fibre/Kevlar monocoque
Stressed engine
Pull rod front and rear suspension - Koni dampers
Speedline aluminium and magnesium rims
Brembo cast iron discs, outboard
Single Brembo four pot calipers - Ferodo pads
Carbon fibre/Kevlar bodywork
2 IPRA water radiators - 2 Secan oil heat exchangers
2 Behr air:air aftercoolers
AP twin plate clutch
Ferrari five-speed gearbox - ZF diff
220 litre fuel cell - 12 litre oil tank
Yuasa battery - Borletti instruments
2760mm. wheelbase; 1797mm. front track, 1663mm. rear
548kg.

In its complete redesign, the Ferrari 156/85 took the path of high aerodynamic efficiency, showing a reduced frontal area, more efficient shape and, above all, high levels of negative lift. The relatively long wheelbase - 2762mm. - indicates the change of direction, which was completed by the M2-style bottleneck plan rear end.

The new monocoque abandoned the half-shell idea and was entirely designed on computer, using CAD/CAM for the first time, in co-operation with the aeronautics company Aermacchi. The two water radiators, one either side, were in

a more forward position, upright, with a marked angle to the longitudinal axis and side venting. Behind, the aftercoolers flanked the rear bulkheads with venting through a grill in the rear deck.

The change in engine design to side-located turbos allowed better positioning of the ECU, which was moved to the area above the fuel tank, immediately behind the roll bar. The suspension was also new, while the model was initially run with conventional brakes, then marked Ferrari's decisive conversion to carbon-carbon discs.

The ban on endplate mounted winglets called for a redesign of the rear wing assembly, which was supported by a horizontal transverse tube formed in carbon fibre. The front wing saw the 'arrow' shape abandoned in favour of a conventional rectangular shape. Great care was devoted to the rear end treatment, with an underwing extending almost to the prescribed overhang limit.

The wheelbase extension was exploited by the incorporation of a new oil tank between engine and gearbox in a single casting. As regards trans-

mission, the transverse five-speed gearbox was retained within the wheelbase, together with ZF cam and pawl differential, though other solutions had been studied; modifications were deferred to a later date.

From the French Grand Prix the engineers started to effect many modifications, beginning with the front suspension. This had new lower wishbones and revised tension link ratio. The underbody was also redesigned while the cooling system was rationalized, by rotating the aftercoolers through 45 degrees towards the water radiators and providing their own side outlets. The oil tank was enlarged. The overall revision was completed just in time for the Italian Grand Prix and the adjustments effected included the following: access plates on the front of the tub to service the dampers; front suspension lower wishbone base reduced in width; side radiator less titled and almost touching the bodywork; bigger aftercoolers with double air outlets; redesigned body sides; new links in the rear suspension and different shock-abosorber mountings; lowered engine shroud; two tier rear wing.

In spite of all the modifications, no tangible car improvements were effected and no appreciable solutions were obtained to the serious problems of poor drive and limited stability. A total of nine examples were produced (078 - 086).

FERRARI F1-86

Ferrari carbon fibre/Kevlar monocoque
Stressed engine
Pull rod front, push rod rear suspension - Koni dampers
Speedline aluminium and magnesium rims
SEP carbon-carbon discs, outboard
Single Ferrari four pot calipers - SEP pads
Carbon fibre/Kevlar bodywork
2 IPRA water radiators - 2 Secan oil heat exchangers
2 Secan air:air aftercoolers
AP twin plate clutch
Ferrari five-speed gearbox - ZF diff
195 litre fuel cell - 12 litre oil tank
Yuasa battery - Marelli instruments
2766mm. wheelbase; 1807mm. front track, 1663mm. rear
548kg.

Construction methods for composite monocoques were making rapid progress. In the case of the F1-86, this was particularly evident from the structural point of view. In the new model, the tub was given more rigidity by being formed as an inverted U with the floor panel bonded on to complete the shell (while using the usual system of bonding and integrating the various components). With this method resistance to torsional and bending stresses turned out to be incredibly high. The best results were noticed in the central area, where the fuel cell is located, and in the front section. This was achieved without any weight increase, and had been enhanced by the use of special alignments for the fibre tissuses and various resin combinations.

The wheelbase was left at the same length as the 156/85, while the front track was widened by 10mm. Strangely enough, in the overall redesign of the rear push rod system, the old rear push rod system was preferred - with the sole justification that the mountings were stronger. At the front, with the pull rod system, the spring/damper assembly had an improved location as it was fitted in a

near horizontal position on the floor, thus solving the always difficult space problem for the drivers' legs, near the pedals. However, at the rear, the positioning of the system in a 45 degree Vee shape above the gearbox showed particular refinement. The upper arms of this suspension were entirely new, built for the first time in carbon fibre with aluminium ribbing. The triangular boxed uprights were also new.

Facing the 1986 season, with the introduction of stricter regulations concerning fuel consumption, the general fixation of the design team was to concentrate its efforts upon aerodynamics in order to reduce rolling resistance (equal speed for less applied power). The frontal area was drastically reduced (according to the values of the non-dimensional coefficient Cx, little margin was left for further improvement) and even a 'sole' shaped car was contemplated. The Ferrari engineers succeeded in lowering the entire fuselage by 40mm, with a narrower and more tapered nose, thinner body sides and a lower rear cowl behind a roll bar incorporated in the chassis structure and fully streamlined in the shape of a cusp. In relation to the maximum height as regards safety, the F1-86 turned out to be as much as 160mm. lower than the '85 car.

A few variations were made to the cooling systems. The longitudinal and vertical water radiators were slightly open towards the front air intake and had wide lateral air outlets. The aftercoolers went back to an exact transverse position with their own venting in the rear deck behind the large periscope compressor air intakes. The underwing was reduced in size and

was fitted with fins. A new type of support for the rear wing was created with twin parallel vertical plates in a composite material. It was not possible to use this to best advantage when a second, lower wing tier was carried.

The F1-86 was originally exhibited with new brake calipers of original Ferrari manufacture, those using Brembo components. It was a six-

piece assembly with a wide slit in the middle for heat dispersal. For the complete assembly, longitudinal rather than transverse bolts were used. Another innovation was an instrument panel with entirely digital instruments, pensioning off the old analogue types. In the new panel, various coloured indicators were rationally positioned to supply indications regarding boost pressure, oil and fuel pressure, besides the most important temperatures, the engine r.p.m. and the fuel consumption.

During the season, several modifications were made to the car. The first, after the failures at Rio and Jerez, concerned the brakes: the Ferrari calipers were replaced by Brembo items. Much work was put into the suspension: a new rear rocker arm was fitted from the Belgian Grand Prix, as well as a new one-piece upright. In the front suspension, the arms were tilted forwared considerably from the French Grand Prix, while various reinforcements were carried out to the rear suspension, with the dampers moved beside the gearbox. With the front suspension arms tilted it was possible to bring the front wheel axis forward by 50mm.; however, at the rear the spacer between engine and transaxle was eliminated (saving 180mm., with the need to displace the oil tank). In the end the wheelbase turned out to be 130mm. shorter (2636mm.), with a shift in the weight distribution and centre of gravity location in the quest for better drivability.

From the aerodynamic point of view, several adjustments were made, both with the manufacture of rear wings with longer and shorter chords and with the fitting of a second wing tier after modifying the central support.

In the final version of the F1-86 seen at Monza the aftercoolers were slightly angled, while umpteen adjustments to the suspension involved fitting new shock absorbers with remote gas containers. Eight examples were produced (087 - 094).

FERRARI F1-87

Ferrari carbon fibre/Kevlar monocoque
Stressed engine
Pull rod front and rear suspension - Koni dampers
Speedline magnesium rims
SEP carbon-carbon discs, outboard
Single Brembo four pot calipers - SEP pads
Carbon fibre/Kevlar bodywork
2 Secan water radiators - 2 Secan oil heat exchangers
2 Secan air:air aftercoolers
AP twin plate clutch
Ferrari six-speed gearbox - ZF diff
195 litre fuel cell - 12 litre oil tank
Yuasa battery - Marelli instruments
2800mm. wheelbase; 1791mm. front track, 1673mm. rear
542kg.

In the planning of the F1-87 (courtesy of Gustav Brunner), the maximum effort was made to further reduce the frontal area. This was a demanding task given the levels already achieved. Maximum effort was made to increase aerodynamic efficiency, besides devoting much energy to redesigning the suspension. The model marked a considerable break with the past as far as transmission was concerned. The transverse gearbox, used since 1975, was put aside and Ferrari went back to the conventional layout of longitudinal gearbox behind the differential. This was in honour of the Great God Aerodynamics, and not for structural or mechanical reasons.

The creation of ground effect follows its own rules and depends on the exact configuration of the lower and rear part of the car. In particular, large areas are required for the underwing flow pattern with the minimum possible central obstruction towards the outlet. The traditional transverse gearbox had created a serious obstacle in this respect.

The transformation marked an important step in bringing Ferrari among the leaders in good aerodynamic characteristics. The F1-87 design excelled in every respect. Its tapering nose was narrower, it had low tub flanks (and wide pod openings) with the smallest possible dimensions for the roll bar and the cockpit opening. Every detail was carefully dealt with. The frontal dimensions were given the utmost care, so much so that the large periscope intakes were replaced by ultra-low intakes, almost level with the lower edge of the side panel. In the ruthless search for unnecessary encumbrances, the rear mirrors were incorporated in the bodywork at the sides of the cockpit area.

An increase in wheelbase length involved a new position for the centre of gravity, in the endless compromise between handling characteristics and car balance on entering and driving through bends. The monocoque was further stiffened as the inverted U shell now incorporated a wide base, with the bonded in floor a mere central strip, producing a very strong structure. The remodelling of the suspension saw a return to a rear pull rod system, in harmony with the front. To match more sophisticated geometries, better mounts and more refinements were incorporated: at the front elliptical section arms were fitted and a vertical positioning of the dampers was again chosen. At the rear, also with vertical dampers, the mountings and the compact design of the control system was improved.

In terms of the general layout of the car, the water radiators and aftercoolers remained in a familiar position, though with more emphasised angles. This was a logical development with the elongated wheelbase for a lowering of the pods. Some attention was also given to the braking system, with the manufacture by Brembo of calipers 350gms. lighter, a particularly important factor for unsprung mass. The remodelling of the cockpit coaming and the upper region of the tank made a new shape advisable for the ECU. The underwing was refined with pronounced fins and was linked to the rear wing endplates. The wing was carried by a thinner, more compact central support.

On the whole it was noticable that the arrival of Barnard had a great influence on the final design solutions. The results showed clearly after the modifications he carried out from Imola. New parts for the suspension were gradually introduced and, during continuous aerodynamic refinement, the following details could be noted: improvements to the nose; redesign of the (very thin) periscope shaped rear brake ducts; front wings with reduced chord for the faster circuits; new rear wing profiles.

For the first half of the Championhsip, emphasis was mainly on the rear wing configuration. Later the second rear wing tier, previously used only on slower circuits, was employed on faster tracks as well. From Detroit onwards the team experimented with the Torsen differential, and often raced the Tilton carbon-carbon clutch. A total of seven examples were produced (095 - 101).

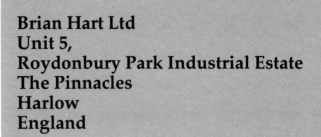

**Brian Hart Ltd
Unit 5,
Roydonbury Park Industrial Estate
The Pinnacles
Harlow
England**

The roots of the Hart Grand Prix engine can be traced back to the Cosworth FVA with which, in 1967, Brian Hart began a long Formula Two involvement, first as driver, then engine builder. The FVA was a Ford based, Cosworth designed and produced race engine: an in line four with a gear driven four valve alloy head that set inlets and exhausts opposite each other at a 40 degree included angle. In '69 Hart established his own company to service the very successful 1600cc. unit and was soon engaged by Ford Competitions to develop the potential of a spin off road/competition engine.

Similarly designed by Cosworth, and homologated into Group Two via the Escort RS1600, the 1000-off derivative married the 1600cc. Ford 'Kent' pushrod engine from the Escort and Cortina ranges to the four valve Cosworth FVA head, this taller unit employing belt drive (hence 'BDA'). The standard Kent camshaft was adapted to drive fuel and oil pumps and distributor and, rather than injected it was fed through two Weber sidedraught carburettors. Hart was charged with the development of an enlarged version for international rallying.

In 1972 Formula Two was confined to homologated Group Two engines of up to 2.0 litre capacity so the FVA gave way to enlarged, fuel injected versions of the BDA. Hart, who by now had hung up his helmet, knew from his rally engine experience that the BDA couldn't safely be taken over 1860cc. and while some of his peers learnt that lesson the hard way he equipped Hailwood's Surtees with the Championship winning 1840cc. engine. Nevertheless, it was only a matter of time before full 2.0 litre engines from rival manufacturers took over so Hart, on his own initiative, had set about development of an alternative alloy block with full 2.0 litre potential. Ford duly bought the rights to the so-called '420S' prototype and homologated it for '73 via another Escort RS1600.

The alloy BDA became the mainstay of the Ford rally programme in the mid to late Seventies but in Formula Two it was quickly outstripped by the iron block BMW M7 in line four, development of which was heavily funded by the Munich marque. In the light of BMW Motorsport's powerful programme Hart took a clean sheet of paper and drew on his BDA experience to design his ideal in line four, compromised only by homologation practicalities. While superficially similar to the alloy BDA, it had a shorter stroke (93.5mm. x 72.6mm. rather than 90mm. x 77.6mm.) and was more rigid if 10kg. heavier. Hart built the prototype in 1975, having a loose agreement with Ford that the 420R (Four cylinder, 2.0 litre Racing) should be homologated as a Mk2 alloy BDA. Alas, the fuel crisis of the mid Seventies scotched that.

Undaunted, Hart developed his prototype as a pure race engine and ran it in a sports-racing car in 1976. The following year he could go Formula Two as the homologation requirement was dropped. However, while the BMW M7 and a newer Renault V6 were heavily funded by their respective manufacturers, Hart 420R development was financed by Brian Hart Ltd of Harlow, Essex. Nevertheless, the privateers serviced by the 420R found it useful, particularly after Renault's withdrawal in 1978, and Hart notched up two wins in '77, four in '78.

For Hart, the turning point was the winter of 1978/79 when along came the ambitious, well financed Toleman team. Toleman undertook to finance Hart development and, running works assisted Ralt chassis, lost the 1979 European Championship by only one point. In 1980, running its own chassis on Pirelli radials, its drivers Henton and Warwick dominated the series, ending a long run of BMW-March success. At this stage the Lucas injected 420R was rated 300b.h.p./9,500r.p.m.

In the wake of the success of the Hart-Toleman came speculation of a joint move up to Formula One. Toleman was warming up for the big time and the emergence of the 1.5 litre turbo engine as a competitive proposition put Grand Prix racing within Hart's reach. In the light of that Hart had quietly started funding 1.5 litre turbo engine research from his own pocket. Having already developed a turbocharged 420S for rallying, Hart's plan was to develop a blown small bore, short stroke 1.5 litre 420R for testing in 1981 then, given sufficient funds, to develop a purpose designed spin off '415T' for the 1982 World Championship.

Meanwhile, Toleman was reluctant to adopt the Cosworth V8 for its graduation in the light of the obvious potential of turbo engines. It had discussions with Lancia, but realistically no major manufacturer was going to entrust its World Championship programme to a team without Formula One experience. Before the end of 1980 Toleman had taken the bold decision to fund Hart's programme. But it was December before Toleman had firmed up team sponsorship arrangements and to keep its momentum going and its sponsors keen it wanted to start racing in 1981.

Hart had casting patterns for the planned 415T, which would have an integral head, but couldn't ready the purpose-designed unit quickly enough for Toleman. The Essex engine builder therefore resigned himself to having to produce the interim, reduced capacity 420R as a stop-gap race engine and to doing development work in public. A further headache was that of confirming a turbocharger deal, while Toleman's inexperience and its decision to continue to run on Pirelli tyres were obvious handicaps, Pirelli having been absent from the World Championship since 1951. In the long term Toleman's exclusive relationships with Hart and Pirelli looked to be strong cards; in the short term such a joint effort was dangerously ambitious, and even the drivers, still Henton and Warwick, lacked worthwhile Formula One experience.

Toleman viewed its plan as ambitious but of high engineering integrity. Consequently, the gamble was primarily commercial: could it maintain sufficient resources to see its engineers through an inevitably long and steep learning curve? There was no major manufacturer to pick up the tab, and few sponsors could be expected to share the patience of Toleman's far sighted Managing Director Alex Hawkridge. Italian domestic appliance manufacturer Candy gave the team the chance to set out on its adventurous climb in 1981, but sought a pay-off in '82.

Hart had the advantage of being able to work closely with Toleman chassis designer Rory Byrne on installation and cooling requirements and found close co-operation from Lucas on injection and ignition systems development. However, he couldn't secure state-of-the-art KKK turbocharger technology, having to rely on off the shelf units from Garrett, the company abandoned by Renault in 1979. Mindful of the response problem inherent in turbocharging he opted for a twin turbo installation, initially trying to feed from each cylinder's siamesed exhaust port to two turbos. A split exhaust manifold proved more practical, the system working well on the bench.

The reduction to 1.5 litres was achieved through a shorter crank, modified piston and alternative liner, with three bore sizes investigated: 93.5mm., 90mm. and 88mm. Hart settled for the 88mm. bore, working with a 6.5:1 compression ratio on pump fuel, injected via the regular (engine load governed) Lucas shuttle metering system. The charge air came through an air:air aftercooler which Byrne slotted into the righthand of two 'wheelbarrow' legs which extended back from his modified Toleman Formula Two car's monocoque to carry the 420S unstressed.

The prototype Hart-Toleman turbocar took to a cold Goodwood track on December 9 1980. The car completed 50 trouble free laps, reaching an estimated 176m.p.h. top speed. In an interview with the author for *Motoring News*, driver Henton, who was familiar with the Cosworth DFV, remarked: "it's the smoothest Hart engine I've ever driven" and expressed himself impressed by its power - "now I know what it was like for Neil Armstrong as he blasted off from Cape Canaveral!"

By the time a purpose-designed Formula One chassis was ready, in March 1981 Hart had concluded that a single, slower revving turbo offered a more practical installation. The turbo was mounted over the transaxle with the aftercooler still in the righthand 'wheelbarrow leg', Byrne retaining rearward-reaching box members to support the drive package. The box members were a proven alternative to A-frames but limited the scope for aftercooler provision. The planned aftercooler was assisted by an engine driven fan, the idea being to maintain cooling irrespective of speed. Alas, early tests revealed a serious charge cooling problem due to a miscalculation somewhere between Essex and Garrett's California base. Inadequate cooling restricted boost, as high as 2.1 bar on the bench, to a mere 1.4 bar.

Due to the 'wheelbarrow legs' Byrne couldn't get sufficient airflow to the aftercooler. He was later to admit that, from the moment the overweight TG181 first scrubbed its Pirelli radials, it was an obsolete chassis. Had a higher aftercooling requirement been specified he would have opted for A-frames. And Hart couldn't see the way to go on engine development until charge temperature was brought under control.

Hart had originally requested a year for development work but Toleman needed to set off for Imola at the end of April. Having been allowed to miss the pre-European season races, to keep on the right side of sponsors and the powers that be it now had to join the fray and to contest each subsequent event. Desperately lacking test time, the team failed dismally to qualify for Imola, and the next race, and the next race...

The team was advised that its aftercooler fan was of dubious legality and action might follow should the car manage to qualify for a race. Hart recalls that at this stage it was hard to get charge temperature below 60 degrees even on a cool day. He was, of course, looking for something in the region of 40 degrees. For the fourth race at Jarama Hart and Byrne relocated the turbo in the airstream atop the engine and switched to air:water aftercooling. The alloy engine was over water cooled at this stage, but it had proved difficult to produce an adequate heat exchanger. Nevertheless, it was worth the effort: charge temperature dropped by the required amount and shorter primary pipes provided improved response. The drawbacks were weight and complexity: the car was now in the region of 620 - 640kg.

Alas, still the DNQ's mounted... By the team's sixth event at Silverstone Hawkridge reckoned the heavily overweight, under-developed package had the potential to qualify, given some luck. At least Pirelli, frustrated by lack of tyre testing opportunity, had by now developed a tyre suited to the cumbersome car. Encouragingly, the following race at Hockenheim saw the it faster than the Cosworth runners in a straightline in spite of its higher drag, but poor acceleration was still evident from the heavy machine.

Hockenheim briefly witnessed the first public outing of the promised 415T. Having an integral head, the 415T was an expensive-to-produce development that offered a lighter, stronger structure. Dispensing with a head gasket eliminated a barrier to the conduction of heat and also removed the thick sections of adjacent faces of two separate castings which can lead to thermal distortion of the structure. The integral head would help check the inevitable tendency for the liners to go oval under the extreme forces involved in extracting over 500b.h.p. from a 1.5 litre engine. It also promised to help keep the valves free from distortion while providing greater freedom in the provision of cooling passages. A long, tall structure doesn't lend itself to be a fully stressed chassis member so Hart designed to 415T to run semi-stressed, carried by conventional A-frames.

Byrne wasn't able to produce a new chassis to take advantage of the 415T and, indeed, due to financial considerations it wasn't the intention to replace the interim engine overnight. The 415T was not seen at the following race on the Osterreichring, then again only the prototype was available, for Henton at Zandvoort and Monza where, at long last, a Hart-Toleman qualified for a Grand Prix. Running on three cylinders for much of the duration, Henton finished a distant tenth.

The real breakthrough came during the off season. At last the team could benefit from a proper test programme and Hart could concentrate upon development work. Detail modifications to camshafts and so forth, a slightly higher compression ratio and a smaller, snappier turbo improved torque and reduced throttle lag. Maximum power was an honest 580b.h.p. at a safe 2.3 bar.

With improved tyres and chassis sorting, comfortable qualifying times were recorded at Paul Ricard. Having experience of the new BMW turbo engine, Surer tried the improved Hart-Toleman package and remarked that, while the Hart hadn't the punch of the German four, it felt stronger than a Cosworth throughout the rev range, with impressive torque. At long last the Hart-Toleman was a real race car. No less than 22 embarrassing DNQs had not, it seemed been in vain.

Nevertheless, 1982 was a season of mixed fortunes, with for the majority of races a chassis developed from the TG181 rather than an overdue new model due to lack of finance. Warwick qualified in midfield for the Kyalami season opener, then neither Warwick nor new partner Fabi T. (Candy's choice) qualified on the bumpy Rio and Long Beach circuits. Candy quit. After struggling at Imola, Zolder and Monaco the team was able to miss two North American races due to 'transport problems'. That welcome break allowed Byrne to produce a further modified TG181'C', and straight away, at Zandvoort, Warwick set fastest race lap! Then, in the British Grand Prix, he moved up from a midfield starting position to hold a remarkable second place before a c.v. joint failed. The Hart-Toleman had arrived. Byrne reflects: "the whole package was being developed. When the tyres suited the circuit and the car was set up well it was reasonably competitive..."

The old TG181 had another four races before it could be honourably pensioned off, but at least 'The Flying Pig' was now a certain qualifier and it took Warwick to a top ten finish in the French Grand Prix at Paul Ricard. At Silverstone in August the long awaited new generation Toleman chassis made its entrance: a lighter, state of the art carbon fibre/Kevlar monocoque car with pull rod suspension. Importantly, it carried the 415T semi-stressed, having A-frames in place of the awkward 'wheelbarrow legs'. The new car was operational only for the last two races of the season, but in the Las Vegas finale Warwick managed a fine tenth fastest in qualifying. Hart was still running less boost than rival turbo engines, under 2.5 bar, but lower boost did mean less engine trouble for Hart.

For '83 the 'TG183' was a flat bottom derivative of the new car featuring a novel aerodynamic package that included front mounted water radiators and side mounted air:air aftercoolers. Feeding the charge air through two matrixes, one either side of the car, the new aftercooling system was designed to save weight over the previous air: water cooler. It helped Toleman reach 575kg. and Warwick was a splendid sixth fastest in qualifying at Rio, fifth fastest at Long Beach. Alas, that early season pace flattered to deceive: thereafter Warwick and new partner Giacomelli were midfield runners, in spite of the development of a twin plug version of the 415T.

Hart was still running pump fuel, which limited the boost that the engine could sustain as flame spread was slow and uneven. The second plug reached into the chamber from a horizontal position, where the head/block interface would have been on a conventional engine, on the inlet side and utilising the space left between valve seat arcs. This upset the form of the chamber a little but allowed the plug, firing at the same time as the central plug, to light an area prone to detonation. It worked very well, and was worth something like a second a lap.

Alas, in '83 ten races passed before Toleman posted a finish, uncharacteristic Hart unreliability partly to blame. Hart explains this as part of the normal "learning process". He was, of course, still working to an extremely limited budget. One particular drawback was lack of turbocharger development, Garrett still supplying off-the- shelf diesel engine units. In the light of that, Hart struck an agreement with Holset. Based in Huddersfield, England, Holset was an old established engineering firm, experienced in diesel engine turbocharging. Practical and enthusiastic, its principals were keen to give Hart full commitment.

The single Holset turbocharger was introduced at the tenth race, on the Osterreichring. Round 11 at Zandvoort brought Toleman its first points, for fourth place, and the team subsequently claimed two sixth, a fifth and another fourth place from the final three races of the season. By that stage, on 2.8/2.9 bar race boost and a 6.7:1 compression ratio the twin plug 415T, still running on Lucas mechanical injection, was producing 630b.h.p. at 10,500r.p.m. Although still low on boost Hart again had a reliable race engine. There wasn't the budget for special qualifying engines - "there was hardly a budget for ordinary engines", Hart notes. "The budget didn't increase with increased performance. We were running engines longer and needed more money to do that".

By the end of '83 Hart reckons to have spent a total of £1.2 million on his Grand Prix programme - a mere fraction of the sums spent by the giants he was up against. Hart, who did the conceptual design while brother Tony worked on the detail drawings, now employed a staff of 24 at his Harlow factory. They worked on a variety of projects, including Ford development work, as at the start of the Formula One adventure when there had been only 15 on the payroll. For '84, having been approached by other teams, Hart reckoned he was in a position to supply additional cars. Meanwhile, Toleman investigated the realistic possibility of using a major manufacturer's engine. Both partners had won respect since those frustrating DNQs.

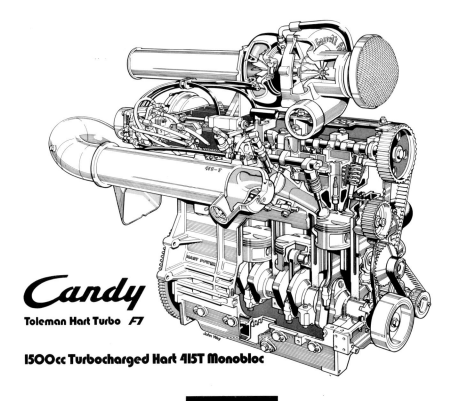

Candy

Toleman Hart Turbo F1

1500cc Turbocharged Hart 415T Monobloc

415T
in line 4

88 x 61.5mm./ 1494.0cc.
1 Holset turbocharger
Aluminium block with integral head
Nikasil coated bores
5 main bearings, plain
Steel crankshaft, 4 pins
Steel con rods
Mahle light alloy pistons
Goetze rings
2 o.h.c., belt driven
4 valves/cylinder, 2 plugs
36mm. inlet valve, 32mm. exhaust
36 degree included valve angle
Marelli ignition
Lucas injection
Compression ratio 6.7:1
Maximum r.p.m. 11,000
120kg.

The heart of the well honed 415T was a stout linerless monobloc with integral head that reached down to the level of the crank axis. It was closed by a lower crankcase that formed the two end main bearing caps, allowing a low crankshaft axis and forming a rigid structure. The block was cast by Sterling Metals in the UK, then was sent to Mahle for the cylinder bores to be Nikasil treated. The combustion chamber had a conventional pent roof by its symmetry was upset by the insertion of the second 10mm. plug. The valve seat inserts were bronze based, as usual.

The regular 'mirror image' flat crank was machined from solid by Allen Crankshafts and nitrided. It was driven through conventional H- section con rods by flat topped, valve clearance notched, three ring Mahle oil gallery pistons. Hart had initially run the 415T with a simple spray to the underside of the crown but by '84 had concluded that an oil gallery piston was a necessity, though it added scavenging problems.

Both the crankshaft and the camshafts ran in five plain Vandervell bearings. The main bearings were of 54mm. (2.125) inch diameter. The 415T had initially run a vibration damper but with crank modifications it had become unnecessary. Camshaft drive was by toothed belt off the nose of the crank. Stainless steel valves were operated through the usual steel bucket tappets. For '84, Hart was investigating Stellite valve seats, Stellite being a class of extremely hard alloys.

Outrigged from the main drive pinion was another pinion which powered an oil pump drive belt. A major change Hart made for '84 was a revised, four pump - one pressure, three scavenge including one for the turbo - system utilising a single sandwich construction combined pump. Located to the left of the block, this was more compact and saved weight. The pump drive belt also turned the water pump, which was mounted on the front of the engine. The alternator and fuel pump were taken off the engine via a cable drive. They were located above the fuel tank.

Sloping down to the ports at 45 degrees, each siamesed inlet tract was fed from above by a Lucas injector. Whereas in the original 415T these had been upstream of the butterfly throttle, now they were on the engine side, the downstream arrangement working better on the dyno. Charge air came from a plenum chamber outrigged to the right of the integral head via a short horizontal feed to the inlet manifold. The manifold carried a butterfly throttle for each cylinder. Hart favoured a four rather than one or five butterfly system. The twin entry turbo was mounted low to the left of the block, at the junction of a steel four branch manifold which was fed by siamesed exhaust tracts.

The 415T employed Lucas ignition and injection. The ignition was Lucas CD with a Monk 'aeroelectric converter' to drive the twin system from a single trigger on the nose of the crank. A Marelli distributor was run on the back of the inlet cam. The metering unit, mounted nearby to the right of the head, was also driven off the inlet cam, via a short toothed belt. The 415T still employed the purely mechanical shuttle system with a cam sensitive to load (throttle opening and boost pressure) but not speed.

Hart was naturally keen to run a micro processor controlled metering system and during '83 had anticipated employing the fully electronic system that was under development by Marelli Weber, having a good relationship with the Italian company. His personal preference was for the superior atomisation offered by electro-mechanical injection and he had asked for the BMW/Bosch system, without success. As '84 approached it became clear that the Marelli-Weber system was running late and that Ferrari would want it on an exclusive basis to tackle the 220 litre ration. Consequently, with Lucas showing no signs of developing a suitable system, at least in the short term, it was a case of DIY.

Hart tackled the problem in two ways: he commissioned Glen Monk to develop an electro-mechanical system and, as that ran into problems, started talking to a new company, ERA with a view to developing a fully electronic alternative. Essentially the problem with electro- mechanical injection was that of finding a servo motor capable of controlling the cam on the Lucas metering unit. Hart explains: "it was asking too much of a servo with the vibration of a four cylinder engine and the incredible response times were we looking for. The Kugelfischer metering unit didn't need such fast response".

While the pile of reject servo motors grew, Hart started talking to ERA (Electronic Racing Aids), a small company based on Lucas' doorstep in Birmingham and run by two ex-Lucas employees Brian

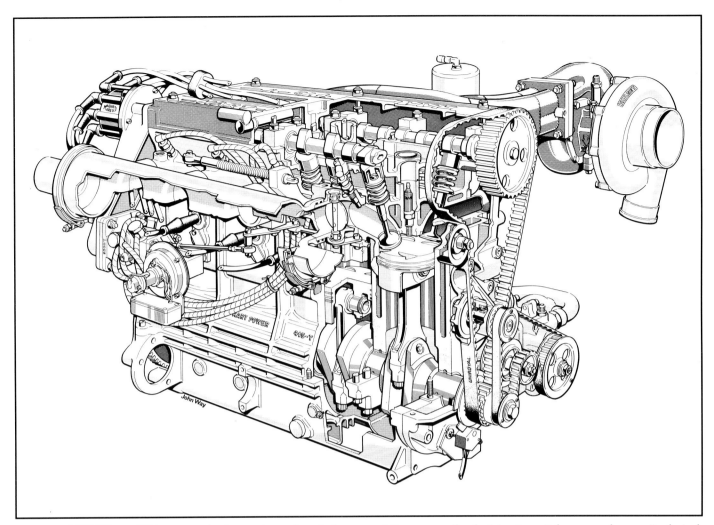

Mason and Bill Gibson. ERA was producing analogue based electronic injection systems and Hart agreed to fund its move into digital (micro processor) control. Work started in late '83 but the system would not be ready for the start of the '84 season.

From the outset the '84 415T benefited from a bigger Holset turbo but the Huddersfield company was still relying heavily upon production based equipment, ill suited to the stresses of mid Eighties Formula One. Now having a maximum of 3.0 bar boost, Hart commenced the season reckoning to race the mechanical engine at something in the region of 640b.h.p. Under development with Lifeline was a system of inert gas injection into the plenum chamber to assist charge cooling and thus help preserve engines during qualifying.

Production of the '84 specification 415T had been somewhat delayed by Toleman Group Motorsport's late confirmation of its order, the team having hung out for the BMW deal that eventually went the way of Arrows. Although Hart had agreed to supply Spirit and RAM, Toleman was still its major source of finance, and would get 'development' engines. While Candy had dabbled again with the team in '83, it was a Toleman team without a major backer and it was starting the season without a new chassis model. The Witney based operation now had a co-operative deal with the Royal Military College of Science at nearby Shrivenham whereby the 25% fixed floor wind tunnel at the college was used with Toleman's rolling road in an on going programme run by R&D Chief Pat Symonds. Byrne's detail design draughtsman was John Gentry, while the team in total employed around 60 on its two car programme, running new recruits Senna and Cecotto.

With two rookie drivers, a chassis inherited from the ground effect era, and neither qualifying engines nor any form of injection control to combat the 220 litre ration, the Pirelli shod, AGIP fuelled Hart-Tolemans, not surprisingly, languished in mid field. Over the first four races the team scored but one point. However, by the fourth race a new chassis was ready, and it could have been race prepared but for the logistical problems of running two models. The team could not be fully equipped until Dijon, by which time it had ended its association with Pirelli.

Hawkridge and Byrne felt that Michelin radials were superior

and Byrne says the decision to switch was made on a "technical basis". However, it was accompanied by public wrangling between Toleman and Pirelli at Imola, and Michelin could provide only for Toleman to run on other teams' cast-off tyres. The TG184's potential was consequently somewhat compromised, yet the car became encouragingly competitive as the chassis was developed and Hart found additional power. The model's career started unimpressively with a midfield pace at Dijon and Monte Carlo, but then down came the rain during the Monaco Grand Prix and Senna excelled in the conditions to claim a splendid second place, closing fast on winner Prost.

Monte Carlo was significant for the introduction of ERA's electronic injection system, which utilised Bosch solenoid operated injectors. Using solenoid injectors allowed four per cylinder, Hart doubling up on the down feed and adding another row of eight to feed up into the tracts. Early tests had employed two, sometimes three injectors per cylinder. Clearly, using more injectors allowed the injection of a greater quantity of fuel in a given space of time.

The ERA system had started running seriously on the dyno early in '84, at first on a single plug engine, the software having been written in late '83. It was a full engine management system, similar to Bosch Motronic; "very similar" according to Mason. Once on the bench, it was a case of patient testing, taking a reading every 250r.p.m. and every 0.25 bar to produce a relatively "coarse" map. Track testing commenced at Easter with a run at Donington. To keep the system free from 'spikes', ERA had separated the ECU from the injector drive, putting the ECU at the nose of the car with a fibre optic link. With electrical and light connections, fibre optics was a complex option, and had not been developed for use on race cars. It caused handling problems and was expensive but kept the ERA system free from noise problems. The electronic Hart ran well and was soon en route for Monte Carlo.

At Monaco Senna reported an encouraging improvement in throttle response from the prototype engine, which he used in qualifying. It offered more progressive power in a wider band, but was new and unproven. The team chose not to race it: Senna was happy with the regular engine, fuel consumption was not a problem at Monaco, and the electronic engine was still undergoing

415T, mechanically injected (as per cutaway on previous page). Note how both distributor and metering unit are driven from the rear of the inlet cam.

development. It was again seen in qualifying at Montreal, then, following shipment back to the UK for a rebuild, was deemed ready to race at Detroit. Alas, it was sidelined by a shunt.

From Brands Hatch the combination of the electronic engine and a revised Holset turbo unlocked far more competitive horsepower from the 415T. The improved turbo featured detail compressor and turbine changes and with electronic injection "unlocked a new area of development in terms of b.h.p., response and fuel consumption", according to Hart. He adds that the additional power also put him in a new area in terms of reliability... An even bigger turbo introduced at the Nurburgring provided the best part of 4.0 bar boost for qualifying and with the electronic engine Senna was able to race at 3.1/3.2 bar boost.

Since Montreal a solid top 10 qualifier, Senna rewarded Hart with a third place finish in Britain. From Dallas until the Estoril finale his was the only Hart car equipped with the electronic engine, and it kept him well up the grid even on the continental power circuits. With it he could never be discounted on race day, though various problems stopped him backing up strong showings with further rostrum finishes. As discipline for an alleged breach of contract, Johansson drove his car at Monza and the Swede finished fourth, albeit two laps down after a late wheel bearing problem. Since Cecotto crashed at Brands Hatch the team had only run one car but Johansson was kept on board and received his own electronic engine for Estoril.

By Estoril, Hart had really got to grips with the potential of the electronic 415T and with a supply of Michelin's best rubber the Hart-Toleman flew. The TG184 chassis had won acknowledgment as one of the best handling in Formula One and Senna managed a resounding third on the grid, just 0.4 second shy of pole. He finished third in the race, while Johansson tangled with Lauda, the

World title claimant having found the Hart-Toleman a real challenge to his Porsche/TAG-McLaren.

The end of season electronic Hart was reckoned to be worth over 800 b.h.p. in qualifying, while it could survive a 220 litre race on 3.3 bar boost, producing around 720 b.h.p. In contrast, the mechanical engine as used throughout by Spirit and RAM was restricted a little on boost and both teams lacked systems experience. Both Pirelli shod outfits were impoverished; neither rose above also ran status.

Spirit Racing Ltd raced with Honda identification and a measure of support from the Japanese manufacturer. Run by the ex-March Formula Two Team Manager and Chief Engineer, John Wickham and Gordon Coppuck respectively, Spirit had been created out of a deal with Honda for Formula Two and had subsequently taken Honda into Grand Prix racing with a converted Formula Two chassis. Late in '83 Spirit had produced a proper Formula One car but it was destined never to be raced in vee six configuration, Honda opting to put all its eggs into the Williams basket for '84.

Honda continued to allow Spirit use of a workshop it owned at Slough and made a small financial contribution to the operation but with no other backer the 15 strong team was the smallest in Formula One and could but operate as a car rental outfit. It secured a Hart contract to cover one car and duly converted its existing Honda chassis, the aluminium honeycomb monocoque, rocker arm suspension 101, introducing a similar second chassis later in the season.

Driven in turn by Baldi and Rothengatter, Spirit's usually Elf (pump) fuelled single entry never qualified higher than 20th place (regularly running a cautious 3.0 bar, according to Coppuck) and failed to score points. Spirit was hit by a shortage of engines which followed a German metal workers strike, Hart unable to get sufficient blocks and pistons from Germany. Consequently, the team ran Cosworth power at Detroit, and failed to qualify as it had done earlier at Monaco. However, on eight of 16 occasions the Hart-Spirit qualified ahead of both Hart-RAMs, and only at the Osterreichring and Zandvoort was the impecunious team's little tested turbocar, following troubled practice sessions, the slowest of the genre. Generally, Spirit got its act together well and, although it scored no points, it managed five top ten classifications from 14 starts, whereas, trying to run two cars on a small one car budget,RAM, which likewise failed to score, only managed four from 27 starts.

Founded by North London motor trader and amateur racer John MacDonald and schoolboy chum Mick Ralph, RAM had run British Formula 5000, British Formula One, and even private World Championship entries out of a Willesden base before moving to Bicester in 1981 to join forces with March for a Grand Prix campaign with jointly developed Cosworth cars. After two undistinguished seasons RAM went its own way with its own Cosworth car, designed by Formula One newcomer Dave Kelly, an aerospace recently turned race car engineer. The 01 was hired by a variety of drivers and, handicapped by its normally aspirated engine and by Pirelli radials developed for turbocars, it frequently failed to qualify.

MacDonald had ended the trying '83 season "skint". Undaunted, by the end of '83 he had secured a deal with Hart to cover one entry and had an evolutionary composite-reinforced chassis designed by Kelly with assistance from Sergio Rinland under construction. He had also signed Alliot, who brought the 28-strong team a small amount of funding. In March, as testing of a converted Cosworth car proceeded, MacDonald helped Palmer scrape together funds for a second car, and together they pleaded to Hart for more engines. Hart had sold RAM four engines and agreed to lend it a further two. Consequently, both the converted Cosworth prototype and the as yet untested 02 model were shipped to Rio for the first race, and at the last minute US Tobacco stepped in with some more money. Some money here, some money there, MacDonald was lengthening the shoestring, but it was still a shoestring. His budget for two cars was a meagre £700,000.

The 02 (with which both drivers were equipped from Zolder) was never better than a backmarker. An early charge cooling problem was sorted for the start of the European season but the 02's 01 design base had left it with a tall tank and poor aerodynamics. And it was low in the Pirelli pecking order. Aerodynamic modifications completed at Montreal brought some improvement, only for the team to face wrecked chassis after Detroit, Dallas and Brands Hatch. Somehow, RAM was still to be found in the Hockenheim paddock...

Come Austria and, having made a tremendous recovery from the seemingly endless carnage, RAM had the 02 chassis working well, MacDonald reckons. However, he admits that it was too big, aerodynamically imperfect, and too heavy, and points out that it always ran on Pirelli tyres of questionable effectivness.

Though RAM never qualified higher than 20th and a race finish was an all too rare occurrence, the 02 was inherently strong and was always well prepared. It ran on a high grade Total fuel, a deal arranged by Alliot. However, running two cars on a pool of six engines wasn't realistic, and there was no spare chassis - the drivers sometimes had to share a car during timed practice.

Happily, there was genuine hope for the future when, just before the Portugese Grand Prix, highly rated designer Gustav Brunner arrived in Bicester. MacDonald had started talking to the Alfa Romeo engineer at Dallas and signing him was a decisive move at a time when RAM looked in danger of disappearing off the grid altogether. MacDonald hadn't firmed up sponsorship for '85, but had asked Brunner to produce a brand new Hart design for 1985 while the team sought the finance to construct and race it. Thankfully, MacDonald's confidence was backed by a renewed, greater commitment from US Tobacco, and with that RAM promised to become a significant second force for Hart.

Senna in the 1984 Hart-Toleman leads the Renault-Lotus of de Angelis at Brands Hatch : by this stage the four cylinder car was flying.

Hart had received Toleman's contribution towards his 1985 programme in good time and undertook a certain amount of repackaging of ancillaries to tuck the large turbo closer to the block, to the chassis designer's advantage. The ignition was changed to Marelli's 'Raceplex' CD system, which employed a different trigger system and could cope with both plugs from one unit, saving bulk and weight. In addition, ERA, now calling itself 'Zytek Systems Ltd', repackaged the engine management system into a pod-mounted three-box system, doing away with the need to carry the ECU in the nose. The ultimate aim was to carry it all in a single yellow box.

Hart, meanwhile, had started work on a small (86mm.) bore engine, having found it impractical to secure funding for an all new six cylinder design, which existed in outline form. The problem was the size of the piston crown. An 86mm. bore was a practical response, but as Toleman ran into a problem finding sponsorship for '85 this development went into the pending file.

Toleman had, ironically, been able to give Byrne the luxury of starting the new car design process much earlier than ever before, and the prototype TG185 was unveiled in January. It was a no compromise step forward from the promising TG184, with a tub produced in Toleman's expanding composite facility and, for the first time the engine shrouded in the interests of cleaner airflow to a necessarily narrower rear wing. "Rory's aerodynamics were more sophisticated", Hart reflects, "he needed an improved flow to the rear wing and running with a cover was not a problem". Alas, since Hawkridge had still to find the finance to run it, and a replacement for Michelin, the attractive car appeared virgin white, sitting on left over tyres.

Hawkridge flew to Japan to talk to Bridgestone and Yokohama, to no avail. Nevertheless, the TG185 ran the Rio test - using three sets of Pirelli race tyres cast off by Brabham. The chassis performed well, Johansson clocking competitive race times. The engine was stronger than ever, but Zytek had a problem: the three-box system wouldn't work. It was no disgrace, Bosch having suffered similar problems with the Porsche/TAG engine. The repackaged system went onto hold...

With sizzling test times, Toleman would clearly be a greater asset to Pirelli or Goodyear than many of its peers but no tyre contract was forthcoming and it continued testing in England on Avon Formula 3000 rubber. Not having a tyre contract, Hawkridge's sponsorship quest was fruitless. He spoke of a conspiracy and in mid March officially withdrew the privately funded operation from the World Championship.

Hart found himself "shot in the leg". He lost all important continuity of development and was left represented by RAM and Spirit. They could afford only 'customer' electronic 415Ts, which were rated "in excess of 740b.h.p." at 10,500r.p.m. in qualifying with "700b.h.p." on 3.2 bar race boost. For qualifying, the inert gas injection system had been replaced by a water spray onto the aftercooler.

For RAM Brunner, assisted by Rinland and Tim Feast (Kelly having moved to Toleman to replace Gentry as Design Draughtsman) had used a carte blanche to produce a radically small, tightly packaged chassis in the interest, primarily, of clean airflow to the rear wing. However, the compact carbon fibre chassis design had not benefited from wind tunnel evaluation, did not offer generous cooling provision, and Hart did not fully approve of the engine installation. The car was engine bay vented with the air exiting through a very tight bottleneck plan tail. The team questioned Brunner on that and, sure enough, the car overheated on its first run at a freezing Silverstone in February. Further cooling problems at the Rio test offset the encouragment of the first day: from 10am. until late afternoon, when the wastegates came off Senna's sticky-tyre-shod Renault-Lotus, Winkelhock held fastest time.

RAM cut the rear of the 03 about but water temperatures hovered around 100 degrees, whereas Hart wanted 80 degrees. The RAM 02 had been adequately water cooled but, while Brunner improved the 03's cooling arrangements for the season, the chassis still didn't offer a generous (Toleman-style) cooler installation.

For its two car Pirelli shod effort with Alliot and Winkelhock RAM had a sensible stock of 12 415Ts running on Shell's doctored Avgas, as used by McLaren so successfully in '84. Alas, the team suffered many problems with its engines. MacDonald and Ralph maintain that the modified 03 offered adequate water and charge cooling provision but, not being generous it was always suspect, particularly in view of the low - below 85 degrees - water temperature the 415T thrived on.

Significantly, at Francorchamps Hart donated some of the toluene based fuel used by Toleman and RAM found a "vast improvement". Toluene tends to reduce temperatures while increasing power - had the 03 offered more generous cooling provision, and had it been run throughout on the elusive 'rocket fuel' it might have realised its potential. Instead, its season broke RAM.

After the first day of the Rio test, the 03 gave a glimpse of its potential at Montreal, where it got as much out of the Pirelli tyre supply as any other car. MacDonald reflects that, "at Montreal the car was good and the package gelled. The potential shown there was never realized - we were changing engines all the time..."

Stock of mechanically injected 415T's in the pits at Imola, 1984. Note the sandwich-construction combined four-in-one oil pump evident on the engine to the right.

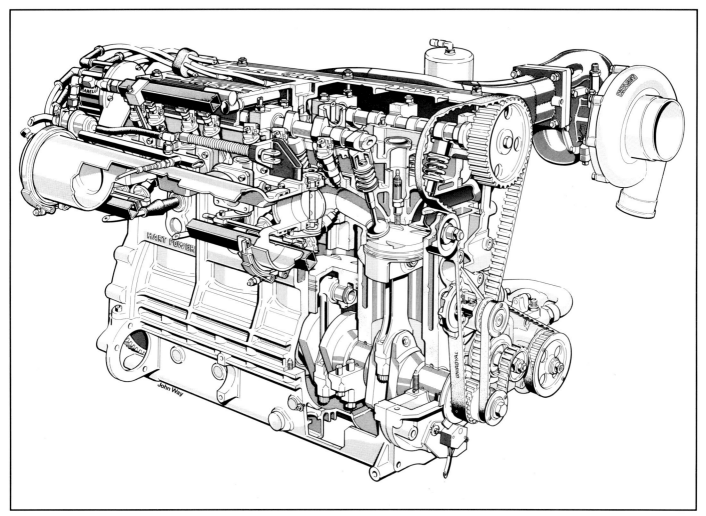

Electronic 415T with four Bosch solenoid-operated injectors per cylinder.
The low pressure, digitally controled injection system was developed by Zytek (nee ERA).

The 03 had been expected to show well in midfield but only at Rio did both drivers qualify in the top 20, and only at Rio did both finish, neither collecting points. RAM failed to score any points in 1985. After Rio, the team's only classified finish was for Winkelhock at Ricard - he came home a relieved 12th, his drive hampered by the ever persistant gremlins. Tragically, the team lost Winkelhock, killed in a sportscar accident just before the Austrian Grand Prix. The number one driver had never despaired of the team's struggle, and had at least qualified in the top 20 on five of nine starts, with a best of 14th at Montreal.

After Winkelhock's death Alliot was joined by Acheson, but the team had just about run out of time. By Francorchamps it was down to only one car due to lack of engines, and MacDonald had been feeling the pinch since Montreal. By Brands Hatch, "'85 had finished us off, mentally as well as financially", MacDonald reflects, "Manfred had been killed, and Brunner was going to Ferrari..."

Hart considers: "RAM had tried to improve its chassis but suffered an inadequate cooling system. It ran out of money for development". Come Kyalami, and the team was missing altogether, its partnership with US Tobacco over.

Spirit had ended its season somewhat sooner. The team hadn't found major backing for '85 but, undaunted by the end of the association with Honda, Wickham had restructured it as Spirit Enterprises Ltd and had found a new home for it in Reading. He set Dave Amey about the design of a new car, Coppuck unhappy with the tight financial restrictions. Amey's new design could not be readied for the start of the season so Coppuck engineered a modified 101 as a stopgap, to be equipped with a Shell fuelled electronic Hart and Pirelli tyres, and once again rented out.

Baldi was the team's first '85 customer and had the task of testing Coppuck's modifications in the heat of the opening race meeting. Bugged by problems, he was the slowest turbo runner by an unhealthy margin. He was a little less uncompetitive at Estoril, but shunted the car during the wet race. A replacement was built up for Imola but again no shakedown was possible; again Baldi was well off the pace. He didn't come back for more. At Reading there had been no progress on the Amey car due to the financial plight and

Wickham had to confess that the team had reached the end of the road. He reluctantly sold his Pirelli contract to Toleman.

Toleman Group Motorsport had continued to operate and had even packed to go to Rio and Estoril, to no avail. At Estoril Goodyear added Zakspeed to its client list and Hawkridge released Johansson to drive for Ferrari. Nevertheless, Toleman reappeared at Monte Carlo, with the Spirit tyre contract, a sponsor in Benetton knitwear and Fabi back in the cockpit. Kelly had quit, but the team was essentially intact. Backer Luciano Benetton had insisted on an option to buy it from Toleman at the end of the year as a condition of his lifeline.

The first four races were unmemorable, Fabi no better than midfield runner. However, the TG185 chassis worked well and the team was getting to grips with it, making up for lost time, as was Hart who had seen the best part of three months development slip away. Importantly, he had been able to procure "advanced fuel" for Toleman from an undisclosed source. 'Rocket fuel' was a necessity in '85. At Paul Ricard Hart re-introduced the three-box Zytek system, after months of facing frequently silent engines on the dyno. It had taken 'Super suppression' MSD leads to coax a three-box managed 415T into life; not to mention endless hours of toil.

The 185T chassis was so good that Fabi was able to run a large turbo and drive around the response problem. Everything clicked at Silverstone, where Byrne introduced a high speed aerodynamic package, including a 'stepped monocoque'. "The TG185 had very strong aerodynamics, and very strong high speed circuit performance", Byrne reflects. Aided by improved Pirelli tyres, and with the sophisticated underbody 185T run radically low, Fabi was sixth in first qualifying at Silverstone: the Hart-Toleman was up to speed. Alas, on Saturday Fabi slipped to ninth and in the race he met with gearbox trouble. Nevertheless, the performance was inspiring and at the Nurburgring Fabi took a splendid pole position on the Friday, which was protected by rain the following day.

Sadly early clutch trouble ended Fabi's German hopes. Never-

Electronic 415T in the 1985 Toleman TG185 Chassis : note Zytek boxes atop the pod ducting. Long radiator helps keep the engine under 85 degrees.

theless, the little Italian was a top six runner on the Osterreichring circuit, again showing the excellence of Byrne's chassis and the progress made by Hart. In Austria, Toleman was able to run two cars once more, Ghinzani joining Fabi - only to over-rev before the re- start. Ghinzani drove to the end of the season but invariably qualified poorly and retired without glory. In contrast Fabi qualified fifth at Zandvoort and was running fifth when a wheel bearing failed. Less impressive speed at Monza and Francorchamps was blamed on lack of top end power. And Fabi never did manage to find good reliability.

For Hart, as the engine was run leaner the main problem was a persistent burning out of valve seats. That took a lot of development to overcome. With an integral head the seats are difficult to access, as are the adjacent water passages. Eventually detail work paid off, but Hart admits that it was not until the end of the year that he got the best out of the toluene based fuel supply. At that stage qualifying at 4.0 bar, the 415T was producing over 800b.h.p.

The TG185 had confirmed Byrne's reputation for good handling cars enjoying plenty of grip: the model's high speed cornering stability was the envy of the paddock. From Silverstone onwards the Hart-Toleman should have been a strong points accumulator and for Toleman it was clear that more could be achieved through exploiting the vast resources of a major manufacturer. This time BMW accepted the team's pitch. At the same time Benetton chose to exercise its option: from New Year's Day the team would be German powered and Italian owned. The all British Hart-Toleman giant killing act was over.

In fact, Hart had lost four teams by the end of '85: RAM, Spirit, Toleman and newcomer FORCE. FORCE was the initiative of two men: Lola's American importer and works Indy Car entrant Carl Haas and James L. Dutt, Chairman of the vast American corporation Beatrice Companies Inc. Haas had met fellow Chicago businessman Dutt in a local restaurant and had talked him in to a massive five year, $80 million sponsorship package covering both Indy Car racing and an ambitious entry into Formula One, long his dream.

Unlike Ron Dennis, who appointed a Technical Director then sought the finance to operate an engineering facility around him, Haas found the finance, then set about the creation of an engineering operation while trying to woo an established Formula One design engineer. Having no British base, he spoke to a number of teams and opted to, in effect, take over a rival Indy Car team, Meyer Motor Racing, which had a home in Woking. Former McLaren bosses Teddy Meyer and Tyler Alexander were keen to get back into Formula One and found themselves in charge of Formula One Race Car Engineering (FORCE) which was to construct and run Lola badged cars on behalf of 'Team Haas USA'.

Haas signed Williams Race Engineer Neil Oatley to take charge of the technical side, and he was joined by fellow Williams technician Ross Brawn who was assigned to look after aerodynamic work while Meyer Motor Racing engineer John Baldwin was made responsible for monocoque design and construction. In the absence of a star designer, Lola boss Eric Broadley was appointed design consultant.

FORCE commenced operation from Meyer's small Woking unit in December 1984, offering attractive inducements to potential employees from other teams, and the Beatrice backing was announced amid much razzmattazz in January 1985. However, while the team had cash and flash, it lacked design experience and had no contract with a leading engine manufacturer. McLaren had quashed a deal with TAG and while talks with Renault and Ford dragged on Meyer put in an order for a supply of the 415T. Fuel would come from Shell, tyres from Goodyear. Goodyear wouldn't confirm as much for this was the time of the Toleman tyre saga, but Akron's links with Haas went back a long way. And Haas was the first American in a long while to pick up Gurney's mantle.

Back in the days of Gurney, Colnbrook meant Bruce McLaren Motor Racing and McLaren's business partners had come home to roost over a brand new 29,000 square foot factory close to the old McLaren base, which opened in July. At that stage they had a staff of almost 70. Since December the design team had been working on a chassis design, evaluating 25% models in the original Imperial College moving floor wind tunnel prior to getting access to the 35% tunnel at Cranfield.

Although he had been unable to tempt a recognised designer, in May '85, while construction of the Hart-FORCE 415T-THL1 proceeded, Haas had upstaged much of the Formula One establishment by clinching a highly sought after deal with Ford to run the forthcoming Cosworth turbo on an exclusive basis, starting in 1986.

In the meantime, five engines purchased from Brian Hart Ltd would see one car for Jones contest only the last four races of '85.

The conventional Hart-FORCE/Lola was first aired in August and made a much hyped Monza race debut with little mileage behind it. Haas was heard to say that if it was a horse he would have shot it. It was that kind of weekend. The car had overheated on its first serious test and a continuing cooling headache hampered efforts to sort the chassis. Jones started the race from the back of the grid between the Hart-RAMs and posted an early retirement after rubbish blocked the radiator, then the distributor failed while the engine was overheating.

While the circus went to Francorchamps, FORCE went off for more testing and sorted out its cooling problem. Oatley explains that casting sand was found in the oil system: it had silted up the heat exchanger! The new car was typically sensitive to pitch and ride height and the characteristics of the Hart engine (with the large '85 turbo) made it difficult to sort: FORCE needed testing time. Come Brands Hatch and Jones still qualified at the back, but admitted that he hadn't made the most of his tyres. He retired with a holed radiator.

After qualifying 18th on the small Kyalami grid Jones missed the politically sensitive South African Grand Prix due to 'influenza'. At home in Australia he lined up 19th, stalled at the start, then charged through to sixth place before the engine went sick. With Cosworth/ Ford testing imminent, Jones made it clear that he was pleased to see the back of the Hart car.

FORCE had suffered an installation problem that wasn't identified until the winter. The car's water cooling system had suffered such a pressure drop that the water pump had stopped working at high r.p.m. Engines hadn't detonated - they had suffered melt down! Although he had lost all his customers, Hart didn't end his development work and for '86 promised more power and improved cooling, having modified the block to improve combustion chambers and waterways. The '86 415T also boasted a new water pump drive to match the increased water circulation and improved electronics,in conjunction with the single box Zytek system. The block was shortened by 12mm. and it required revised chassis mounting points.

Most important of all, Hart had managed to bring the 86mm. engine to a high state of development. The early 86mm. engine had been a modified '84 spec. 415T: for '86 Hart laid down a batch of new blocks in 88mm. and 86mm. configurations, the small bore engine having a simple single plug head and a 34 degree included valve angle (16 - 18). It ran new a crank, new rods and pistons and its block featured split exhaust tracts. The 420R's siamesed outlet had made a twin turbo installation awkward - the 86mm. engine was specifically designed for twin turbos and its response was highly encouraging. Further, the split tracts assisted cooling. Running on 'rocket fuel', and an 8.0:1 compression ratio, the 86mm. engine offered a wider power band and could run a 195 litre race on 3.7 bar boost, producing over 800b.h.p: a highly competitive output.

Hart calculated it would cost £1.6 - £1.7 million to service a two car team. He clung to "a glimmer of hope" with two possibilities in addition to RAM, which was down but not yet out. A consortium of Australian businessmen was interested in backing a single car effort by MacDonald. As an exploratory venture it backed RAM's participation in the February Rio test. By that stage MacDonald had lost Brunner to Ferrari, Rinland to Williams and Feast to the aspiring Ekstroem Formula One team. He took Amey on board to run an existing 03, modified to accept the revised (88mm.) 415T and driven by Perth- raised, New Zealand born Thackwell. Alas, the more powerful engine further taxed the cooling capabilities of the RAM 03, in spite of the team having modified its water system. It was an unhappy test which led to ill feeling in both camps.

Thankfully, late in the day, FORCE put in an order as the Cosworth V6 had met delays. The team needed more engines to run Jones and new recruit Tambay as a stopgap measure and leased 88mm. engines with '86 modifications. Having run a Toleman specification in '85, it opted for the smaller '84-standard turbo slightly modified and, with the revised water cooling system, the THL1 was much more encouraging.

A third 'interim' chassis had been constructed to start Ford testing and this was converted to take the '86 specification Hart and was driven by Jones at Rio. Both Jones and Tambay qualified strongly in midfield. Five storming laps, then Jones succumbed to distributor failure. Tambay carefully worked his way into the points at one third distance, then his alternator failed.

Both race cars had '86 specification 88mm. engines at Estoril, but the THL1s slipped back in qualifying, bugged by a fault in the fuel system. However, while Jones was taken out by an accident, Tambay finished, albeit well adrift following a brake problem. Tambay got the final THL1 drive at Imola, where Jones debuted the new Cosworth/Ford. The 88mm. engine boasted modified turbo and electronics and with 11th fastest time Tambay comfortably outqualified Jones. However, having shot into the top six, on lap five a piston failed. Mahle had made a modification that allowed fuel to get trapped alongside the skirt. The diagnosis came too late.

Hart gamely plugged on with development work through the summer, amassing adequate test evidence to the effect that the 86mm. engine would make a fine 4.0 bar weapon. Alas, there were no takers. By 1987 engineering integrity alone was insufficient - Formula One had outpriced a realistic privateer turbo effort. A tremendous initiative was over: David would have been proud of Hart's performance against the massed Goliaths of the world's motor industry.

Electronic 415T in the 1985 Force THL1 Chassis. The car has a conventional underwing with diffuser section extending beyond the gearbox.

FORCE THL1

The Hart-FORCE was a strikingly clean machine, with a relatively long, squat tank to keep the fuselage profile low and relatively short transaxle. The rearward engine situation did not cause a rearward weight bias, Oatley quoting a 42 - 58 front - rear split: similar to that with which he had worked at Williams. The car made generous cooler provision within side and engine bay vented pods and featured an under-stated bottleneck- plan tail and a long, conventional diffuser rising under a central post supported rear wing. Clearly, having started the design from scratch, Oatley and aerodynamicist Brawn drew heavily upon their experience at Williams. However, the team had been able to conduct a significant amount of wind tunnel work and the THL1 was far from an adapted Williams.

The monocoque formed the cockpit flanks and the tank shroud, the tank broad shouldered but low set and topped by a conventional roll hoop. A fairing behind formed engine shroud, pod lids and rear deck, while a front fairing covered a flat scuttle. Leaving a horizontal surface above the driver's legs did nothing to harm monocoque rigidity and cutouts allowed easy access to the front suspension and pedal box. The monocoque employed aluminium honeycomb and carbon fibre skins, with just a small amount of Kevlar, in the pedal box area. It was produced in upper and lower halves and had composite bulkheads, other than those carrying the front suspension which were machined alloy.

The sidepod layout saw the aftercooler (on the left) and the water radiator (on the right) set on edge lengthwise and splaying away from the tub, extending alongside a portion of the cockpit. A forward portion of each cooler vented through a large square aperture in the adjacent side panel while the remainder vented through the engine bay. The turbo was fed from a NACA duct in the pod lid, while the heat exchanger sat on the opposite side of the engine bay.

The engine was supported by regular A frames picked up by the short transaxle, which was an integral FORCE design with the oil tank extending from the bellhousing back over the diff housing. The magnesium transaxle case carried small yokes to support the push rod rockers and contained a FORCE modified FGB with DGB c.w.p. and a FORCE modified Salisbury diff, accessed via a single sideplate.

The THL1 was equipped with cast iron discs as SEP was finding it hard to meet the demand for its carbon-carbon products from its existing teams, leaving the newcomer low on its list. The THL1 first turned its Dymags at Snetterton in August '85. Two examples were produced for the team's short season and the suspension was revised to incorporate anti-dive for Kyalami. A revised heat exchanger overcame the early oil cooling problem and the water cooling system was improved for '86. The third THL1 produced for that year's stop-gap Hart campaign had originally been equipped with Ford engine mounts but had been converted to Hart specification as the winter V6 testing went by the board.

FORCE carbon fibre monocoque
Semi-stressed engine
Push rod front and rear suspension - Koni dampers
Dymag magnesium rims
AP cast iron discs, outboard
Single AP four pot calipers - Ferodo pads
Carbon fibre bodywork
1 Secan water radiator - 1 Secan oil heat exchanger
1 Secan air:air aftercooler
AP twin plate clutch
Hewland/FORCE six-speed gearbox - Salisbury diff
220 litre ATL fuel cell - 10 litre oil tank
Saft battery - VDO instruments
2794mm. wheelbase; 1803mm. front track; 1626mm. rear
540kg.

RAM 02

Ralston Auto Tech carbon fibre/Kevlar and aluminium monocoque
Semi-stressed engine
Pull rod front and rear suspension - Koni dampers
Speedline aluminium and magnesium rims
SEP carbon-carbon discs, outboard
Twin AP two pot calipers - SEP pads
Carbon fibre/Kevlar bodywork
1 Behr water radiator - 1 Secan oil heat exchanger
1 Behr air:air aftercooler
AP twin plate clutch
Hewland six-speed gearbox - Salisbury diff
220 litre Marston fuel cell - 10 litre oil tank
Saft battery - Smiths and VDO instruments
2769mm. wheelbase; 1765mm. front track, 1607mm. rear
565kg.

RAM's first Hart car was the converted Cosworth chassis with which it commenced turbo testing. Aside from engine installation, the conversion entailed a longer, taller tank which, in conjunction with the Hart block added 77mm. to the wheelbase. Significantly, the definitive 02 was 20kg. lighter, thanks partly to the use of carbon-carbon brakes. It also had a lighter, stiffer monocoque thanks to the incorporation of carbon fibre and Kevlar, the 01 design having had a purely aluminium skinned RAT tub.

The '84 monocoque was produced in two sections: the exposed lower half was of aluminium honeycomb construction while the upper section had carbon fibre/Kevlar skins over an aluminium honeycomb core. The two halves were glued and riveted together around five aluminium bulkheads. The tub design followed the pattern of the converted 01 chassis.

The Hart engine was carried between regular steel A-frames picked up by a RAM oil tank/bellhousing, designed for the 01, to which was bolted a Hewland FGB with RAM end cover. Crossmembers carried the suspension. The differential was a Williams modified Salisbury, the team doing a certain amount of sub-contract work for Williams.

Running between the front and rear wheels were unusually long sidepods, with straight side panels. The pod lids blended into a deck that spanned the width between the rear wheels, with either side an unusual fence which followed a rounded wheel clearance instep. The rear treatment left the engine completely concealed. Cooling was taken care of by an aftercooler in the left-hand pod and water radiator on the opposite side, both running lengthwise along the respective slab sided pod and slanted upwards to top vent. The heat exchanger sat behind the water radiator, opposite the turbo, while on the left a side panel duct provided the compressor feed.

The bodywork came in three sections - nose; cockpit coaming/tank cover/pod lids; engine shroud/rear deck. With a high tank and awk-ward lines, the 02 didn't look particularly elegant. It carried its rear wing via a horizontal post between end-plates and no diffuser was provided. The team didn't have the budget for wind tunnel work and essentially carried over its '83 aerodynamic package, adapted to turbo requirements.

After a brief Silverstone shakedown, the first proper 02 was sorted in the heat of the Brazilian Grand Prix and, like the modified 01 sister car quickly discarded its engine shroud. Louvres were cut in the rear cover for Kyalami but still charge temperatures were too high. Consequently, for Zolder, which saw the introduction of a second 02 model, there were fundamental cooling modifications. The cooler rake was increased from 15 to 30 degrees and the bodywork was altered, the car featuring modified sidepods, shorter with higher leading edge. A reshaped, more rounded rear cover to improve flow to the rear wing was planned but could not be introduced before Montreal due to the pressures of the race programme.

As the season progressed the cars were shedding rear bodywork on a regular basis, Hart recommending an unshrouded engine. Carbon-carbon discs were only run in qualifying. The rear suspension was beefed up after a failure at Kyalami and front suspension geometry was revised between Detroit and Dallas, the re-design work carried out by Nigel Stroud on a consultancy basis. In Dallas the original carbon fibre/Kevlar top monocoque was written off; 02/03 was duly prepared for Brands Hatch.

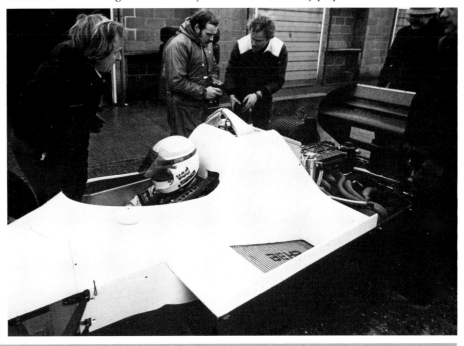

RAM 03

Ralston Auto Tech carbon fibre/Kevlar monocoque
Semi-stressed engine
Pull rod front and rear suspension - Koni dampers
BBS aluminium and magnesium rims
AP cast iron discs, outboard
Single AP four pot calipers - Ferodo pads
Carbon fibre bodywork
1 Behr water radiator - 1 Secan oil heat exchanger
1 Behr air:air aftercooler
AP twin plate clutch
Hewland/RAM six-speed gearbox - RAM diff
220 litre ATL fuel cell - 10 litre oil tank
Varley battery - VDO instruments
2794mm. wheelbase; 1778mm. front track, 1626mm. rear
540kg.

For Brunner, the RAM 03 followed his ATS D6 and D7 designs, the former pioneering the concept of carefully sculpturing a composite monocoque to form cockpit coaming. The 03 took his innovative thinking further along the same lines, in the light of what he had learned at Alfa Romeo, where he had enjoyed access to a wind tunnel for the first time in his Formula car career. He started work for RAM in late October '84, having arrived with outline plans. For budgetary reasons he had to produce the 03 without reference to tunnel research.

The 03 was a brand new car - every last nut and bolt was new - making extensive use of carbon fibre. It featured a new integral magnesium transaxle case produced by Kent Aerospace Castings. Brunner's narrow case had only one side-plate, which accessed a unique cam and pawl- type diff entirely designed by him and built in house. The c.w.p. was also bespoke, while gearbox internals were repackaged, heavily modified FGB with only 3rd, 4th and 5th standard Hewland gears, the others produced by RAM. The monocoque was again made by RAT. It had an aluminium honeycomb core and was moulded as upper and lower sections, with carbon fibre/Kevlar bulkheads inserted. It formed the entire fuselage shape ahead of the engine, aside from nose cone and short pods.

Brunner kept the 03's monocoque as small, as slim as possible - the cockpit was a narrow as was practical and the front tapered sharply ahead of a bubble-shaped cockpit wind deflector. Behind the driver the tank top blended into a roll pyramid while its lower portion, hidden below sidepod level, was notched in each flank. The notches tapered in plan to the width of the Hart block. Thus, the rear bulkhead was T- shaped. The notches allowed the coolers, set on edge lengthwise either side of the tank and splayed outwards, to be recessed, tucking them closer to the centreline. The notches left an awkward-shaped tank cavity, requiring an irregularly shaped 220 litre cell to be produced by ATL.

The cooler area Brunner provided was not generous, nor was the ducting. The coolers were relatively small, helping keep the pods short and low. Tucked in at the rear end, they almost touched the block and they vented into an enclosed engine bay. The pod lids and side panels were closed and the side panels swept inwards in pronounced bottleneck-plan fashion, dramatically narrowing the air escape channel. The idea was that the wake behind the car would be strong enough to suck the hot air out of the small rear opening around the gearbox.

Designed to allow the rear fuselage to be as unobtrusive as possible, the rear of the car was very tightly packaged indeed. Brunner set the aftercooler on the right for a clean exit channel while a heat exchanger plumbed into the radiator piping was made wide and flat so it could be crammed in above the turbo. The engine sat between conventional A frames picked up by the new RAM transaxle, which supported the rear suspension with the anti roll bar actually passing through the bellhousing. The cramped engine bay was closed by a tight fitting, all enveloping cover that splayed to form flat pod lids and narrow tail deck.

The 03 sported a typical vee-six-type wing and underbody package, with conventional front and rear wings, plus a diffuser rising under the bottleneck tail. It rolled on Speedline-pattern BBS wheels in recognition of a deal between Winkelhock and the German wheel company, and ran cast iron discs for reasons of economy. However, there was also a tactical consideration - should the horde on carbon-carbon run into problems, RAM would be well set.

The prototype 03 barked in anger for the first time at Silverstone in February, just prior to shipment to the Rio test, and overheated in spite of freezing temperatures. In the heat of the southern sun, the rear cover was extensively cut about and the oil heat exchanger was switched for a conventional oil radiator accommodated in a cutout in the right side diffuser tunnel lest it was contributing to high water temperatures. However, the problem persisted, to the extent that the rear cover had to be dispensed with altogether for extended running.

Back at base, Brunner revised his cooler layout for the second chassis which emerged at Donington in mid March. It had modified inlet ducting and longer coolers which were no longer set on edge, but which slanted upwards from the horizontal plane, RAM 02 fashion. This allowed longer coolers, and louvres were set into the rear cover, while the tail shroud was shortened for better air extraction. For hot Rio, the diffuser was removed for the same reason. Assisted by an aftercooler water spray, the new cooler arrangement kept water and charge temperature under control. The prototype having been sent to Rio as modified at the test with additional water radiators replacing the diffuser, it was actually overwater cooled, and it was modified to match the newer car after the first day's running.

The diffuser was replaced for the rest of the season, over which the car remained essentially in its revised cooling guise. It occasionally sported a two tier rear wing and only on rare occasions were carbon-carbon discs fitted. A spare car was available from Imola while chassis number 4 was brought on stream at Silverstone. It featured a tub with revised composite construction for marginally improved rigidity as a natural progression from the original design.

For '86 the chassis received new coolers and a water system to Hart specifications, plus revised mounts to accept the modified Hart block.

SPIRIT 101B

John Thompson aluminium honeycomb monocoque
Semi-stressed engine
Rocker arm front and rear suspension - Koni dampers
Dymag magnesium rims
AP cast iron discs, outboard
Single AP four pot calipers - Ferodo pads
G.r.p bodywork
2 Serck water radiators - 1 Serck oil radiator
1 Behr air:air aftercooler
AP twin plate clutch
Hewland six-speed gearbox - Salisbury diff
220 litre Marston fuel cell - 10 litre oil tank
Varley battery - Smiths instruments
2718mm. wheelbase; 1956mm. front track, 1600mm. rear
560kg.

The prototype 101B was an adaptation of a chassis designed to accept a fully stressed vee-six engine. Coppuck designed a neat adapter plate to bolt to the back of his outmoded monocoque and incorporated a tube in the base of the casting to take the charge from the compressor to the aftercooler which, unusually, was to the right of the engine. The car shunned conventional sidepods and the aftercooler ran on edge lengthwise, alongside the block, angled back from the rear bulkhead towards the rear wheels. Consequently, its top exit lay close to the Hart plenum chamber. This simple, functional layout offered short plumbing, minimising throttle lag.

Water and oil radiator positioning reflected the

aftercooler location, flanking the block to the left, the concept of exposed rear mounted coolers echoing '83 Brabham practice. The engine was carried between conventional A-frames which linked the adapter plate to a new bellhousing with integral oil tank, to which an FGB gearbox was bolted. Wide transaxle yokes provided rocker pivot support.

With the longer block of the in line four the wheelbase grew from 2540mm. but the alloy 415T and lack of sidepods saw the car to weigh a full 25kg. less, in spite of the engine cradle. The existing monocoque accommodated a 220 litre tank and an extension of a detachable tank cover shrouded the engine bay from cooler to cooler. A single tier rear wing was supported between end-plates by a horizontal post.

The 101B was first run at a wet Brands Hatch in January '84, then was promptly shipped to Rio where the heat dictated removal of the rear cover. Subsequently, Coppuck designed a new fairing that concealed the tank and flared out to meet the coolers, but was cut away over the block. Of this Hart approved, and in this guise the car raced at Rio. For Kyalami there was vertical post support for a revised rear wing, and the underbody was shortened.

A second 101B chassis appeared at Zolder, purpose built as a Hart car with a tidying up of details where appropriate. Whereas the weight of the original car had been shaved down to 556kg, this came in at 550kg. It was due to have sported a new pull rod front suspension but lack of funds had left that development on the drawing board. 'B2' commenced its career as Spirit's race car at Monte Carlo, while, faced with a Hart engine shortage, Coppuck buckled down to the task of converting B1 to Cosworth power.

The conversion job involved reversion to a

Honda-type rear end with short sidepods housing a water and an oil cooler for each cylinder bank. Dubbed '101C', the modified chassis was only required at Detroit and was subsequently converted back to Hart specification, to continue spare car duties. At the Nurburgring 'B' specification was altered through the installation of a 50mm. wheelbase spacer between the engine and oil tank.

101B1 was pensioned off at the end of the season and Coppuck modified B2 to produce '101D' with push rod front suspension and revised rear end aerodynamics. The suspension utilised the existing mounts while the rear end modifications involved revised cooler positions.

The water radiator (left) and aftercooler (right) were each set alongside the tank, on edge lengthwise and splayed outwards across a short pod. The square cut pods were side and rear vented, and, extending no further back than the tank, the entire engine bay was left open. The oil radiator sat behind the aftercooler, the turbo behind the water radiator. Air was fed to the compressor from a funnel shaped inlet set into the adjacent pod side panel. The undertray blended into a short diffuser.

Raced at Rio and Estoril, Baldi's shunt in the latter race left the 101D1 tub a write off, and it was replaced by the third Thompson 101 monocoque for Spirit's final event, at Imola.

TOLEMAN TG184

Advanced Composite Technology carbon fibre/Kevlar monocoque
Semi-stressed engine
Pull rod front suspension, push rod rear - Koni dampers
Dymag magnesium rims
AP cast iron discs, outboard
Single Brembo four pot calipers - Ferodo pads
Kevlar bodywork
1 Behr combined water and oil radiator
1 Behr air:air aftercooler
AP twin plate clutch
Hewland/Toleman six-speed gearbox - Salisbury diff
220 litre Marston fuel cell - 10 litre oil tank
Saft battery - Smiths instruments
2692mm. wheelbase; 1816mm. front track, 1676mm. rear
540kg.

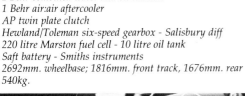

The TG184 was a development from the 1983 model with which Toleman started the '84 season. The TG183B had its roots firmly in the ground effect era, being an adaptation of a 1982 design to flat bottom specification. It was a 2692mm. wheelbase car with ACT monocoque, modified Hewland FGB and pull rod suspension which carried its 415T semi-stressed via A-frames. Its conversion to flat bottom specification had introduced a radical aerodynamic and cooling package, incorporating a diffuser at the front. As that upset the flow to the sidepods Byrne had positioned the water radiators on it, ahead of the front wheels. Small aftercoolers sat in short pods either side of the tank, and the car featured a unique twin rear wing arrangement.

The TG183B had been little changed for the '84 season: there was improved gearbox cooling, a revised fuel system and a consumption read out for the driver. Design of the replacement TG184 had started late in '83, the team awaiting confirmation of its engine deal and completion of its rolling road wind tunnel at Shrivenham. Due to budget constraints, and lack of in house facilities, the TG184 retained the existing, 1982 vintage monocoque, which had upper and lower sections moulded by ACT and Toleman's own composite bulkheads. The core was aluminium honeycomb, except around the fuel tank area where Nomex was employed as insulation to help slow the chilled fuel's temperature rise.

Like the 183, the new car carried an FGB main case with Toleman side plates and end cover, which was bolted to a new magnesium oil tank/bellhousing. The wheelbase remained the "106 inch" measurement preferred by Byrne. The suspension was completely new, front and rear, as was the engine systems layout and the aerodynamics. In the light of the fuel restriction Byrne sought improved cooling without additional drag, top end power not the Hart's strong suit. Using the new tunnel, Byrne and Symonds found a claimed 25% downforce improvement for the TG184, with improved cooling and no drag penalty.

The TG184 abandoned the distinctive front radiator set up for greater control over front end aerodynamics and less pitch sensitivity, improving drivability. It sported conventional front wings, with an unusual treatment of their trailing edges, which were swept back. The TG184 located all its coolers in lengthened sidepods that ran alongside the cockpit. It was a pioneering

design in its employment of vertically mounted coolers; aftercooler on the left, water/oil radiator on the right. The coolers were generous in proportion and, splaying away from the tank ran to full sidepod length. The pods were left open at the rear, the coolers venting into an engine bay that was left uncloaked at Hart's behest.

With a 700mm. span for each cooler, the TG184 had a larger cooler surface area than any rival car. Byrne explains: "we went conservative on cooling. The Hart needed to run at 80 degrees centigrade - 15 degrees lower than any other engine - requiring more cooling capacity. And we were now running the water radiator behind the front wheels".

While the bodywork stopped short just aft of the tank, the underbody extended back, below the transaxle, not to form a prominent diffuser but to carry Byrne's unique twin rear wing package. Mindful of the 1000mm width restriction behind the rear wheel axis, Byrne placed a wider wing immediately ahead of it. Its end-plates, reaching down to the undertray, curved around the front of the wheels. The curved end-plates isolated the wing's underside flow from the high pressure caused by tyre rotation. Byrne additionally placed a lower, 1000mm. wide wing

behind the rear wheel axis, its end-plates connected by links to the primary wing's end-plates.

The TG184's monocoque carried an integral nose box and was angular with wedge shaped nose topped by wedge shaped scuttle, while a flat, broad shouldered tank carried a tubular roll hoop. It was completely shrouded, a single moulding concealing the tub and forming flat, closed pod lids. The compressor feed was from an oval duct in the rear of the left-hand pod.

The TG184 was first run at Brands Hatch soon after the Kyalami race and took part in pre-race testing at Zolder, if not in the race itself. As a result of the early tests vents were set into the upper region of each side panel to assist hot air extraction. Three chassis were prepared for the model's Dijon debut and a fourth was introduced at Brands Hatch, allowing 01 to assume the role of team test car. A fifth chassis was introduced at Hockenheim, with a single rear wing carrying fashionable winglets. The twin rear wing had created high downforce, but at a relatively high drag penalty. The high speed aerodynamic package was the only significant alteration to the basic specification.

TOLEMAN TG185

Toleman carbon fibre/Kevlar monocoque
Semi-stressed engine
Pull rod front suspension, push rod rear - Koni dampers
Dymag magnesium rims
Brembo front, AP rear cast iron discs, outboard
Single Brembo four pot calipers - Ferodo pads
Carbon fibre/Kevlar bodywork
1 Secan water radiator - 1 Toleman/Serck oil heat exchanger
1 Behr air:air aftercooler
AP twin plate clutch
Hewland/Toleman six-speed gearbox - Salisbury diff
220 litre Marston fuel cell - 9 litre oil tank
Saft battery - VDO instruments
2692mm. wheelbase; 1816mm. front track, 1682mm. rear
540kg.

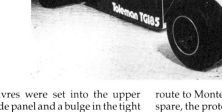

Byrne was able to start the production of the TG185 six months before the start of the new season, to produce a monocoque in house, and to produce an integral transaxle case. Unlike its immediate predecessor, the TG185 was a no compromise car and it inherited only its clutch pedal. With the Shrivenham tunnel operational for a year it benefited from; "a lot more wind tunnel work".

The TG185's monocoque shell was produced as a single moulding using vacuum bag and oven rather than an autoclave. It had an aluminium honeycomb core and was designed so that one piece bulkheads could be threaded into it. Whereas the previous ACT tub had been taper sided in response to wing car considerations, the in house production was slab sided, and formed the cockpit coaming (offering a wedge shaped scuttle) and tank shroud-cum-pyramid roll hoop.

Behind the monocoque, the engine was a little more heavily stressed and the bespoke transaxle case was slimmer, with a smooth exterior. Produced by Sterling Metals, its integral design made it stiffer and lighter, saving perhaps 5kg. Gearbox internals were again modified FGB, while the engine bay was shrouded for the first time. Byrne admits that the unshrouded engine had been a penalty in terms of aerodynamic efficiency, one that was intolerable given the narrow rear wing dictated by the '85 regulations. The TG184's efficient cooler layout was retained, with a water-only radiator in the right-hand pod, an oil heat exchanger to Byrne's design behind it.

Unlike the TG184, the TG185 continued its clothing back behind the coolers, the pod cover sweeping inwards to blend with a snug fitting engine shroud which extended as far as the

bellhousing. Louvres were set into the upper portion of each side panel and a bulge in the tight rear cover told of the location of the plenum chamber.

Byrne did not shroud the transaxle, but set short diffuser tunnels either side of the diff housing and a wing further back, at gearbox level. This wing, operating in ground effect was part of a three tier wing package, the tiers connected via joint end-plates and the assembly supported by the ground effect wing's connection to the gearbox. The effect of that low-set wing was to help draw air through the diffuser tunnels, though it created quite a bit of downforce in its own right.

At the front, Byrne's typically innovative aerodynamic package allowed for a vee-plan underbody step that cut the air like a snow-plough, deflecting it to the sides of the car to help create low pressure over the flat bottom. Located under the nose, the step (which echoed the vee plan formed by the trailing edges of the TG184-type front wings) was about 25mm. deep. It was kept in reserve, until the campaign reached the fast circuits.

While the TG185 retained Brembo front calipers, Byrne switched to AP at the rear, considering its smaller, lighter unit was more appropriate.

The TG185 prototype was shaken down at Silverstone in January, running on old Pirelli tyres found in the store room. Lapping on Brabham cast off Pirellis at the Rio test proved its cooling was efficient and that it was potentially very competitive. Alas, little progress could be made thereafter until May, when Pirelli tyres were made available. Chassis 03 was the first run under the new deal, in a test at Paul Ricard en

route to Monte Carlo. In Monaco Fabi had 02 as spare, the prototype having been assigned to the test team. A fourth chassis allowed 02 to be replaced from Paul Ricard while a fifth chassis appeared with the arrival of Ghinzani at the Osterreichring. The model was not significantly modified over the season, other than for the use of a high speed aerodynamic package which featured the underbody step plus wing refinements. It was first fitted at Silverstone. Larger, heavier Brembo calipers were run at the rear on heavy braking circuits.

By Allan Staniforth

Honda Research and
Development Co. Ltd.
Wako
Nr. Tokyo
Japan

If the word "inscrutable" had not already been in the dictionaries for some years, somebody would have had to invent it for the Japanese. At a push, "incomprehensible" might have deputised for Western minds, right from the secretive beginnings of Honda's fabulous 1.5 litre turbo engine, through the short-lived deal and parting from Spirit, up to the parting of the ways with Frank Williams and his world-beating team. The announcement, in March 1983, of the much rumoured Formula One power unit, probably one of the biggest single investments in research in the history of the company, was stark to the point of emaciation. Technical information since then has been sparse. Early in 1988 Formula One Project Leader and Chief Engineer Osamu Goto was able to kindly supply some engine facts to *Racecar Engineering*. However, his superiors dictated that, in addition to the usual veil over bore and stroke and compression ratio, there should be secrecy regarding piston material and number of rings, liner material and coating, valve angles, sizes and operation, type of main bearings and even the weight of the engine.

It was not much different if we go back to the very beginning, well over 20 years ago. Vastly experienced and hugely successful with motorcycles, the bedrock of Soichiro Honda's massive enterprise, in the early Sixties the company decided to attempt the same domination on four wheels. By 1964 work was well advanced - in secret, of course - on an approach it knew best; a multi-cylinder, multi-cammed and valved, highly complex unit with tiny pistons achieving almost unheard-of r.p.m. At the end of the year RA-271 was announced: an unblown 1500cc. V12 to be installed transversely behind the driver in Honda's own chassis.

During the winter of '64/'65 Honda looked for an experienced driver who would be unknown in Europe, and found Ronnie Bucknam to conduct the modified RA-272. This was said at the time to be in accord with a "low key approach" but for the unfortunate American it meant only "low results" - two points for a single fifth place finish, to be exact. It was not actually anywhere near as bad as that as the construction of a second car for Ritchie Ginther, an American driver of world calibre, produced victory in Mexico, with contemporary press remarks like "potentially dominating".

Nobody will ever know, as the winter of '65/'66 saw Formula One regulations changed to 1500cc blown/3000cc normally aspirated. Honda decided in favour of the latter option and in quite remarkably short order produced RA-273: a complex 90 degree V12 with 48 valves, roller bearings everywhere, massively bulky with weight to match, officially producing 420b.h.p. at 10,000r.p.m. Its debut season brought the first mention of Yoshio Nakamura, who was then not only master-minding the current 1.0 litre, 16-valve screamers pushing Jack Brabham and Denny Hulme to 11 consecutive victories and the Formula Two title, but had spent much of the previous winter laying out the Formula One V12 as well.

RA-273 was, in essence, two 1500cc. V6s end-to-end, with the power take-off in the middle, and Nakamura was to draw on the memory for his Eighties turbo engine. Working with him in '66 was Nobuhiko Kawamoto, who would 20 years later be President of Honda R and D, while his older colleague had retired to honoured but still active consultancy.

Late to get going, and carrying a gigantic 150/200kg. reputed overweight despite an alloy monocoque chassis, the RA-273 powered 'F-101' was nevertheless driven by Ginther to determined fourth and fifth place finishes plus a fastest lap before a massive accident at Monza left it written off. That necessitated the hasty construction of F-102 and F-103. A major re-think by Honda about the problems of drivers, car building and race teams operating on the other side of the world brought into being a deal with John Surtees for 1967.

Surtees was not only a motorcycle world champion of immense stature, but was a successful convert to four wheels. He would set up his own base in Slough with Kawamoto and another engineer and would soldier on with faithful RA-273/F-102 (and 103 as the spare car) while building a new chassis. Heavily drawing upon Eric Broadley's Lola T190 Indy Car, the replacement took rapid shape, with a new version of the V12 in the back, coded RA-300/1. It was a formidable year, both in work and achievement. The F-102 chassis was persuaded to work with radical modification and managed some useful placings. The RA-300/1 powered car did not debut until Monza but did so in impressive fashion, winning the Italian Grand Prix. Over the season as a whole Surtees collected sufficient points to claim fourth place in the World Championship. Considering the difficulties to be overcome, both technical and in the distance between Tokyo and Slough, it was an impressive performance.

The winter of '67/'68 found Honda not only further developing its existing engine, but also creating a totally new 3.0 litre V12, this time a 120 degree engine to be carried by an all-new Japanese chassis and air cooled: RA-302. The 1968 season began with much promise, ingenuity and developing success, but was marred with tragedy and finally spelled Honda's exit from Formula One for more than a decade. Using the water cooled car, Surtees took pole at Monza and was runner up in the French Grand Prix, but sadly during that meeting Frenchman Jo Schlesser had a massive accident in the air cooled car and died from his injuries.

Designer Len Terry was called in to draw a replacement for the air cooled machine, but it was too near the end of the season for full development and the marque declined to compete in 1969. It had decided that consolidating world car markets was more important than flag waving in Formula One. Kawamoto and Nakamura slotted back into Honda's separate and largely independent R & D department at Wako to nurture a new generation of engineers. It was to be 12 years before the name of Honda was even whispered in connection with Formula One, and 14 before it showed its hand.

Early Eighties turbo engines were meeting every type of difficulty from electronic injection, engine management, high boost, structural failure, heat and still more heat. Not to mention the dreaded throttle lag. Honda recalled the painful lesson of jumping in at the deep end in distant 1964 and had decided to slide sideways back onto the European scene via 2.0 litre Formula Two. They had an excellent iron block 80 degree V6 for that project, on which to build a Formula One future. The engine was designed by Nakamura, and was built and developed by a team of young engineers.

Training promising engineers through the tough battleground of motor racing was an important motivation behind the project, aside from flag waving, as it had been in the Sixties. The team supervised by Nakamura travelled to Europe to work with an old ally of his, Ron Tauranac - partner of Jack Brabham in the good old 1.0 litre Formula Two days. The 350b.h.p. RA-263 Formula Two engine was unveiled mid season in 1980 at Silverstone and went on to win the 1981 European Championship with Ralt, and not a little advice and work put in by John Judd (in spite of problems with Bridgestone tyres and Bosch electronic injection, switched for Lucas mechanical). Spirit, a new team created by March Formula Two Team Manager John Wickham and Engineer Gordon Coppuck had also used the Judd-assisted engine.

By 1982 work was well advanced on a 1500cc. turbocharged spin-off of RA-263. Behind closed doors, discussion took place with Ralt and Spirit as to a deal to race the Formula One engine. Having sold Brabham to Bernie Ecclestone many years before, Tauranac admit-ted at the time that he had Indy Car racing rather than a return to Formula One as a personal ambition. It may well not be pure coincidence that a Honda Indy engine project subsequently surfaced, linked with John Judd and one of Brabham's sons. That V8 evolved into the Judd Indy and (3.5 litre) Formula One engines.

Spirit was keen to get into Formula One, and was given a deal, though after, one suspects, delicate approaches to established teams had not met with any great enthusiasm? On the Formula Two front 1982 was a disappointing year, but by the end of it the prototype turbocharged engine was track testing in a converted Spirit Formula Two car. The wraps officially came off RA-163-E at the Geneva Motor Show in March 1983.

It was a low-key unveiling on the Honda stand: an engine looking very much like a contemporary Formula Two V6 with a turbo system added, a few smiling Japanese faces, and a press pack containing three stapled sheets of A4 paper and four black and white photographs. A few hours later Porsche/TAG generated rather more excitement in a packed conference room downstairs with a panel of recognisable personalities and a glossy press pack to help to announce its brand new 80 degree V6 Formula One engine. However, again hard engine facts were scant.

The Honda technical information could not cover a single sheet of A4 paper - it admitted only: liquid cooled, four-valve d.o.h.c. 80 degree V6; CD ignition; dry sump; dry multi-plate clutch; Honda Electric Fuel Injection / PGMFI (Programmed fuel injection system - developed for F2 and F1 engines and also used in City-turbo); twin KKK type K 26 turbochargers; maximum output over 600b.h.p. Much of this was fairly obvious to anyone not covering the show with the help of a white stick and guide dog, and "over 600b.h.p." was the going turbo rate for the time.

The external similarity to the Formula Two engine suggested Honda had retained its 90mm. bore in search of high revs and that left 39.35mm. as the stroke that would give the quoted displacement of "1.5 liters" (sic). Were these correct? Polite oriental silence. Study of the cam covers suggested wide angle valves - perhaps a 40 degree included angle - and an ultra large bore. "Didn't they?" The silence remained unbroken.

There was nothing wrong with Honda's timing: 1982 had seen turbo cars at last taking a decisive 1st, 2nd and 3rd at Monza, the last race in Europe. In 1983 the Cosworth cars would fight a gallant rearguard action - but lose. Spirit tested extensively prior to a debut at the Brands Hatch Race of Champions, then joined the World Championship trail at Silverstone, still employing a converted Formula Two chassis. It contested six Grands Prix, finishing in three albeit well down the field. However, Honda had already decided upon a parting of the ways, having announced in mid season that it would be changing horses. It was apparent that Spirit was too new and too small an outfit to cope with Honda and its high ambitions. For three full seasons, starting with 1984, Williams Grand Prix Engineering would get free engines and maintenance.

Through the ground effect era Williams had established itself as a Top Team, winning three world titles in four years with Cosworth powered cars. However, 1982 World Champion Rosberg found his 1983 FW08 hopelessly under-powered: a new era had dawned. Having struck the agreement with Honda, Williams and his Technical Director Patrick Head decided to get in on that era as soon as possible, preparing the first Honda-Williams RA-163-E-FW09 for a debut in the season-closing Kyalami race.

With some furious design and build work they made it - just - despite the engines arriving virtually bare. Head was later to reflect: "we had to improvise a lot. Honda hadn't the least idea of heat generated or air consumed once the engine was in a car. We had to do the whole installation ourselves. The FW09 chassis was not particularly good, but the problem was not lack of rigidity (the criticism at the time) but the transition from Cosworth to turbo - starting to try and put 800/1000b.h.p. through wheels of limited size".

WGPE successfully got the latest, "D-spec" RA-163-E not only onto the grid, but into the points with fifth place for Rosberg. Probably as much due to Rosberg's incomparable talent with a virtually untried new car equipped with a power unit that went off like a bomb when the power came in. It was a considerable feat which provided a wealth of information for winter development. That included Rosberg's view, not only that the (considerable) power came in "explosively", but that it was confined to a tiny powerband, and there was bad throttle lag.

RA163-E
80 degree V6

Bore and stroke undisclosed
2 IHI turbochargers
Iron block, aluminium heads
Liner material and coating undisclosed
4 main bearings, plain
Steel crankshaft, 3 pins
Steel con rods
Honda pistons, material undisclosed
Honda rings
4 o.h.c., gear driven
4 valves/cylinder, 1 plug
Valve sizes undisclosed
Included valve angle undisclosed
Honda ignition
Honda injection
Honda engine management system
Compression ratio undisclosed
Maximum r.p.m. 12,000
Weight undisclosed

Honda took the attitude that its engine could only be as good as its turbocharger and engine management system and consequently produced as much as possible in house, while popping round the corner for turbochargers rather than continuing to rely on general supplier KKK. The Ishikawajima Harima Heavy Industries (IHI) company was willing to do special development work for the programme. Separation of the engine into effectively two banks with a plenum chamber above each fed by its own turbo was discarded experimentally in favour of a single plenum chamber. A lengthy series of experiments over the winter of '83/'84 included comparisons of butterflies against slides, in single, twin and multi versions to each inlet port. Plenum chambers were split, joined, tapered, buffer-ended. Injectors were doubled, pointed upstream and downstream, relocated and variously pressured.

Specific fuel consumption on the bench was poor but even this did not prevent a series of spectacular piston failures, later repeated under race conditions. And, worst of all, the block was showing clear signs of unhappiness at having its already excellent race output doubled. Any flexing would obviously lower reliability, as well as producing handling problems in any car in which it was a stressed member, having to cope with suspension, shock and torsion loads of large magnitude.

The casual observer of later triumphs tends to forget that Honda was by no means an early steamroller over the opposition, but suffered a vast range of horrific and expensive problems during initial development. High on Patrick Head's list for the '84 version FW09 was a six-speed gearbox to deal with a powerband reputedly lying only between 10,300 and 11,400r.p.m. on these early 'D-spec' engines. But the car in which it was to be mounted would stay an aluminium honeycomb conception as there was more than enough for Williams to handle shoe-horning the heavy, untidily packaged and only partly developed Honda in. Formula One had an even greater obsession with being overweight than a top model and Honda was at this point some 20kg. heavier than the seven year old slimline Renault V6, and it did not make Head's job one little bit easier.

With total responsibility for the technical side of WGPE, Head had lost the freedom to discuss an engine problem by telephone within seconds, or even resolve it with a quick rush to Northampton for the afternoon to see Keith Duckworth's team. There was not only half a world between Didcot and Wako, there was a nine hour time difference as well. Engines would have to go back and forth for rebuild and modification for it would be another 18 months before Honda would set up a base within the Didcot factory, and 1984 really highlighted the reasons why.

Early track testing with the IHI turbos rapidly showed one thing. Whatever power they gave, it still came in like a sledgehammer, though the bottom end of the power band was edging downwards towards 9,500r.p.m. Throughout its early life, the RA-163-E had been equipped with Hitachi electronics, but as with KKK turbos Honda was not totally happy with this. The job of developing the engine management system was taken over by Honda-owned Kikaki, which ensured that secrets went on staying in-house.

The 1984 season opened on a high note: second place "out of the box" at Rio for Rosberg, though teammate Laffite had to call it a day after 15 laps due to "electrical trouble" - still more than enough to induce palpitations in the hearts of the opposition. They need not have worried, at least not for this year. Although there was an even better first place at Dallas in mid season, again down to Rosberg, combined with a handful of lowlier placings, the rest of the year was total disaster.

The FW09 chassis - one of the "last of the metal honeycombs" - gained a probably undeserved reputation at the time for flexibility and gross understeer. Hindsight later pointed to both violent power with throttle lag and doubtful engine rigidity as the more likely culprits. The "instant" power characteristics of the short stroke V6 were giving the front tyres inputs of such suddenness and magnitude that they found it barely possible to cope. Further, the block was probably insufficiently rigid to hold the back end and suspension in precise place. The Goodyear shod, Mobil fuelled FW09 started as a short stubby car based on the earlier 08 and in mid season underwent a radical 125mm. wheelbase extension, while a lot of research, as usual, went into aerodynamics, but now additional downforce was desperately needed to deal with what was defined as "wheelspin anywhere, in any gear at almost any speed".

Aerodynamic improvement was assisted in mid season by the relocation of the twin turbos through a revised exhaust manifold, and WGPE produced the improved but still troubled FW09B. Throughout, the car was equipped with a dash board boost control and a very sensitive fuel gauge, capable of giving both a consumption rate figure and the amount of fuel remaining. Two way radio, battery operated via a small whip aerial gave the driver and pit direct communication with each other at all times.

Honda had taken eight engines to Rio, still using the 'old' split plenum chamber, but with twin injectors for each inlet tract to each cylinder. Over the course of the season the RA-163-E powered Rosberg to seven starting positions from the top two rows (two of them from outside pole) and just those two worthy rostrum finishes. In total, Rosberg managed nine points finishes, Laffite two. A total of 23 D.N.F.'s, 13 of them in one unlucky unbroken run, was not entirely Honda's fault. There were chassis failures, too, but broken exhausts, turbos, electronics, pistons or otherwise shattered engine parts littered the year and Honda's museum of horrors. This despite thousands upon thousands of hours of work and experiment by Honda and Williams engineers and technicians.

By the time of the last race at Estoril (Rosberg, engine failure at 39 laps; Laffite 14th) the more unkind paddock wits were joking that "it looks like fall-on-your-sword time" for the Japanese. Whether they heard or understood such an irreverent Western jibe, it made no difference. The battle had been lost. The war was still on.

Back at the ranch, Honda was reputed to have built 25 different engine specifications for its winter test programme, each a significant variation on the theme, as part of a ferocious attack on its shortcomings. It would produce a massively modified (yet still officially "D-spec") engine with lowered and re-sited turbos, modified exhaust system, flattened plenum chamber, inlet tract alterations, not counting those invisible refinements to combustion chambers, piston tops, turbo wheels, scrolls and materials, valve timing and electronics. Simultaneously, Williams was making the leap to its first advanced composite chassis, moulded in-house and tailored to new and stiffer engine mountings due on the 1985 engine.

Honda engineers, in a rare admission of defeat, had been unable to improve on the brilliantly ingenious top engine mounting brackets devised by Duckworth for the DFV - triangular, angled plates bolted to the cam covers that gave total rigidity in the planes in which it was needed, while still flexing to accommodate expansion and contraction under heat of the whole engine. Similar devices had appeared on the Honda cam boxes.

The awful season of 1984, far from crushing the Williams team had galvanised it in all sorts of directions. They embraced advanced materials and production techniques, together with a major aerodynamic study programme for the new FW10 chassis. New driver Mansell (replacing Laffite) brought with him highly valuable experience of the rival Renault turbo. While the opening season results of 1985 were not dramatic, perceptive watchers soon spotted the major difference. The cars were crossing the finishing as well as the start line, and both Rosberg and Mansell were moving the better handling FW10 up the grid in practice. It spelled a massive improvement in reliability. The power band, however, was still all-too-sudden in its arrival; it even caught out the lightening reflexes of Rosberg, putting him off the road in Portugal, which left him with a broken thumb.

Still down the pipeline at that stage was a fundamentally new engine incorporating not only all the lessons learnt to date, but a seriously stiffer block, skilfully employing cast-in ducts and piping to add to its structural strength. Much rumoured, and highly likely but never confirmed was a move to a much smaller bore: it is believed to have gone from 90mm. to 82mm. Certainly the rest of the world's Formula One V6 engine builders were moving to the region of 80 - 82mm. At this stage "ceramics/coatings" were the in-words, but they are two-edged weapons where heat is concerned. Clearly they can protect against heat, but can also trap it, and under fierce heat ceramic materials can shatter. Honda denied the use of ceramics.

What was not denied was the arrival of the new "E-spec" RA-163-E at Francorchamps. With that race called off, it's debut was Montreal (4th and 6th place) followed by Detroit, where Rosberg won convincingly. He then took pole position at Silverstone where *Racecar Engineering* contributor Enrico Benzing used his well

Aluminium honeycomb FW09 chassis (above, in Rosberg's hands at Rio) gained a poor reputation, probably due to characteristics of the '84 spec RA-163-E (left).

proven check of speed read-outs and wind tunnel model tests to calculate 1070b.h.p. for that performance, with 810b.h.p. in race trim, and Williams did not dismiss that out of hand... Benzing offers bore and stroke of 82 x 47.2mm for the E-spec engine. Perceptive ears at Silverstone reckoned the rev range had been further improved.

This new strength coincided with the opening of a purpose-built engine 'shop within the Williams factory at mid-season. It could not have come at a better moment, playing a vital role in curing a series of bottom-end failures, but security remained tight. The notice on the door said in clear English block capitals "Honda Personnel Only" and Occidental faces (except perhaps that of John Judd) were strictly not admitted. It was a case of wheeling the used ones (and any wreckage) in through the first double door, and picking up a new plastic packed replacement by the same route.

Honda's involvement not only in the engine, but also in the electrics and electronics had produced an ultra-sophisticated computerised fuel read-out telling the driver precisely how many litres were left in the tank. For the late-season races the overall engine height was reduced via a flattening of the plenum chamber by a remarkable 100mm., helping Williams improve airflow to the rear wing. And finally, after all those years, it all came good: Brands Hatch, Kyalami and Adelaide - three convincing triumphs.

Overall, the tally for 1985 included three pole positions, four fastest laps and 14 points finishes, eight of them on the rostrum. With those three consecutive end of season wins the writing was on the wall. The drawings were on the board for the FW11 and yet another radically new engine was on the dyno to face the new 195 fuel litre ration.

The 25 litre fuel cut was partly offset by the continuing development of "heavy" toluene based fuel, which Mobil was supplying for the Honda-Williams. For 1986 the Anglo-Japanese package looked like being heavily revised, with a new chassis, a new driver (Piquet replacing Rosberg) and on the engine front new lower plenum chambers with double inlets to a single body, new low body air intakes for the compressors, relocated injectors, not to mention a new number - RA-166-E/ "F spec". The electronics had on it telemetry links to the pits, capable of unfolding an instant-by-instant account of what was happening during practice or the race, from water temperature to ignition advance and boost pressure. Apart from its obvious values, it also allowed the pits to tell the driver what might be wrong if he had a problem, and whether it promised to be fatal or might finish the race.

Under questioning during the season Engineer Sakurai managed a couple of masterly ambiguities, admitting to *Sport Auto* Editor Gerard ('Jabby') Crombac that the pistons were of "composite metal" and "no change in bore or stroke at this time". This week, this month or this engine, one might ask? Benzing, whose estimates in these matters are the best guide we have, reckons the bore had been reduced for '86 to give 80 x 49.4mm.

An intriguing development seen in '86 was an aftercooler bypass: under certain conditions of air pressure and temperature air was sent direct to the plenum chamber to improve throttle response. Turbo development was relentless, including VGS - variable geometry scrolls - in the turbines as a method of adjusting the gas intake to vary the engine's torque characteristics. Also tried, but later removed, was watercooling for the turbo. There were still piston and turbo failures but they were rare.

One deceptively simple and "driver friendly" fitting was a four position switch for boost control. Linked very sensitively to the engine management system, electronically altering the complete engine map, it had come a long way from winding pressure up and down on a spring while watching what happened on the gauge. A flick switch gave: 1 - fuel saver; 2 - low race boost; 3 - high race boost; 4 - an extra 100b.h.p. for overtaking. It was easier on the driver, monitorable on the telemetry links and more in accord with real life during a race, with a complex and instant resetting of ignition, fuel flow, temperatures and power.

Williams called the FW11 "a logical development" of its FW10 design, yet it was totally new: lower and more compact with revised aerodynamics. With the "166" engine it was crushingly successful, and one of the biggest tributes to Frank Williams as a leader is the fact that, although a the tragic road accident put him in a wheel chair with serious paralysis just before the start of the season, the team he had created went on to new heights and new levels of success. His cars started from pole position on four

occasions and, more impressively, took 19 points finishes, 17 on the rostrum including no less than eight wins to sweep the constructors championship.

The 1986 season was very much the season of the Honda-Williams, with no other engine capable of the same level of race power. It had taken Honda six years and untold millions for that achievement - and it had successfully guarded its secrets in the colander world of Formula One.

One of those secrets had been a plan to move out of Didcot, to Honda's own factory in Slough, some 40 miles away. Mysterious? Not if the engines were no longer to be going solely to Williams, now at the end of the original three-year contract, but to Lotus as well. And essential if no engines at all were to be destined for Williams...

From Slough Honda prepared a total of 60 "4.0 bar" engines for the two teams, fitting a single pop-off to each at a point in the inlet manifolding that looked very much as if it was, in effect, a venturi throat... The 1987 "G-spec" engine pushed revs, initially to 13,000r.p.m., though a later "GE" version brought this down to 12,000, with superb economy and reliability. Project Leader Goto was prepared to confirm that his team produced four different types of engine in '87 in the quest for better fuel consumption, though details of each had to remain confidential. The piston was still a conventional flat top design, running in a four valve, single plug serviced cylinder and driving a four bearing, three pin crank, but other internal details remained a secret. However, a reliable source confided that Honda ran plain, rather than roller or ball, big end and main bearings

Goto could reveal that, while the compressor wheel was aluminium, the turbine wheel was Inconel. Inconel is an ultra high temperature tolerant alloy metal that is very hard to work (but did appear in Indy Car exhaust systems). For '87 Honda adopted a distributorless ignition system, like Ferrari following the lead of Renault. This enhanced ignition control, helping to run closer to the detonation threshold. Crucially, throughout '86 and '87 Honda appeared to be able to race closer to that threshold than almost

The E-spec RA-163-E, first raced at Montreal in '85 (above right) gave the Honda-Williams challenge new strength. At Silverstone (below) output was over 1000 b.h.p.

anyone.

For Williams, 1987 was another crushing success, this time with a World Championship for Honda favourite Piquet as well as the constructors title. Piquet was keen on the Williams ride leveller system and behind the scenes poured thousands of miles onto it. Bit by bit the programme that would sense and correct ride height in braking and acceleration as the 200kg. fuel load slowly diminished was put together and polished, and two thirds of the way through the season it was considered fully race-worthy. Piquet debuted it at Monza with pole position, and won. Indeed, he was so enamoured of its qualities that he kicked up considerable fuss when it was not taken to Mexico or Japan for "logistical reasons".

Nevertheless, Mansell took the classic RA-166-E-FW11B from pole position to win the Mexican Grand Prix, while Piquet claimed the runner up slot and fastest lap. That was the ninth WGPE win of the season, and turned out to be its last. Honda's top brass gathered at Suzuka to witness another of the many triumphs, only to see Mansell crash in practice, ending his efforts for the season, while Piquet coasted to a halt with a broken engine after looking far from a race winner. At this stage, Cosworth reckons it had at last overtaken Honda race power after two seasons development, while Ferrari had surged into contention, and won the final two events.

There was no denying, however, the excellence of the WGPE record for 1987: 10 pole positions, and 22 points finishes, 18 of them on the rostrum. And the overall tally for Honda was 11 pole positions and 11 wins, thanks to the efforts of Team Lotus.

With a switch to the all conquering Honda engine, Lotus enthusiasts might have expected more than one pole and two wins from the team's 99T, particularly in view of the excellence of its earlier Ducarouge chassis. However, Lotus had replaced the Renault V6 engine with a less svelte and heavier replacement, of which it lacked installation experience and had further burdened its chassis development effort by incorporating a revolutionary suspension system, the likes of which had not been seen before in Grand Prix racing.

There are only 24 hours in each day and Lotus' "active ride system" promised to take most of them after Senna tested it during the winter and said, in effect, 'let's not waste time in the past: I will only drive "active". Any Formula One car is a near miracle of compact packaging but the 99T had to find extra room for a 3000p.s.i. hydraulic pump, a microprocessor, a hydraulic ram at each wheel and so forth, all linked by a mass of hydraulic pipes and wiring looms weighing some extra 20kg. Circuit know-how that had previously been coil rates, roll bar settings and wing angles suddenly had become literally millions of fragments in the computer. The amount of data was colossal, interpreting it a mega-task, even for a handful of test laps. A totally new programme from scratch for every Grand Prix circuit in the world was needed and on top of the other race demands it promised a failure of impressive size. It didn't come, even though the team was up against Williams in one of its Great years.

By the end of the season, the active computer was making 250 million decisions a race, by no means all of them perfect but with Senna using them all to best advantage. The results for a car of such complexity were staggeringly good: two wins plus another six rostrum finishes, and three fastest laps. Also, without being unkind to Japanese Formula One rookie Nakajima - placed in the team by Honda - who was dogged in his efforts and modestly placed in the points on four occasions, it was the achievement of a one man team.

Senna and "active" showed at their very best, as expected, on the streets of Monaco and Detroit. On the swooping billiard tables of Silverstone or Hockenheim with their minimal suspension movements, the old gang with coils, roll bars and dampers could hold their own, at least partly thanks to the standard wear Goodyear tyres. Ducarouge stresses the system was safe and reliable, if heavy and complex and says the more the team tested the more it learned: "we achieved a lot in our first year". He dismisses the 8-12 Honda horses it sapped as "almost insignificant".

There were plenty of those horses in 1987 - at least 950 on race day, and they galloped Honda towards its goal of being the best in the world, irrespective of team. The day it does that to its own satisfaction may well be the day it disappears from the sport as suddenly as it arrived in the mid Sixties, perhaps leaving behind only "Judd" on Formula One camboxes, and the still puzzled "gaijin" (or round eyes).

Inscrutable is certainly the word.

Honda engine in Lotus chassis: the Japanese V6 lent around 10 b.h.p. to drive the 99T's 'active' suspension system, which proved its worth at Monaco and Detroit.

LOTUS 99T

Lotus carbon fibre/Kevlar monocoque
Stressed engine
Pull rod front and rear suspension - Koni dampers
Dymag magnesium rims
SEP carbon-carbon discs, outboard
Single Brembo four pot calipers - SEP pads
Kevlar bodywork
2 Secan water radiators - 1 Secan oil heat exchanger
2 Secan air:air aftercoolers
AP quadruple plate clutch
Hewland/Lotus six speed gearbox - Salisbury diff
195 litre ATL fuel cell - 8 litre oil tank
Yuasa battery - Honda instruments
2720mm. wheelbase; 1790mm. front track, 1640mm. rear
560kg.

Although it was outwardly little changed from its Renault powered predecessor, Ducarouge describes the 99T as a "totally new car". It was however, based on the same design philosophy and was structurally similar with aluminium bulkheads inside a moulded composite shell and a one piece magnesium transaxle casing. Both monocoque and transaxle had been redrawn and the latter contained the six speed gearbox introduced in '86 and now considered fully proven. Like Williams, Lotus was supplied a 5 1/2 inch AP clutch by Honda. The suspension was a refined version of the regular systems.

The Honda liaison gave Lotus access to the Honda-sponsored 40% rolling road tunnel at Imperial College. Aerodynamically, the 99T was a new departure with a revised cooler layout, the aftercoolers flared like the water radiators (though still engine bay vented) within narrower pods. Lotus was not supplied by Honda with its coolers and the aftercoolers produced by Secan to meet its cooling and airflow requirements turned out 40mm. higher than the items run by Williams. The fuselage shroud was still one piece with a smaller cover required by the Honda V6. Naturally, the underbody was also new, with each diffuser tunnel fed by a twin exhaust outlet.

The 99T was checked in a new, higher speed fixed floor St Cyr tunnel prior to its shakedown at Donington in February. It went to the Rio test with an exciting new development: active suspension. The system was powered by a hydraulic pressure pump driven off the rear of the left-hand bank's exhaust camshaft and sapping around 10b.h.p. A fluid accumulator was incorporated in the bellhousing, mounted above the oil tank, to maintain pressure at low revs. Fluid pipes ran from the accumulator to an 'actuator' for each wheel where an electronically controlled 'Moog' valve controlled hydraulic pressure felt by the jack controlling wheel movement. Wheel movement was precisely controlled via a central processor fitted under the driver's seat and programmed to react in given ways to inputs from a variety of sensors monitoring wheel movement, chassis attitude, steering input and air speed. The system added around 20kg. but was sufficiently promising to be run throughout the season.

Seeking to save weight, Lotus keenly adopted the Tilton carbon-carbon clutch, running it regularly. Small revisions to underbody and periscope turbo intakes appeared at Monaco and Detroit, while there was a new body for Hungary to reduce frontal area. The main saving was in lowering the aftercoolers to bring them in line with those of Williams, which had greater experience of running the Honda V6. In addition to lower pods, the cockpit surround was lower and narrower and the dorsum was also lowered a little thanks to a tighter engine shroud.

Over the course of the season the team switched to OZ rims. Six 99T chassis were built, of which five were utilised by the race team, while the sixth was written off in testing.

WILLIAMS FW09

Williams aluminium honeycomb monocoque
Stressed engine
Pull rod front and rear suspension - Koni dampers
Dymag magnesium rims
AP cast iron discs, outboard
Single AP four pot calipers - Ferodo pads
Carbon fibre/Kevlar bodywork
2 Behr water radiators - 1 Behr oil heat exchanger
2 Behr air:air aftercoolers
AP twin plate clutch
Hewland/Williams five-speed gearbox - Williams diff
220 litre ATL fuel cell - 9 litre oil tank
Panasonic battery - VDO instruments
2667mm. wheelbase; 1829mm. front track, 1676mm. rear
540kg.

The FW09 emerged in 1983; autumn testing led to two cars being run at Kyalami to help the team get to grips with the Honda power it would enjoy the following season. The car was an evolution of the regular Cosworth machine, retaining the same aluminium honeycomb chassis base, albeit with a slightly longer wheelbase. The tub was consequently angular, and had a triangulated scuttle, low cut cockpit flanks and a boxy tank of which the long flat roof carried a tubular roll hoop. The aluminium structure carried conventional pull rod front suspension and was completely shrouded by a fuselage fairing which extended as far as the rear wing. Forming a high, bulbous dorsum which concealed the roll hoop as well as the engine, the fuselage shroud formed the lids of short pods which extended either side of the tank.

The sidepods set upward and forward slanted, top vented water radiators ahead of upright, engine bay vented aftercoolers flanking the rear bulkhead. The pods had straight side panels running as far back as the rear wheels: there was no attempt to produce a bottleneck rear plan and a flat rear deck filled the width between the rear wheels. This deck worked in conjunction with short underbody flip ups, while the exhaust pipes passed straight back through the suspension. The rear wing sat on a central post supported by a two-piece transaxle case, the main case split from the oil tank/ bellhousing and supporting a rocker arm suspension via sturdy yokes.

The FW09 was a relatively short, stubby car with a blunt nose (detachable with the front wings) and a bulkier rear shroud than originally anticipated due to the size of the version of the Honda V6 supplied. Both examples run at Kyalami were updated to 1984 specification, which essentially consisted of a new main case to carry a pull rod rear suspension and Williams modified, FGB based internals, together with Williams' own diff. The '84 engine, initially, came with a higher exhaust exit, and like the '84 'production' chassis was reckoned to be a little lighter, bringing the entire package to 540kg.

From the outset the team played with Hitco carbon-carbon discs, but raced iron, employing various combinations of single four pot and twin two pot caliper. The handling problems experienced in '84 led to early suspension geometry alterations and, for Monaco, a reversion to the '83 rocker arm rear suspension which necessitated the older main case, containing essentially standard FGB internals. A sixth FW09 chassis was introduced in time for Montreal with revised exhaust system, repositioned turbos and heat exchangers and 'waisted-in' rear shroud. However, the exhaust revision caused an engine problem and the car was put back to standard after the race.

Brands Hatch re-introduced the bottleneck plan-style rear end, the exhaust having been further modified and designed to work with a prominent diffuser. The turbos were again repositioned, and a 120mm. spacer was set between engine and transaxle, allowing pronounced rear waisting. The spacer also improved weight distribution, handling and rear wing location. Of the nine FW09 cars completed by the end of the '84 season, six were either of 'B' spec, or converted to it.

WILLIAMS FW10

Williams carbon fibre/Kevlar monocoque
Stressed engine
Push rod front suspension, rocker arm rear - Koni dampers
Dymag magnesium rims
SEP carbon-carbon discs, outboard
Single AP four pot calipers - SEP pads
Carbon fibre/Kevlar bodywork
2 Behr water radiators - 1 Behr oil heat exchanger
2 Behr air:air aftercoolers
AP twin plate clutch
Hewland/Williams six-speed gearbox - Williams diff
220 litre ATL fuel cell - 9 litre oil tank
Honda battery - Honda and VDO instruments
2794mm. wheelbase; 1803mm. front track, 1651mm. rear
540kg.

After the poor showing of the first full season with Honda, Head took a major step using the team's newly built in house autoclave to produce its first 'black' tub. This incorporated aluminium and Nomex honeycomb cores and carbon fibre/Kevlar skins, with all but two bulkheads composite. The two machined from solid aluminium bulkheads carried a new push rather than pull rod suspension, a little further forward for improved weight distribution (the engine/transaxle spacer was deleted). The tub formed the cockpit coaming with a detachable nose fairing ahead and the engine cowl concealing the top of the tank, which carried a conventional roll hoop and Honda electronics.

In overall shape the FW10 was reminiscent of its predecessor and it retained a similar cooler layout, with new aftercoolers and turbo system helping produce a cleaner bottleneck plan rear end. Williams produced a new main case to carry a six-speed gearbox but retained rocker arm rear suspension. Damping was now dealt with by new Penske/Monroe oil/air units which employed remote mounted air reservoirs that could be independently topped up to any required pressure level.

The car featured a two tier rear wing, supported by a short post to the lower tier. First run at Brands Hatch in March '85, it was designed to run SEP carbon-carbon brakes from the outset but cast iron was reverted to at Detroit and Adelaide. A double floating disc carbon-carbon design from AP was tested.

The strength of the new tub was amply proven by serious crashes for both Mansell and Rosberg from which they emerged virtually unscathed. Initially, the team was only able to complete two cars, an FW09B acting as spare until Imola where FW10/03 appeared. An FW09 continued service in Japan as an engine test machine. FW10 specification saw little alteration other than stiffer rocker arms, prior to Brands Hatch.

Brands Hatch witnessed the emergence of a redesigned, pull rod rear suspension carried by a new integral transaxle case and incorporating new uprights. In conjunction with this came a slimmer and lower dorsum allowed through Honda's modification of the plenum chambers, improving flow to the rear wing. The modified cars were known as FW10B. Three of the seven 'black' cars built were converted.

WILLIAMS FW11

Williams carbon fibre/Kevlar monocoque
Stressed engine
Push rod front, pull rod rear suspension - Penske/Monroe dampers
Fondmetal magnesium rims
SEP carbon-carbon discs, outboard
Single AP four pot calipers - SEP pads
Carbon fibre/Kevlar bodywork
2 Secan water radiators - 2 Secan oil heat exchangers
2 Secan air:air aftercoolers
AP twin plate clutch
Hewland/Williams six-speed gearbox - Williams diff
195 litre ATL fuel cell - 9 litre oil tank
Honda battery - Honda instruments
2794mm. wheelbase; 1803mm. front track, 1651mm. rear
540kg.

While Williams called the FW11 a "logical development" of its '85 car, it was totally new. Thanks to the smaller, 195 litre tank and side vented pods it was lower and more compact. Head came up with his own approach on the side-venting theme, splitting the flow vertically as usual so that the outer slice of a marginally smaller pod's tunnel fed a side vented water radiator. Naturally the water radiator was set upright and splayed away from the tank; the novelty was in giving the aftercooler a similar stance. Staggered behind, the aftercooler vented through the engine bay.

The FW11 retained familiar suspension with revised geometry, continuing with the integral transaxle case introduced in late '85. Wing profiles and hub assemblies were new, in addition to the monocoque and bodywork. The tub was formed as a single shell less floorpan, the bulkheads - all composite on the FW11 - being fed in through its base, with the floor bonded in afterwards. The cockpit opening was smaller and the tank shroud was a tighter fit, the latter possible thanks to an expanding use of CAD/CAM facilities. The turbo continued to be fed through a side panel duct while the rear wing was again two tier, supported by a conventional central post. A longer diffuser was standard.

Three cars were ready for the start of the '86 season and at Rio twin disc carbon-carbon brakes were raced by Mansell for the first and only time. Thereafter, through the summer the race car specification remained substantially unaltered. The team produced chassis 05 for Ricard a little lighter and aerodynamic experiments included the pure aircraft approach of small tubes within the rear wing designed to "clean off" at least some of the "dirty" air. The c.v. joints were strengthened for Monza and periscope compressor intakes were first run at Estoril. In total, six cars were produced, only 04 being crash-damaged.

WILLIAMS FW11B

Williams carbon fibre/Kevlar monocoque
Stressed engine
Push rod front, pull rod rear suspension - Penske/Monroe dampers
Fondmetal magnesium rims
SEP carbon-carbon discs, outboard
Single AP four pot calipers - SEP pads
Carbon fibre/Kevlar bodywork
2 Secan water radiators - 2 Secan oil heat exchangers
2 Secan air:air aftercoolers
AP twin plate clutch
Hewland/Williams six-speed gearbox - Williams diff
195 litre ATL fuel cell - 9 litre oil tank
Honda battery - Honda instruments
2794mm. wheelbase; 1803mm. front track, 1651mm. rear
540kg.

The FW11B was a refined version of a World Championship winning car, fundamentally unaltered. The main improvement was a slightly less intrusive dorsum to clean the flow to the rear wing. The driver was reclined a little more, the roll bar was lowered and the rear bodywork was dropped and slimmed. The turbos and their periscope intakes were revised but the staggered cooler arrangement went unchanged. The front wing endplates doubled in size, the rear edges contoured as closely to the front tyre edges as turning lock would permit - an aerodynamic tweak several other teams would copy.

The most exciting development was well out of sight: it was only installed on a test car. This was Head's very personal approach to "active", or computer aided suspension. Essentially, he iso-

lated perhaps the most important and most difficult problem then facing the Formula One designer - total and continuous control of the car's ride height. His approach was to control the length of the suspension unit, effectively making it longer or shorter hydraulically, as required, a computer sorting out "when, where and how much". It could be seen as a variable top mounting which kept the front up under braking and the rear up under acceleration as well as - and still more important - adjusting steadily throughout the race for a reducing weight of fuel. Refinement took all spring and summer: the system did not appear until Monza in September. Piquet's pole and race winning car had it fitted.

Like Lotus, Williams had found the hardware

a lot easier than the programme for the computer responsible for making large numbers of correct decisions at the right time. Two chassis were tailor made for the system with integral hydraulic piping and were only run in Europe for logistical reasons. A third chassis, however, was modified at Adelaide after the parts had been specially flown out. Six 'conventional' suspension chassis appeared over the season, and were not fundamentally modified. A shorter wheelbase, bringing the front wheels 35mm. back to put more weight on them, was tested but not raced. The team developed a low drag compressor intake ducting air from the pod inlet and on occasion substituted this for the usual periscope.

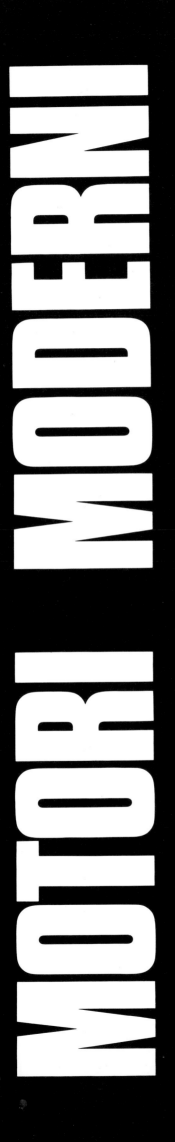

MOTORI MODERNI

Motori Moderni SpA
Via E. Fermi 3
Novara
Italy

In the summer of 1984 Carlo Chiti got a telephone call from Giancarlo Minardi. Minardi was a Faenza (near Imola) Fiat dealer with a Formula Two race team and influential friends, among them Chiti's one time boss Enzo Ferrari. In 1976 Ferrari had given Minardi the privilege of running a factory prepared Formula One car for Giancarlo Martini and more recently he had granted him a supply of 2.0 litre V6 engines as a possible alternative to his regular BMW pool.

Minardi had built his own Formula Two cars since 1980, starting with a BMW-March based device engineered by one time Ferrari Formula One technician Giacomo Caliri's Fly Studio. For 1981 Caliri produced the Minardi Fly 281 and Alboreto used it to take some strong results in the European Championship, including victory at Misano. Minardi and Caliri found they worked well together and, as Minardi had set his sights on Formula One Caliri bought a stake in the team, becoming its Technical Director.

Caliri designed a composite tub-car for 1983 (the 283) as the basis of a Cosworth powered Formula One challenger but during that year it became clear that a turbo engine would be essential for the step up. In the summer of 1984 the team unveiled a spin-off Grand Prix challenger equipped instead with an Alfa Romeo V8 engine.

Alfa Romeo had offered a loan of its engine for testing, and had talked of the possibility of a deal for '85 races. But the V8 was clearly too thirsty and, with Alfa Romeo having second thoughts, Caliri had designed the M184 to accept any possible engine, including an in line four. One possibility was to turbocharge the 60 degree Dino-based Ferrari V6 but that would call for the production of a stronger block. Better to start with a clean sheet of paper. Hence the 'phone call.

"It was simple to decide to leave Autodelta", Chiti recalls. Nevertheless, the disillusioned engineer had been at its helm for 21 years, and his association with Alfa Romeo did stretch right back to the mid Fifties. An aeronautical engineering graduate, Chiti had worked in the marque's experimental and racing departments from 1953 (soon after leaving Pisa University) until he had joined Ferrari in 1956. He went on to become Ferrari's Technical Director.

Although he had been part of the mass Maranello walkout at the end of the 1961 season, Chiti hadn't made himself an enemy of Enzo Ferrari. He sought the Old Man's advice before resigning from Autodelta (and it was clear that Minardi would need some more favours). Chiti had been sitting uncomfortably at a desk job since he had been ousted from the Alfa Romeo Euroracing pit in mid season, and he resigned as from October.

Another of Minardi's influential friends was the wealthy financier Piero Mancini. With the Minardi team's graduation to Formula One Mancini had become Vice-President of the organisation, taking one-third of its shares, and he supported the creation of Motori Moderni specifically to produce a turbocharged engine for Minardi. Mancini was also heavily involved in the Novamotor company and 61 year old Chiti set up shop in a new factory close to Novamotor's Novara base. He immediately started work on a state of the art V6 turbo engine. By February Chiti had a unit ready to run, boasting he had broken the record he set with the Alfa Romeo V12 - "that took six months".

Produced so rapidly, did the engine draw in any way upon the Alfa Romeo V8? The rotund Tuscan quakes with laughter at such a preposterous suggestion, and draws attention to the head bolt pattern. The V6 has a pair of studs each side of each cylinder, whereas the V8 set only one pair between neighbouring cylinders. The 6VTC was a clean sheet of paper design. Given restricted fuel, an eight cylinder engine was clearly too thirsty, while Chiti now reckoned the in line four "a valid concept, but there are installation problems". His preference was for a V6, and in practical terms Ferrari's offer of its discarded Lucas based V6 electro-mechanical injection system put any other configuration out of the question. Minardi was once again going Formula One with a helping hand from his friend in Maranello.

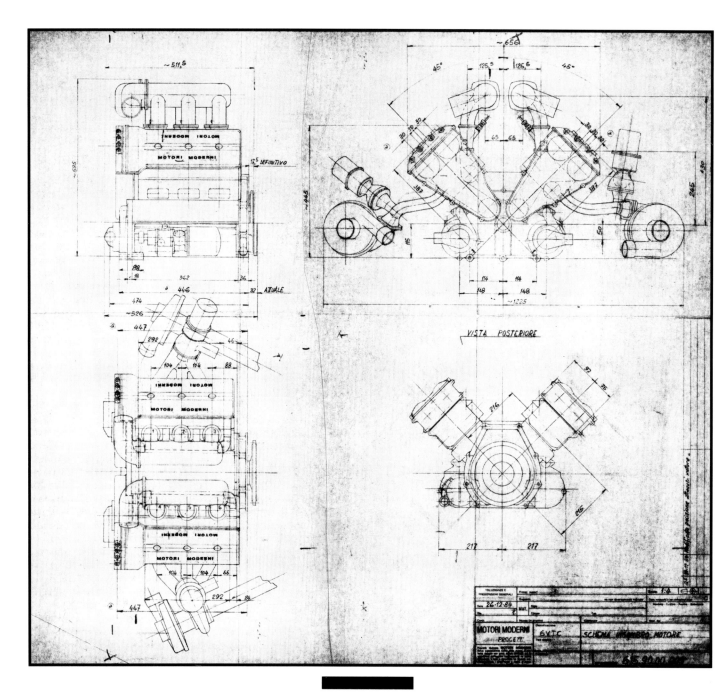

6VTC
90 degree V6

80 x 49.7mm./ 1498.9cc.
2 KKK turbochargers
Aluminium block and heads
Nikasil wet aluminium liner
4 main bearings, plain
Steel crankshaft, 3 pins
Titanium con rods
Mahle light alloy pistons
Goetze rings
4 o.h.c., belt driven
4 valves/cylinder, 1 plug
28mm. inlet valve, 23mm. exhaust
27 degree included valve angle
Marelli ignition
Lucas-Ferrari injection
Compression ratio 7.0:1
Maximum r.p.m. 12,000
154kg. including turbos and wastegates

Chiti plumped for a traditional 90 degree vee rather than the Honda and Porsche favoured 80 degree angle, saying that the balance characteristics are the same and that (in the absence of wing car considerations) personal preference dictated the former option. The block was designed to be run fully stressed and at Caliri's request Chiti incorporated Cosworth-copy chassis and gearbox attachment lugs.

The crankcase was split at the centreline with the lower half of each main bearing support formed by the sump casting, original DFV style. Eight studs, one either side of each main bearing, passed from the block right through the sump, rigidly tying the bottom end together. As we have noted, each head was pulled down by twelve studs. The cams ran in a detachable cam carrier.

Chiti plumped for a relatively small 80mm. bore for his conventional Nikasil cylinders, this choice echoing the new reduced-bore (80.1mm.) Renault EF15 engine. Oil jet cooled Mahle three ring, valve clearance notched, flat top pistons were employed, weighing 440gms., complete with steel gudgeon pin. The H-section con rod was of titanium and weighed 460gms. complete with two steel bolts and nuts. It drove a forged steel crank through a plain Vandervell bearing, that three-pin crank having six extended balance webs. It had 40mm. diameter, 19mm. wide crank pins and 60mm. diameter, 25mm. wide journals for the plain Vandervell main bearings. The crank weighed 11kg.

The overhead cams ran in four plain Vandervell bearings and each bank was driven by its own belt from a pulley either side of the power take-off at the front of the crank. The usual co-axial valve springs came from Schmitthelm. The valve angles from vertical were: inlet 13 degrees 50, exhaust 13 degrees 30.

The pumps, inevitably mounted Cosworth-style either side of the crankcase, were also driven off the nose of the crank and were headed each side by a water pump for the respective bank. Ignition was Marelli Raceplex CD, with the distributor driven off the back

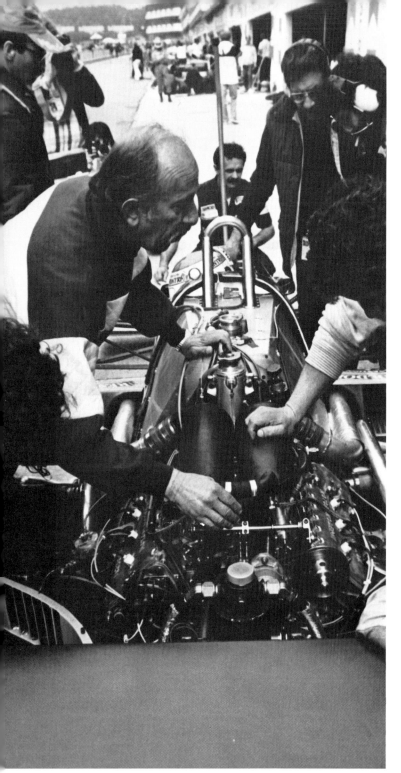

Ermanno Cuoghi (left) tends the 6VTC on its debut at Imola, 1985 in the Minardi M185 chassis with aftercoolers ahead of the water radiators.

tyres and AGIP fuel. The entire package was somewhat over-weight at 585kg., and lacked serious testing. However, the proto-type had run reliably straight out of the box, in trials at Imola then Misano, and it behaved itself in Imola qualifying, Martini setting an extremely encouraging 19th fastest time. Alas, in the race a turbo problem cost 17th place after only 70km.

Early development saw qualifying boost reach 3.9 bar, while race boost was the maximum 3.2 bar the Lucas-Ferrari injected engine could cope with on 220 litres. The claimed 720b.h.p. was a modest figure by '85 race standards. Yet even at that level, without com-puter control the last four laps of a typical 220 litre race would be marginal. Not that Martini seemed able to get that far, due to mechanical mishaps, and some mishaps of his own making. However, having persistently qualified outside the top 20 after Imola, he was eventually classified, outside the top 10 and five laps down, at the Nurburgring, then at Francorchamps. He finished the season with eighth place, four laps adrift (after a spin had cost over a lap) at Adelaide.

During '85 Chiti spoke of a plus-800b.h.p. race potential, if only he had the right electronic control. For '86 there was something of a breakthrough: the Marelli-Weber injection system introduced by Ferrari in 1984. Used with two injectors per cylinder, this was also loaned and overhauled by Ferrari, and was first tested on the 6VTC at Ferrari's Fiorano test track in February '86. Motori Moderni also benefited from an improved, now toluene-based AGIP supply, and an improved KKK turbocharger model. Chiti's relatively low compression engine was essentially unmodified internally and, with Motori Moderni unable to afford extensive engine mapping, needed to run a relatively rich mixture to preserve its pistons. However, given that it would be unlikely to complete as many laps as the winning car it could race at 3.3/3.4 bar, sometimes as high as 3.7 bar. On 3.7 bar the power output was officially quoted as 840b.h.p./11,300r.p.m., with torque 53kg.m./9,000r.p.m. Chiti produced a specific qualifying engine with a 6.5:1 compression ratio, different cams and a few minor modifications and (given the need preserve engines) that was boosted to a maximum of 4.3 bar, at which it was rated at 950b.h.p.

On a dozen leased engines, Minardi ran two Pirelli shod cars throughout '86, for Nannini and de Cesaris. The chassis was a mildly modified M185, still overweight at 575kg., though Cesaris got an evolutionary 567kg. M186 model for the last half dozen events. Minardi was reckoned to spend $3.5 million in '86, of which $2 million went to Motori Moderni. That was a drop in the ocean compared to the Reparto Corse's budget.

Chiti estimated the cost of each engine as "150 million Lire". He had hoped for contracts to additionally furnish the Ekstroem and Osella teams, but those fell through early in the season for lack of cash (though not before Osella had produced a Motori Moderni chassis, subsequently converted to Alfa Romeo power). However, he had found a late season customer in AGS and also had a project to produce an F3000 engine based on the Lamborghini Jalpa block. With a staff of 12 headed by engineers Nicolazzi and Bernardoni, Chiti expressed enjoyment at life as he approached retirement age: "the money is less on my own, but the satisfaction is much greater - it is very difficult working for a big, nationalised company like Alfa Romeo..."

Over at Minardi, the technical staff had been strengthened by the arrival of Tommaso Carletti, ex-Ferrari and Renault, as Caliri's right-hand man and things had started well in April with Cesaris lapping Fiorano a second quicker than the best time managed by Ferrari in '85. Alas, this year the team again failed to score a single World Championship point, its best result once more eighth - that was Cesaris in Mexico, two laps down. And that was the team's first finish of the year, engine and turbo failures particularly rife. It was clear that, with its small budget and small staff the Motori Moderni company was somewhat overstretched.

Progress was made, however, in terms of qualifying speed. At Imola Nannini broke the M185 into the top 20 again (18th place this year) then the model was regularly seen around 19th/20th slot, usually thanks to Nannini's effort. Nannini got up to 17th at Budapest, then Cesaris put the new M186 16th on the grid in Estoril and a splendid 11th at Adelaide, to finish the year on a resounding note.

At the last two European races (Monza and Estoril) there was that second Motori Moderni team, AGS. Automobiles Gonfar-onaise Sportive was a well established French Formula Two/3000

of the left-hand cylinder bank's inlet cam, while the alternator was belt driven off the back of the opposite bank's inlet cam. The metering unit for the Lucas-Ferrari electro-mechanical injection system was mounted behind the alternator, within the vee and fed a single injector at the base of each trumpet. Separate plenum chambers for each bank were linked at the back by a balance pipe.

Motori Moderni utilised off the shelf KKK turbos: only one, compromise race and qualifying model was available to it. And with the '83-vintage Lucas-Ferrari injection in place the new engine would be badly handicapped in terms of control: Chiti had left digital engine management technology behind at Autodelta. The new engine was officially rated 720b.h.p./11,300r.p.m., with maxi-mum torque 46kg.m./9,000r.p.m. on 3.2 bar.

The 154kg. 6VTC was ready to race at Imola, Minardi having contested the first two Grands Prix of '85 with Cosworth power for Caliri's conventional, adaptable chassis, now dubbed the M185. The team's sole driver was the inexperienced Martini (Pierluigi, no relation to Giancarlo!) but with Ermanno Cuoghi heading the spanner men there was no shortage of experience in the pits.

The Motori Moderni-Minardi ran on a six-engine supply, Pirelli

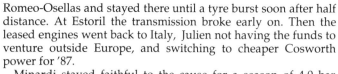

operation with big ambitions. Run by Henri Julien, the Gonfaron-based equipe had drawn a Cosworth engined Formula One car in the early Eighties but lack of funds had kept designer/engineer Christian van der Pleyn's handiwork on paper. Julien hadn't given up hope - and had subsequently ordered a BMW engined design. Finally, along came the funds that had allowed a Motori Moderni car to be both drawn and built...

AGS acquired its cash through Italy's Jolly Club, an organisation that could offer both management expertise and sponsorship connections. In the summer of '86 AGS unveiled the product of van der Pleyn's third Formula One design - a low line machine based around equipment bought from the defunct Renault team.

The Brabham BT55-influenced JH21C ran on AGIP petroleum and Pirelli tyres, dusting its radials for the first time six weeks behind schedule, on August 12 at Paul Ricard. Retired driver Pironi gave it a whirl, then handed it to regular pilot Capelli who expressed it easier to drive than the Renault-Tyrrell he had previously tasted. Unfortunately, only 200 miles of testing were possible prior to the Monza debut desired by the Italian sponsors, but the car didn't reveal any major weakness. At Monza a turbo blew on each day's first timed lap yet Capelli got into the race ahead of the Alfa

Romeo-Osellas and stayed there until a tyre burst soon after half distance. At Estoril the transmission broke early on. Then the leased engines went back to Italy, Julien not having the funds to venture outside Europe, and switching to cheaper Cosworth power for '87.

Minardi stayed faithful to the cause for a season of 4.0 bar competition, with the impressive Nannini promoted to team leader and joined by rookie Campos. Both were equipped with the M186, lightly modified. In mid season it was finally equipped with carbon-carbon brakes, which brought weight down to 550kg. The only engine modification for '87, Chiti confirms, was an integral plenum chamber serving both banks from the usual twin aftercoolers to allow for a single pop-off valve. The valve was mounted on the back of the chamber, which mid season was split internally to divide the flow to each bank ahead of the valve. The 6VTC retained the same turbos and '84-technology injection system, the latter the "big problem", according to Chiti, who still didn't have the resources to do extensive mapping, and couldn't afford uprated parts. Ignition was still not mapped. On 4.0 bar qualifying boost he quoted the author "850b.h.p.", estimating "760b.h.p." at a typical 3.6 bar race boost. That was within 5% of the official power figures for '86, Chiti saying he had the same engine, the same turbos and the same power in '87 as he had in '86.

The 6VTC-M186 worked well at Monaco, Detroit, Estoril and Adelaide, but poorly on the slippery Budapest circuit, suggesting a lack of downforce. The engine supply was again unreliable, oil too often found in the water, and Minardi found a big variation in engines between meetings. Team leader Nannini qualified in the top 15 on ten occasions, with highs of 13th position at Monaco and Adelaide, while Campos' best grid slot was 16th. He failed to make the Monaco cut and from 31 starts there were only four finishes, none in the top ten. Engine and turbo failures were frequently to blame and Minardi not surprisingly switched to Cosworth power for '88.

For Chiti, after three under-funded, struggling years of turbo Formula One, there was hope on the horizon in the form of an agreement struck when the circus visited Suzuka. The elderly Tuscan was approached by the Subaru company to develop a new Formula One engine: a flat 12 for the 1990s.

The 1986 M185 featured a conventional cooler layout with side vented radiators. In 1987 the 6VTC had a single pop off valve (lower photo).

AGS JH21C

MOC carbon fibre/Kevlar monocoque
Stressed engine
Push rod front and rear suspension - Koni dampers
Speedline aluminium and magnesium rims
SEP carbon-carbon discs, outboard
Single AGS four pot calipers - SEP pads
Carbon fibre/Kevlar bodywork
2 Secan water radiators - 1 Secan oil heat exchanger
2 Secan air:air aftercoolers
AP twin plate clutch
Renault six-speed gearbox - Salisbury diff
Riche 195 litre fuel cell - 10 litre oil tank
Yuasa battery - Marelli instruments
2873mm. wheelbase; 1810mm. front track, 1654mm. rear
540kg.

Van der Pleyn began work on a low line Motori Moderni chassis in October 1985 and when it was unveiled ten months later he was not disheartened by the disappointing performance of the BT55. Convinced that had nothing to do with the basic concept of Murray's radical chassis, he asserted: "I prefer the Brabham solution, on paper it is the fastest car".

The JH21C had a fuel tank cross section that kept to the frontal dimensions of the Motori Moderni V6; no taller, no wider. That left an overall height (excluding roll bar) of 830mm. - mid way between that of the BT55 and a conventional car, such as the Honda-Williams FW11. The AGS was a full 30mm. lower than the similarly propelled Minardi, which featured a prominent bubble behind the driver, in accordance with a different aerodynamic philosophy. The AGS's unobtrusive fuel tank was of inverted-T cross-section and its small cross-sectional area left it longer than normal, which in turn pushed the wheelbase beyond conventional limits. The JH21C had a wheelbase fully 165.5mm. longer than that of the Minardi M186 which was introduced one race before it. Van der Pleyn considered neither his wheelbase nor his extremely reclined driving position to be a drawback.

In lesser formulae van der Pleyn had made a wide track his hallmark and consequently his designs tended to shine on street circuits and in the wet. There was no question of his Grand Prix design being distinctive in this respect - with a conventional front and rear track the JH21C was at the limit of Formula One width regulations.

Along with Renault parts, AGS had acquired a useful amount of technical help, and the Gonfaron equipe was able to benefit from a relationship that had grown between the Regie and MOC, a French military equipment manufacturer which had a considerable amount of expertise in advanced composites. MOC had produced noses and underbodies for the RE60 and had geared up to produce the monocoque for the still born RE70. It adapted that design to suit van der Pleyn's requirements and below the waist the JH21C was clearly of the Renault mould.

Van der Pleyn had tested models of his design in the same St. Cyr wind tunnel used by Renault and was able to benefit from Renault underbody moulds. Although he would not admit to it, a member of the AGS organisation whispered that van der Pleyn had done consultancy work for a major Formula One team - most likely Renault, post-Tetu.

The AGS' Renault based, angular monocoque was shaped to form most of the cockpit coaming, with only a small, detachable scuttle fairing over the dashboard roll hoop and anti-roll bar. Ahead, a short, stubby rounded nose supported the front wings while to the rear the engine cover (sloping down from engine to gearbox height), the squared-off sidepods and the underbody were detachable as a single unit. The rear wing was mounted on a central post.

Cooling followed the RE60B layout with side vented radiators and engine bay vented aftercoolers, a flattening of the water pipes as they crossed each aftercooler revealing the Renault origins of the equipment. A single Secan oil heat exchanger was placed over the bellhousing, adjoining the oil tank. Van der Pleyn resorted to louvres to assist the extraction of air from the side vents and joined Minardi in the use of snorkel compressor feeds.

AGS used a tall, narrow Renault transaxle with Renault six-speed gearbox and a choice of Torsen or Salisbury diff. Brakes were ex- Renault SEP discs used in conjunction with AGS's own machined-from- solid, titanium and aluminium calipers, which the team had started developing before F3000 regulations had banned carbon-carbon brakes. Driveshafts, in titanium, and uprights and wheels were from the RE60 programme but although the general layout of the suspension (push rod with vertically mounted de Carbon dampers) followed Renault practice, the detail design was by van der Pleyn and was specifically to suit Pirelli radials.

Although the prototype was late for pre-Monza testing, the team did manage to assemble the parts from which 002 could be rush built in the event of any mishap during its debut meeting. In the event, 001 ran Monza and Estoril and was the only AGS chassis to carry the Motori Moderni engine.

MINARDI M185

Minardi aluminium and carbon fibre/Kevlar monocoque
Stressed engine
Pull rod front suspension, push rod rear - Koni dampers
Essen aluminium and magnesium rims
Brembo cast iron discs, outboard
Single Brembo four pot calipers - Ferodo pads
Carbon fibre/Kevlar bodywork
2 Citroen water radiators - 2 Behr oil coolers
2 Behr air:air aftercoolers
AP twin plate clutch
Hewland/Minardi five-speed gearbox - Salisbury diff
220 litre ATL fuel cell - 6 litre oil tank
Yuasa battery - Contactless/Veglia/Minardi instruments
2607mm. wheelbase; 1813mm. front track, 1661mm. rear
585kg.

As we have noted, Caliri had designed Minardi's 1983 Formula Two car as the basis of a Cosworth Grand Prix machine. Like many designers in the early Eighties wary of the pure carbon fibre tub in terms of driver safety, Caliri plumped for an inner skin of carbon fibre/Kevlar mix and an outer skin of aluminium sandwiching an aluminium honeycomb core. Without the cuts and folds that characterised the traditional all-aluminium tubs employed by his Formula Two rivals, Caliri saw his in-house produced monocoque as extremely rigid, relatively light and, should the worst happen, very safe.

Minardi had constructed its own small autoclave to work the advanced composites and had attracted attention from a major car manufacturer that could see an application for its aluminium and plastics combination on future road cars. The M283 monocoque was carried over to the prototype Grand Prix car (christened the M184 when it was unveiled with dummy Alfa Romeo V8 in the summer of '84), this turbo machine adapted from the Cosworth car drawings.

The M184 retained a familiar pull rod front suspension which was hung on a double row aluminium dashboard bulkhead assembly. The monocoque formed a distinctive arch over the driver's headrest (topped by the roll bar) and high cockpit walls but there was a detachable sloping scuttle panel blending into a detachable wedge nose (which carried the front wings). Behind the arch of the monocoque was an extensive rear shroud that splayed to form the rear portion of the pod lids and reached as far back as the gearbox forming a plump dorsal bulge and slim rear waisting.

In overall shape the M184 was influenced by the McLaren MP4, Caliri admits, but the car had to be adaptable. Thus, in downward swept pods the aftercoolers lay ahead of the water radiators and were angled forward to be top vented through the rear portion of the lid while the radiators stood upright and transverse to be vented through the engine bay and the oil coolers were set flush with the pod instep, just ahead of the rear wheels. The logic of this layout was that if a Cosworth engine should have to be accommodated after all, the surplus aftercooler flow could be diverted by a modified rear cover to feed the air box. Similarly, Caliri could adapt to suit an in line four - the destined power plant was by no means certain at the time of drawing.

Compared to the M283, the rear end of the M184 was revised structurally as well as aerodynamically. Naturally, whereas the four cylinder BMW had been supported by A-frames, the eight cylinder Alfa Romeo could be run fully stressed, and Caliri also changed the rear suspension. This was switched from a rocker arm to a push rod system with the dampers mounted in a wide-angle vee over the Minardi transaxle case, which carried Hewland FGB gearbox internals. The rear wing was mounted on a central post and the tail layout allowed a wide diffuser upsweep either side of the narrow bottleneck.

Interestingly, the rev counter was produced by hand locally, while the wheels were supplied on an exclusive basis by the Japanese company Enkei - they were similar to three piece Speedlines. They first turned at Misano in the summer of '84, courtesy of Alfa Romeo power before

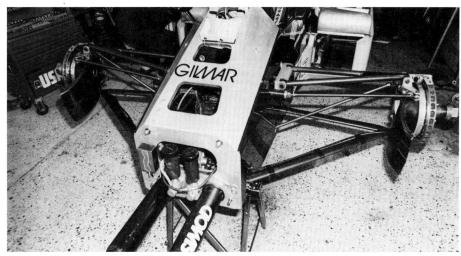

the car made its Cosworth propelled race debut. To convert the car to Motori Moderni specification was a relatively straightforward job, given the similar engine mounting. Of course, the 6VTC was somewhat shorter than the classic engine it replaced: the loss of one pair of cylinders left Caliri around 120mm. to play with. Consequently, 40mm. was added to the bellhousing while 80mm. was left between engine and monocoque to allow for the passage of charge plumbing. Each compressor was fed from a side panel duct while the turbine exhausted into its respective diffuser tunnel.

Following winter work in the Fiat wind tunnel the diffuser had been shortened for '85 but Caliri was later to regret this, concluding that he had been misled by the fixed floor of the full-sized facility. The team prepared a second chassis (confusingly, 003) for its Imola turbocharged debut, taking along the Cosworth car as a spare, albeit with empty engine bay. The 003 chassis was eventually written off in Monaco. Chassis 002 was fresh for the aborted Francorchamps race, where Caliri experimented with rear wheel

air deflectors. The concept was subsequently abandoned as it called for further wind tunnel testing, which the team simply could not afford. The team was granted a Fiorano track session in June but overall there was a crying lack of funds for tunnel and track testing.

The original chassis was badly damaged in qualifying at Montreal but was repaired for Paul Ricard, while a fourth example was ready for Silverstone, allowing the '84 car to be pensioned off. However, it had to be resurrected after Martini wrecked 002 during the Zandvoort race. Over the season specification changes were few. Snorkel turbo intakes were tested at Silverstone and a low rear wing (level with the shortened diffuser) was run at the Osterreichring, then in the last five races. The front suspension geometry was revised at Brands Hatch.

Caliri penned a new car for 1986 but the team didn't have the funds to be able to prepare it for the start of the season. Indeed, it was Budapest before the M186 made its entrance. In the meantime many of the new model's features were incorporated in the existing design, which saw

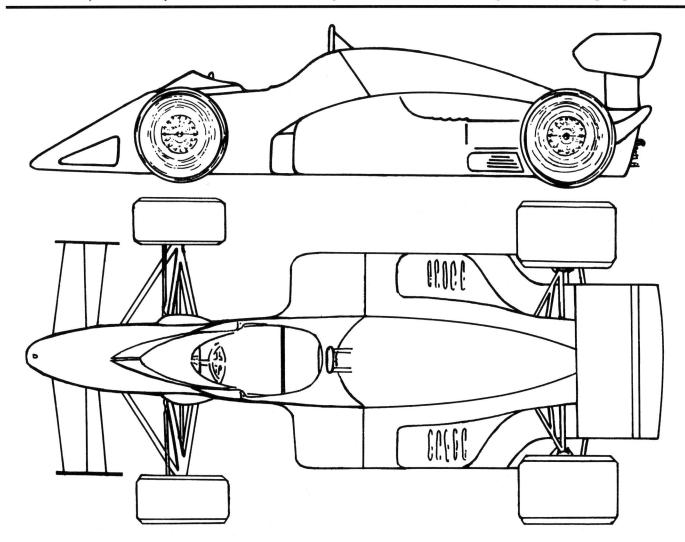

service right to the end of the season. Three M185 chassis were prepared for the team's expansion to a two-car operation and only one M186 came into service for the late season races. Of the three M185 chassis, one was built around a fifth monocoque and was given the 003 chassis plate from the Monaco wreck while 001 and 004 were familiar runners with updated parts, Caliri recalls.

Modifications introduced from the start of the new season comprised revised front suspension for better turn in, revised pods and a new transaxle case. The suspension modification incorporated a new rocker arrangement to alter the ratio of wheel to spring movement. Whereas previously the rocker arm had pivoted about its inner end with the pull rod acting on its outer end and the spring/damper located in between (in conventional fashion), now the rocker pivoted about its outer end, the pull rod acted in the middle and the spring/damper was compressed by the inner end.

The revised sidepods transposed the coolers to reduce the length of aftercooler plumbing, thereby improving throttle response. Further, the radiators were side rather than top vented to keep the pod lids closed - the Cosworth car had demonstrated a higher top speed with its sealed lids. Naturally the radiators, now Valeo items, were splayed outwards while the aftercoolers (similarly upright) were transverse and vented through the engine bay. Oil cooling was now taken care of by Secan heat exchangers, these expensive lightweight items (one either side of the block) reducing the oil tank requirement to 4.5 litres while lowering engine oil temperature by 15 degrees.

The new transaxle was an integrated Minardi production with Minardi's own, Hewland pattern gearbox in which only second and fifth gear sets were of Hewland origin. Designed to save weight, the case was cast by Italian helicopter manufacturer Agusta in an American developed metal with a magnesium base but the strength of aluminium: MSR. Unique to Minardi in Formula One, this material allowed a 4mm. rather than a 7mm case wall, gaining around 10kg. over the standard magnesium case. Aluminium plates were bolted to it to carry the rear suspension. The in house gearbox was approached as a commercial venture, with Cosworth car application in mind. Caliri admitted that it was "on the limit" for Formula One turbocar use.

With its 57kg. transaxle, the revised M185 was closer to the weight limit (575kg.) but the team could not afford the carbon-carbon discs that would have shaved off a good portion of the remaining excess. However, lighter Brembo calipers introduced in mid season added up to a 6kg. weight saving. Significant modifications were not seen until the late introduction of the M186 and lack of funds for wind tunnel and track test programmes was still a major drawback. The low wing was removed for fast circuits and a snorkel turbo intake was reintroduced at Monza, where the model received M186 rear suspension.

MINARDI M186

ATR carbon fibre/Kevlar monocoque
Stressed engine
Pull rod front suspension, push rod rear - Koni dampers
Essen aluminium and magnesium rims
Brembo cast iron discs, outboard
Single Brembo four pot calipers - Ferodo pads
Carbon fibre/Kevlar bodywork
2 Valeo water radiators - 2 Secan oil heat exchangers
2 Behr air:air aftercoolers
AP twin plate clutch
Minardi five-speed gearbox - Salisbury diff
195 litre ATL fuel cell - 4.5 litre oil tank
Yuasa battery - Digitex/Veglia instruments
2708mm. wheelbase; 1813mm. front track, 1581mm. rear
567kg.

As we have seen, many aspects of the M186 design appeared first on the updated M185 trio for '86, including front suspension, pod layout and transaxle. Even the new model's rear suspension was first tested on an M185, just before the Budapest launch. Indeed, due to the incorrect manufacture of a component by a sub contractor the new car had to make its entrance with the old suspension and both M185 and M186 models were equipped with the new design at the same time, for Monza.

The new suspension featured a clever double-action operation offering increased damper movement, enhanced spring rate progression. While the top of the spring/damper was attacked by the push rod's crank in the normal manner, the unit was angled just a little from the upright position so that its lower end could be attacked by the forward arm of the lower wishbone. This arm having been suitably reinforced, the damper picked up a short distance from its transaxle pivot.

The basis of the M186 was a new monocoque, skinned entirely in carbon fibre/Kevlar. In 1980 Minardi had been offered a carbon fibre wing by ATR, a small company based in Teromo near Pescara and run by two brothers. The Pierantozzis' credentials were good, as evidenced by work for a number of important clients in the aviation world and gradually they had come to do more work for the team. Now Caliri felt the time was right to abandon the aluminium outer skin for a lighter, ATR produced tub, the brothers offering the team an exclusive contract for motor racing.

The new tub moulding incorporated the front and tank bulkheads but the scuttle bulkhead was the familiar aluminium structure. The overall shape of the car was retained, Caliri's aerodynamic philosophy requiring a 'bubble' behind the driver's head. However, a 195 litre tank allowed the distinctive dorsum to be lowered and this, together with lowered pods put the rear wing in cleaner air. A step under the pedal box allowed for the installation of a Toleman-style air deflector. An interesting safety feature was a dished driver head restraint produced from the polyurethene material used widely on road car dashboards.

While sharing running gear with the M185, the lower, 10kg. lighter newcomer featured a 99mm. longer wheelbase and an 80mm. narrower rear track. The prototype was rush-produced for Budapest and was the only example run in '86. It was tried with a stepped nose at Budapest but this development was another to have to be shelved for lack of wind tunnel test time. As the M185, the newcomer appeared with the new rear suspension and snorkel intakes at Monza.

The M186 continued in service into '87 with three new monocoques joining the original. These were two or three kilos lighter thanks to a more sparing use of resin. In addition, a couple of kilos was shaved off the bodywork by employing less skins. Essentially, the design was unchanged though further work in the Fiat wind tunnel led to slightly revised front and rear wings and a major test at Estoril in February confirmed the value of a slightly extended diffuser. The front suspension was slightly revised, as was the five speed gearbox. The 'box benefited from an improved selector fork arrangement for faster changes. For the new season, the team gave up an experiment with Torsen differentials, not having the resources to develop a suitably rugged case for the sophisticated unit.

After Rio (where Nannini lost a rear wheel due to a wrongly calibrated air bottle leading to an inadvertent over-torquing of the bolt!) the rear suspension was modified. The drawbacks of the original design were that the activating wishbone link was heavy, was expensive to produce and was hard on its bearing, while with a more conventional system the lower wishbone could have a wider base to improve rigidity. Consequently a conventional lower wishbone with a further forward reaching arm was adopted, while the base of the spring/damper unit was naturally anchored to the transaxle.

A new rear wing was introduced at Monte Carlo - a little shorter, this pushed the centre of pressure back. A three tier wing was introduced for the late season races outside Europe. An important gain came at Ricard with the first use of carbon-carbon discs, supplied by SEP, which put the car down to around 555kg. However, it was not until Monza that both drivers were able to enjoy the benefit. Following a shunt at Monza 002 was replaced by 004.

PORSCHE/TAG

By Mike Lawrence

**Dr. Ing. h.c.F. Porsche AG
Entwicklung (R&D)
Porschestrasse
7251 Weissach
West Germany**

By 1979 Ron Dennis had built an enviable reputation as a team manager. His company, Project Four, not only ran Marlboro-sponsored cars in Formulae Two and Three but had been responsible for building most of the BMW M1s used in the Pro Car series. Project Four, too, had run Niki Lauda in Pro Car. For a man of Dennis' drive and talent, the next logical stage was Formula One.

At the same time John Barnard was feeling discontented. He had been working for Jim Hall's Chaparral team in the USA and his design, the 2K, had set new standards for Indycar performance but Hall's team was not up to making it a consistent winner and, worse, Barnard was receiving little credit for his work. When Dennis approached him with the idea of a new Formula One car, he jumped at it. He would have time to consider the problem at length and not be distracted by meanwhile having to develop an existing car in parallel, which is the lot of most Formula One designers.

Dennis had staked his future in racing on his judgement of Barnard's ability and then had to find the wherewithal to back it. It so happened that Team McLaren was in the doldrums and in danger of losing its sponsor. Dennis is a shrewd businessman and McLaren showed all the signs of a company ripe for either a complete take-over or, at the very least, an injection of capital and fresh talent.

Dennis was able to buy 50% of McLaren's equity and in October 1980 became joint Managing Director, with Teddy Meyer, of a brand new company called McLaren International. John Barnard (who already had a ground-breaking chassis design under development for Dennis) joined the board as Technical Director and the remaining directorships were held by Tyler Alexander (ex-Team McLaren) and Creighton Browne. This arrangement was to last for two years at which point the position would be reconsidered and despite speculation to the contrary, Dennis maintains that the partnership worked well.

Just before the 1981 season M.I.'s first car was unveiled, the Cosworth-powered McLaren MP4/1. At first glance, Barnard's design appeared fairly conventional: a smooth, beautifully detailed and packaged, state of the art Formula One wing car. Where it broke new ground was with its monocoque which, for the first time in motor racing, was of carbon fibre. The tub was manufactured by the Research Division of the Hercules Corporation of Salt Lake City, Utah, and the fibres were bonded to 0.40in. thick aluminium honeycomb base built by M.I.

Hercules was chosen because, though carbon fibre originated in Britain, no British company was found to undertake the work (at the time the McLaren tub was said to be the largest object ever made of the material) and, indeed, some even believed that carbon fibre was so unpredictable under certain types of impact that it might disintegrate to powder in an accident. Since McLaren's number two driver, de Cesaris, had no fewer than eighteen shunts in 1981, he deserves credit for single-handedly proving the product.

The new car immediately proved an improvement over the existing McLaren M29F, and Watson finished third from his fifth start in it, second from his sixth and he won his seventh, the British Grand Prix at Silverstone. However, even as the design of the MP4 was being finalised, it was becoming clear that the days of the Cosworth DFV were numbered.

It was one thing to believe a turbo engine was necessary for the future, and quite another to obtain one. For a time, the BMW unit was seriously considered, for an exclusive option BMW had with Brabham was coming up for review but Barnard was not convinced of the long term potential of any in line four. The same went for the iron block Renault V6, a development of an old sports car and Formula Two engine, which was seriously considered. Heidegger's straight six project, which was being hawked around, was quickly rejected on the grounds that its configuration was unsuitable to be central to a competitive package.

More than anything else, however, Barnard disliked the compromise inherent in designing a chassis around an existing engine. Rather, he had in mind an integrated package which would be the ultimate ground effect machine. This vision, however, required a bespoke engine and the problem was who could, and would build it.

Dennis had always declared that his function was to provide the means whereby Barnard could provide success and he was soon engaged in discussions with a number of possible sources of supply, including Honda, Toyota and General Motors. Cosworth Engineering was also approached, and was prepared in principle to undertake a commission to design a new engine but its declared lead time to produce it was unacceptably long.

Dennis then approached Porsche, which operates an engineering consultancy division.

In retrospect Porsche may appear to be an obvious solution, for it is difficult to think of any company, outside the ones Dennis had already approached, with the resources and expertise to undertake such a project no matter how much money was on the table. It has to be said, though, that while Porsche had a remarkable reputation, it had been gained through sports car racing where it had never faced the depth of competition which existed in Formula One and where the engineering requirements were markedly different. Most of its competition designs had, in truth, been compromises; an air-cooled boxer unit is not optimum for racing at its hardest edge (as Porsche discovered in 1962 when it essayed a Formula One car) but makes sense if you are selling air-cooled boxer engined production cars.

On the other hand, Porsche had unrivalled experience of turbocharging, had excellent relationships with key suppliers of ancillaries, and as the paying customer M.I. would be able to insist on the basic package. An approach was made in August 1981 and Porsche listened with interest for it was being offered a chance to enter Formula One with someone else paying.

Porsche suggested that a three year development programme had the right ring to it, Dennis and Barnard replied it was to be ready by the end of the following year. Two months later, on October 12, a contract was signed to cover the first, six month, phase of development and work began at Weissach under the direction of Porsche's chief racing car designer, Dipl. Ing. Hans Mezger. McLaren's existing sponsors underwrote the first stage of development but it was up to Dennis to find the backing to implement the remaining work. As a precaution there were clauses in the contract which made the work the exclusive property of M.I. so had he failed to find a further sponsor no other team could have taken over the project.

The prototype engine was ready in December 1982, by which time Dennis had come to an agreement with Meyer and Alexander to buy out their equity in McLaren International. He had formed a relationship with TAG (Techniques d'Avant-Garde) a company which had been established in 1977 'to institutionalize commercial activities between Europe and the Middle East' (i.e. to invest Saudi oil revenues). TAG, which had been a sponsor of the Williams team, had interests in a wide range of enterprises, from agriculture to aircraft, and from cement to art galleries. It was a new company, TAG Turbo Engines, which signed the contract with Porsche to instigate Phase Two of the programme and it would be TTE which would sell engines to McLaren International.

One very important factor in raising the considerable amount of money required to finance the project was that Dennis had persuaded Lauda to come out of retirement and drive for McLaren. The importance of this coup in setting up the overall team package cannot be underestimated.

While Porsche was looking after the engine, Barnard was pressing ahead with a new aerodynamic package for his second generation car. Again, in this he was assisted by Dennis who learned that the National Physical Laboratories at the National Maritime Institute was interested in exploring commercial outlets for its expertise. Dennis was able to arrange a deal whereby M.I., which had previously used the 25% rolling road wind tunnel at Imperial College, would use the Institute's larger-scale tunnel, supplying its own rolling road equipment to complement the facility.

Testing of a 33.3% model showed that Barnard's concept would initially produce at least 30% more downforce with no increase in drag. In fact so good were the projected cornering forces that it was highly probable that the drivers would have to wear 'G' suits. Barnard says, "We were getting a lift to drag factor of 9 or 10 to one, and from the point of view of a designer, the potential was tremendous. The fact that the drivers' heads were going to be ripped off as they went through the corners was something to be dealt with when it happened!"

It was a problem the team never had to face for, by the time the first engine was ready to run, FISA had abruptly introduced the 'flat bottom' ruling, so Barnard's idea of the ultimate ground effect package was in ruins. Worse, the engine, designated TTE-P01, had compromises, such as the location of the exhaust pipes, which were no longer necessary. Barnard estimates that the flat bottom rules wiped out 50% of the advantage of building a 'ground up' new engine.

The team had undertaken to have a turbo car running in 1983, as part of its commitment to its sponsors. Barnard consequently designed an interim car, the MP4/1E, and that went against the grain as the MP4/1 series had been designed as a Cosworth package, the MP4/2 series as a turbo package and he disliked the idea of mating together two different concepts.

Barnard had to acquiesce, however, and in late August 1983 the 80 degree V6, twin turbo TAG engine made its competition debut at Zandvoort in the hands of Niki Lauda. By Barnard's standards the car was a poor compromise which had not been properly wind tunnel tested and refined. In a straight line the Porsche/TAG-McLaren was as quick as anything but it still had essentially a Cosworth chassis designed for about 530b.h.p., not the 100 more Lauda had on tap. While it was fast between corners, the car's aerodynamics could not use the power and the brakes proved inadequate.

Using a Cosworth engine in the right package, Watson qualified 15th to Lauda's 19th and lasted the distance to finish a fine third while Lauda retired, in 14th place, on lap 26 with the brake fluid boiling.

Another car was completed for Watson to use at Monza and iron discs were substituted for the team's regular carbon-carbon items. At Monza, Lauda qualified 13th with Watson 15th but Watson quickly picked up places in the race and was lying seventh after 13 laps when the valve gear broke and the engine died. Lauda meanwhile had problems with the electrics and was in 20th, and last, place when he retired after 24 laps.

For the European Grand Prix at Brands Hatch there were revisions to the turbochargers, radiators, and exhaust pipes, and larger rear wings. Watson qualified 10th and both he and Lauda were in 10th place when they retired (rear wing and engine failure respectively). For the 1983 finale at Kyalami the cars featured improved aftercooling, but still did not look promising in qualifying. Running at 3.0 bar the engine was now producing 700b.h.p. at 12,000r.p.m., whereas at Zandvoort it had run at 2.5 bar, developing around 630b.h.p. at 11,500r.p.m.

Watson was disqualified for an incorrect starting procedure after his car had stalled at the start of the warm up lap but Lauda drove steadily through the field to take second place from Piquet eight laps from home after the BMW-Brabham driver had felt the World Championship within his grasp and had eased off to guarantee a finish. Alas, Lauda's race did not last long after that due to electrical problems. But a glance at lap times made interesting reading. Piquet's BMW-Brabham had set the fastest lap by a clear margin, and early in the race at that, but second quickest lap went to Lauda's Porsche/TAG-McLaren. That provided plenty of food for thought for anyone contemplating the 1984 season.

TAG P01 80 degree V6

82 x 47.3mm./ 1499cc.
2 KKK turbochargers
Aluminium block and heads
Nikasil wet aluminium liners
4 main bearings, plain
Steel crankshaft, 3 pins
Titanium con rods
Mahle light alloy pistons
Goetze rings
4 o.h.c., belt driven
4 valves/cylinder, 1 plug
30.5mm. inlet valve, 27.5mm. exhaust
29 degree included valve angle
Bosch ignition
Bosch injection
Bosch engine management system
Compression ratio 7.5:1
Maximum r.p.m. 12,000
148kg.

Barnard's ground effect package had demanded a compact engine, either a V6 or a V8, with a maximum angle between the banks of cylinders of no more than 90 degrees. In order to clear the underfloor profile of a ground effect car, the exhaust pipes would leave horizontally, and Barnard had drawn a head on silhouette within which all components had to be housed.

Thus, the two water and two oil pumps, which were driven by spur gears from the crankshaft were on the front of the block, within the silhouette, and so too was the single fuel pump, driven by one of the camshafts, at the back of the block. When Porsche proposed a cowling for a bolt which would slightly transgress the silhouette, it had been told to find an alternative. In order to have some known variables, the mounting of the engine was to be similar to the Cosworth DFY engine which M.I. was currently using, and this had resulted in a slightly higher crankshaft line than was strictly necessary.

Mezger chose the 80 degree vee which, coincidentally, was the same lay-out that Honda had adopted for the Formula Two engine which went on to become its Formula One unit. Bitter experience with the Porsche Indianapolis project had led Mezger to prefer a V6 rather than a theoretically more powerful V8 (given, as at this time, unlimited fuel) on the grounds that an engine which was too good could find itself facing rule changes, such as the maximum number of cylinders permitted, which could make it obsolete. Since Renault and Ferrari both had V6 engines it had been a politically safe decision.

The base engine would finally fit almost exactly into a two foot cube with a length of 600mm. (24.0in.), height of 620mm. (24.8in.) and maximum width of 610mm. (24.4in.). Complete with exhaust pipes and turbochargers it tipped the scales at only 149kg thanks to a well designed alloy block and a magnesium lower crankcase.

The mechanicals broke no new ground, though were as advanced as any. The block was cast by regular Porsche race engine sub contractor Honsel Werke AG while the conventional steel crank was produced by Maschinenfabrik Alfing Kessler, another long standing Porsche ally. The crank ran in four plain Glyco bearings (lead bronze in a steel shell) and the twin overhead camshafts were driven by straight cut spur gears from its front end. As usual, there were four valves per cylinder - the two 30.5mm.

diameter inlet valves were inclined at 14 degrees, the two 27.5mm. diameter exhaust valves at 15 degrees. Made by Glyco, the valves were of Nimonic steel and were sodium cooled, as was long Porsche practice. There were two Bosch solenoid-operated injectors per cylinder angled downwards at 30 degrees in the intake tract, positioned between the throttle butterfly and the valves.

In order to protect the exhaust valves Porsche first experimented with ceramic inserts, the settled for drilling minute waterways between the valves. Further internal cooling was provided by oil gallery pistons. Each three ring piston's crown was slightly concave with valve clearance notches.

Bore and stroke dimensions of 82.0 x 47.3mm. gave a capacity of 1499cc. and after appearing in 1983 with a compression ratio of 7.0:1, this was increased for 1984, varying from circuit to circuit but hovering around the 7.5:1 mark - the highest run by any six cylinder engine. The available b.h.p. had increased to a quoted 750 at 12,000r.p.m. on 3.2 bar, with maximum torque of 466Nm.

A total of 56 engines were made with, at any one time, 24 in the race/test programme and eight in the development programme. On average each engine took 155 man-hours to rebuild. The production specification for 1984 had been finalised over the winter of '83/'84 and only involved a few details such as changing some steel studs to titanium ones and casting the inlet manifolds instead of fabricating them. In line with this, the name of the engine was changed from TTE- P01 to TAG-P01.

It has often been assumed that one of the particular advantages of employing Porsche was that M.I. automatically locked into the long standing relationships Porsche enjoyed with key suppliers such as Bosch and KKK. In fact, before Bosch came into the picture, M.I. had spoken to a number of other firms, such as Magnetti-Marelli, about the supply of an engine management system and throughout the life of the TAG Turbo was always prepared to listen to other suppliers for both the management system and the turbochargers.

Bosch, indeed, had initially been reluctant to become involved (it was already busy working with BMW) and only agreed to do so when Porsche's persuasion became insistent. Once it had made its commitment, however, Bosch insisted on a fully electronic management system as a useful further stage in its own research for it already supplied Porsche with a relatively crude version of the Motronic MS3 system for use in its 956 Group C cars, in addition to the electro- mechanical systems it was developing with BMW.

The term relatively is important because in 1982 the Motronic system was one of the most advanced in the world, and Formula One had yet to see digitally controlled solenoid injectors with integrated ignition timing. The requirements of Group C racing were not as subtle as those of Formula One and the progress which Bosch was to make over the next five years was extraordinary. Eventually its management system would not only provide a tailored mixture for every single r.p.m. but would take into account such factors as altitude, humidity, whether the engine was accelerating or decelerating, and how much torque load was being supplied.

KKK was another matter : it took them, Barnard fulminates, a full 18 months and a lot of money to come up with 'mirror image' turbos.

Within days of the encouragement afforded by the '83 finale at Kyalami Dennis pulled off another coup, snapping up Prost. M.I. therefore faced '84 with two drivers who were not only among the greatest in motor racing history, but both of them were first class test and development drivers. However, events at the start of the year did not suggest that the team's crushing 1984 performance could have been in the wildest dreams of any of its members.

Pre- season testing at Rio with the MP4/1Es had been a fiasco when the cars refused to start, perform, or run cleanly. In common with other electronic management systems, Motronic MS3 initially suffered from 'spikes' (electro magnetic impulses) playing havoc with it, and had to be painstakingly isolated from them. On other occasions, basic components which had been borrowed from proven production car systems, had vibrated apart. This shook the Bosch team more than a little, an attitude no doubt reinforced by John Barnard's famous temper, as it faced up to the realities of Formula One.

Bosch had been used to dealing with major manufacturers and in such dealings there are ways of doing things and lines of communication. For some time it held out against dealing directly with

McLaren, it knew Porsche, and while TAG was ultimately paying, its commission had come from Porsche. Bosch knew who Porsche was, but had no idea how to cope with a comparatively tiny outfit which seemed so unnecessarily insistent. To its credit, however, Dr Zucker's team immediately grasped the situation and, though chastened by the Rio experience, when it returned home it buckled down to work.

By the time the MP4/2 appeared for testing at Paul Ricard, many of the bugs had been ironed out. It was by any standards an impressive response and Dr Zucker and his team deserve more credit for the success of the Porsche/TAG-McLaren than has normally been given for they not only delivered the goods but they had to adapt to methods of operating which previously had been foreign to them.

When McLaren returned to Rio for the race it must have been crossing its fingers and everything else but even though he could do no better than fourth on the grid, Prost emerged the winner. Lauda, who had qualified sixth, had led between laps 12 and 37 before retiring with an electrical problem caused by a faulty power connection.

Despite the fact that McLaren was to win more races than any other team in the period 1984 - '87, its drivers only occasionally started from pole and, indeed, Lauda, something of an expert in setting pole times, won his third World Championship with an average starting place of about sixth on the grid.

It became something of a hallmark to see the cars on the grid, near the front, rarely quickest, but always in contention. There even grew a widely-held belief which said that McLaren was relatively slow in qualifying and that the TAG engine would not take 'qualifying boost'. To set the record straight, if you add up every driver's qualifying time in every race over the four year period, to create a hypothetical grid, you will discover that Prost sits on pole. He rarely made actual pole position for a race but was wonderfully consistent.

This consistency is the true hallmark of McLaren in the period. From the start Dennis had declared he was not going to build sacrificial engines in order to impress on the grid. He staked his team on the fact that the right fuel-efficient package could win regardless of who led into the first corner. In truth, it is only at circuits such as Monaco and Detroit where pole as opposed to, say, sixth on the grid is likely to be critical and on such circuits McLaren's drivers found time in the chassis rather than the engine.

In those cases where teams ran special high boost engines, and even bespoke cars for qualifying, there was a major manufacturer picking up the tab, while the position at M.I. was that the team was paying TAG for its engines and there were simply not enough spare parts or spare dyno time to make the investment in mapping the units to achieve a few minutes at ultimate power. In any case, it would have involved not merely the turning of a screw, or a replacement chip, but a lot of expense to develop new turbochargers.

Having said that, engines were run to different specifications for qualifying and racing and in 1986/'87 that resulted in a difference in power of about 200b.h.p., but McLaren did not push the engine to its ultimate possible performance.

When the team arrived for its second race at Kyalami, the engine did not run smoothly at the high altitude, but the problem was cured by fitting smaller turbochargers. From then on, three different sizes of turbines and two sizes of compressor were used and these were used in different combinations depending on weather conditions, the individual circuit, or whether the cars were running in qualifying or the race itself. Larger turbos gave more power at a cost of response, something critical at Monaco but less important at Silverstone.

Another key to McLaren's success was revealed at Kyalami when Prost's car developed a misfire and he had to start the race from the pit lane in the team spare. On that occasion he finished second to Lauda but later would come times when Prost would win in a spare car fired up at the last minute. It was this rare ability not only to give equal treatment to two top-line drivers but also to have a spare car prepared to race standard which marked out the team. Barnard's brilliant design was backed by Dennis' equally gifted team management.

For Monaco KKK delivered specially commissioned turbocharger casings which tightened internal tolerances. They were standard fitting from then on and later lightweight, thin wall turbine housings were introduced.

During qualifying for the French Grand Prix the team suddenly suffered a spate of broken pistons through detonation, a problem which was later traced to the fuel being used. Until mid-way through 1985, McLaren ran a 40/60 mixture of Avgas and pump fuel but after that Shell came up with a more sophisticated, denser toluene based fuel. The doctored Avgas had originally been provided by Shell's nearest laboratory to a given circuit, but after the failures in France supply was exclusively in the hands of the German branch.

Although in retrospect that 1984 season appears to have been a case of there being only one team in the business with the right package, M.I. suffered its share of racing luck. In France, for example, Prost lost second place when a front wheel came loose when a combination of tolerances led to the disc retaining bolts being proud of the wheel mounting surface so the wheel was pressed against the heads of those bolts proud of the wheel mounting surface. This led to two lengthy pit stops. During the second stop, the offending bolts were removed (they do not constitute part of the drive) the wheel was replaced and from there Prost put in a heroic drive to seventh place, just out of the points.

What marked out McLaren, and its associates such as Porsche and Bosch, was that the team more quickly adapted to running fuel-restricted turbo cars than any other outfit and the drivers both possessed extraordinary intelligence as well as talent and determination.

During 1984 M.I.'s main opposition had come from Piquet's BMW-Brabham which was probably the quickest car in the field but the BMW engine was being stretched to stay in contention, and its larger single KKK turbo was over-stressed, and more often than not Piquet retired, generally through engine or turbo failure. Further, whereas McLaren was running two great drivers, Piquet was teamed with one or other of the Fabi brothers, neither of whom looked like a race winner.

By 1985 the opposition was stiffer as other marques, particularly Renault and Honda, made long strides while M.I., Porsche and Bosch concentrated upon detail refinements. With increased opposition, Lauda and Prost had to work harder and their brakes in particular suffered stress. Barnard refers to this as the 'year of the brake duct' and at Detroit both cars ran out of braking. By mid-season the problem had been identified as acute transfer of heat to the brake fluid and, once identified, the problem was cured.

Dr Zucker had redesigned the Bosch management system using the mass of data gathered from the MS3 system and this was now housed neatly in one box. As part of the package, the on-board computer read-out included the number of laps at current boost which the car could complete.

From the German Grand Prix onwards the cars had the 'mirror image' KKK turbos which gave the design team more space to play with as well as cleaning up the gas flow to the right-hand turbo.

In race trim, the engine is quoted as having run 3.3 bar, producing 800b.h.p. with torque increased to 497Nm., while for qualifying 890b.h.p. was available. Part of this increase came from the improved management system, part from the mid season introduction of 'rocket fuel'. The TAG PO1-MP4/2B remained the most competent all-round package but while Prost finally clinched a World Championship title with five wins (a sixth win at Imola was discounted when it was discovered his car was 0.7kg. underweight - less than the weight of the fuel it had used on its slowing down lap) Lauda managed only three finishes from 14 starts.

There were those who suggested that Lauda suffered as all the team's effort went into Prost's Championship challenge but since that has been discounted by Lauda himself one can only put his season down to racing luck and in a couple of instances, driver error. In the Dutch Grand Prix, however, Lauda used all his race craft to keep Prost at bay to win his 25th (and last) Grand Prix victory.

Lauda's right hand was injured during practice for the Belgian Grand Prix when his throttle stuck open and he hit a barrier. This left him a non starter in Belgium and his place in the following European Grand Prix at Brands Hatch was taken by Watson who discovered that in the two years he had been out of Formula One, development had been such that he could not make up the lag with a couple of test sessions and one race.

Lauda retired at the end of the season and his place was taken by Rosberg. While Lauda and Prost liked their cars set up to remarka-

TAG PO1 V6 powered Barnard's MP4/2 chassis to a hat trick of World Championship titles. Detailed photographs of the ultimate MP4/2, the 2C of 1986 appear on page 32.

bly similar specification, which made preparation of the team spare easy, Rosberg's more flamboyant style required completely different settings and this slightly altered the delicate balance within the team.

Again, Barnard chose to refine his existing design rather than break new ground. The twin turbochargers were repositioned again, this time so that they took air from close to the radiator inlets. KKK also produced new turbines which enabled more boost to be delivered without suffering a penalty in back pressure, which had previously been the case. Indeed, in one early test session M.I. had turned the boost right up to see what would happen and the car went no faster.

From Hockenheim onwards, Bosch came up with an improved engine management system, designated MP1:7, and KKK came up with a new turbocharger, the HHB. These improvements allowed both cars to run 3.9 bar at Hockenheim and Rosberg and Prost were able to take over the front row of the grid though in the race the fuel read-out failed and both cars ran out of fuel when lying second and third. Normal race boost was officially 3.3 bar in spite of having 25 litres of fuel less, and at this level the engine developed 850b.h.p. at 12,800r.p.m. with an increase of torque to 519Nm.

By this time all was not well in the Dennis/Barnard relationship. Barnard was becoming increasingly frustrated and was looking for fresh challenges. There was a suggestion that he would go to BMW to design a BMW Grand Prix car but BMW's board of directors decided not to proceed with the project. He eventually left M.I. at the end of August and went to work for Ferrari. The departure of its Technical Director might have severely damaged another team but Ron Dennis held everything together and Steve Nichols, number two in the design team, was able to step into the breach with apparently little trouble.

During the mid part of 1986, McLaren began to suffer a fuel pick-up problem which defied easy diagnosis. This problem was solved, after Barnard had left, by the addition of three fuel pumps within the tank. For the last three races of the year, the McLaren cars had more fuel to use and so went faster. The explanation for this improvement given by observers at the time was that the TAG engine had benefited from a major internal modification.

1986 was really the year of the Honda-Williams as Honda made remarkable strides with its management system but Prost again had a very consistent season. He retired only twice, won four races, and was disqualified once when the officials at Monza decided he had been too slow in changing to his spare car when his race car refused to start due to the failure of its mechanical fuel pump. In fact, at Monza Dennis kept Prost on the track while he remonstrated with the officials but then suddenly withdrew his objections as on lap 28 Prost coasted to a halt.

While it is true that had Mansell not had a tyre blow in the final round at Adelaide and had been able to maintain his third position for the remaining nine laps, he would have won the World Championship, it is also true that he had thrown away vital points earlier in the year. The title is won by consistency over a whole season, a fact ignored by the British news media which concentrated on Mansell's spectacular puncture. This made good copy and Mansell achieved the 'heroic loser' status so beloved by the British but it missed the point of the Championship.

Thus, Prost emerged Champion for a second year, albeit with one less win than Mansell. It was the first time since 1959/60 that a driver had won consecutive titles and the first time ever that a team had provided the cars for a hat trick of drivers' titles. M.I. had to relinquish the Constructors Cup to Williams but by the end of 1986 it could boast 22 wins from 48 races in the three years since the introduction of the MP4/2.

Rosberg retired at the end of the year and was replaced by Johansson, sacked by Ferrari, whom Dennis had run under Project Four back in 1980 when he had won the British Formula Three title. In the last race of '86, Rosberg's engine had run an 8.0:1 compression ratio and this became standard for 1987. Again, the modification was allowed by a combination of the management system and fuel. For the engine's final year power in race trim went up to 900b.h.p. at 13,000r.p.m. running 3.5 bar (3.8 bar in qualifying) with maximum torque increased to 527Nm.

To cope with the increased compression ratio, the pistons themselves became heavier, had heavier gudgeon pins and the con rods too were changed and became slightly heavier. These apparently minor modifications increased reciprocating weight which led to vibrations which caused other parts to break. Calculations had suggested that the modifications could be accommodated by the engine but the calculations themselves were at fault since they had been based on adding all the additional weight together and not compounding the individual additions in weight. This was cured for Hockenheim by re-balancing the crankshaft.

Prost won the last race of 1986 and the first of 1987. In the interim McLaren had moved lock stock and barrel to a new factory and Gordon Murray had joined the team as Technical Director. It is a further demonstration of the remarkable strength of the entire team that these upheavals did not affect it.

At Hockenheim Prost led from half distance, with Johansson taking third a little later, but he was robbed of his 28th Grand Prix win, and the points which would have taken him to within a point of the top of the Championship table, by a broken alternator belt. This had previously happened early in the San Marino Grand Prix when he was lying second and at Paul Ricard when Johansson lost sixth, and a belt had broken during testing at Silverstone as well.

After four years of reliable performance this spate of failures was a mystery but a cure was effected by a redesigned twin belt assembly rapidly supplied by the American firm Gates.

Although a deal with Honda for 1988 was announced in September, engine development continued and as late as Mexico there were visible modifications when, to service a revised version of the on-board computer, the cars sprouted small telemetry aerials.

While the Honda-Williams was the cream of the field in 1987 Prost had emerged as the driver of his age. By his own standards, three wins in a season was below par but he was almost always among the top four qualifiers (typically Johansson would be half a dozen places lower down).

Failures of the alternator belt lost Prost a win in Germany and a possible second place at Imola. A first lap incident with Piquet in Mexico on the first lap in Japan lost him other possible points. That puncture in fact lost him two laps but in what Ron Dennis describes as his finest drive he unlapped himself once but was rewarded only with seventh place. It is interesting that his fastest lap (1m 43.844s) was 1.696 seconds better than anyone else.

In Australia both cars were fitted with thicker carbon-carbon discs and both retired with loss of brakes around the two-thirds mark. That was the last race for the TAG P01 engine and it seemed likely to be consigned to history since a further possible application in helicopters was eventually ruled out on the grounds of unit cost.

Throughout its effective life of four seasons the combination of McLaren and Porsche/TAG had been a major force as a total of three World Championship titles and 25 Grand Prix wins demonstrates. Had his luck been slightly different, it is possible that Prost might have given the team a fourth drivers' Championship as a fitting swan song to the engine.

McLAREN MP4/2

Hercules Corp. carbon fibre monocoque
Stressed engine
Push rod front suspension, rocker arm rear - Bilstein dampers
Dymag magnesium rims
SEP carbon-carbon discs, outboard
Twin AP two pot calipers - SEP pads
Carbon fibre bodywork
2 Unipart combined water/oil radiators
2 Behr air:air aftercoolers
AP twin plate clutch
Hewland/McLaren five-speed gearbox - ZF diff
220 litre ATL fuel cell - 9 litre oil tank
Yuasa battery - Contactless instruments
2794mm. wheelbase; 1816mm front track, 1676mm. rear
540kg.

Barnard's turbo car, the MP4/2, bore a striking similarity to the earlier Cosworth and hybrid MP4/1 series but then he had always resisted change for the sake of change. As before the monocoque was made by the Hercules Corporation but was enlarged behind the driver to accommodate a fuel bag 30.5 litre larger than on the MP4/1 since 1984 saw a 220 litre race ration.

The monocoque was fully shrouded to allow maximum aerodynamic flexibility and consequently was of angular form. It set a wedge shaped scuttle behind an aluminium nose box and had relatively low-cut cockpit flanks and a long, boxy tank, upon the flat roof of which was a conventional tubular roll hoop. Slots set into the lower section of each tub flank allowed a duct to take cooling air from the inlet of each relatively long sidepod to the engine bay without encroaching upon the cooler tunnel space.

The combined water/oil matrix was slanted upwards and forwards alongside the front section of the tank to top vent while the aftercooler for each bank flanked the rear bulkhead, venting through the engine bay. The side panels were formed with the undertray and were pinched in as they ran back alongside the engine, leaving prominent horizontal fins formed by the full width undertray immediately ahead of each rear wheel. The side panel in-sweeps met a narrow tail shroud, with a wide diffuser rising either side of it through the suspension: Barnard's pioneering bottleneck plan rear end.

The diffuser was exhaust activated from the first race. Compressor intakes were set into the horizontal fin ahead of each rear wheel as here tyre rotation flung air downwards causing high pressure. Louvres were set into the deck above each turbo to assist heat extraction. The rear deck was formed at the base of a bulbous, bubble-shaped dorsal shroud which concealed both tank and engine, leaving only the tip of the roll hoop exposed. A wedge shaped nose/scuttle shroud was detachable from the rest of the fuselage fairing, which extended as far as the rear wing's central post (forming high swept fore-

decks ahead of the pod lid apertures).

The wing post was supported by an integral magnesium transaxle case which contained an oil tank in the bellhousing and carried the rocker arm suspension via yokes. Transmission internals were modified FGB with a cam and pawl diff.

The most obvious difference of the evolutionary '84 car, so far as external differences were concerned, was a larger rear wing supplemented by three-piece winglets. The bottleneck plan was more pronounced, thanks to a more compact engine package, while the pod inlets were higher and narrower than before, with a pronounced inward curve at the leading edge.

Suspension remained as on the MP4/1 series and McLaren was still the only team using Bilstein dampers, which it had adopted at the beginning of 1983. Bilstein had come into the reckoning in 1982 when McLaren was running ground effect and massive springs. The Koni dampers that everyone except Renault was using were unpressurised and sensitive to heat, and Barnard disliked the idea of having to add ducts to cool dampers. Bilstein was at that time one of few makers of pressurised gas dampers and while they were not instantly adjustable they did maintain their damping ability consistently over much higher temperature range, and could be used for race after race.

When McLaren proved so successful, other teams wanted anything on their cars which they could share (Barnard once threatened to put a rubber duck on the nose cone to see how many would copy it) but Bilstein was so pleased with its relationship that it signed an exclusive deal with M.I.

Another area where McLaren went its own way was with brakes. In 1982 Lauda ran solid carbon-carbon discs in a test session at Donington. Barnard says: "The performance against iron brakes was stunning. As a measure you are talking about banging on iron brakes at the 100 yard board and, with the best composite brakes available at the time you are talking about banging them on at the 60 yard board."

The key to carbon-carbon brake performance is temperature control and throughout '83 and '84 McLaren constantly had to rethink ducting and airflow over the discs. Having run solid carbon-carbon discs at most races in '83, SEP, having been impressed by M.I.'s commitment had cooperated in the development of ventilated discs, and these had appeared at Kyalami.

Using the new disc material which generated far higher levels of heat showed up some shortcomings in the AP calipers M.I. was using. Barnard therefore designed new twin caliper units which he had machined from a solid forged billet of aluminium alloy to obtain a higher grade of material. These calipers had more surface area, the better to dissipate heat, and included refinements such as a finned end to the piston to lower the temperature of the fluid. They were first raced at Kyalami in '84, where they were used only at the rear. Thereafter they became standard fitting all round.

Barnard suspected that a lot of his car's handling problems had originated from the cam and pawl differential it was using. One of the McLaren engineers suggested the Gleason Torsen unit might solve the problem and Dennis negotiated an exclusive arrangement with the New York company. At Monaco McLaren used the Torsen diff for the first time and its smoother operation in the appalling weather conditions made the MP4/2 more controllable and thereafter the Torsen diff became standard McLaren equipment.

Also in time for Monaco, KKK delivered specially commissioned lightweight turbocharger housings with tighter internal clearances. They were standard fitting from then on. At Zandvoort compressor feeds were set into the adjacent side panel. A total of four MP4/2s were built, two of which formed the mainstay of the team's effort. 03 was the team spare car while 04 was used only for testing.

McLAREN MP4/2B

Hercules Corp. carbon fibre monocoque
Stressed engine
Push rod front and rear suspension - Bilstein dampers
Dymag magnesium rims
SEP carbon-carbon discs, outboard
Twin McLaren two pot calipers - SEP pads
Carbon fibre bodywork
2 Unipart combined water/oil radiators
2 Behr air:air aftercoolers
AP twin plate clutch
Hewland/McLaren five-speed gearbox - Torsen diff
220 litre ATL fuel cell - 9 litre oil tank
Yuasa battery - Bosch/Contactless instruments
2794mm. wheelbase; 1816mm. front track, 1676mm. rear
540kg.

For 1985 M.I. produced a car which was recognisably still a development of the original 1981 MP4. In common with all other makers, the front end of the monocoque had been revised to accommodate the new nose box regulations and this resulted in a longer nose. Again, the regulations called for a smaller rear wing and to service it the sidepods were 100mm. shorter, and the rear bodywork was 33mm. narrower.

There were new front uprights and the former rear rocker arm suspension was replaced by a push rod system which was stiffer and lighter and allowed small gains both in geometry and aerodynamics. Although M.I. had had to switch from Michelin tyres to Goodyear, it was a smooth transference largely because Goodyear's radial technology had reached a par with the French firm.

When M.I. was formed it inherited the existing Team McLaren transaxle which was basically standard Hewland FGB internals in an integrated bellhousing/main case that had originated from Team Tyrrell. In 1982, as part of a general weight saving programme, some steel components were replaced by titanium ones but by 1984, when around 800b.h.p. was being fed through it, the transmission started to show signs of strain. At first the problem was dealt with by shortening the working life of components and then M.I. started to have special gears made by EMCO of Chicago.

McLaren was able to specify a higher grade material and the gear teeth were ground, rather than shaped and shaved, to give better surface contact. Arrow gears was approached to make a stronger ring and pinion. These internals were fitted into what was still basically the old Tyrrell case, though it had been thickened up here and

there. For 1985 McLaren had a new, slimmer case and while the 'box followed FGB principles, 70% of the internals were unique to McLaren.

Out of work on the gearbox came revisions to the c/v joints because that was one of the areas which was showing most stress due to the increase in power. Further, with the conventional design it was difficult to seal in the grease and sometimes it leaked and got onto the brakes. Barnard solved the problem by incorporating the c/v joints with the rear hubs and switching them from taper roller to ball bearings. At first the idea seemed as though it was going to be expensive for already c/v joints were being thrown away after every race and it was feared that the rear hubs would have to be scrapped too. In fact, the unit being much stiffer, proved to have a considerably longer life.

Having created new c/v joints, Barnard began

to examine their geometry. Most joints derive from road cars and have to be more flexible in their geometry than is required for racing. By tailoring the geometry of his own c/v joints to his specific needs, Barnard was able to find significant improvements not only in the life of the component but also in its torque carrying capacity. This led him to look carefully at the lives of other components to see if they could be lengthened so that the team would have fewer headaches as when races followed each other on successive weekends.

As part of this general policy of control, to-

wards the end of the year M.I. took over the monocoque moulds from Hercules and from MP4/2- 06 on, all McLaren monocoques were made in the team's works at Woking though using materials supplied by Hercules.

Silverstone saw a subtle front suspension geometry modification through altered pick-up points which made the '85 version more controllable, and this was balanced by a subsequent rear geometry change. From Hockenheim onwards, the cars had 'mirror image' KKK turbos which gave the design team more space to play with as well as cleaning up the air flow to the right-hand

turbo. M.I. toyed with front wheel turning vanes, and sparked off the aerodynamic front brake duct craze.

Lauda's title winning MP4/2 had been pensioned off, but the remaining three '84 cars had been updated to 'B' specification. All five 'B' cars produced saw race action during the year with Lauda mainly driving the last '84 car (04) which had previously been reserved for testing. A new car (05) was generally used by Prost, and he used the first McLaren monocoque car for the last two races.

McLAREN MP4/2C

McLaren carbon fibre monocoque
Stressed engine
Push rod front and rear suspension - Bilstein dampers
Dymag magnesium rims
SEP carbon - carbon discs, outboard
Twin McLaren two pot calipers - SEP pads
Carbon fibre bodywork
2 Llanelli combined water/oil radiators
2 Behr air:air aftercoolers
AP twin plate clutch
McLaren six-speed gearbox - Torsen diff
195 litre ATL fuel cell - 9 litre oil tank
Yuasa battery - Bosch/Contactless instruments
2794mm. wheelbase; 1816mm. front track, 1676mm. rear
540kg.

Although the '86 regulations restricted fuel capacity to 195 litres, Barnard decided against radical change to the existing monocoque but he did take the opportunity to seat the driver in a more reclined, lower position and to put the gearchange inside the tub instead of over the top of the right-hand side. In order to accommodate the smaller ATL fuel cell, internal panels were added to the monocoque. Apart from these small modifications, there were no significant revisions to the car.

For 1986 a six-speed McLaren gearbox was fitted as standard and as well as the extra cog, there were improvements to the transmission's lubrication system.

McLaren's excellent relationship with SEP had led to the development of a carbon-carbon clutch, first tried in 1985. Apart from the inherent characteristics of carbon-carbon, it weighed half the weight of the regular AP unit. Distortion-free plates made for very clean gear shifting but racing starts were more difficult, because take-up was more critical and therefore the driver had to be more sensitive.

The carbon-carbon clutch was used in the '86 development programme but was not raced and before it could be put into service Tilton came along with an off-the-shelf unit which included some improvements in assembly and design, whereas Barnard had basically made a carbon-

carbon version of a metal clutch. Subsequently AP came to an agreement with SEP to produce its own purpose-designed carbon-carbon clutch using SEP friction material. McLaren, however, would run conventional AP clutches throughout '87 as well as '86.

Five new MP4/2C tubs were made during the year, all by M.I. at Woking. Rosberg used /02 exclusively while Prost did most of his races in /03, did single events in /01 and /04 and finished the last three races in /05. MP4/2C/04 was damaged when Prost was involved in Arnoux' incident in Hungary and was not taken to races again.

McLAREN MP4/3

McLaren carbon fibre monocoque
Stressed engine
Push rod front and rear suspension - Bilstein dampers
Dymag magnesium rims
SEP carbon-carbon discs, outboard
Twin McLaren two pot calipers - SEP pads
Carbon fibre bodywork
2 Secan water radiators - 2 Secan oil heat exchangers
2 Behr air:air aftercoolers
AP twin plate clutch
McLaren six-speed gearbox - Torsen diff
195 litre ATL fuel cell - 9 litre oil tank
Sonnenschein battery - Bosch/Contactless instruments
2794mm. wheelbase; 1841.5mm. front track, 1676mm. rear
540kg.

In August 1986 John Barnard had left McLaren International and Steve Nichols had moved up to oversee the development of the '87 car. Later, Gordon Murray and Neil Oatley joined the design staff. Nichols decided on a conservative approach, one of development rather than radical change, but he did take full advantage of the 195 litre fuel limit by making the monocoque lower and slimmer behind the driver's head and redesigning the aerodynamic package. The dorsum was noticeably less intrusive but equally as significant was a switch to side venting.

Previously, wind tunnel testing had shown that the lower drag achieved by side vents, with their lower pods, had been negated by reduced downforce from the rear wing and since it had

been a straight trade Barnard had decided to make life simpler by maintaining the status quo. Instead of combined Llanelli water/oil radiators slanting upwards and forwards, Nichols specified vertical Secan radiators splayed away from the tank. Between the radiators and the aftercoolers, Nichols placed small Secan oil heat exchangers.

Apart from Secan replacing Llanelli, one other component supplier was changed. A Sonnenschein battery replaced the Japanese Yuasa which came from motorcycle racing and was anyhow made under licence from Sonnenschein.

A total of six MP4/3s were made during the year, 05 being built up for Johansson to replace his regular race car, 04, which was destroyed

during practice at the Osterreichring when he collided with a deer. The sixth car was purpose-built to take the Honda V6 engine which McLaren would have in 1988, while one of the earlier monocoques was taken out of the race programme and re-jigged to provide a second Honda-powered test car.

**Renault Sport
Usine Amedee Gordini
1, Avenue du President Kennedy
91170 Viry-Chatillon
France**

Bernard Hanon gave the go-ahead for the first turbocharged Grand Prix car of the mid engine era on July 21 1976. Renault's Chairman saw the benefit to his giant corporation in terms of image, publicity, technical spin-off and sheer inspiration for all its engineers. On the other hand, with the turbocharging of road racing engines a relatively unexplored science, the programme was nothing if not ambitious. And there would be an additional burden for its bold advocates: Hanon dictated that Renault Sport, the marque's new competition wing directed by Max Mangenot, must simultaneously pursue its similarly challenging Le Mans programme to a successful conclusion. Hanon's decision came a few weeks after the failure of a turbocharged Renault prototype to win the Great French race at a first attempt.

Although the Renault-Alpine had retired from Le Mans, its performance had been worthy enough to convince the Francois Castaing headed Renault Sport technical team that it had the basis of a potential outright winner in its V6 engine. That was something Castaing hadn't even dreamt of when he had designed the V6 as a 2.0 litre normally aspirated race engine back in 1972.

The V6 had been born of a meeting of Castaing's bosses Christian Martin (member of the main board), Jean Terramorsi (director of Gordini, Renault's competition and high performance engine wing) and Claude Haardt (manager of the Usine Amedee Gordini at Viry Chatillon, just south of Paris) with Francois Guiter of Elf. The State owned petroleum company was actively supporting the competition programme run by Jean Redele's *Automobiles Alpine* concern at Dieppe. Alpine based its competition and high performance cars around Renault engines and on its behalf Elf was keen to support a new Renault race engine.

Renault agreed that Gordini should produce a 2.0 litre unit following the general architecture of the 2.0 litre V6 'PRV' road engine that was under development as a joint project between Peugeot, Renault and Volvo (hence PRV). Castaing had his 90 degree vee, d.o.h.c., alloy head, iron block V6 running on the bench by the end of the year.

Meanwhile, and in no connection with that work, Alpine's engine preparation chief Bernard Dudot was exploring the potential of turbocharging. Up at Dieppe he had prepared a single Holset blown Alpine 1600 rally car which promptly won the '72 Criterium des Cevennes. It was, says Dudot: "a small test; a simple installation with no wastegate and no special injection adaptation. We were simply trying to find a way to increase the power of a limited capacity rally engine".

Castaing's V6 was unveiled by Renault in January 1973, named the Gordini CH1 in tribute to Claude Haardt who had been killed testing a Renault propelled powerboat. It was destined for the European 2.0 litre sportscar series, powering an Elf sponsored Alpine prototype. Although the first season was not a success, that didn't stop Terramorsi and Guiter aspiring to 3.0 litre honours. The World Championship equated 2.1 litres turbocharged to 3.0 litres atmospheric, and Porsche had now demonstrated the awesome road racing potential of turbocharging through its 917 Can Am car.

Before the year was out Dudot had been recruited by Gordini and had been dispatched to California to further investigate turbocharging, and to look at supercharging, the other alternative. "I went to California with no idea of the technical choice. I visited a lot of small companies, and also Garrett, the biggest turbocharger company. At the same time I had a look at the Porsche Can Am car. At the end the choice was turbocharging - it was the most efficient solution".

In 1974, exploiting a reliable 305 b.h.p. at 10,800 r.p.m., the 2.0 litre Renault-Alpine A441 was fast enough to dominate the European title chase. Meanwhile, Dudot and fellow Gordini engineer Jean-Pierre Boudy had further developed the turbocharged 1600cc. in line four to extend their knowledge. Dudot recalls that he didn't yet believe it would be possible to do a competitive 1.5 litre turbocharged Grand Prix engine. Nevertheless, Gordini and Elf were already toying with the idea of a radical Grand Prix engine, perhaps a 3.0 litre W9 or a 1.5 litre V6 turbo? Ken Tyrrell was invited to meet Terramorsi with Tyrrell team sponsor Guiter at Paul Ricard and was asked his opinion. He favoured the turbo.

Already, in May '74 Dudot and Boudy had turned to the V6, with intent to produce a turbocharged 2.0 litre sportscar engine. Dudot recalls: "we had taken the bull by the horns and we worked like idiots. By the beginning of 1975 we had tested our engine for the first time. Jabouille was in despair - he dared not tell us the thing was undriveable". In fact, Jabouille later likened its throttle response to pushing a button to call a lift...

Dudot and Boudy persevered and found improvement, mainly through adaptation of the turbocharger; in particular the size of the turbine and compressor housings. Their CH1 was blown by a single Garrett turbocharger, using standard production equipment intended for diesel engine application. The block ran non-standard pistons to lower the compression ratio and had improved lubrication, improved water flow around the heads to cool the exhaust valve seats and sodium filled exhaust valves. The fuel injection system incorporated a Kugelfischer metering unit and this was equipped with a pneumatically controlled 3D cam to adjust flow to match boost pressure, as well as throttle opening.

The improved engine was slotted into a suitably modified Alpine A441 to contest the 1975 sportscar World Championship. The debut race at Mugello brought victory but the balance of the season was a disaster. Meanwhile, at Viry Chatillon Boudy was already working on a reduced stroke 1500cc. version. The exercise had been commissioned by Elf, which had ordered two so called 'EF1' engines for evaluation purposes. The idea was to race a Renault turbo powered Tyrrell six wheeler in the 1976 World Championship.

The first EF1 was fired up on the bench on July 23 1975. The second was measured at 360 b.h.p. during a test of August 8. Dudot says: "we very quickly reached 500 b.h.p., using 2.5 bar boost". On November 18 the engine was track tested in an A441 prototype at Paul Ricard. However, its development was being bugged by failures stemming from the fact that the production based Garrett was not up to the strain of the 500 b.h.p. output necessary to match 3.0 litre normally aspirated engines.

Nevertheless, Renault, assisted by Garrett, was now dedicated to both Le Mans and Formula One turbo engine development. Renault took over Alpine and incorporated its competition activities with those of Gordini, creating 'Renault Sport' under the direction of Mangenot and the management of Gerard Larrousse, Terramorsi having been forced to stand down due to ill health. Castaing was Technical Director of the Viry Chatillon based operation, which was liaising closely with Garrett, Elf and Michelin as it pursued its far reaching programme into 1976. Tyrrell's reluctance to commit his operation to the turbo route found Martin studying a report on the feasibility of an in house Grand Prix team, ready to brief Hanon....

On March 23 1976 the EF1 was tested on Michelin's Ladoux test track in a *Laboratoire* Alpine single seater. Then, in June, the sister 2.0 litre prototype made its ill fated Le Mans debut. The sole entry suffered detonation caused by the strain of running the Mulsanne. Nevertheless, Le Mans project manager Dudot reported that he felt sure he had the basis of a future winner.

Sadly, soon after Hanon's historic decision Terramorsi died, not having had a chance to see Le Mans conquered, or to hear Renault bring a distinctive new exhaust note to the Formula One scene. But his aspirations continued to unfold and on September 16 a Formula One operation was consolidated at Viry Chatillon, leaving Alpine's Dieppe factory as the base for the Le Mans programme. Engine testing included evaluation of an alternative 80mm. bore EF1,

without definite conclusion. Boudy stuck with the regular 86mm. bore.

On December 18 Ken Tyrrell, hedging his bets, signed an option for the supply of the EF1 from 1977 until the end of the decade. Tyrrell designer Maurice Phillippe began work on a six wheeler Renault design while production of Renault's own Formula One car had already begun. Following wind tunnel tests of a straightforward four wheel chassis at St Cyr, construction of the aluminium monocoque Renault RS01 commenced in January 1977.

The first half of '77 saw the heavy (iron block, turbo laden), radial shod Renault Grand Prix car test and the Renault Le Mans car fail again to beat Porsche due to piston failure. The RS01 made its famous race debut at Silverstone in mid July: Jabouille qualified 21st and retired when the induction manifold split. In any case, the car would have run out of fuel. Tyrrell was meanwhile concentrating on his regular Cosworth car...

Renault Sport took a deep breath for further development, then tackled four more Grands Prix. Blown at 2.7/2.8 bar whereas the Le Mans engine was run at 2.0 bar, the car continued to lack speed and reliability. Tyrrell let his option lapse.

The Renault Grand Prix programme continued into '78 with a single car for Jabouille and a high at Kyalami, where the altitude helped secure sixth fastest qualifying time. There was little else to report until mid June when, having won Le Mans, Renault Sport could close the resource-sapping prototype department, increasing the size of the Viry Chatillon workforce from 136 to 176.

With Le Mans out of the way an air:water aftercooler was brought into play. With the previous air:air aftercooler charge temperature had varied with ambient temperature - since the pneumatic control over the metering unit was sensitive only to pressure, it had been fooled as charge density varied with charge temperature. The mixture had been liable to become over-rich, sometimes diluting the oil film in the cylinder to a disastrous degree. The air:water aftercooler provided a steadier charge temperature thanks to better low speed cooling and a decrease of peak temperatures, and helped improve throttle response.

Toyed with at Monaco, the air:water cooler became standard equipment from the Austrian Grand Prix, in which Jabouille was a splendid third quickest. Monza saw the RS01 fastest in a straight line, though throttle lag, excess weight and lack of dependability were still hurdles to be overcome. Nevertheless, the *Regie* collected three World Championship points at Watkins Glen in October.

Renault Sport ran two cars in '79, Jabouille joined by Arnoux, at first in the RS01 design which took pole at Kyalami this time around. Then came the RS10 ground effect design master minded by Michel Tetu, who had joined in 1976 from the Alfa Romeo Autodelta prototype team, having previously worked on Ligier GT cars. The Tetu chassis was effective and for Monaco was equipped with a twin turbo engine, the pair of smaller, lighter turbos (one per bank) offering faster response and a wider power band. As Garrett had wanted an understandably long lead time to develop the new hardware, Castaing had turned to Porsche twin turbo supplier KKK. He had also improved the induction system, and had introduced oil jets to spray the underside of the piston, reducing crown temperature. Thermal problems affecting pistons and rings had been a major headache.

"At the start", says Dudot, "the engine was a new problem for the sub contractors. For the piston and ring suppliers, the temperature was so high it was beyond their experience of other engines. For example, we tried many new solutions to decrease the temperature of the piston. Mahle had no experience of oil circulation in such a small bore piston. It eventually developed the oil gallery piston, which it then could make for everyone..."

Run as high as 3.0 bar, the 7.0:1 compression ratio twin turbo engine was officially rated at over 600 b.h.p. with a maximum of 11,000 r.p.m., enjoying a significant power advantage over 3.0 litre normally aspirated engines. However, weight, turbo lag and reliability still left scope for improvement. Piston failures continued, this time due to inadequate charge cooling which demanded two stage aftercoolers incorporating a primary air:water matrix and a secondary air:air matrix. There was also a valve spring problem caused by the savage cams necessary to get the required valve opening which was tackled in conjunction with supplier Schmitthelm.

Michelin was on a steep learning curve too, its radial tyres not yet consistently competitive. And the weight handicap was around

EF4
90 degree V6

86 x 42.8mm. / 1492cc.
2 KKK turbochargers
Aluminium block and heads
Nikasil wet aluminium liners
4 main bearings, plain
Steel crankshaft, 3 pins
Steel con rods
Mahle aluminium pistons
Goetze rings
4 o.h.c., belt driven
4 valves/cylinder, 1 plug
29.8mm. inlet valve, 26.1mm. exhaust
21.5 degree included valve angle
Marelli ignition
Kugelfischer injection
Compression ratio 7.5:1
Maximum r.p.m. 11,000
160kg. including turbo system, clutch and starter

30kg., which put a burden on brakes, in particular, due to the lack of engine braking, while the impressive torque of the twin turbo 'EF2' was unkind to the transmission. Nevertheless, the first victory came in 1979, at a memorable French Grand Prix.

As Renault Sport strode into the Eighties having inspired Ferrari and Alfa Romeo to follow the turbo route, Dudot took over its technical direction, Castaing quitting over a policy dispute. In 1980 Renault was a serious World Championship force with its RE20 propelled by a revised EF2 that boasted Nikasil rather than steel liners for better heat rejection and improved water circulation. Running 3.0 bar boost, or thereabouts, Arnoux won at Rio and Kyalami, Jabouille won at the Osterreichring. Elsewhere mechanical failures were rife, and Michelin radials still proved a handicap on occasion. And the same weight and throttle lag penalties had to be faced, and once again valve springs proved troublesome...

1981 saw an engine with better response, but apparently lacking the power and response of the first rival Formula One turbo engine, the 120 degree V6 from Maranello. However, reliability was improving and a valve seat problem that reared its head in the summer was rapidly overcome. Renault was competitive and took third place in the constructor's championship. Nevertheless, the season's tally for Arnoux and new boy Prost was still a total of only three wins.

In 1982 the same pairing took two wins each but Renault reliability had slipped again and the team could not better third in the constructors league. It could count 10 pole positions but no less than 26 retirements from 32 starts. An injection control problem was the most easily pin pointed weakness, following the introduction of a more flexible, more frugal engine at Monaco.

The EF3 introduced both DPV (as later used by Boudy on the Peugeot Turbo 16) and electro-mechanical injection. The cam on the Kugelfischer metering unit was controlled by a servo motor which responded to signals from a microprocessor based ECU. The system was not, Dudot admits, as sophisticated as that on the rival Kugelfischer injected BMW engine, for the processor developed by Bosch for BMW could cope with more than the five parameters dealt with by Renault's black box. Nevertheless, the in house system brought major improvement. Alas, there was a long delay in supply of the servo motor ordered from an aeronautical company. Dudot says: "it was ordered right at the start of '82 but was not available until September. Before that we had to use a Japanese servo that could not adopt to Formula One conditions".

The Japanese motor found it hard to survive in the environment of a hot, high revving race engine. Servo failures cost the team two wins and the World Championship. At least by the end of 1982 the current RE30 chassis was down to 580kg., with more to come through an advanced composite monocoque for '83. Consequently, with reliable electro-mechanical injection and lighter, more aerodynamically efficient air:air aftercoolers Renault could enter the new flat bottom era full of confidence. Prost (now partnered by Cheever) had matured into an outstanding driver and come mid '83 he looked certain to win the World Championship, in spite of a late entrance by the composite RE40.

The RE40 had been accompanied by a new alloy block cast by sub contractor Messier that replaced the familiar spheroidal graphite casting from Renault's own foundry, saving a further 12kg. The switch to alloy was simply to save weight, Dudot confirms, and the alloy EF3 brought the RE40 right down to the new 540kg. minimum. Renault followed Ferrari in running water injection to assist charge cooling and supplied the EF3 to Lotus in a new agreement. An initial problem of block rigidity soon overcome, the EF3 was rated a healthy 650b.h.p./10,500r.p.m. on 3.2 bar race boost.

In qualifying Renault used 3.4 bar boost and water-sprayed its aftercoolers but didn't match Ferrari or BMW turbo power. And just as Prost looked to be sailing to the title, BMW made a surge in race power, to which Renault failed to respond. Piquet pinched the World Championship and Renault could only look to runner up positions in both drivers and constructors championships as its best ever results.

Prost had severely criticised the alloy EF3 engine for not having evolved fast enough to match BMW progress: Dudot set about to remedy that with the evolutionary, higher compression EF4 for '84. Heart of this electro-mechanical unit was an aluminium block from Renault's own foundry, one that still bore a strong resemblance to the original CH1 iron casting. However, it had been completely redrawn and had a slightly greater wall thickness.

Like the CH1, the EF4 block was closed by alloy heads and an alloy lower crankcase that supported the main bearings. The heads carried separate cam carriers with cam bearing caps formed by the cam cover. Compared to the Messier EF3 casting, the in house block had strengthening at the main bearings and head attachment. Block/head sealing was achieved via a composite metallic gasket for gas sealing with Viton ring seals for oil and water passages. The liners were located at the top of the cylinder, being free to expand at the lower end where two 'O' rings provided a seal.

The crankshaft, incorporating extended balance webs, was machined from solid and nitrided and rotated in Glyco bearings. The smooth running unit required no vibration damper. The camshaft drive was taken off the front of the crank, a gear on its nose driving a gear either side, one per bank. The drive was then transferred via external toothed belt, the belt looping down around a lower crankcase mounted pulley on its own side. The low set pulleys drove oil and water pumps neatly tucked, Cosworth style, either side of the crankcase.

Lubrication was taken care of by a pressure pump, a main scavenge pump and a scavenge pump for each turbo, while water circulation was ensured by a centrifugal pump for each cylinder bank. Drives for the alternator, distributor and the Kugelfischer metering unit, all located within the central valley of the block were taken off the camshafts via short toothed belts. The distributor and alternator were at the front and were driven off the front end of the left bank's inlet cam while at the other end the metering unit was driven off the back end of the right bank's inlet cam. The main fuel pump was run off the nose of the crankshaft.

The crankshaft was turned by nitrided steel con rods through

Renault - Lotus EF4 - 95T with fuselage shroud off, revealing the cooler layout : twin water radiators ahead of the aftercoolers, one per bank.

plain big end bearings secured by two high tensile steel bolts. Steel gudgeon pins were free floating in the three ring pistons, which had flat tops pocketed for valve clearance. The combustion chamber was modified from the design run in '83 for "improved thermodynamic efficiency in the light of the 220 litre fuel ration". In essence, the piston was taller to come higher up the bore at T.D.C., increasing the compression ratio. The inlet valves were still at 10 degrees from the cylinder axis, the exhaust valves at 11.5 degrees. The sodium filled valves were closed by conventional coaxial springs and were operated by steel bucket tappets housed in the cam carrier. Each steel camshaft ran in four plain Glyco bearings.

The inlet tracts were siamesed, unlike the exhaust tracts. Each siamesed tract was fed compressed air from the plenum chambers atop the engine, one per bank. The engine stood 640mm. high to the top of the induction manifolding and was 640mm. wide between cam covers and 480mm. long. Designed to be run fully stressed, tub mount pick ups were situated under the heads and at the foot of the crankcase. Tyrrell had complained about these cantilevered mounts back in '76 and Lotus ran additional bracing struts from the tub.

The capacitor discharge ignition was Marelli's 'Raceplex' system and its electromagnetic pick up was positioned in the bellhousing. It was independent of the injection ECU. The firing order was 1 - 6 - 3 - 5 - 2 - 4. The electro-mechanical injection system was still Kugelfischer with Renault Sport control, as developed in 1982. One injector fed into each siamesed inlet tract.

The EF4 retained the Renault Sport licensed DPV system to improve compressor performance. According to Dudot, this had been "very important for turbo lag". However, he admits that, with continuing development reducing lag in other ways, he cannot say how significant DPV was come the mid Eighties. Renault had started developing electronically controlled injection with DPV on the engine and were continuing with it. The drawback was a slight pressure loss through the DPV unit at each compressor entry.

Each compressor blew through an air:air aftercooler to its respective plenum chamber and each chamber was injected with water from a central injector, the flow rate adjusted to match boost pressure. Boost was controlled by Renault's own wastegate positioned at the junction of the three manifold branches, immediately upstream of the turbine entry. The '84 exhaust system mounted the wastegate and turbo lower with the turbo shaft parallel to the longitudinal axis and the compressor facing forward, and provided for an underbody exhaust exit, whereas in '83 the exhaust had sometimes been used to blow the rear wing.

For 1984 the turbochargers were once more Garrett rather than KKK units. Dudot: "in '83 we had a lot of turbo development to do but KKK didn't want to assist. It believed its turbos were OK. Ferrari and Renault had the same turbo - it was correct for the Ferrari engine, but not for our engine as we had a higher airflow". In crude terms, the turbos were too small to deliver the necessary flow at full power. In contrast, the Porsche/TAG engine had arrived with bespoke KKK turbochargers.

Renault signed a three year technical agreement with Garrett. "We needed special constructions - it was very difficult to get specialist turbos from KKK. We knew the possibility of development working with Garrett. Garrett was completely implicated in the project and developed turbine wheels from special steels and a high speed compressor wheel machined from solid in a special aluminium".

With turbochargers employing exotic materials and advanced processes, Renault had insured itself against the hammering that would be dealt by lean running 220 litre race conditions. With aftercoolers designed to be positioned upright either side of the rear bulkhead (Porsche/TAG-McLaren style) rather than angled alongside the tank, the '84 turbo system was more compact and its plumbing was shorter, providing improved response and better full throttle running. The lighter turbo system and a more extensive use of magnesium and carbon fibre, in particular in the inlet manifold, contributed to a weight saving of 12kg. for the EF4 package.

Renault admitted that the most fundamental improvement of the EF4 engine was its turbo system. In addition, it planned to introduce fully electronic injection. Dudot wanted the superior control offered by low pressure solenoid injectors and work started on a full engine management system at the start of '84. However, it would take some time to complete. Meanwhile, in electro-me-

Renault EF4 showing the camshaft drive, exposed at the front end.
The tub picks up at the crankcase base and outside each head.

chanical form Renault quoted a maximum torque of 49m./kg. at 8,500r.p.m. with maximum power 660b.h.p. to 750b.h.p. "according to configuration". Race boost was 3.0 - 3.2 bar.

While the EF4 engine was the responsibility of the staff under Dudot's technical direction at Viry Chatillon (where Boudy, off to Peugeot, had been replaced by Jean-Jacques His), in the spring the race team moved to nearby Evry, where Tetu was technical director. This hesitant move towards autonomy for the chassis/gearbox department reflected a concern of Prost, who had taken nine of the team's 15 wins during a three year spell.

Although he had developed into a remarkable driver, Prost hadn't been the ideal Renault employee - he had made his criticisms of the corporation's Grand Prix effort too widely known. Of course, it was conventional wisdom that the team was too cumbersome to be a truly effective fighting force: it operated under the shadow of a cumbersome committee based organisational structure; it was conservative in its approach to a dynamic environment; it tried to cope with engine and chassis development in the same breath. Prost had pressed for a separate, tighter, sharper, more flexible race team based at Paul Ricard and engineered by Lotus' saviour Gerard Ducarouge. Frustrated, he got out.

Warwick and Tambay were recruited to replace Prost and Cheever at Renault Sport, of which the director was still Mangenot, the manager, Larrousse, with Jean Sage Race Team Manager. Larrousse said he was moving with the times by making the race team semi-autonomous - he no longer saw the place for an all-embracing Technical Director, such as Ferrari had in Forghieri. Sage's operation was 70-strong (but did not enjoy in house wind tunnel or autoclave facilities) and was joined by Tambay's Ferrari engineer Tommaso Carletti, while Dudot's engine department employed 85, producing 40 engines and preparing 15 of them for the works team (customer engines being sub-contracted).

Aerospace company Hurel Dubois at Velizy manufactured Renault's composite chassis - an evolutionary design for 1984,

rather conservative as Tetu's previous, effective offerings had been. The RE50 offered improved rigidity and weight distribution as well as improved aerodynamics. Naturally, it was Elf fuelled and continued to exploit Michelin tyres, as had its highly competitive predecessor, while the conservative approach extended to the retention of cast iron discs.

The season got off to an encouraging start with Warwick seemingly destined for victory at Rio when his suspension broke 10 laps from the finish, legacy of an earlier bump with Lauda. Only at Dallas would things look so rosy again. The rival German engines surged to the fore at Kyalami, then Ferrari similarly overshadowed Renault at Zolder. Thereafter, it was German horsepower all the way, with the exception of Dallas - and that freak race went the way of Honda...

If in qualifying Renault often had to take a back seat to customer Lotus' Goodyear shod, Ducarouge engineered chassis, on race day Tetu's car generally had the upper hand. Tambay managed to lead at Dijon and Monza - but on both occasions found himself overhauled by Lauda. A higher compression engine introduced at Monza followed a heavily revised unit introduced at Dallas which had featured new camshafts and pistons and revised electro-mechanical injection.

It wasn't until after Monza that Renault was able to test fully electronic injection, the technology exploited so well by Porsche/TAG. It was clear that lack of the late arriving 'Renix' system had put it at a disadvantage. Generally it had been strongest on slow circuits where consumption is less of a problem. The early races had been a struggle with fuel waxing: it was chilled to 30 degrees below zero and fuel line heaters had to be introduced to overcome misfire in the early laps.

At Dijon larger aftercoolers reduced charge temperatures, while revised Elf fuel was said to offer a much needed 4 - 5% consumption improvement. Just before the home race Larrousse had declared that the works team would withdraw temporarily for further development if consumption hadn't been improved by mid season. He was clearly trying to galvanise the effort to produce an engine management system to match Bosch Motronic. Poor fuel consumption was deeply embarrassing to a company selling mass

141

Tetu directs operations in the Renault Sport encampment at Dijon, 1984.
Note low height of engine relative to the tank, with charge plumbing removed.

market road cars. Nevertheless, it was Estoril before the long awaited Renix equipment was ready to race.

Renault might have looked to Kugelfischer owner Bosch for electronic injection but knew that both its German rivals had a very close relationship with the German company. Consequently, with the 220 litre ration looming, it had resolved to produce its own answer to Motronic. In 1978 Renault had formed *Societe Renix* in conjunction with the American Bendix electronics corporation and, based at Toulouse, this concern developed and produced all its electronic systems. It was briefed to develop a low pressure system that would offer control of injection timing and duration, with integrated ignition control.

Suitable solenoid actuated injectors were procured from Marelli

Weber, one per cylinder to be run initially. The system was based around a more powerful processor than that used to control the superseded electro-mechanical injection and incorporated more sensors. Dudot considers: "the Motronic system was a little more sophisticated than the Renix system, but it was very close". With Renix in place, Renault reckoned it had finally achieved fully competitive race power.

Earlier fuel consumption deficiencies aside, the RE50 had proved poor at extracting the best from Michelin's offerings on bumpy surfaces. Its push rod rear suspension was suspected - the similarly shod McLaren MP4 appeared to ride bumps better and it had a more compliant rocker arm rear suspension. Nevertheless, Tetu considered his chassis mechanically sound if aerodynamically imperfect (and a number of aerodynamic modifications followed the early installation of larger coolers).

Not surprisingly, a four turbo engine that had tested at Kyalami

RENAULT

before the season got underway hadn't re-surfaced. "It was a two stage system", Dudot admits, "but we had no time in which to develop it. There was much work to do to develop completely this installation".

Designed to tackle the 220 litre race ration, the EF4 didn't respond as well as the lower compression EF3 to the stimulant of higher boost and the older engine had been raced on the rare occasion when fuel consumption was of little concern, and frequently exploited in qualifying. Between them Renault and Lotus took three pole positions, of which two were down to the customer team. And Tambay's morale boosting Dijon pole was one protected by Saturday rain. The Renault V6 had come close to 4.0 bar in qualifying by mid season and Renault started its own cars from the grid top 10 on all but four occasions but only once from the front row.

1984 was the first year since 1978 in which Renault failed to win a race. From 32 starts (Tambay withdrew from Montreal due to leg injury but a third car was run for test driver Streiff at Estoril) the team amassed 33 points, with rostrum finishes for Warwick at Kyalami (third), Zolder (second), Brands Hatch (second) and Hockenheim (third) and for Tambay at Dijon (second). Only half a dozen retirements were down to chassis failure, mainly of the drivetrain. Another half dozen retirements were caused by engine breakage or excessive thirst, while eight were due to shunts or spins, and a turbo failed once, leaving only 11 race classifications.

If Renault was on the way down, Lotus was on the way up. Recruitment of Ducarouge, fired by Euroracing, in mid '83 had been the turning point. When Ducarouge, whose talents had been squandered by Euroracing, unpacked his bags at Ketteringham Hall in rural Norfolk in June '83, Lotus was struggling with the 93T. That car had taken it from the Chapman/Cosworth era into the Renault age. Within five weeks Ducarouge had prepared a lighter, more agile chassis based on the previous year's carbon fibre/ Kevlar monocoque. It retained unfashionable rocker arm suspension, yet was as competitive as its Pirelli radials allowed - competi-

Monaco 1984 - first corner of the race. A relatively low speed shunt caused this damage to the carbon fibre/Kevar monocoque of Tambay"s car.

tive enough to outqualify the Renault works team at the Oster-reichring, Zandvoort and Brands Hatch, where de Angelis took pole and Mansell mounted the rostrum.

Ducarouge's technical direction lifted Lotus out of the floundering situation in which it had so often found itself between Chapman breakthroughs. Having, for example, been upstaged by Williams and Ligier (under Ducarouge) in the exploitation of wing car technology, Lotus now found itself uncharacteristically honing the racer's edge rather than the pioneer's axe.

One year on from the loss of its founder in December 1982, Lotus was a compact, 60-strong operation enjoying a promising on-going relationship with Renault. Team director Peter Warr renewed his driver contracts but switched from the inconsistent Pirelli radials to Goodyear rubber - just as Akron was in the process of switching from crossply to radial-ply. Unlike McLaren, Brabham and Williams (the other British top teams), it had to pay directly for its engines and, backed by long time sponsor Imperial Tobacco, it

Warwick's Renault in full flight at Zolder, 1984, en route to six points. Note how engine cooling scoops flank the tank.

operated on a relatively tight budget. It had nowhere near the financial resources of the Renault works team but it did have an in-house composite production facility, one that in '81 had produced the first ever carbon fibre/Kevlar skinned monocoque. From the Ketteringham autoclave came the first Ducarouge monocoque, for the 95T, penned by 93T designer Martin Ogilvie.

An elegant development from the compromise 94T, the 95T was equipped with a Renault engine/turbo installation serviced by Mecachrome at Bourges where 15 technicians looked after a common pool of 24 engines on behalf of Lotus and Ligier. Ducarouge explains: "development was through Renault Sport with Mecachrome rebuilding engines. We had a lot of trust in Mecachrome, which worked to aerospace standards. We never had any problem and had the same performance as the works engines".

Like Ligier, Lotus could run only one Garrett equipped car in the early races. It introduced a fuel warming heater before Renault, at Zolder, but had to wait until Imola before both cars could run Garrett qualifying turbos and until Montreal for the larger after-coolers seen on the works cars at Dijon. Prepared by a team headed by Bob Dance, the 95T emerged as the most competitive Goodyear runner of a Michelin dominated year. If, in the final analysis, Ferrari came out with a higher Constructors Championship total, that was thanks to a slightly superior finishing record.

In the drivers table de Angelis took the honour of highest placed non-Porsche/TAG-McLaren driver thanks to a string of solid finishes in another promising but winless year for Lotus. Highlight of the year for de Angelis was right at the start: pole at Rio, while Mansell took pole at Dallas. Both drivers generally qualified solidly in the top ten and de Angelis managed 11 points finishes, four on the rostrum, Mansell five, two on the rostrum. However, neither driver climbed above the lowest rung, though de Angelis received six points following Brundle's Detroit disqualification.

The 95T handled well and its aerodynamics were clearly sounder than those of the RE50, which it outqualified on 12 occasions. It was a superb chassis handicapped by a lack of race power and often by inferior race tyres. It did not frequently outrun the RE50 on race day, probably due to Goodyear's lack of radial experience. Zolder was a rare Goodyear weekend but saw Ferrari rather than Lotus profit. The the next spurt of Akron competitiveness came at Monte Carlo where there was a new construction front and Lotus went to the top of its client list. From the front row, Mansell would probably have won the wet race but for driver error. Hockenheim brought a very competitive dry race tyre and this time de Angelis led - only for his engine to fail after a mere eight laps.

Engine and turbo breakages each cost six finishes, while transmission failure cost four, brake failure two. Three incidents left a tally of 17 finishes from 32 starts compared to the works team's dismal record of 11. In terms of qualifying speed and points gathering, Lotus was the top Renault team of '84 and its chassis was arguably the equal of the McLaren MP4. Certainly it was the best on Goodyear and the best with Renault power.

Ligier, by way of contrast, had the poorest of the three Renault chassis. A newcomer to the V6, the team should have been moti-

Mansell's Renault-Lotus at Zandvoort, 1984. The EF4 propelled Lotus 95T was a well balanced chassis with good grip : arguably the best on Goodyear tyres.

vated by a 120 degree Matra V6 turbo, a successor to the marque's classic 3.0 litre 60 degree V12. However, designed by George Martin with backing from the Talbot/Peugeot PSA Group, the 1.5 litre Matra turbo only made it as far as the test bench. Performance wasn't the problem - it was a political dispute between Matra and PSA that left it stillborn. That meant Talbot could no longer offer its *Automobiles Ligier* team a competitive engine. Guy Ligier heard the news at Monza in '82 and went straight to Renault.

Ligier was well connected and was a well established part of the French Grand Prix effort. The former gentleman Grand Prix driver had, in essence, taken over the Matra Grand Prix programme in the mid Seventies, acquiring its sponsor (SIETA, the national tobacco company), its engines and many of its key personnel, led by Ducarouge, the 'crew chief'. Together Ducarouge and Michel Beaujon had engineered a series of highly competitive machines, of which the Cosworth cars of 79/80 came very close to claiming the

Ligier began its Renault adventure at Rio in 1984. This is rookie Hesnault getting to grips with its A.C.T.-monocoque, long wheelbase chassis.

ultimate accolade for France.

Ligier was offered the Renault V6 to replace his Matra V12 for '83 but, having lost the partnership of Talbot, found he could not raise adequate finance. His team's second switch from Matra to Cosworth power was in striking contrast to that made for '79. Inexplicably, Ligier had let his association with Ducarouge lapse in '81 and while Ducarouge was revitalising Lotus fortunes, Ligier saw even his FOCA travel concession slip from his grasp...

For '84, Ligier acquired Renault engines on the same basis as Lotus, the state lottery 'Loto' helping ensure an adequate budget. Michelin agreed to continue supplying the Abrest, near Vichy based team and even new number two driver Hesnault could offer good freight rates through his family's shipping company. The 70-strong equipe took on de Cesaris as number one driver and Beaujon and Claude Galopin produced its first composite chassis. In no way handicapped by a long term friendship with President Mitterand, Ligier was now in a position to strengthen the national Grand Prix effort...

Other than for a tub from Advanced Composite Technology, Ligier made most of its chassis in house: it emphasised that only wheels, tyres, brakes, gearbox internals, fuel bag, steering rack and instruments came from outside. That allowed tight control over quality of manufacture. The JS23 was a brand new model, with a rearward weight bias and only its long wheelbase in common with the superseded Cosworth car. Alas, getting to grips with turbo power proved a struggle and the team was completely overshadowed by the other Renault runners.

Ligier's most encouraging performances came at Monaco and Montreal where Cesaris used the rear-weight-biased JS23 's traction to break into the top ten qualifiers. Elsewhere the car was a midfield qualifier, and everywhere it was a midfield runner. For the last few races the team introduced a heavily revamped JS23B, this move indicative of the weakness of the original design, which had been hacked about without solving fundamental problems: lack of grip, excess weight and inadequate cooling. The 'B' spec belatedly introduced Renault's larger specification aftercoolers but did nothing to improve Ligier's struggling status.

From 31 starts Ligier managed a dozen finishes, only one in the top six: Cesaris was fifth at Kyalami. The effort had been weakened early on by an ill judged diversification into CART racing that had fizzled out by mid season, later by industrial problems that had left Ligier too busy fighting the labour unions in his city runabout factory to motivate his team. Yet following a breakfast rendezvous with Larrousse during the Estoril finale there was renewed hope for the future...

On behalf of Renault, Larrousse had started talks with Lauda at Detroit and into the autumn it had looked increasingly likely that the Austrian would accept the challenge of the slumped works team. Chairman Hanon gave the nod but a story in the French press alleged that employing the star would cost a king's ransom and in the face of poor productivity and hostile unions the deal fell through.

Larrousse sat in an awkward position between the bureaucracy and politics of Paris and the reality of racing. He felt uncomfortable running Renault Sport in the wake of the rejection of the Lauda deal and spoke of increasingly trying conditions. The Ligier team offered fresh motivation, and before the year was out Tetu had asked to move with him down the road to Vichy. Larrousse's departure made way for an executive who held more sway on the main board - Hanon's brother in law Gerard Toth.

Quality control director Toth was known as a decision maker and an achiever. With Mangenot retiring at the end of the year, he moved into Renault Sport as combined President and General Manager. But there was a catch: he had no experience of motor racing. On the other hand, nor had he any grudge against the Tyrrell team. Stuck with Cosworth engines, as an anti-turbo activist Tyrrell had, somewhat ironically, become a thorn in Renault's side. Nevertheless, Guiter approached Toth on behalf of his old associate and Toth agreed to Tyrrell's recruitment, provided it represented a viable commercial proposition for Renault Sport. Toth pointed out that more funds would be available for overall development, and that eight cars would give Renault more chances to win. Consequently, the Mecachrome workforce was expanded to match a larger customer pool, though Tyrrell's supply could not be arranged until the summer, and at first the newcomer would have to accept engines based on the old iron block.

EF15
90 degree V6

80.1 x 49.4mm./ 1492cc.
2 Garrett turbochargers
Aluminium block and heads
Nikasil wet aluminium liners
4 main bearings, plain
Steel crankshaft, 3 pins
Steel con rods
Mahle light alloy pistons
Goetze rings
4 o.h.c., belt driven
4 valves/cylinder, 1 plug
29.8mm. inlet valve, 26.1mm. exhaust
21.5 degree included valve angle
Marelli ignition
Weber injection
Renix engine management system
Compression ratio 7.5:1
Maximum r.p.m. 12,000
154kg. including turbo system, clutch and starter

In spite of the enthusiasm for the electronic EF4, it had been recognised that the V6 needed a major update for '85. The EF4's architecture was inherited from its 2.0 litre ancestor and in conjunction with Renault's Rueil R&D Department Dudot's team set about evolving a longer stroke version to challenge younger generation rivals. That entailed heavy revision of the V6, the modified, (80.1mm. rather than 86.0mm.) small bore block incorporating improved waterways.

With a revamped combustion chamber and smaller piston crown Renault was looking for improved combustion and a shorter heat flow to the cylinder wall to assist heat dissipation. Of course, a longer throw crank promised more torque, and the unit would keep maximum revs as 12,000r.p.m. Race boost went up to 3.5 bar from the outset. Renix engine management was now standard, this year operating two injectors per cylinder. The ECU was programmed to keep the wastegate setting within certain limits, though ultimate boost control lay within reach of the driver in the form of a five position switch. The driver was also provided with a switch specifically to produce a spurt of power for overtaking. He could keep this switch pressed, but had to use it with caution...

The new EF15 was 20mm. lower overall, and was 40mm. narrower at the top: the inlet trumpets were angled inwards so the plenum chambers came closer together and were lower set. Each cylinder's Weber-Marelli injectors appeared on the outside at the base of the inlet manifold with attendent fuel feed lines necessitating a bulge in any close fitting engine shroud. Revised exhaust plumbing tucked the turbos and wastegates closer to the block with the turbo shaft at 45 degrees to the longitudinal axis, while larger aftercoolers were standard. The new installation was 6kg. lighter and the upper monocoque attachment points had at last been revised, now picking up on the cam covers, Cosworth style.

Mindful of qualifying engine requirements, an updated EF4 was developed alongside the EF15. This so called EF4*bis* was equipped with the revised turbo installation and with certain EF15 internals, and was reckoned to contain around one third new parts. It was produced in both low (7.0:1) compression, high boost qualifying trim and higher compression, more economical race configuration since the EF15 would initially be in short supply.

The '85 engine track test programme got underway at Rio in February, with Lotus as the factory team didn't yet have its '85 chassis and the EF4*bis* wouldn't fit an '84 car due to the revised turbo installation. The modified, interim engine was found to be down on power and poor in throttle response. However, with a revised exhaust system it was running properly at Rio in March for both Lotus and Renault. In qualifying trim it was found to fly without wastegates, Garrett's '85 qualifying turbo pushing out a solid 4.5 bar boost: around 1000b.h.p.

The Evry race team was now living under a dark shadow. Upon his appointment Toth had been faced with uncertainty over the tyre situation in the wake of Michelin's withdrawal but on November 8, three days after starting work, he concluded the anticipated deal with Goodyear. Then had come the real worry: Hanon was replaced as Chairman of Renault by Georges Besse - a man with a cost cutting axe to wield. During '84 it had been announced that Renault was studying a brand new four cylinder engine in anticipation of the mooted 1.2 litre formula. Now each and every project was under the closest scrutiny and even the long term future of Renault Sport in Formula One could not be counted upon.

Things looked better in the short term. The Evry operation had expanded and been reorganised under Toth, and was provided with at least a temporary base at Paul Ricard, a 500 square metre workshop just 100 yards from the Signes curve for use during testing. The team still had to hire the circuit on a day to day basis but was able to install its own permanent timing sensors at strategic points around the track.

Rather than attempting to recruit a 'name' designer to replace Tetu, Toth opted for internal promotion, reckoning that his organisation should not have to share the credit for any success that might come its way. Admitting the risk inherent in this policy, Toth promoted Tetu's righthand man Jean-Marc d'Adda to the post of chief designer while putting Bernard Touret in overall charge of the Evry technical team, in which Jean-Claude Migeot headed aerodynamic research.

Rear of the Renault RE60B monocoque with aftercoolers either side of the rear bulkhead. The mounts accept the EF15, with cam cover pick up.

Renault EF15, with 12-bolt AP Racing 7 1/4 inch clutch and Garrett turbochargers. Note twin solenoid-operated injectors per cylinder.

D'Adda, Touret and Migeot developed the preliminary RE60 design left behind by Tetu, producing a straightforward development of the '84 car with strengthened transaxle, suspension to suit Goodyear tyres and aerodynamics that took advantage of the repackaged turbo system. Race preparation was headed by Patrick Ratti and while Carletti ran Tambay's car, Warwick was rejoined by John Gentry, his Toleman race engineer who had spent a very brief spell at Euroracing.

This year there would, in effect, be two works teams, for Hanon had promised Lotus 'works' status - it would get Renault Sport developments as soon as the works team. Ducarouge pledged to stay with Lotus at least until the end of the '87 season and produced a refined 95T in the 97T which retained Goodyear tyres. While de Angelis stayed on to drive it, Mansell's contract was not renewed. Warr had lured Senna from the Toleman team, offering the Formula One newcomer number one status. Senna requested joint number one status, as Tambay and Warwick shared at Renault.

Of the four Renault leading lights, Senna shone most brightly. Poor Tambay and Warwick didn't have a chance, burdened with an uncompetitive chassis that left them floundering in midfield. In contrast, Senna took over from Piquet as King of Pole Position and broke Lotus' long winless streak. Before the season was very old he had established himself as a more equal number one than de Angelis, the team gelling around him.

Warr was quoted by team confidant Gerard Crombac in *Sport Auto* telling de Angelis that (just as the Lotus chassis could get a quicker lap time out of a given boost level than Renault's offering) Senna could get a quicker lap time out of a given boost level. End of argument. And certainly Senna was a revelation, early on dominating the streaming wet Portuguese Grand Prix: in that performance driving skill was everything, power was insignificant.

Renault was always short of race power, even with the EF15 which offered more torque and greater fuel efficiency but was in very limited supply at the start of the season. Only one car could be equipped at Rio; Lotus had to wait until Imola, where His noted that there was still plenty of development to come from the new unit. Senna's Estoril performance highlighted the smoothness and drivability of the superseded engine. However, the stronger EF15 was reckoned to be 4-5% more fuel efficient. And that still wasn't good enough by '85 standards. Renault introduced 'periscope' compressor air collectors in mid season and race boost went as high as 3.8 bar but the EF15 never looked as efficient a race engine as the title winning Porsche/TAG and towards the end of the season Honda overshadowed both Renault and Porsche/TAG.

Lotus introduced a fuel consumption read out for the driver (as run by Renault since Rio '84) in mid season, along with a pits to car radio. Clearly the equal of its predecessor, its 97T was a superb chassis, and it enjoyed consistently good qualifying tyres and plenty of qualifying power from the low compression EF4*bis* with wastegates removed. While the KKK blown BMW four offered more qualifying power, it was less drivable and Brabham was often let down by its Pirelli tyres. Overall the most successful qualifying combination was that of Senna, the Lotus 97T, Goodyear tyres and the Garrett equipped EF4*bis*. Renault-Lotus took a total of eight pole positions and was unrepresented on the front row on only half a dozen occasions.

The 97T chassis worked well almost everywhere, the exception to the rule the Osterreichring where Lotus had not attempted to test. Ducarouge recalls that, "some fuel efficiency was lacking but in general Ayrton considered it a good car".

If the 97T was a first class chassis, clearly the EF15 race engine was another matter. It served both 'works' teams and Ligier from the aborted Francorchamps meeting and, equipped with it from Monaco, Senna led more laps than anyone else but, frustratingly, winning was often just out of reach. After Estoril, he won only one more race, in the damp at Francorchamps, while de Angelis, who adopted a tortoise rather than a hare policy, inherited victory at Imola. Using an EF4*bis*, Senna had run out of fuel while leading, and on no less than eight other occasions he was let down by engine or ancillaries. It did look as though Renault was trying to run too many cars.

For its part, Lotus not only produced a superb chassis (and was

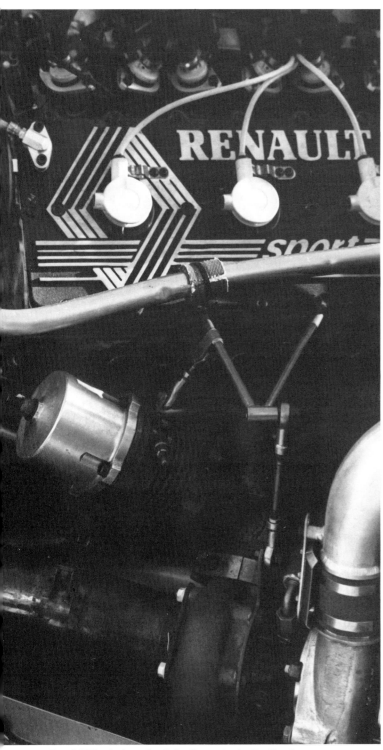

Renault EF15 turbocharger installation. Note wastegate at junction of manifold, just ahead of turbine entry, and rotor shaft bearing oil feed.

of hope at Estoril and both at Estoril and at Imola Tambay found himself on the lowest rung of the rostrum. Thereafter, apart from some encouragement at the aborted Francorchamps meeting, on the North American trail and at Zandvoort, Renault was simply a midfield runner. The introduction of a heavily revised 'B' spec RE60 at Paul Ricard didn't buck the trend, and come the second visit to Francorchamps, neither driver could reproduce the promising time set by Tambay earlier in the season: while others went quicker, Renault went 1.5 seconds slower...

At Estoril, then in North America Warwick qualified sixth fastest, a feat matched by Tambay at Zandvoort. Hardly significant achievements when Senna was setting pole position after pole position. In the Zandvoort race the RE60Bs suddenly looked more competitive than before - but following a warm up suspension failure full tank running was perhaps ill advised and, significantly, neither car ran the distance. Both officially retired with "transmission failure".

If nothing else, the Renault chassis was generally dependable, aside from its FGB-based transmission. Like Lotus, during the course of the season it decided it would be prudent to switch to a DGB-based transaxle, but unlike Lotus it did not complete the work before the end of the campaign... And on six occasions its transmission certainly broke. Four times the engine or its ancillaries failed. Add on five retirements due to 'incidents' and that left 14 finishes from 31 starts (which included a camera car driven by Hesnault at the Nurburgring, the team missing Kyalami). Finishes in each of the first four races brought points, but thereafter only another three events added to the poor tally. The post-Tetu Renault was a flop.

Often it was a pig; occasionally it handled well, yet would still lack pace. Why remained a mystery. Warwick tried a Lotus 97T in the autumn and reported eye opening front end adhesion and high speed corner stability. While it offered greater responsiveness to chassis alterations than its predecessor, the B version had only represented a marginal improvement over the disappointing original design. It brought Renault down to the weight limit from a starting point in excess of 570kg., improving already good acceleration, but did little to tackle the fundamental problems of lack of grip and poor turn in. And it could not accept EF4 chassis mounts, so required a qualifying version of the EF15 which was never as strong as the big bore engine.

While Renault slumped without Larrousse and Tetu, Ligier started to pick itself up. The team had, of course, been reorganised around the Renault defectors, Beaujon heading the drawing office while Galopin was in overall charge of race preparation. Hesnault had gone, to make way for Laffite, and though the state lottery had to stand down as it planned to let punters gamble on Grand Prix races, the national tobacco company was back in evidence, along with Candy. Ligier's state connections were clearly still important and it was understandable that the team should bow to the official line by boycotting Kyalami, like the state owned team.

Throughout the season the JS25 model produced by Tetu was a good midfield runner, well capable of collecting useful points (unlike its predecessor). Tetu hadn't had sufficient time to produce anything other than a heavily compromised derivative of the existing car but concentrating upon aerodynamics and front suspension paid off. Excess weight, the introduction of difficult Pirelli tyres and lack of pre- season testing were high hurdles to overcome; Tetu steadily pared weight off one of the heaviest cars on the Rio grid and Pirelli tyres improved as the season wore on. Interestingly, Cesaris was the fastest Pirelli qualifier at Estoril - probably as the weight of the JS25 helped put heat in the rubber. He was, after all, only eighth on the grid.

Going into a season without a chance to learn about the car was a significant drawback for newcomer Tetu, and a succession of accidents by Cesaris hampered the chassis development effort - no sooner had the team four complete chassis than Cesaris would put another out of action! Not only operational difficulties but also a financial headache arose and apparently Ligier suggested Cesaris pay for repairs out of his retainer. From Monza the Italian was replaced by Streiff. Whereas Cesaris' only finish had been fourth at Monaco, Streiff managed third at Adelaide and at Brands Hatch gave the team its '85 qualifying highlight with fifth fastest time. In contrast, Laffite only once (and only just) made it into the grid top ten, though he did finish in the top six on five occasions, taking to the rostrum at Silverstone (third), Hockenheim (third) and Ade-

the first team to employ tyre warmers) but achieved excellent reliability - only twice in 31 starts was chassis than engine failure to blame for retirement. De Angelis's tortoise policy paid off with 11 points finishes and early on, after Imola he had found himself leading the drivers championship. However, of all his finishes only three put him on the rostrum, whereas Senna managed six finishes each on the rostrum. Together the hare and the tortoise amassed 71 points for Lotus - an equal number to Honda-Williams but less than Ferrari and Porsche/TAG-McLaren, if somewhat closer to the title winner than in '84.

With sweet handling, good grip and excellent reliability, Lotus had the right chassis and tyres, and adequate power if inadequate fuel efficiency. Renault, on the other hand, although similarly using the dominant Goodyear tyres, had its worst ever composite chassis. Of course, it didn't help running a Tetu-sired design without the man himself, and Toth's reluctance to go for an established design engineer looked a misjudgement.

From Rio the RE60 proved uncompetitive. There was a glimmer

laide (second).

Those rostrum finishes perhaps flattered the car, though by Brands Hatch the chassis was performing well, an understeer problem having been traced to a lack of mechanical rather than aerodynamic grip. Steady progress over the season gave Ligier's new regime a firm foundation upon which to build in '86.

Tyrrell also made progress, though from a lower level, having absolutely no experience of turbocharged Formula One. Designer since the memorable six wheeler days of the mid Seventies, Maurice Phillippe had drawn Tyrrell's first composite car, the 012 of 1983, as the basis of a turbo machine. BMW engines were a strong possibility but no contract was forthcoming and by '84 the team had become an embarrassment to a turbocharged Grand Prix circus. Ken Tyrrell was the only participant standing to lose through retention of the 220 litre fuel limit, shelving a planned cut to 195 litres for '85. Come mid '84 and his participation had been outlawed in controversial circumstances.

Tyrrell and FISA buried the hatchet in March '85, Tyrrell having set up as a turbo performer and FISA having failed to prove more than minor indiscretions against him. Alas, the team was without a major sponsor. For the Renault installation Phillippe rush-produced an uprated version of the existing car, a simple but effective design based on an aluminium and carbon fibre skinned tub. The first Renault engine arrived in May '85 and the 014 made its race debut at Paul Ricard, after a limited amount of testing, equipped with an iron block based EF4 engine.

For the first four races there were only sufficient engines for one entry - Brundle drove in France and Britain, teammate Bellof in Germany and Austria. Austria marked the end of an era, Brundle understandably failing to qualify a 500b.h.p. atmospheric car (without even appropriate tyres) on the high speed circuit. Zandvoort became the first Grand Prix since 1967 without a Cosworth/Ford car in the paddock. Tragically, Bellof was killed

Dijon 1985 brought the Renault RE60B, with heavily revised aerodynamics in an attempt to drag the slumped works team into competitiveness.

soon afterwards in a sportscar event. Tyrrell ran one car at Monza and Francorchamps, then invited Capelli and Streiff to take turns for the three remaining races.

Sadly, the 014 wasn't competitive and in 14 starts the model made one top six finish - fourth at Adelaide. It was a difficult transitional season for the under financed team with so much to catch up on. The main problem was finding adequate traction. Phillippe recalls, "we had to start late and to rapidly adapt to the Renault engine. The engine programme was very expensive and the car represented 'value engineering'. We had to produce the it in very short order".

The 014 understeered too much early on, but moving the front wings 75mm. forward improved that. Nevertheless, it never qualified higher than 16th, though as development progressed it began to look more promising in race trim. Lack of budget, lack of testing had left Tyrrell in a difficult situation but a continuing relationship with Renault and fresh sponsorship allowed the team to anticipate a more suitable '86 chassis, designed to make fuller use of Renault power.

The factory team was less fortunate. Toth had been warned that substantial outside sponsorship was required if the Evry operation was to continue in 1986. He didn't find it and two days after the Dutch Grand Prix Besse' axe fell. Later, at the end of October, Toth himself came in for the chop. The following year he was charged with diverting monies paid by Tyrrell into his own Swiss account.

Pierre Tiberghien took over as President of Renault Sport and later Bernard Casin was appointed General Manager. These appointments led to Renault Sport becoming more closely integrated

The combination of Senna and the Renault-Lotus was devastating in 1985 : in only his second season of Grand Prix racing, Senna took eight poles.

with the Paris HQ and its bureaucracy. Having missed the South African Grand Prix on political grounds, the condemned team had only gone to Australia thanks to commercial backing secured by long time manager Sage. Sage made an attempt to raise backing to acquire the assets of the team and run it as his own operation, but didn't come up with sufficient funding to do the job properly. Subsequently many of the assets from the Evry workshop were sold to AGS, while Sage moved to the Viry Chatillon engine department.

Among those leaving Renault were Migeot, who went down to Ferrari, Carletti, who went to Minardi and Gentry, who had already joined Brabham. Viry Chatillon lost His, another to move to Ferrari. Down at Maranello, although he found a smaller staff and smaller budget, he expressed himself well pleased with the depth of racing experience and the response time within the factory.

Dudot's operation still had to equip six cars, even though Ligier's original contract had expired at the end of '85. During the course of the season Ligier had been informed, first that it would only be renewed at a significantly higher price, then that it would not be renewed at all. A furious Guy Ligier was certain Lotus was behind that. He enlisted the help of his high level contacts and pressure was brought to bear on the state owned company while Minister of Sport Alain Calmat offered a cash contribution via the National Sports Development Agency, which didn't please all French athletes. With Renault receiving money from the state and from Elf on its behalf, Ligier was able to continue paying the same amount as Lotus and Tyrrell for an '86 supply.

Of course, Lotus was the number one team, receiving its engines direct from Viry Chatillon. A van was sent from Norwich to Paris to collect qualifying engines for each (European) race while Renault would take the race engines direct to the circuit. Senna (now undisputed number one, with rookie Johnny Dumfries in the

second car) used the same qualifying engine both days in the spare car, which was set up specifically for his pole seeking efforts, while he would run a different race engine in his race car in each day's untimed session to compare possible units for the race.

Renault actually began the '86 effort at Paul Ricard late in '85 where Senna was able to sample a number of exciting developments. It was a crucial test for both Lotus and Renault were desperate to avoid losing his services, the competition for which was extremely hot...

Senna sampled developments that eliminated both valve springs and the distributor. He was sufficiently impressed to stay. However, as a condition of his continuing association he insisted that the second Lotus should not be driven by a top liner - hence Dumfries' big break. Senna understandably reasoned that as a driver was at the mercy of his equipment as never before, nothing should detract from the attention lavished on his by Ducarouge and Dudot.

French sources reckon Renault had spent around $27 million on engine development in '85, and out of Viry Chatillon had come the radical *distribution pneumatique* valve closing system. Its origins could be traced back to the early Eighties, when Renault ran into valve spring problems. Valve springs are subject to fatigue and surge. Surge is tackled by running coaxial springs but the interference that damps surge increases the likelihood of fatigue. And maximum revs are limited by the weight of the valve plus part of the weight of the spring. Renault looked at desmodromic timing but was put off by the extra weight and complication involved. However, in '84 emerged the clever concept of using compressed gas rather than springs to close the valves.

A flange on the valve stem formed a piston which ran in a nitrogen filled chamber. Each chamber was part of a central network, pressurised to 1.2 - 1.8 bar. Compressed by the flange as the valve lifted, subsequent expansion of the nitrogen closed the valve in a very positive fashion. Overcoming the mechanical limitations of conventional springs, the system offered improved reliability and more scope with cam profiles, helping the quest for fuel efficiency. Further, a self damping effect reduced a potential source

Early in 1986 Renault introduced this 'dromedary-style' plenum chamber for the RE15, with central input. Pressure went over 5.0 bar in qualifying.

Ducarouge's evolutionary Lotus 98T featured a ride height adjustment device to compensate for diminishing fuel load and made good use of Renault's 13,000 r.p.m. EF15*bis*.

of vibration.

Clearly the threat to the system was loss of gas pressure. Consequently, the nitrogen network was monitored by an automatic valve which could let in more gas from a 1/2 litre reserve bottle stored in the central valley of the engine. Intriguingly, increasing gas pressure was equivalent to fitting stiffer springs and, in effect, allowed the use of very stiff springs at no weight penalty. "It was possible to go to 13,000r.p.m.", Dudot explains, pointing out that there was also an added measure of security as a driver could over-rev without dire consequence: "It was possible to get very high r.p.m". How high? "Sometimes in excess of 13,500r.p.m. without problem..."

From the start the system allowed the EF15 to go to 12,500r.p.m. and come '86, the regular limit was 13,000r.p.m. The so called EF15*bis* also benefited from the distributor free ignition system.

The revamped ignition provided a high tension coil for each plug, which was built into its cap. Each spark could then be individually controlled by the ECU via a low voltage signal. There were no moving parts or H.T. leads to leak away current and there was more programming flexibility promising more efficient combustion. In particular, there was the potential to run just that little bit closer to the detonation threshold. "We could adjust the timing according to more parameters", Dudot explains, "making it more accurate. That was very important for fuel consumption. For fuel consumption you must run as close as possible to the limit of detonation".

While the EF15 had incorporated an ignition pick up in the bellhousing, the pick up was henceforth carried on a 50mm. spacer between engine and bellhousing so as to avoid the necessity to re-time whenever the transaxle was removed. However, although longer, the EF15*bis* had a lower centre of gravity, 2.5kg. saved at the top end via *distribution pneumatique*. Fuel injectors were now supplied by Bosch and engine management system development was no longer the responsibility of Renix. Instead, the work was carried out by a small team at Viry Chatillon. Bosch injectors were used for commercial reasons, while Renix' involvement was no longer necessary, Dudot explains.

In '85 Renix had fielded an on-board data logging system which could monitor ten functions for a limited amount of time or two over race duration - logically revs and boost pressure. For '86 there was a more accurate fuel read out for the driver.

With its 13,000r.p.m. potential the EF15*bis* could be adapted as a fine qualifying engine, allowing the EF4*bis* to be laid to rest. In qualifying the EF15*bis* was similarly used without wastegate. Come Estoril, and a new turbo was offering an honest 5.0 bar boost.

Right at the end of the season Adelaide saw a high of 5.2 bar - and well over 1100b.h.p.

For race day Elf had denser fuels, including some based on toluene, which added 10kg. to a tankful. Elf was never in the forefront of 'rocket fuel' development, but Dudot says he was content with its progress. In '86 race boost was in the region of 3.7 - 4.0 bar. A total of 50 EF15*bis* engines were prepared for the '86 teams, Mecachrome servicing Ligier and Tyrrell and, as usual, each team having a race engineer and two Renault mechanics. Engine developments included a 'dromedary' style, central input plenum chamber introduced at Jerez and new wastegates for Paul Ricard.

By that stage all the teams had EF15*bis* race engines whereas only a handful of the new units had been readied for the start of the season - at Rio only Senna enjoyed EF15*bis* qualifying and race engines. At Jerez there were still only three race engines - two for Senna, one for Ligier, but all Renault cars had EF15*bis* qualifying units.

No doubt about it, the 13,000r.p.m. qualifying unit on which Lotus spent 40% of its engine budget was hugely successful and Senna comfortably retained his crown as King of Qualifying with no less than eight poles. The Brazilian always qualified his 98T - a refined version of the previous year's car - in the top 10 and only at Monza and the Osterreichring missed out on the top two rows. Lotus exploited the potential of underbody downforce to the full, and Senna's low riding Q car set a fashion for rubbing skid plates on the track. "We were probably the first people to run lower to get some advantage", Ducarouge reflects; "the cars were evolving and the 98T responded well to running low in qualifying. The driver responded too..."

While the Renault-Lotus was a superbly effective qualifying car, the massive amount of engine testing Lotus did for Renault meant that, in Senna's opinion, the chassis wasn't as finely honed as it might have been. Nevertheless, the design was sound and didn't require significant modification over the season. The real weakness of the package was the original EF15*bis* race engine. It demonstrated excellent low down power and throttle response but couldn't properly exploit its r.p.m. bonus - poor fuel consumption cost acceleration and top speed. Consequently, time had to be made up in the corners, which was hard on tyres and hard on Senna. However, at least the *distribution pneumatique* system allowed a gear to be held a little longer, sometimes avoiding an unsettling mid corner shift and thus doing something towards alleviating tyre abuse. Nevertheless, Renault simply didn't have the fuel efficiency of Honda and it is significant that Senna won at Jerez and Detroit, slow circuits on which fuel consumption is less of a problem.

Renault had a real problem on faster circuits and mindful of that a 'C' version of the EF15 was developed featuring revised heads. "It was a problem of the temperature in the combustion chamber", Dudot admits, "we changed the cylinder head for improved water circulation. The C specification was much better". Of course, compression ratio increases were behind the problem, the geometric ratio moving towards 8.0:1, probably beyond. The C specification additionally included re-profiled inlet tracts, modified injectors and exhaust.

Having been only briefly tested at Silverstone, the first EF15C was rushed into service for the French Grand Prix as Senna's race engine. He found it a definite advantage and opted to race it. Alas, it did not quite bridge the gap to Honda and Senna was forced to revert to an EF15*bis* at Brands Hatch, the Hungaroring and the Osterreichring, each time due to a misfire. "It was a problem in the harmony between ignition and injection", Dudot reports, "on the bench it was OK but sometimes in the car it arose".

Dudot reckons the EF15C got "very close" to the Honda engine and could have been the basis of a highly competitive offering for '87. In '86 Renault engines rarely let Lotus down when it mattered most, the EF15*bis* and EF15Cs only causing four of 15 retirements, the majority of which befell Dumfries. A six speed gearbox introduced at the start of the season proved to be a weak link and was never raced by Senna. C.v. failure afflicted both cars at Imola, caused by faulty uprights. Although Senna was rarely able to get to grips with Honda power, from 16 starts he managed ten points finishes, and although he took only two wins he was only twice off the rostrum. Missing the Monaco cut, Dumfries made 15 starts, only three of them from (just) inside the grid top ten, and he scored points only twice, contributing a mere three to Lotus' total of 55. That left it a distant third in the constructors championship, overshadowed by Honda-Williams and Porsche/TAG-McLaren, both

End view of Ligier's 1986 transaxel, gearbox endplate removed.
Ligier fed Renault power through a six-speed modified Hewland DGB.

of which ran two competitive cars.

Ligier managed fifth in the points league (behind Ferrari), one position higher than '85 indicative of its steady climb with Renault power behind it. Loto was once more a sponsor in '86, along with Gitanes and Elf while Laffite was joined by Arnoux and young hopeful Alliot was taken on as test driver, the aim being to run a test team for the first time. Alas, that did not come about - finance was tight in the wake of the cost of Renault engines and retainers for two star drivers. There were now 81 employees at Abrest, from which emerged a development of the JS25 rather than the all new chassis that Tetu would rather have produced, given adequate time and money.

Nevertheless, considering Ligier's secondary status in the Renault camp and the use of Pirelli rather than Goodyear tyres, the JS27 showed itself a sound design. Its potential was best exploited at Detroit where at one stage the boys in blue headed the race. Laffite and Arnoux earned their retainers over the first half of the season, then an accident at Brands Hatch left Laffite on the sidelines and team morale slumped. Ligier planned a switch to Alfa Romeo power and asked Tetu to concentrate upon a brand new four cylinder chassis for '87 while Larrousse planned to set up his own team. Meanwhile, Benetton had established itself as Pirelli's favourite and the JS27's potential wasn't properly developed. From Hockenheim to Adelaide midfield performances by Arnoux and stand-in Alliot were reminiscent of the struggles of '85.

Laffite had made nine starts (including the aborted Brands Hatch race), qualifying in the top ten on five occasions and scoring points on five occasions, including second at Detroit and third at Rio. Arnoux contested all 16 races, qualifying in the top ten on all but four occasions and scoring points on six occasions. Not once on the rostrum, his race record didn't match a worthy qualifying record. Alliot scraped into the top ten twice and scored a point in Mexico.

The switch to Alfa Romeo power followed lack of assurance from Renault for the future, in spite of the team's encouraging progress early in the season. The Italian connection was announced in July and came as a breath of fresh air as the relationship with Renault soured. The team did not receive a C-spec EF15 until Hockenheim.

Tyrrell had to wait even longer, until Mexico. The Ripley team had secured a major backer for '86 in US computer giant Data General, but hadn't had its engine situation clarified until November and consequently wasn't able to ready its 015 model until the season was well underway. This season Streiff partnered Brundle and together they made six starts in 014s - untested over the winter - from which two points were collected, by Brundle at Rio. The model was still qualifying near the back of the grid and the 015 replacement couldn't come quickly enough...

The 015 was a brand new design that appeared at Jerez in Brundle's hands and immediately qualified 12th on the grid. Alas, accidents postponed its race debut until Monaco, where Brundle qualified tenth. That effort was not equalled again until Adelaide, Tyrrell, last in the Renault pecking order, failing to break out of mid field. Its late build programme and those early shunts hampered the development process somewhat and consequently the 015 never merited a rostrum finish, and it never achieved one. Encouragingly, got its power down better than the 014 and handled better, and was worth two or three seconds a lap. Nevertheless, it didn't perform well on bumpy tracks, or on high speed circuits, recording poor top speeds.

Although the 015 chassis was generally dependable, engine failure, turbo failure, electrical failure and fuel system failure contrived to a high retirement rate and from 25 starts only five points finishes were achieved, adding nine points to Brundle's Rio score. Come the end of the season and Tyrrell was the only runner left in the Renault camp.

In switching to Honda, Lotus was terminating its contract one year early but Renault had already transgressed the conditions of contract in accommodating Tyrrell. Having lost Lotus and Ligier Renault courted McLaren. However, that deal was vetoed by Shell. Without a top team to supply, Besse added the Formula One engine to his list shortly before he was killed by terrorists late in '86. The refined EF15C on Dudot's drawing board was destined never to see the light of day. In the wake of Ligier's early divorce from Alfa Romeo Besse's successor Raymond Levy stated categorically that Renault was not interested in another turbo Formula One adventure...

LIGIER JS23

Advanced Composite Technology carbon fibre/Kevlar monocoque
Stressed engine
Pull rod front and rear suspension - Koni dampers
Speedline aluminium and magnesium rims
Brembo cast iron discs, outboard
Single Brembo four pot calipers - Ferodo pads
Carbon fibre/Kevlar bodywork
2 IPRA water radiators - 2 IPRA oil radiators
2 Secan air:air aftercoolers
AP twin plate clutch
Hewland/Ligier six-speed gearbox - Salisbury diff
220 litre ATL fuel cell - 12 litre oil tank
Yuasa battery - Contactless instruments
2810mm. wheelbase; 1778mm. front track, 1626mm. rear
585kg.

Ligier's first, British produced composite monocoque was of unusual design, its shell extending ahead of the front bulkhead over the master cylinders, even though a detachable nose box was carried. It formed the cockpit coaming, an arched scuttle bulging awkwardly out of a narrow convex pedal box shroud, while the similarly arched tank blended into a roll pyramid. The tank shoulders were no wider than the V6 behind and a bulbous engine cowl fitted the cam covers so snugly that the plugs had to project through cutouts. With a tapering nose cone, the JS23 had a distinctive central fuselage shape, and its wheelbase was longer than any rival car, other than the Brabham BT53.

The transaxle case was an integral Ligier production, high and narrow incorporating a bellhousing oil tank and specifically designed to carry a new tension link rear suspension. Engine

installation and turbo system were to Renault norms, and the water radiators were positioned at a slant to top vent, ahead of the upright, engine bay vented aftercoolers. A small oil radiator rode piggy back on the lower end of each water radiator. The pods were short (only just reaching into the cockpit zone), and relatively low and blended into a relatively wide tail deck that shrouded the transaxle. Each compressor was fed through a square aperture in the adjacent side panel.

Rear bodywork was simplified above the side panels which were formed with the underbody, the engine cowl extending to form the wide tail and the pod lids. Just ahead of the rear suspension the exhaust pipes popped through the rear deck to activate the rear wing. The wing was carried on a central post above a prominent diffuser. The front wing assembly was moulded

with the nose cone and formed a delta plan projecting ahead of the tip of the nose. Adjustment was provided via flaps.

The prototype JS23 was run briefly at Paul Ricard in January '84 prior to testing at Rio where the team had an embarrassing introduction to turbo power, facing a number of broken suspension parts. The car re-appeared at Paul Ricard with beefed up wishbones and mounts and a Lotus-type bracing strut from the upper corner of the rear bulkhead to a point midway along the adjacent cam box. That might have reduced chassis flex under acceleration, but the drivers still complained of excessive understeer.

Gone at Paul Ricard was the '83 Renault-style activation of the rear wing by the exhaust: Ligier was now up to date with an exhaust blown diffuser. Following a second understeer-plagued trip to the Southern hemisphere, for its third race at Zolder the model sported revised front suspension, with new uprights and re-positioned steering rack, and a revised nose with square-cut front wings.

At Zolder chassis 04 replaced 03, the original prototype having been followed by two race cars. 03 was back to replace 01 as spare car at Dijon. Monaco saw reinforced rear suspension pick up points. Chassis 03 was put out of action in Detroit (leaving the team without a spare for Dallas) and was subsequently converted to 'B' specification while 01 returned to spare car duties.

Heavily revised, 03B tested at Paul Ricard after the Dutch Grand Prix. It featured new suspension and aerodynamics. The front suspension was converted from pull to push rod operation, while at the rear there was a revised transaxle case to accommodate rocker arms. The aerodynamics were revised around the bigger coolers introduced by Renault earlier in the season, which called for larger pods. In addition, the nose was wider, the dorsum was higher and the rear end waisting was tighter. Cesaris opted to race 01 at Monza, confining 03B to the transporter, but following further testing used it at the Nurburgring and Estoril.

LIGIER JS25

Advanced Composite Technology carbon fibre/Kevlar monocoque
Stressed engine
Push rod front suspension, rocker arm rear - Koni dampers
Dymag magnesium rims
SEP carbon-carbon discs, outboard
Single Brembo four pot calipers - SEP pads
Carbon fibre/Kevlar bodywork
2 IPRA water radiators - 2 IPRA oil radiators
2 Secan air:air aftercoolers
AP twin plate clutch
Hewland/Ligier five-speed gearbox - Salisbury diff
220 litre ATL fuel cell - 12 litre oil tank
Yuasa battery - Brion Leroux instruments
2835mm. wheelbase; 1790mm. front track, 1662mm. rear
585kg.

Tetu didn't get his feet under a Ligier desk until November 20: it was too late to produce a new monocoque or transaxle case. The '85 model was built around the existing core with yet longer wheelbase, (longer than any save the Brabham BT54). The monocoque mould was remodelled in Derby to suit Tetu's requirements and he retained (revised) push rod front, rocker arm rear suspension, as featured on the JS23B. A push rod system would have been preferred at the rear, but was not practical within the constraints of the existing transaxle case.

Tetu, in the limited time available, concentrated upon front suspension and aerodynamics and while the monocoque remained substantially unaltered the shape of the central fuselage was considerably modified through the production of new fairings. Where the JS23 had left its scuttle exposed, Tetu added a fairing to blend the nose into the cockpit coaming with a uniform gradient. The nose itself was slightly reworked with a deeper prow. The dorsum was also modified, and was shaped by separate engine and tank shrouds. The tank shroud formed a bubble behind the driver's head which concealed all but the tip of the roll pyramid while a bulbous engine shroud formed a separate step, tightly encasing the V6. However, the plugs were no longer visible, a slight bulge over each cam cover leading back from a scoop that collected cooling air for the V6 alongside the higher EF4bis/15 engine mounts. With the improved engine attachment there was no longer a bracing stay to each cam cover.

The JS25 followed Renault's new side-vented radiator layout, with longer and lower pods than the superseded model, their flat sealed lids blending into a bottleplan tail having modest waisting. The engine and tail fairing was detachable separately from the the pods, which featured louvered side panel exits. NACA ducts set into the pod lids fed the compressors. The wing and diffuser package was conventional. Although the model ran carbon-carbon discs from the outset, it was closer to 600kg. than 540kg. - evidence of its heavily compromised design.

The prototype was ready to run in March and was aired at a wet Paul Ricard prior to the major Imola pre-season test, which ended a few days before the trip to Brazilian Grand Prix. At Rio the prototype was joined by a second race car that had only been run at a local aerodrome, plus a virgin T car. A priority was weight reduction and for the San Marino Grand Prix 01 appeared for Cesaris with lighter bodywork, saving 10kg. A fourth chassis replaced it at Monaco, this lighter still thanks to a brand new monocoque rather than one adapted from '84, saving 12kg., plus lighter rear suspension and coolers.

The lighter rear suspension and coolers were fitted to 01 which returned as a stop gap car for Laffite, until 05 could be fielded at Ricard, leaving the prototype T car, 02 and 03 having been set aside. Cesaris all but destroyed 01 at the Osterreichring and was not allowed to use his 04 chassis in the subsequent Zandvoort race, being allocated the hastily prepared 03 instead! 01 was rebuilt and resumed T car role for the final two races of the year, in which Cesaris' replacement Streiff drove 04 rather than 03.

Other than lightening, Tetu toyed with pod winglets from Imola, and ran front wheel turning vanes from Silverstone, periscope compressor intakes from the Nurburgring. On occasion a two tier rear wing was raced.

LIGIER JS27

Advanced Composite Technology carbon fibre/Kevlar monocoque
Stressed engine
Push rod front and rear suspension - Koni dampers
Fondmetal aluminium and magnesium rims
SEP carbon-carbon discs, outboard
Single Brembo four pot calipers - SEP pads
Carbon fibre/Kevlar bodywork
2 Chausson water radiators - 2 Secan oil heat exchangers
2 Secan air:air aftercoolers
AP twin plate clutch
Hewland/Ligier six-speed gearbox - Salisbury diff
195 litre ATL fuel cell - 12 litre oil tank
Yuasa/Varta batteries - Contactless instruments
2835mm. wheelbase; 1790mm. front track, 1662mm. rear
560kg.

As Ligier's expensive '86 Renault deal was confirmed late in the day Tetu was again short on design time and the JS27 monocoque had to come from the existing mould, with cut down, 195 litre tank. Tetu would have liked to have lengthened the tank to lower the centre of gravity but the extra 50mm. required for Renault's '86 package put paid to that. The JS27 retained the JS25 wheelbase and track dimensions. Tetu had three major goals for the JS27: to save weight, to ease maintenance and to improve aerodynamics, and the rear end shape was completely reworked. The top of the tank was chopped and the tank and engine cowling was revised, along with the pods, rear wing and diffuser. Once the engine deal had been confirmed a full sized

mock up was tested at St Cyr to cross-check the results of moving floor 25% modelling.

While the monocoque was little changed, the transaxle case was new, designed for push rod rather than rocker arm suspension and to carry a six-speed gearbox. Six speeds offered a potential fuel consumption advantage, but at a weight penalty and it proved a struggle to keep the JS27 as light as the JS25 which had been pruned to just under 550kg., let alone to gain on that. Secan heat exchangers saved a few kilos and were positioned either side of the integral bellhousing oil tank, just ahead of the dampers. The push rod front suspension was reworked to match the push rod rear.

Interestingly, the aftercoolers, upright as usual, were hung from the front of the engine rather than the back of the tub, integrating the engine/turbo installation. Together with dry-break fluid couplings and other such short-cuts, this made for faster engine changes, easing maintenance in the field.

The JS27 inherited its predecessor's sidepod layout. However, its overall shape was cleaner, with slimmer nose (and no ugly flares to conceal upper rocker supports) and slimmer, lower dorsum without an ungainly hump behind the roll pyramid. The rear wing was a two-tier affair, the lower tier at rear deck height, and it shared end-plates with the diffuser, the entire assembly

supported directly by the gearbox, without the need for the usual central post.

The prototype JS27 made a brief appearance at Paul Ricard, immediately prior to shipment to the final Rio test. Three chassis were readied for the Grand Prix, 03 serving as spare. 04 initially appeared briefly at Imola with a Citroen based hydro-pneumatic suspension system.

First seen on the JS21, the Citroen system replaced the conventional coaxial spring and damper with a combined air spring/damper unit. In this cylinder a constant mass of air was compressed/expanded to provide the suspension medium while a varying quantity of hydraulic fluid kept ride height constant. An engine driven pump supplied the fluid under pressure to an accumulator from which it went to each wheel cylinder through a levelling valve.

Tested on the JS21 then, much modified, on a JS25 at Estoril in December '85, the system promised a consistent angle of attack but drawbacks included lack of development and a 6kg. weight penalty. It was taken off 04 before it re-appeared at Francorchamps and was not seen again on Ligier's Renault cars.

A fifth chassis was introduced for the North American tour, along with more compact water radiators. Imola had seen a modified engine cowl to accommodate Renault's dromedary plenums, plus reinforced driveshafts which followed failures at Jerez. Problems across the Atlantic saw modified brake scoops at Ricard, but otherwise there were no significant alterations. Having started life at around 560kg., the model finished up there.

LOTUS 95T

The first Lotus Ducarouge was able to design around his own monocoque was an elegant evolution of his compromise 94T, slimmer and lighter, with longer wheelbase and pull rod front suspension. Of conventional design, Ducarouge called it a "classical car". The wheelbase extension was slight, through perpendicular rather than angled driveshafts which reflected the clean sheet of paper approach. The new monocoque retained composite skins and Nomex core and was still produced by folding up panels to form upper and lower halves of the shell into which machined-from-solid aluminium bulkheads were inserted.

Shrouded by a central fuselage fairing, the monocoque was still of functional form, but its angular scuttle tapered more gently to a wedge nose while its boxy tank (carrying a tubular roll hoop) was chamfered at the back. Ducarouge was not happy with the standard Renault EF4 mounts and ran a stay back from the tank to the middle of each cam cover.

The rear suspension boasted unique combined rocker arm and pull rod operation: the spring/damper unit was attacked from both ends. Ducarouge says the main reason was to reduce the parts necessary to attach the suspension to the existing Lotus transaxle case: "mounting was the key - it was neat and clean; a light and tidy layout". The transaxle was split between main case and oil tank/bellhousing and had no sideplates hence it was necessary to separate it to access the diff. The gearbox internals were FGB modified by Lotus.

The 95T carried the standard Renault aftercooler layout and top vented radiators. Having no experience of heat exchangers, Ducarouge stuck with existing lightweight combined water/oil radiators. Aerodynamic research was carried out using 25% models in the Imperial College rolling road tunnel. The rear end was of under-stated bottleneck plan with the transaxle shrouded. The pods extended no further forward than the tank and the entire fuselage shape was provided by a single Kevlar moulding that formed nose, cockpit coaming, tank/engine/

transmission cowl and pod lids.

The fuselage fairing provided a wedge nose, an arched scuttle blending into a cupped, integral windscreen and a long, gently swept dorsum that curved down under the rear wing with a small bulge either side to clear the plenum chambers. Formed with the underbody, the pod side panels each contained a rectangular aperture to feed the respective compressor. The underbody incorporated a generous, exhaust blown diffuser above which was a conventional central post supported wing. The front wings were unusual with converging leading and trailing edges.

Unveiled in December '83, the 95T first ran at Donington the following month. The prototype's monocoque was quickly pensioned off, Ducarouge explaining that, "it was too weak by our standards". Thereafter a different lay-up was employed. Aerodynamic tests were carried out in the St Cyr 100% fixed floor tunnel and an alternative pod shape with an inward curving leading edge to the side panel was subsequently seen on occasion. Extensive pre-race tests of the 95T took place at Rio, Paul Ricard and Kyalami and 01 then went back to Rio to serve as T car

alongside 02 and 03.

An interesting aerodynamic tweak seen on slow circuits was a horizontal lip jutting out from the lower edge of each side panel. This increased downforce marginally but made the car more pitch sensitive. Generally, only wings were changed from race to race. There were no significant chassis design modifications, the original design sound.

A fourth chassis took over from the prototype at Dijon and Lotus had to wait until Montreal for its larger aftercoolers. Having been raced by Mansell at Rio, SEP carbon-carbon brakes did not re-appear until the Nurburgring, then in conjunction with Lotus' design, Brembo manufactured calipers. Ducarouge had been convinced carbon-carbon was the way to go but had lacked time to develop calipers specifically for the new material.

Early gearbox problems - broken gears and dogs - prompted the development of a DGB based five speed gearbox in a new case with new lubrication and selector systems. A lot of work resulted in only a slight weight penalty - around 2/3kg. The unit was ready for a Monza debut.

Lotus carbon fibre/Kevlar monocoque
Stressed engine
Pull rod front suspension, pull rod and rocker rear - Koni dampers
Speedline aluminium and magnesium rims
Brembo cast iron discs, outboard
Single Brembo four pot calipers - Ferodo pads
Kevlar bodywork
2 IPRA combined water/oil radiators
2 Secan air:air aftercoolers
AP twin plate clutch
Hewland/Lotus five-speed gearbox - Salisbury diff
220 litre ATL fuel cell - 11 litre oil tank
Yuasa battery - Contactless instruments
2720mm. wheelbase; 1800mm. front track, 1600mm. rear
540kg.

LOTUS 97T

Lotus carbon fibre/Kevlar monocoque
Stressed engine
Pull rod front suspension, pull rod and rocker rear - Koni dampers
Speedline aluminium and magnesium rims
SEP carbon-carbon discs, outboard
Single Brembo four pot calipers - SEP pads
Kevlar bodywork
2 IPRA combined water/oil radiators
2 Secan air:air aftercoolers
AP twin plate clutch
Hewland/Lotus five-speed gearbox - Salisbury diff
220 litre ATL fuel cell - 11 litre oil tank
Yuasa battery - Brion Leroux instruments
2720mm. wheelbase; 1816mm. front track, 1620mm. rear
540kg.

To follow up the superb handling 95T chassis, an evolutionary approach was clearly in order. Nevertheless, the refined chassis Ducarouge masterminded for '85 was a brand new car - no parts were interchangeable. He reckons it; "really a development of a reasonable car", benefitting from work on suspension geometry and aerodynamics aimed at reducing understeer and improving the lift:drag ratio. The main development was side vented radiators - "although Renault and Ferrari simultaneously appeared with them, it was our own idea. Side venting provides better cooling and better aerodynamics, clearing the flow to the rear wing".

The monocoque was of familiar design but was stronger and stiffer; after the still born 96T Indy Car it employed aluminium rather than Nomex honeycomb. The transaxle carried the DGB-based gearbox introduced during the '84 season in a reinforced case. The Torsen diff was perceived as far heavier and in need of much development work while Lotus found the ZF cam and pawl well suited to street circuits, substituting it for the Salisbury as appropriate.

While the 97T's wheelbase was unchanged, its track was fractionally wider, extending to the maximum. SEP discs were now standard, in conjunction with standard '85 Brembo calipers. Lotus had an on-going technical liason with the Italian company.

The major departure from the 95T was in terms of packaging, with the side vented radiators and the '85-style Renault turbo layout. Lower profile pods led into a more tightly waisted rear cover. While the aftercoolers flanked the rear bulkhead, the radiators now splayed away from the tank, reaching forward into the cockpit zone and necessitating longer pods. A short inward sweep to the front of each side panel was reminiscent of the 'low drag' 95T inlet duct. The flat, closed pod lids were again part of an all-embracing fuselage shroud, similar in general shape to that of the previous car. In accordance with '85 Renault practice, the compressors breathed through apertures in the pod lids.

The 97T was unveiled at Donington in February, where it had a brief shakedown prior to dispatch for the Rio test. The car proved quick from the outset but its rear suspension geometry was revised prior to the second Rio test to make the back less nervous. For the Brazilian Grand Prix the prototype acted as T car alongside two fresh race cars.

Two interesting aerodynamic novelties were unveiled at the Grand Prix - front wheel turning vanes and pod lid mounted winglets. Neither was claimed to be of more than marginal benefit and the winglets were rarely raced. Again, no fundamental change was made to the chassis over the course of the season - the hallmark of a good design. A two tier wing was toyed with in mid season while a four tier wing dreamt up in '83 was tried at Brands Hatch but was not raced. An experimental rear suspension with pull rod only operation was seen in tests during the summer and was fitted to the T car at the Osterreichring, Monza and Brands Hatch.

A fourth chassis was introduced at Monaco, while periscope compressor intakes appeared at Silverstone and a cockpit fuel consumption read out was developed for the Nurburgring, where pits-to-car radio was first adopted.

LOTUS 98T

Lotus carbon fibre/Kevlar monocoque
Stressed engine
Pull rod front and rear suspension - Koni dampers
Speedline aluminium and magnesium rims
SEP carbon-carbon discs, outboard
Single Brembo four pot calipers - SEP pads
Kevlar bodywork
2 IPRA combined water/oil radiators
2 Secan air:air aftercoolers
AP twin plate clutch
Hewland/Lotus six-speed gearbox - Salisbury diff
195 litre ATL fuel cell - 11 litre oil tank
Yuasa battery - Brion Leroux instruments
2720mm. wheelbase; 1816mm. front track, 1620mm. rear
540kg.

The 97T having proven itself another sound design, Ducarouge was content to produce a refined version for '86. Many hours in the wind tunnel led to a further developed underbody and a device was introduced to adjust ride height to compensate for fuel load lightening. A cockpit control governed a hydraulic ram set atop each spring/damper unit. The installation of the ram was possible thanks to a simplified rear suspension - a pull rod only system. It had never been conclusively proved that the pull rod and rocker system offered a performance advantage.

Ducarouge maintained his preferred 2720mm. wheelbase, in spite of the extra length of the '86 Renault package. The rear suspension was carried by a new one piece magnesium transaxle case into which a six- speed DGB was slotted.

This gearbox benefited from "a huge action for weight saving", according to Ducarouge. It offered six speeds in response to the more stringent fuel limitation and the higher revs of the 'DP' engine at no weight penalty.

Although the monocoque still had an aluminium honeycomb core and aluminium bulkheads, its manufacture was by a different technique. Rather than fabricated from two folded up panels, the shell was moulded to shape. As composite materials evolved, so the method of manufacturer had to be modified. As a consequence the product was lighter and more rigid. Naturally the fuel tank was smaller and its reduced height allowed the Renix equipment to be stored on top, simplifying the loom and easing access. Otherwise, the general layout of the car followed that

of its predecessor.

While the 98T was visually very similar and dimensionally identical to the 97T, its one-piece fuselage shroud extended to incorporate the pod side panels, offering maximum access upon removal. Another feature was an improved fuel consumption read out, based on an additional processor. The car was launched with single tier rear wing and without either front wheel turning vanes or winglets.

The 98T was first run at Paul Ricard in February, and was then dispatched to the Rio test. Four examples were prepared for the season, with 01 as T car and 04 for the test team. After Senna's Ricard shunt in 03, his regular race car, it swapped roles with 04. Front wheel turning vanes were run on occasion, as conditions dictated.

Senna shunned the six-speed gearbox, running a five speed DGB in the new transaxle case. Ducarouge explains that; "the problems were small details. The six-speed gearbox needed a lot of test miles to ensure it was problem-free". Dumfries was charged with its development and problems with it contributed to his Monaco DNQ. Following that it was taken out of the race programme until the summer.

C.v. failure at Imola was at first blamed on driveshafts found to be 4mm. too long. However, a post-Monaco test at Ricard revealed insufficient rigidity in the uprights so these were redesigned. Reinforced uprights were not available in time for Francorchamps so the cars reverted to the 97T rear suspension for one race. During the course of the season one piece Speedlines were tested and subsequently a switch was made to Dymags, saving a couple of kilos.

RENAULT RE50

Hurel Dubois carbon fibre/Kevlar monocoque
Stressed engine
Pull rod front and rear suspension - De Carbon dampers
Speedline aluminium and magnesium rims
Brembo cast iron discs, outboard
Single Brembo four pot calipers - Ferodo pads
Carbon fibre/Kevlar bodywork
2 Secan combined water/oil radiators
2 Secan air:air aftercoolers
AP twin plate clutch
Hewland/Renault five speed gearbox - Salisbury diff
220 litre Superflexit fuel cell - 12 litre oil tank
Marelli battery - Renault instruments
2680mm. wheelbase; 1802mm. front track, 1670mm. rear
540kg.

Tetu was given clearance to replace his ultra-competitive RE40 with a brand new car for the 220 litre formula and attended to rigidity and weight distribution as well as aerodynamics. Weight was saved and weight distribution was altered through a shorter wheelbase and shorter pods containing lighter coolers. Weight was grouped towards the centre of the car, reducing the moment of polar inertia.

Unlike the superseded item, the new carbon fibre/Kevlar over Nomex honeycomb monocoque with composite bulkheads (only the second from Velizy aerospace company Hurel Dubois) offered integral cockpit coaming. Its tank rose well above the height of the plenum chambers and cowling for the black box set atop it enclosed the lower portion of a tubular roll hoop. The tub tapered conventionally from tank top to a detachable, crash tested nose box.

The rear suspension was carried by Renault's own transaxle case, new for '84 and carrying FGB internals, a Salisbury diff and Renault's own strengthened crown wheel. A bracing strut ran from the damper support to the rear of the neighbouring cam carrier. The rear pull rod system was inherited from the RE40, while the front suspension was switched from a rocker arm to a pull rod system. The car was provided with stronger

anti dive and anti squat and it was planned to continue experiments with a hydraulic ride height levelling system, as tested but never raced on the RE40.

The new cooler layout for the EF4 set aftercoolers vertically either side of the rear bulkhead and ahead of them upward slanted the radiators, and a horizontal plate was set in each pod to divide the upper (radiator) and lower (aftercooler) flows. However, the radiator flow was not top vented in conventional fashion, but exited over the aftercooler through the engine bay.

Sitting, of course, just behind the aftercoolers, the forward facing compressors were fed at right angles from side panel ducts. The side panels swept only gently inwards and the closed lid pods blended, with a downsweep, into a deck which extended no further back than the engine. The transaxle was unshrouded and the inward

sweep of the pod side panels met the width of a conventional, exhaust blown diffuser. The leading edge of a domed engine cowl bulged slightly from the tank forming a flank scoop to collect cooling air for the concealed V6.

The RE50 carried a conventional wing package inherited from the RE40, with the rear wing on a single, central post. The prototype was ready for a pre-Christmas shakedown at Paul Ricard, prior to shipment to the Rio test in which it registered uncomfortable water temperatures. Tetu had to look to top venting for better hot air extraction, compromising his aerodynamic package. Over the season the RE50 would qualify with the original package for superior top speed while racing with extractor hatches set into the pod lids for adequate long distance cooling.

The ride height leveller was seen only in early tests, the drivers complaining of a lack of chassis

feedback. However, two significant gadgets were adopted for the new season - a pits/car radio and a dashboard fuel consumption read out. Chassis 01 was used only for testing: there were three fresh cars for the Brazilian Grand Prix. 02 was the T car and the early introduction of 05, at Zolder, left it unraced. Dijon saw the introduction of larger aftercoolers. Warwick crashed during the French race and the lower left wishbone - strengthened since wishbone failure at Rio had cost his retirement - penetrated the tub.

The punctured tub, 04, was replaced by 06 for Monaco, where both drivers were involved in a first corner pile up and this time Tambay's tub, 05, suffered wishbone penetration. Warwick, likewise at slow speed, suffered primary and secondary impacts and his tub split just behind the front bulkhead. The team hastily prepared three uprated cars with steel and aluminium reinforcements around the pedal box for North America (03 modified, 04 repaired and modified and a new example, 07). However, at Detroit a shunt once again saw 04's cockpit penetrated by a wishbone arm. 02 was uprated as T car for Dallas where larger water radiators were slotted into 100mm. longer pods, allowing more boost at some cost to drag. A small additional oil radiator was mounted on each water/oil radiator and an oil capacity increase called for a revised bellhousing tank. Dallas also saw a narrower, elongated nose.

The British Grand Prix introduced a new, carbon fibre only tub (08) with thicker honeycomb and thicker side panels, and beefed up front bulkhead with further reinforcement around the pedal box. A second such chassis, the last of the RE50 series, was introduced at Hockenheim, where new, more efficient oil radiators were brought into play. For the '84 season, Renault had produced its own calipers (requiring modified wheels) to be run in conjunction with SEP carbon-carbon discs but it stayed with cast iron discs until Monza.

RENAULT RE60

Hurel Dubois carbon fibre/Kevlar monocoque
Stressed engine
Push rod front and rear suspension - de Carbon dampers
Speedline aluminium and magnesium rims
SEP carbon-carbon discs, outboard
Single Renault four pot calipers - SEP pads
Carbon fibre/Kevlar bodywork
2 Secan water radiators - 2 Secan oil heat exchangers
2 Secan air:air aftercoolers
AP twin plate clutch
Hewland/Renault six-speed gearbox - Salisbury diff
220 litre Kleber fuel cell - 8 litre oil tank
Marelli battery - Brion Leroux instruments
2800mm wheelbase; 1800mm. front track, 1650mm. rear
540kg.

Having decided to uprate to a DGB based transaxle in the middle of '84, Renault hadn't managed to finish the work prior to the last race. However, the new tall, slim integral unit was ready for the Tetu sired, committee developed RE60. While heavier, it was more rigid and provided all mounts for a new push rod suspension.

While suspension was new front and rear and it sat on a 120mm. longer wheelbase, the RE60 was based around a similar tub to that of the uprated RE50. The nose followed the later, narrower RE50 pattern but the sidepods were remodelled with side venting and a more pronounced bottleneck rear end plan. Setting the turbo shaft at 45 degrees to the car's main axis (rather than parallel to it) made way for a pronounced sweep of the side panel.

Unlike the RE50, the new car enclosed its transaxle, the side panels almost kissing the dampers then extending back through the suspension, bridged via a narrow tail deck. Ahead of the aftercoolers, the side panels distinctively curved inwards (under the flat pod lids) to meet the rear, inner end of a smaller, water only radiator, positioned upright and splayed towards the front. Each compressor was fed from a duct set into the side of the engine cowl, which again

integral with the pod lids and extended to form the tail fairing.

Although it carried lighter radiators and a single oil heat exchanger mounted over the bellhousing and ran carbon-carbon discs as standard, with its 25kg heavier transaxle the longer RE60 was nearer 600 than 540kg. It was systemchecked at Montlhery in February '85, then ran the major Rio and Imola tests, again the prototype acting only as test car. It was short on grip and the team tried using the exhaust to activate the rear wing rather than the diffuser, without success. However, with an eight pipe outlet into the diffuser (a three branch main pipe plus the wastegate pipe either side) a 10% downforce gain was claimed.

The Imola test saw RE60 01 adopt an original, wide RE50 nose, a fashion followed by the three cars prepared for the race team. Estoril saw front wheel turning vanes inspired by Lotus and a

smaller radiator outlet while Imola saw the compressor feed taken from a rectangular aperture in the pod lid to slim the engine cowl. The San Marino Grand Prix also introduced a modified exhaust system and stiffer front uprights and rear damper mounts.

Monaco introduced smaller, lighter radiators and lighter bodywork, bringing weight down to 570kg. with the 6kg. lighter EF15 installed. Meanwhile with a lighter, five rather than six speed gearbox, chassis 05 was introduced at 555kg. It was more rigid with revised tub and front suspension, and responded better to set up adjustments. The other chassis subsequently received the suspension modifications.

More drastic modification was required as the model was still off the pace - hence the introduction of chassis 06, the first RE60B, at Paul Ricard. It was down to 540kg. with modified transaxle case offering the option of a lighter five speed gearbox, new suspension parts front and rear (retaining standard geometry), new hubs, Dymag wheels and lightened bodywork. Its aerodynamics were revised, with a slimmer, tapering nose, lower, shorter sidepods housing new coolers, lower dorsum and abbreviated tail (exposing the transaxle). Although the rear wing was initially mounted on a horizontal post, a vertical post was quickly reinstated.

The RE60B's lower pods and dorsum were made possible thanks to better space utilisation. Flattened water pipes where the radiator feed crossed the aftercooler allowed the pod lids to be lowered while relocating the black box from tank top to cockpit provided the scope to lower the dorsum. While the monocoque was of regular design, it was moulded only to accept RE15 mounts.

A second B spec car emerged at Brands Hatch, the final example at the Osterreichring. The RE60B demonstrated further responsiveness to chassis settings and was not significantly modified as a doomed team played out its final, demoralised phase...

TYRRELL 014

Tyrrell carbon fibre/Kevlar and aluminium monocoque
Stressed engine
Pull rod front and rear suspension - Koni dampers
Dymag magnesium rims
AP cast iron discs, outboard front, inboard rear
Single AP four pot calipers - Ferodo pads
Carbon fibre/Kevlar bodywork
2 Unipart water radiators - 2 Secan oil heat exchangers
2 Secan air:air aftercoolers
AP twin plate clutch
Hewland/Tyrrell six speed gearbox - Tyrrell diff
220 litre ATL fuel cell - 10 litre oil tank
RS battery - Brion Leroux instruments
2756mm. wheelbase; 1765mm. front track, 1638mm. rear
565kg.

The 014 was a rapidly produced chassis - the team didn't strike its engine deal until the end of February 1985. It was a completely new car but its basic structure was similar to that of the 012 and it still represented what Phillippe describes as "value engineering". In particular, the team didn't have the budget for extensive aerodynamic research, and in this case there was little time for any sort of study before the design had to be finalised.

The 014 chassis featured top and bottom carbon fibre/ aluminium honeycomb mouldings and aluminium/ aluminium honeycomb side panels. Tyrrell didn't have the capacity to manufacture a full carbon fibre tub in house and with sub contracted work "couldn't guarantee the integrity of the material", Phillippe explains. The compromise composite tub was fitted with machined-from-solid aluminium bulkheads. It was noticeably angular with a steeply raked

scuttle rising high above a tapering snout and characteristic cut down cockpit flanks. The flanks were exposed while a humped scuttle fairing was integral with a bullet-headed nose fairing.

The front and rear pull rod systems were adopted from the 012, with the rear suspension carried by Tyrrell's own magnesium transaxle case. This was new for the Renault project but followed the pattern of the advanced one-piece magnesium case Phillippe had designed for the wing car era. It contained modified FGA gearbox internals and Tyrrell's own clutch-pack diff, both items developed over many years and offering a lighter package than the usual combination of FGB plus Salisbury diff. Uniquely, the rear brakes were mounted inboard, with the calipers hung on the transaxle case, restricting rear suspension layout and underbody design.

Inboard rear brakes were favoured on the score

of traction and curbed diffuser upsweeps. Phillippe says: "we knew bigger upsweeps would be beneficial but the regular brake and suspension layout was an expediency - we had to produce the car very quickly..." The rear end was left uncommonly naked. A narrow dorsum fairing ran back from the headrest enclosing the base of the roll hoop and the electrics tucked in behind, sweeping down to shroud the plenum chambers. And that was as far as the slab sided pods reached.

The pods adopted Renault's '85 cooler package with side vented water radiators ahead of rear vented aftercoolers and ran alongside the tank and cockpit, reaching further forward than those of the RE60. Behind the aftercoolers the side panels were angled inwards following the slant of the turbocharger, but extending only as far as the engine left a wide gap for the aftercooler to vent through. The flat pod lids were low set,

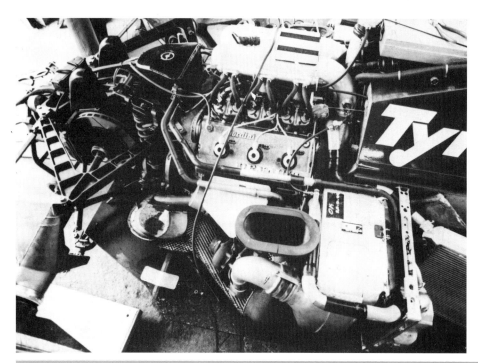

anticipating the soon to be announced RE60B, and the car sported the periscope compressor feeds introduced with the RE60B.

The 014 carried a simple wing package and the first example was shaken down without diffuser at Silverstone prior to its Paul Ricard race debut, for which 02 was on hand as spare car. The EF4-equipped car re-appeared at Silverstone with two tier front wings, deeper rear wing end-plates and a short diffuser, blown only by the main pipe. Silverstone also saw carbon-carbon discs, while Hockenheim witnessed new front uprights, the Osterreichring a bigger rear wing.

Chassis 03 made its entrance at Monza with 200mm. shorter pods to save weight and improve aerodynamics: the pod was abreviated without a reduction in radiator core size. There was also revised rear suspension geometry for increased camber change aimed at improving traction from slow corners, the main complaint of the drivers. That was subsequently standardised while a revised steering rack made the model lighter and easier to drive. From Brands Hatch the 014 also ran a two tier rear wing. Chassis 01 having been written off at Francorchamps, 04 was introduced at Adelaide and the model continued service into '86 unmodified, save for adaption to take the EF15.

TYRRELL 015

Tyrrell carbon fibre/Kevlar and aluminium monocoque
Stressed engine
Push rod front and rear suspension - Koni dampers
Dymag magnesium rims
AP carbon-carbon discs, outboard
Single AP four pot calipers - AP pads
Carbon fibre bodywork
2 Llanelli water radiators - 2 Secan oil heat exchangers
2 Secan air:air aftercoolers
AP twin plate clutch
Tyrrell six-speed gearbox - Tyrrell diff
195 litre ATL fuel cell - 9 litre oil tank
RS battery - Brion Leroux instruments
2756mm. wheelbase; 1765mm. front track, 1651mm. rear
545kg.

In spite of much publicity given to a deal with Data General for CAD/CAM facilities, the Tyrrell design office was not thus equipped until the 015 was well into its career. And Phillippe was not able to benefit from extensive rolling road wind tunnel testing in the evolution of a new model. However, according to Phillippe, the 015 was "a new design throughout" and Tyrrell's 86 Renault chassis benefited from some work in MIRA's 25% rolling road tunnel and featured a significantly improved rear end layout.

The regular construction monocoque retained a familiar angular shape, other than for the upper portion of the tank which was distinctively barrel vaulted. A combined nose/scuttle fairing was still carried but the tank arch was left exposed. The monocoque and a new transaxle case both carried push rather than pull rod suspension and with the improved EF15 engine mounting system the chassis structure was more rigid. The integral case retained FGA-based internals, Tyrrell's long development programme having produced a lightweight gearbox that could cope with turbo power. With carbon-carbon brakes the question of unsprung weight was less significant and with the new case the brakes went outboard offering more scope in terms of aerodynamics.

With the wishbones repositioned and the brakes tucked inside the wheels there was scope for a conventional diffuser, blown by four pipes either side. The wings were inherited from the 014 but the pod and rear end treatment featured a more extensive engine cowl and top vented radiators (again produced by Llanelli, now sold off by Unipart). The engine cowl carried the arched dorsum over the plenum chambers and, leaving the transaxle exposed, was formed with the rear portion of the pods, aft of the aftercoolers. The pod ends were sharply bevelled, tightly encasing the turbocharger.

While the aftercoolers were familiarly sited, the water radiators were positioned to vent through the lid of the forward section of the slab sided pod. The idea was to package the coolers into a shorter if taller pod, reducing plan area. McLaren was successfully exploiting top venting. Side panel apertures fed the compressors while slatted cooling vents were set into the lids, above the turbos.

The prototype 015 sprang into life at Silverstone in April, then was shunted at Jerez and Imola, postponing its race debut. Chassis 02 was introduced at Monaco but was written off prior to the North American trip and 03 was introduced at Detroit. Tyrrell planned to run double disc brakes in North America, having tested the AP system at Francorchamps and a subsequent Brands Hatch test day. However, in qualifying at Montreal an overheated caliper caused a shunt, curtailing the project. The team had put "quite a bit of time and effort" into it, says Phillippe, primarily in the quest for weight reduction. "In the end you adapt to what the drivers want": there was a question mark over the reliability of the new system.

Chassis 04 was new at Hockenheim. The 015 was generally raced with a two tier rear wing and underwent no fundamental modification.

ZAKSPEED

Zakspeed Rennsport GmbH & Co KG
Brohltalstrasse
D-5471 Niederzissen
West Germany

Erich Zakowski went as far as he could with Ford. From 1300cc. club racing Escorts to the factory Sports-Prototypes of the mid Eighties. A Prussian based near the Nurburgring, Zakowski built up a solid Niederzissen Ford dealership before he prepared his first racing Escort, in 1968. On August 17 of that year one Michael Kranefuss gave him his first win, at the 'Ring. The Eighties found Kranefuss head of Ford's worldwide racing programme and Zakspeed running Ford Prototypes on both sides of the Atlantic. The growing German concern had handled works competition cars since 1976, the year Ford closed its European competition department.

Zakowski had taken over a production car based programme, developing increasingly radical silhouette (Group 5) cars and introducing turbocharging in 1978. The first Zakspeed turbo engine was based on the BDA race/rally in line four and, with a single KKK turbo pushing 2.0 bar, around 400b.h.p. was extracted from 1400cc. By 1980, with 2.7 bar and aftercooling power was officially up to 560b.h.p., which spelt Formula One potential. Indeed, Zakowski publicly expressed a desire to develop his turbo engine (based on his own alloy casting) in association with Ford and an established Grand Prix team, saying: "such a small engine, with high output and reliability belongs in Formula One".

Meantime, the silhouette programme had culminated in a blown 1.7 litre spaceframe Capri with over 700b.h.p. on tap. Ever working with Ford-based in line four engines, Zakspeed subsequently developed a 2.1 litre turbocharged derivative of the USA's 2.3 litre single cam production engine for IMSA competition. Based on the standard five bearing iron block this fuel injected special featured a Zakspeed belt driven twin cam head and (like the Capris) Zakspeed CD ignition. It was, however, only a stop gap measure.

Rather than a conventional mid-engined IMSA Prototype, Ford had commissioned a radical front engined, Mustang-styled coupe for the 1983 Camel GT series. Having an iron lump in the front spoiled weight distribution: Kranefuss had ordered an aluminium block replacement from Zakowski. Although for marketing reasons this had to reflect the architecture of the belt driven Detroit four, to all intents it could be considered a purpose-designed turbocharged race engine.

Only 31 years old, designer Norbert Kreyer had joined Zakspeed in 1982 to pen the 2.1 litre iron engine's twin cam head. Assisted by former Ferrari and Alfa Romeo technician Gianni Marelli, he was working for a well connected, successful and highly ambitious company. Perhaps he would be called upon next to draft the inevitable turbocharged Cosworth DFV successor?

By mid '83 Zakowski knew that Kranefuss had given Keith Duckworth the Formula One brief (which, initially, called for an in line four). Zakowski felt that (through its profitable liaison with Ford) his company had learnt enough about turbocharged four cylinder engines and electronics, and even (through a specialist sub-division) about composite materials to be able to produce its own Formula One machine. The challenge was irresistible.

Zakowski called Kreyer, business partner Siegfried Vogel, Technical Director Helmut Barth (a 35 year old local who had worked on the first Zakspeed race car), Chassis Designer Paul Brown and Chief Mechanic Bruno Bunk into his office. Part of the Niederzissen factory was to be partitioned off; 45 other employees were to be kept in the dark...

Kreyer didn't lean on the emerging IMSA engine and there wasn't any money from Ford. The two turbocharged straight fours under development for 1984 would at best be superficially similar. The 2.1 litre unit was to be promotable as the ultimate development of a production engine, was belt driven. Given a free hand Kreyer plumped for more precise gear drive.

Kreyer points to other fundamental differences - for example the stroke:bore ratios were very different. With a ratio of 0.789:1 the IMSA engine shared dimensions with its iron predecessor; the Formula One engine was to be far more oversquare at 0.527:1. While the IMSA engine was confined to 9000r.p.m., the Formula One unit would scream towards 11,000r.p.m. The IMSA engine was essentially an evolution of the stop-gap iron block (with the same Kreyer-designed head but revised lubrication and revised belt drive) and was equipped with dry steel liners, whereas the purpose-designed 1500cc. unit would employ state-of-the-art Nikasil cylinders. However, the single KKK blown IMSA engine was to benefit from a highly sophisticated Ford engine management system, and in Formula One that costly technology was exclusive to Cosworth. With Bosch disinterested, Kreyer's 'no compromise' four would have to await Zakspeed's own electronic control...

Zakowski's project, targeted at a Nurburgring '84 race debut, was nothing if not ambitious. Indeed, when news of it was announced early in 1984 some sighed that such a scheme to produce the first all-German Grand Prix car since the 1962 Porsche sounded more worthy of a certain fictional Spaniard than a proud Prussian. But that was to underestimate the solid technical resources Zakowski had built up, and his Prussian resourcefulness.

ZAKSPEED in line 4

90.4 x 58.25mm./ 1495.0cc.
1 KKK turbocharger
Aluminium block and head
Nikasil wet aluminium liners
5 main bearings, plain
Steel crankshaft, 4 pins
Titanium con rods
Mahle light alloy pistons
Goetze rings
2 o.h.c., gear driven
4 valves/cylinder, 1 plug
34mm. inlet valve, 31mm. exhaust
22 degree included valve angle
Zakspeed ignition
Kugelfischer injection
Compression ratio 6.5:1
Maximum r.p.m. 10,500
125kg.

Zakspeed turbo (the engine was given no other model designation) :
note the neat front adapter plate which mates perfectly with the rear bulkhead.

This was Zakspeed's first clean-sheet-of-paper turbocharged race engine and, mounting all pumps externally, Kreyer produced a notably slim in line structure, for maximum car layout flexibility. The crankcase was split at the waistline, with the block integral with the upper half and having Nikasil coated aluminium liners inserted. The block was designed to be run semi-stressed and featured slightly larger bores than the rival BMW engine. The head and cam box were individual castings and the head was tied to the block by 10 primary studs. The lower crankcase formed the five main bearing caps.

The crank, forged by an undisclosed German company, was turned in SKF bearings by conventional titanium con rods, in turn driven by oil spray cooled three ring pistons designed in conjunction with supplier Mahle. The gear drive was taken off the front end of the crank. The gear on the end of each camshaft was turned by a central gear mounted on the front of the head and that in turn was driven by two intermediate gears from the crank pinion. Two ancillary drive belts were mounted out in front of the gear train and a cleverly designed casting both isolated the two drives (concealing the gear train) and doubled as an engine mounting structure, having been given the exact form to mate with the rear of the tub.

One ancillary drive belt was turned by an extension from the upper intermediate gear and wrapped around a gear at each bottom corner of the tub-width casting. These gears turned external driveshafts, a bank of pumps lying each side of the lower half of the crankcase. In addition to the water pump, the shafts drove four oil pumps - one pressure, three scavenge, including the turbo - and a mechanical fuel pump.

A second ancillary drive belt turned by a further pinion on the same extension reached to the top right-hand corner of the casting to drive the metering unit, which was tucked under the inlet manifold . A third belt was driven off an extension from the crank pinion and drove the altenator, located at the top left-hand corner of the casting. The distributor was mounted at the back of the cam box, to be driven directly off the inlet cam.

There was no electronic control for the injection system, but Zakspeed's own electronics division had fully electronic injection part of a micro processor based engine control system under development. With the high pressure Kugelfischer system, there was one injector per cylinder, the injectors high mounted in the inlet tracts which were on the right of the head. The plenum chamber was offset at 45 degrees from the horizontal, slightly increasing the overall height as well as the girth of the entire package. To the other side of the block, the turbo was mounted low, but was outrigged, and was angled so that its axis, while horizontal, splayed away from the crankcase.

Initially, only one size of KKK turbo was available to the team. It was used in conjunction with regular air:air aftercooling and a conventional wastegate. Weighing 125kg. without turbo system, the base engine was 5kg. lighter than the 2.1 litre aluminium IMSA unit. Delayed by the '84 German metalworkers' strike, the first example wasn't ready for bench testing until September, at which time the prototype Brown-penned '841' chassis was also nearing

163

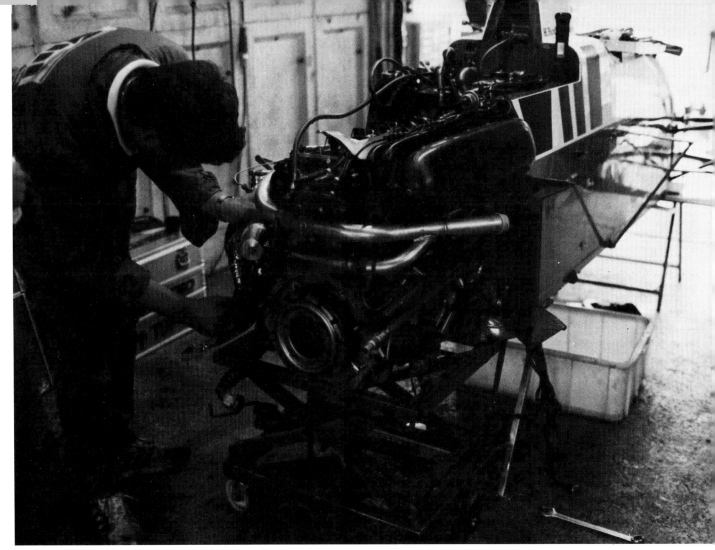

Zakspeed turbo in the 186 chassis : note how pods are fully detachable for ease of maintenance. The new Motronic box sits atop the fuel tank.

completion. The 841 was the product of over 600 20% scale model runs in the Aachen Institute of Technology's rolling road tunnel. By the time of the Nurburgring race Zakspeed had a car and two spare engines (a total of 12 engines was planned for '85) but lack of testing ruled out an entry. Instead, the car was publicly unveiled to coincide with the Grand Prix and once the meeting was over Winkelhock began the shakedown process on the local circuit.

The car gave no bothers and set a midfield race pace on race tyres. Zakowski might not have had the resources of Renault or Fiat/Ferrari (and he talked of having only a dozen technicians working full time on the project) but he wasn't tilting at windmills, that was for sure.

Barth recalls how, the first day, "we ran through until it was dark...we were all surprised that a Formula One car was like any other race car - there were no big disasters..." However, the team was under no illusions. "We also realised that to make it competitive would be hard work..."

That work continued in private at the Nurburgring and Misano, then, in public, at Paul Ricard just before Christmas. The car ran smoothly throughout, the only hitch an inadequate oil tank which cost a couple of engines. That had been remedied by Ricard, where Zakspeed did not disgrace itself. Palmer had taken over cockpit duties from the guest test driver after the initial runs and was sufficiently encouraged to sign for '85, during which Zakspeed would contest only the European races with a lone entry running on Shell fuel - doctored Avgas, as used by McLaren in '84 - and Castrol oil.

Throughout a generally drama-free six month test period the 841 sported a silver livery but just two weeks before Estoril Zakowski clinched a sponsorship deal which turned it the red and white of the Golden Gate Tobacco Corporation's West brand, injecting much needed funding. Come the first race and Zakspeed still only had its prototype chassis, but six engines were now in service. Maximum revs were 10,500 and power at 3.5 bar was reckoned to be in the region of 800/820b.h.p.

Engine development had released encouraging top end power but performance lower in the rev range and throttle response were less impressive, the effort badly hampered by a continuing reliance upon mechanical injection. And chassis development had been hampered by a reliance on old tyres, and by the need to tame, then refine the engine. Barth reflects: "early on the biggest job was to make the engine work..."

Nevertheless, the team looked well prepared as it made its entrance, and it even had a Goodyear tyre supply, to the chagrin of the beached Toleman operation. Clearly Akron valued a long association with the Ford USA-blessed team. In spite of master switch failure wiping out second qualifying, Palmer was 23rd fastest at Estoril, then was 17th on the grid at Imola, and then made the 20-car Monaco cut with penultimate place, going on to finish only the third race for the all- new car. Alas, he fell back with the less competitive rabbits on the faster European circuits that followed, and the team lost its Monaco reliability.

Ricard saw a second chassis, then the long overdue in house electronic injection and engine management package arrived for Silverstone. However, it only ran on the T car, not reproducing its bench performance on the track at this stage. "It is difficult to do such development work during a season", Barth sighs. In any case, in August Bosch agreed to supply its well proven Motronic equipment for the following year. "Bosch had so much experience. Trying to do everything yourself is very difficult", Barth points out. Zakspeed's computerised system might not have been raced in Formula One, but it later found success, both technically and commercially, in American racing, including the IMSA and CART arenas.

Over the summer the compression ratio had been increased to 7.0:1, and another important performance gain was an 11,000r.p.m. ceiling, achieved through camshaft work and attained in time for the Osterreichring. However, the summer was bugged by persistent gear breakages in the camshaft drive which hampered the effort at races and led to a shortage of engines for testing. It was a vibration problem. In line four cylinder engines are notoriously bad vibrators and naturally Kreyer had taken that into account. However, the precise nature of the Zakspeed four's crankshaft vibration hadn't been fully anticipated and a suitable crankshaft damper had to be incorporated. This development took many weeks - modified engines were not available until late August.

The end of August found Palmer hospitalised by a sportscar

accident and consequently the team missed Monza, then Danner finished the season. Writing in *Fast Lane* (October 1985) after his accident, Palmer was able to report: "the Zakspeed engine is almost able to hold its own with the less competitive cars, on power if not response; that is, I feel, a superb achievement in the team's first year... I have been faster than in the RAM last year virtually everywhere, by up to three seconds on some circuits".

Over the season as a whole Zakspeed's highlights remained the Imola qualifying performance and the Monaco finish (Palmer having come home four laps down for the outfit's sole '85 classification). By the end of its European trail, the car was qualifying at 3.7/3.8 bar, but there was still no qualifying turbo, let alone a qualifying engine, and mechanical injection was clearly a major handicap.

Estoril in December was the turning point, Palmer trying the car with Bosch electronic injection. He declared it transformed, showing improved throttle response and more power at low revs (hence better drivability), while it offered improved fuel consumption. Three months of busy mapping on the dyno later, the team was back at Estoril with a full Motronic system (having mapped ignition as well as injection) and a revised, lighter (but still overweight) and somewhat more refined chassis, the 861.

Zakspeed had a low pressure Motronic system as favoured by Porsche: BMW preferred high pressure electro-mechanical injection but a fully electronic four cylinder system had been developed by Bosch with the planned Alfa Romeo engine in mind. With inlet and exhaust pipes tuned to maximise its potential, Kreyer says Zakspeed's four was able to race at 3.5/3.6 bar (around 850b.h.p.) while qualifying as high as 4.5 bar, on occasion.

There had been no major alterations to the base engine for 1986. General development work had paid much attention to cooling, piston cooling in particular and there were now two nozzles spraying the underside of each piston. The turbo system was slightly revised with the rotor axis now north-south and angled upwards. The original plan was to run a single car, for Palmer again, in all World Championship races but from Imola the team also accommodated Rothengatter, who brought useful extra cash at a penalty of somewhat stretched resources.

At Imola a BMW-style compressor inlet control butterfly was introduced and from Monaco onwards the team had a choice of two sizes of KKK turbo. Montreal saw an experimental engine with three injectors per cylinder and this became standard from Brands Hatch. In mid season the team phased in toluene-based fuel, brewed by BMW supplier Winterschall. This allowed the compression ratio to increase to 7.5:1. At the Osterreichring the team tested a Garrett turbo and a switch was made for Estoril. The motivation, Barth explains, was that following BMW's defection KKK wasn't offering the right sort of development programme.

By late '86 Zakowski was talking of the magic 1000b.h.p. in qualifying, while indicating that he would be prepared to take on a customer team the following year. Progress had been somewhat stifled by financial considerations, the team lacked testing time and in '86 failed to achieve its target of scoring World Championship points. Palmer would have collected sixth in Mexico, but for a few litres more...

Fuel economy and reliability: the major posers of '86. Palmer managed to qualify his still significantly overweight car in the top 20 on eight occasions, on two occasions as high as 16th, and he and Rothengatter posted ten finishes, of which all but one were over two laps adrift. Getting competitive was proving hard work, particularly given both engine and chassis to cope with.

Like other four cylinder engines the Zakspeed unit, with its single turbo, was rather peaky and with increasing power levels the chassis was ever more prone to break away when the power chimed in. In any case, with the more mature Motronic engine the basic chassis design had been found wanting; hardly surprising in view of its 1983 vintage. Says Barth: "it was too big and had too much drag. It was time to do a new chassis". Brown departed late in '86 and IMSA chassis designer Chris Murphy was recalled from the USA to draw up lighter, more aerodynamic replacement.

To help make the 871 a smaller car with markedly better airflow to the rear wing the plenum chamber was relocated below sidepod lid height, with inlet tracts feeding upwards. Unfortunately the prototype 871 wasn't ready to test until after Rio but Brundle debuted it at Imola (Palmer having moved to Tyrrell for the season) where he qualified 14th and gave the team its first points for fifth place.

Two cars were run throughout the year for Brundle and Danner, the latter getting an 871 at Monaco, where Brundle again qualified 14th. Thereafter, the 871 duo slipped down the grid, only cracking the top 15 at Detroit, until Mexico, where Brundle qualified in Zakspeed's best ever position - 13th. The final qualifying performance of note came at Suzuka - 15th. Imola remained the only points finish, but the team managed a total of eight top ten finishes from 30 starts, Danner disqualified at Monaco for his driving during qualifying and failing to make the Estoril restart after a shunt. Engine failure cost four finishes, turbo failure five, and transmission failure five.

The engine still hadn't been fundamentally altered but with Garrett turbo and Motronics and more than two years' careful honing it was now able to race at 4.0 bar on certain circuits. Bosch allocated an engineer to the team and Zakspeed was satisfied with '87 engine reliability and drivability. Brundle proved very quick in the wet. However, while response was good and top end power was reasonable, Brundle found a lack of mid range punch. Over the second half of the season, improved engine maps brought better fuel efficiency (from the Osterreichring) and more power (from Mexico).

Over the season as a whole development had apparently been somewhat stymied by lack of funds: for example, mid season Brundle expressed in print some dissatisfaction at the amount of engine development and wind tunnel work that had been achieved. That wasn't for any lack of effort by the crew. Running three cars in 16 races, Zakspeed was employing only 50 people on both engine and chassis preparation and development. Clearly more could have been achieved with more money, but such is always the case. The fact is that on limited resources and a huge amount of resourcefulness Zakspeed developed both an engine and a chassis in which it could take pride.

Zakspeed engine, 1987 with pop-off valve underneath the plenum chamber, which feeds upwards to minimise height of engine shroud ; note twin-entry turbine.

ZAKSPEED 841

Zakspeed carbon fibre/Kevlar monocoque
Semi-stressed engine
Pull rod front and rear suspension - Koni dampers
BBS aluminium and magnesium rims
AP cast iron discs, outboard
Single AP four pot calipers - Ferodo pads
Kevlar bodywork
2 Behr combined water/oil radiators
2 Behr air:air aftercoolers
AP twin plate clutch
Hewland/Zakspeed five-speed gearbox - Salisbury diff
220 litre Marston fuel cell - 12 litre oil tank
Bosch battery - Zakspeed instruments
2820mm. wheelbase; 1800mm. front track, 1600mm. rear
565kg.

Zakowski had been well prepared to construct his first ever single seater. He had his own plastics department and a designer, Brown, who was ex-March, Maurer, Chevron and UK advanced composite specialist RK Fibres. Barth's chassis team started out in mid '83 with a solid knowledge of the new materials and employed Hexcel in Belgium to test the composition and cooking of various carbon fibre/Kevlar weaves. The 26kg. end product, which was produced in the Zakspeed Advanced Composites' autoclave in May/June '84, had an aluminium honeycomb core shell and composite bulkheads, with Nomex core for the bulkheads sandwiching the fuel tank.

Meanwhile, Barth had been studying aerodynamics, having been able to produce a 20% scale wind tunnel model from Brown's drawings as early as December '83 to test in the Aachen Institute of Technology facility. To keep the pods as low as possible, Barth's team opted for a complex and unique (in four cylinder terms) radiator and aftercooler arrangement. The combined water/oil radiator in the right-hand pod and the aftercooler in the left-hand pod were both split, having a forward part sloping upwards and forwards alongside the fuel tank for top venting and a rear part upright for engine bay venting. Giving the 841 the appearance of a six cylinder car, this called for some tricky plumbing. Established using mock-up radiators, it was identified as more aerodynamically efficient than any conventional four cylinder solution.

An inherent drawback of any in line car is lack of symmetry but the overall shape of the 841 resembled a typical vee six runner from wedge nose to bottleneck plan rear end. However, the pods were short, the right-offset plenum chamber protruded through the engine canopy and the waisting wasn't particularly tight, and only extended as far as the bellhousing. The integral magnesium transaxle case was a Zakspeed production, and housed modified Hewland DGB gearbox internals. The in line block was supported by conventional A-frames and the way its front casting mated with the rear of the tub illustrated the advantage of producing the entire package from scratch in-house.

The monocoque formed a high walled cockpit coaming and carried conventional pull rod suspension with magnesium uprights. The rear suspension was hung on the transaxle case with two small yokes over the diff housing. The rear wing sat on a single central post supported by the gearbox and a short diffuser tunnel emerged either side of the 'box. The fuel tank, engine and pod shrouding was a one-piece in house moulding (in Kevlar with Nomex honeycomb), while the side panels were formed with the undertray. A conventional dorsal curve was cut away behind the fuel tank, a step leading down to a flat panel over the cam cover. This notch was reckoned to allow better airflow to the rear wing.

Located behind the split aftercooler, the turbo was fed from a duct in the side of the left pod and exhausted through the suspension, above the left-hand diffuser tunnel. Interestingly, instrumentation was fully digital, with a memory, offering information call up and pre-set warning lights for critical readings, this system developed by Zakspeed for the IMSA programme.

During early tests the wheelbase was extended by 80mm. through an engine/transaxle spacer and it was established that the oil tank was inadequate - its capacity was too small. Consequently a revised transaxle case was produced, 80mm. longer with oil tank capacity increased from nine to 12 litres, the breather arrangement then having to be modified. The car naturally made its debut at Estoril without winglets. Having been designed for '84 regulations, Zakspeed reckoned its newcomer suffered more than most from the '85 rear wing restriction.

Only the prototype chassis was available right up until the French Grand Prix and it benefited from revised pod top vents for better cooling at Imola and titanium springs and roll bars at Monte Carlo (where the team started playing with front wheel turning vanes). The car's weight was still over 600kg. as it had been conservatively designed and there remained a lot of steel to be replaced by lighter materials.

Chassis 02 featured subtle revisions to the tub and bodywork form and although stiffer and a little heavier in the tub was lighter overall, if not under 600kg. Used in conjunction with a six-speed gearbox, it relegated 01 to the role of spare. Further modifications included revised suspension geometry at the Osterreichring, smaller, lighter radiators in slimmer pods at Francorchamps and a transaxle case incorporating the starter motor at Brands Hatch (where a two-tier rear wing was first employed).

ZAKSPEED 861

Zakspeed carbon fibre/Kevlar monocoque
Semi-stressed engine
Pull rod front and rear suspension - Koni dampers
BBS aluminium and magnesium rims
AP cast iron discs, outboard
Single AP four pot calipers - Ferodo pads
Kevlar bodywork
1 Behr water radiator - 1 Secan oil heat exchanger
1 Behr air:air aftercooler
AP twin plate clutch
Hewland/Zakspeed six-speed gearbox, Salisbury diff
195 litre Marston fuel cell - 12 litre oil tank
Bosch battery - Zakspeed instruments
2820mm. wheelbase; 1800mm. front track, 1600mm. rear
560kg.

The 861 was a straightforward evolution of the 841 taking advantage of a smaller (195 litre) fuel tank bulk to improve airflow to the rear wing and designed to save weight wherever possible. The new model abandoned the split cooler arrangement for a single radiator and single aftercooler set up which, Barth admits, was a little less aerodynamically efficient. Although the new arrangement was lighter, Barth says the main motivation was a logistical one: the ideal solution had been so complex it had lacked operational practicality. For the same reason revised sidepods were individually detachable, no longer moulded with either rear canopy or undertray. The tank and engine fairing was split and, overall, the 861 was designed by Brown as an easier package to run.

In the 861 the coolers stood upright and the water radiator splayed outwards along an increased pod span so that its front portion could be side vented while its rear portion was engine bay vented. Oil cooling was now taken care of by a Secan heat exchanger (positioned behind the water radiator) which saved a few precious kilos. With the air:air aftercooler symmetrically splayed across the opposite pod and engine bay vented, the pod tops were flat and fully closed. Louvres were employed to help draw air through the radiator's side vent.

The rear end featured tighter waisting and

turbine and wastegate pipes exited into the diffuser under a lightly modified rear suspension. Suspension geometry was modified both front and rear, while the car adopted the 841 transaxle. Importantly, weight was genuinely down to the region of 575kg. with more extensive use of titanium and careful pruning throughout.

Two cars were ready for the '86 season and early modifications included side venting for improved heat extraction from the aftercooler and a snorkel intake for the turbo. A two-tier rear wing became regular wear from Jerez, and in Spain the car appeared with modified rear suspension geometry. Monaco saw the introduction of a third chassis (the team up to two drivers since Imola) and with this new car carbon-carbon brakes were phased in, though they were not raced until Hockenheim. During the season the team dabbled with pod mounted winglets and a Williams-influenced nose shape, to no avail.

With the Motronic engine it had quickly become clear that the chassis' 1983 design base had run out of development. The replacement could not be readied in time for the start of the '87 season so the 861 trio lived on with modified suspension geometry, cooling and rear aerodynamics, the '87 engine revisions allowing the plenum bulge to be deflated, while the compressor intake snorkel was replaced by a scoop at the junction of pod top and tank side. The model raced at Rio and, alongside the first 871, at Imola. Subsequently it continued in a T car role until Detroit, where Brundle shunted his 871 and consequently gave the car its final fling.

snug fitting, 60mm. lower engine/tank shrouding behind a pyramid roll hoop. The hoop was formed as an integral part of the revised upper tank portion of the monocoque. With the lowering of the dorsum, the driving position was a little more reclined. Airflow to the rear wing was enhanced and the entire aerodynamic package was subtly modified following off-season wind tunnel work at Aachen. Thus, there was a slightly wider nose, there were new wing and underbody profiles (with the left diffuser tunnel now blown by the exhaust), while rear wheel turning vanes (mirroring those at the front) were situated in the increased gap between rear bodywork and wheel.

With the turbo installation slightly modified the compressor now took its feed down from a duct flush in the top of the left-hand pod. The

ZAKSPEED 871

Zakspeed carbon fibre/Kevlar monocoque
Semi-stressed engine
Pull rod front and rear suspension - Sachs dampers
BBS aluminium and magnesium rims
AP carbon-carbon discs, outboard
Single AP four pot calipers - Ferodo pads
Kevlar bodywork
1 Behr water radiator - 1 Secan oil heat exchanger
1 Behr air:air aftercooler
Sachs twin plate clutch
Hewland/Zakspeed six-speed gearbox - Salisbury diff
195 litre Marston fuel cell - 12 litre oil tank
Bosch battery - Zakspeed instruments
2820mm. wheelbase; 1800mm. front track, 1600mm. rear
550kg.

As we have noted, the 861 was perceived as too big, and even with carbon-carbon discs was badly overweight. With the increasingly widespread use of the more exotic materials there was no obvious way to slash weight but naturally careful design of a new chassis could pay dividends. And clearly there was room to reduce the cross sectional area of the fuselage to further enhance airflow to the rear wing. Consequently, the broad shouldered 861 monocoque was radically reshaped above the waistline to produce a significantly lower, slimmer upper fuselage.

Gone were the high flanks and the roll pyramid: topped by a tubular roll hoop the revamped Zakspeed tub was far less bulky in the tank region, while the cockpit coaming (which it continued to form) was likewise trimmer. In conjunction with the re-sculptured tank, the lowering of the plenum chamber allowed for a much less intrusive dorsal hump, and gone was the turbulence created by a prominent plenum bulge. Interestingly, the dorsal slope stepped down over the engine, as on the 841.

Heat extraction from radiators and engine bay was improved by a revised pod design - under a flat lid inward stepped vertical slats reached right back from the rear of the respective cooler (splayed as on the 861) as far as the bellhousing. The overall shape of the 871 had been finalised in the light of extensive wind tunnel testing and naturally included a revised wing and under-

body package to work with the new fuselage and pod forms. Initially, at least, that package abandoned wheel turning vanes and reverted to a single tier rear wing.

The Murphy-penned 871 featured altered monocoque and bodywork and refined running gear, while carrying a familiar powertrain package. Suspension geometry was further revised and Sachs dampers and clutch were introduced. Zakspeed had built a good relationship with Sachs over a number of years and the fellow German company was now keen to enter the Grand Prix arena. It offered gas dampers and a conventional 7 1/4 inch twin-plate clutch. BBS supplied improved wheels designed to help speed tyre stops. Overall, the 871 was a lighter (genuinely 565kg.), more elegant car with significantly more downforce, yet less drag. Its

aerodynamics, as usual based on Aachen-tested models, were the responsibility of Heinz Zollinir, who in mid season was given access to BMW's 100% fixed floor tunnel.

Shaken down on the Nurburgring, just prior to Imola, the 871 had a little drag was added by the early introduction of front wheel turning vanes and a two tier rear wing, these becoming regular fitments. The most significant modification over the season was a revised rear suspension, introduced at Hockenheim, and there was a further suspension revision for Estoril. Only three examples of the '87 car were produced, 01's San Marino debut followed by the introduction of 02 at Francorchamps while 03 was new at Ricard allowing 01 to take over spare car duties from the superseded model.

CHASSIS INDEX